STEP FORWARD 4

SECOND EDITION

STANDARDS-BASED LANGUAGE LEARNING
FOR WORK AND ACADEMIC READINESS

SERIES DIRECTOR
Jayme Adelson-Goldstein

Lesson Plans

198 Madison Avenue
New York, NY 10016 USA

Great Clarendon Street, Oxford, OX2 6DP, United Kingdom

Oxford University Press is a department of the University of Oxford.
It furthers the University's objective of excellence in research, scholarship,
and education by publishing worldwide. Oxford is a registered trade
mark of Oxford University Press in the UK and in certain other countries

© Oxford University Press 2018

The moral rights of the author have been asserted

First published in 2018

2022 2021 2020 2019 2018

10 9 8 7 6 5 4 3 2 1

No unauthorized photocopying

All rights reserved. No part of this publication may be reproduced, stored
in a retrieval system, or transmitted, in any form or by any means, without
the prior permission in writing of Oxford University Press, or as expressly
permitted by law, by licence or under terms agreed with the appropriate
reprographics rights organization. Enquiries concerning reproduction outside
the scope of the above should be sent to the ELT Rights Department, Oxford
University Press, at the address above

You must not circulate this work in any other form and you must impose
this same condition on any acquirer

Links to third party websites are provided by Oxford in good faith and for
information only. Oxford disclaims any responsibility for the materials
contained in any third party website referenced in this work

ISBN: 978 0 19 474834 6

Printed in China

This book is printed on paper from certified and well-managed sources

ACKNOWLEDGMENTS

Back cover photograph: Oxford University Press building/David Fisher

CONTENTS

Pre-Unit
The First Step 2

Unit 1
It Takes All Kinds! 5

Unit 2
Breaking News 32

Unit 3
Going Places 56

Unit 4
Get the Job 82

Unit 5
Safe and Sound 107

Unit 6
Getting Ahead 133

Unit 7
Making Ends Meet 159

Unit 8
Satisfaction Guaranteed 186

Unit 9
Take Care! 210

Unit 10
Get Involved! 235

Unit 11
Find Us Online! 260

Unit 12
How Am I Doing? 286

PRE-UNIT

The First Step

Lesson Overview

MULTILEVEL OBJECTIVES

On-, Pre-, and Higher-level: Greet others, use various verb tenses, and identify word families

LANGUAGE FOCUS

Grammar: Parts of speech (noun, adjective, verb, adverb)

Vocabulary: Country names and adjectives

For vocabulary support, see these **Oxford Picture Dictionary** topics: A Classroom, pages 6–7; Prepositions, page 25; Meeting and Greeting, pages 2–3

READINESS CONNECTION

In this lesson, students process instructions by working together to complete activities.

PACING

To compress this lesson: Conduct 2A as a whole-class activity.

To extend this lesson: Brainstorm word families and write sentences. (See end of lesson.)

And/or have students complete **Multilevel Activities 4 pages 13–16.**

Lesson Notes

CORRELATIONS

CCRS: SL.1.B (d.) Explain their own ideas and understanding in light of the discussion.

SL.2.B Determine the main ideas and supporting details of a text read aloud or information presented in diverse media and formats, including visually, quantitatively, and orally.

R.1.B Ask and answer such questions as who, what, where, when, why, and how to demonstrate understanding of key details in a text.

R.7.B Use information gained from illustrations and the words in a text to demonstrate understanding of the text.

L.1.B (b.) Explain the function of nouns, pronouns, verbs, adjectives, and adverbs in general and their functions in particular sentences. (l.) Produce simple, compound and complex sentences.

L.1.C (f.) Use verb tense to convey various times, sequences, states, and conditions.

L.4.B (e.) Use glossaries and beginning dictionaries, both print and digital, to determine or clarify the meaning of words and phrases.

RF.4.B (a.) Read grade-level text with purpose and understanding.

ELP: 8. An ELL can determine the meaning of words and phrases in oral presentations and literary and informational text.

Warm-up and Review
10–15 minutes (books closed)

Tell the students a little bit about yourself. Then ask them questions in different tenses. *Where do you work? Are you taking any other classes? Where did you last study English? What were you doing at this time last year? How long have you attended this school? What will you do when you finish this class?* As you ask questions, learn the students' names and write a sentence on the board. For example: *[Name of student] works in/at [place]. [Name of student] is taking a [subject] class.*

Introduction
5 minutes

1. Say: *Now we know something about a few people. It's time for more of us to get to know each other.*

2. State the objective: *Today we're going to get to know each other, review verb tenses, and talk about word families.*

1 Get to know your classmates

Presentation I
20–25 minutes

A Direct students to look at the picture. Ask: *Where are these people?* [in class] *What are the people talking about?* [the seat/if it's free] *How do you know?* [She's pointing at the empty chair.]

B 1. Read the instructions and question aloud. Direct students to read the conversation silently and listen for the answer to the question: *Where are Ara and Estela from?* Call on a volunteer for the answer. Point out Armenia and El Salvador on a world map.

2. Play the audio. Ask comprehension questions: *Is anyone sitting in the seat?* [No, the person left.] *How long has Estela been in the United States?* [two years] *How long has Ara been here?* [four years]

Answer
Ara is from Armenia and Estela is from El Salvador.

Guided Communicative Practice I
10–20 minutes

C 1. Read the instructions aloud. Model the activity with a volunteer using your own information.

2. Have students practice the conversation in pairs using their own information. Then have pairs join another pair to practice with two more students.

3. Call on volunteers to tell the class about their partners.

2 Review verb tenses

Guided Communicative Practice II
10–20 minutes

A 1. Introduce the new topic: *Now we're going to review verb tenses.*

2. Direct students to study the timeline. Use the sentences on the board from the *Warm-up* to check comprehension. Elicit the verb and tense of each sentence.

3. Direct students to work individually to write the correct tense for the sentences under the chart. Call on volunteers for the answers.

Answers
1. simple present
2. present continuous
3. simple past
4. past continuous
5. present perfect
6. future

B 1. Direct students to look at the picture. Ask: *Do you think they know each other? Why or why not?*

2. Read the questions and have students repeat them. Ask them to work with a partner to identify the verb tense and then ask and answer the questions. Monitor and provide feedback. Call on volunteers to tell the class about their partners.

Answers
1. present continuous
2. simple present
3. present perfect
4. simple past
5. future

3 Word families

Presentation II
15–20 minutes

A 1. Introduce the new topic: *Now we're going to learn about word families.* Write *Noun*, *Adjective*, *Verb*, and *Adverb* on the board. Elicit an example of each and write the words in the correct columns.

2. Direct students' attention to the first chart on page 3. Point out that the example words are all related and are called a word family.

3. Ask students to work individually to complete the sentences below the chart and then compare answers with a partner. Go over the answers as a class.

4. Refer students to the words on the board and elicit the complete family for each word. Point out that not all words have a "family member" in every part of speech.

Answers	
1. student	3. studious
2. studies	4. studiously

Guided Practice
15–20 minutes

B 1. Ask students to look up the word *help* in their dictionaries.

2. Direct them to work individually to complete the sentences in the chart and then compare answers with a partner. Go over the answers as a class.

Answers	
1. help	3. helpful
2. help	4. helpfully

> **TIP**
> Make a transparency or copies of the page from the dictionary that lists *help* and look at the parts of speech as a class. Point out other useful features in the dictionary, particularly example sentences. Encourage students to use an all-English learner's dictionary.

Communicative Practice
20–25 minutes

 1. Read the instructions aloud. Assign a time limit (ten minutes). Ask students to work with their partners to find a word family in the dictionary.

2. Tell students to complete the *Word* and *Part of speech* columns in their charts and write an example sentence for each word. Tell them not to use the example sentence from the dictionary.

> **MULTILEVEL STRATEGIES**
>
> Adapt 3C to the level of your students. Explain that you will be watching them so that you can determine their levels and target your instruction to their individual needs.
>
> • **Pre-level** Provide these students with the following sentences for *care*.
>
> *The teacher _____ about her students. Please drive _____. You have to be _____ when you walk down the stairs. When you are sick, you need medical _____.*
>
> Tell students that if 3C is difficult, they can use the sentences on the board.
>
> • **Higher-level** Tell these students to find an additional word family and write sentences for it.
>
> Monitor student practice and make a note of which students will need extra help or extra challenges.

 Call on volunteers to write two of their sentences from 3C on the board. Ask the class to identify the parts of speech. Then have the volunteers write their charts on the board so the class can check their answers.

Evaluation
10–15 minutes

Dictate several sentences using word families and different tenses. *Maria drives to school every day. That driver is talking on the phone. He has always worked very slowly. We came home the slow way. Will you please slow down?* Ask students to label the verb tenses and to identify the parts of speech for the words related to *drive* and *slow*. Collect and correct the dictations.

> **EXTENSION ACTIVITY**
>
> **Brainstorm**
>
> Brainstorm word families. Call on volunteers to say the related words—for example, *act-action-active-actively, comfort (v.)-comfort (n.)-comfortable-comfortably.* Write the words on the board. Have students work with a partner to write sentences for the words. Tell them to use at least three of the tenses from 2A. Call on volunteers to share their sentences with the class.

UNIT 1 It Takes All Kinds!

Unit Overview

This unit explores personality types, learning styles, and issues in education, and contextualizes simple present and present continuous structures.

KEY OBJECTIVES

Lesson 1	Identify and describe personality types
Lesson 2	Identify learning styles and write a paragraph describing them
Lesson 3	Use action and stative verbs
Lesson 4	Ask and answer questions about education
Lesson 5	Describe symptoms of and strategies for test anxiety
At Work	Ask questions when you don't understand something
Teamwork & Language Review	Review unit language

UNIT FEATURES

Academic Vocabulary	*assessment, communication, concentrate, emphasize, expert, focus, maximize, minimize, strategy, stressed, visual, visualize*
Employability Skills	• Locate information • Infer information • Analyze information • Determine how to talk with your roommates about a problem • Understand teamwork • Work with others • Solve problems • Manage time

Resources	**Class Audio** CD1, Tracks 03–12
	Workbook Unit 1, pages 2–8
	Teacher Resource Center
	    Multilevel Activities 4 Unit 1
	    Multilevel Grammar Exercises 4 Unit 1
	    Unit 1 Test
	Oxford Picture Dictionary Succeeding in School

LESSON 1 VOCABULARY

Lesson Overview

MULTILEVEL OBJECTIVES

On-level: Describe and talk about personality types and learning styles

Pre-level: Identify personality types and describe learning styles

Higher-level: Explain personality types and learning styles

LANGUAGE FOCUS

Grammar: Adjectives (*She is adventurous.*)

Vocabulary: Personality types and learning styles

For vocabulary support, see this **Oxford Picture Dictionary** topic: Succeeding in School, page 10

STRATEGY FOCUS

To match vocabulary and definitions, look for words that are related to the new words you want to learn.

READINESS CONNECTION

In this lesson, students understand teamwork by conducting research together.

PACING

To compress this lesson: Conduct 1C as a whole-class activity.

To extend this lesson: Have students role-play a conversation between a learner and a teacher or guidance counselor. (See end of lesson.)

And/or have students complete **Workbook 4 page 2** and **Multilevel Activities 4 Unit 1 pages 18–19**.

Lesson Notes

CORRELATIONS

CCRS: SL.1.B (d.) Explain their own ideas and understanding in light of the discussion.

SL.2.B Determine the main ideas and supporting details of a text read aloud or information presented in diverse media and formats, including visually, quantitatively, and orally.

SL.4.B Report on a topic or text, tell a story, or recount an experience with appropriate facts and relevant, descriptive details, speaking clearly at an understandable pace.

SL.6.B Speak in complete sentences when appropriate to task and situation in order to provide requested detail or clarification.

R.1.B Ask and answer such questions as who, what, where, when, why, and how to demonstrate understanding of key details in a text.

R.2.A Identify the main topic and retell key details of a text.

R.4.B Determine the meaning of general academic and domain-specific words and phrases in a text relevant to a topic or subject area.

R.5.B Know and use various text features to locate key facts or information in a text efficiently.

R.7.C Interpret information presented visually, orally, or quantitatively and explain how the information contributes to an understanding of the text in which it appears.

W.7.A Participate in shared research and writing projects.

L.1.B (l.) Produce simple, compound and complex sentences.

L.3.B (b.) Recognize and observe differences between the conventions of spoken and written standard English.

L.4.B (a.) Use sentence-level context as a clue to the meaning of a word or phrase. (e.) Use glossaries and beginning dictionaries, both print and digital, to determine or clarify the meaning of words and phrases.

RF.4.B (a.) Read grade-level text with purpose and understanding.

ELPS: 2. An ELL can participate in level-appropriate oral and written exchanges of information, ideas, and analyses, in various social and academic contexts, responding to peer, audience, or reader comments and questions. 5. An ELL can conduct research and evaluate and communicate findings to answer questions or solve problems.

Warm-up and Review
10–15 minutes (books closed)

Tell students what you like and don't like to do in your free time—for example, *cook, read, play basketball*. Then use adjectives to describe why you like or don't like the activity. (*I like to cook because it's relaxing. I don't like to do rock climbing because it's dangerous.*)

Elicit things that students like and don't like to do and write them on the board. Write a separate list of adjectives.

Introduction
5 minutes

1. Ask students which of the activities on the board a musical (or artistic or athletic) person might like to do and why. (*An adventurous person might like to rock climb because it's dangerous.*) Tell them things we like to do in our free time are a reflection of our personalities and also of our learning styles.

2. State the objective: *Today we're going to learn about personality types and learning styles.*

1 Identify personality and talent vocabulary

Presentation I
20–25 minutes

A 1. Write *words for personalities* on the board, and elicit examples from the whole class (e.g., *quiet*). Write a list on the board of the words your students identify.

2. Have students identify the types of people they find it easiest to get along with. Elicit ideas and put a checkmark next to the adjectives they mention. Elicit one or more reasons for each one.

B 1. Copy the first two rows of the chart onto the board.

2. Model the task by "thinking aloud" about the first word in the chart and marking the first column appropriately. Work with a volunteer to demonstrate completing the last two columns.

3. Direct students to review the vocabulary independently, marking the first column of the chart in their books.

4. Pair students and ask them to complete the last two columns of the chart together.

Guided Practice I
10–20 minutes

C 1. Direct students to look at the first question and answer. Then read question 2 aloud. If students struggle to answer, direct their attention to the *Vocabulary Note*. Ask if there are any words in the question that are related to the vocabulary from 1B. Elicit the answer [*numbers* and *mathematical* are related].

2. Set a time limit (five minutes). Direct students to continue working with their partners to complete the activity. Have a volunteer from each pair give their responses. Check answers as a class.

Answers	
1. h	5. g
2. f	6. c
3. b	7. e
4. d	8. a

D Prepare students to listen by saying, *Now we're going to listen to someone describe her classmates. While you listen, check your work in 1C.* Ask students to circle the items in 1C that don't match the listening passage. Elicit those items and play them again, focusing on clues to meaning in the 1C questions.

E 1. Tell students they are going to hear the audio again. Ask students to take notes on the people the speaker describes, their personalities, and the things they like to do or are good at as you play the audio.

2. Have students form pairs and take turns reporting what they heard about one of the classmates.

3. When students finish, have each pair join another pair and compare notes.

2 Learn about learning styles

Presentation II
10–20 minutes

 1. Direct students to look at the website. Introduce the new topic: *We've talked about personalities. Now we're going to talk about learning styles.*

2. Elicit the names of the people students see on the website.

3. Ask students to work individually to complete the chart. Go over the answers as a class.

4. Check comprehension. Ask: *What kind of learner likes learning from lectures, music, and video tutorials online?* [an auditory learner] *How does a kinesthetic learner remember?* [by trying new skills]

Answers		
Antonio	Auditory	Calls a friend for advice
Trang	Kinesthetic	Tries to fix the problem
Ria	Visual	Reads the instruction manual

Guided Practice II
10–15 minutes

 1. Model the conversation with a volunteer. Model it again using other information from 2A.

2. Set a time limit (three minutes). Direct students to practice with a partner.

3. Call on volunteers to present their version of the conversation for the class.

> **MULTILEVEL STRATEGIES**
>
> Adapt 2B to the level of your students.
>
> • **Pre- and On-level** Pair pre- and on-level students for 2B. Assign pre-level students part A for the first round, and then have them switch roles.
>
> • **Higher-level** Pair students and direct them to create a conversation for all three learning styles.

Communicative Practice and Application
20–25 minutes

 1. If students will use the Internet for this task, establish what device(s) they'll use: a class computer, tablets, or smartphones. Alternatively, print information from the Internet before class and distribute to groups.

2. Write the questions from 2C on the board. Explain that students will work in teams to research and report on these questions. Ask: *Which question requires research?* [possibly 1 and 3] *Which search terms or questions can you use to find the information you need?* ["learning styles"; "learning types"] *What information will you scan for?* [characteristics, strategies] *How will you record the information you find?* [table, checklist, index cards] Remind students to bookmark or record sites so they can find or cite them in the future.

3. Group students and assign roles: reporter, manager, administrative assistant, and IT support. Verify students' understanding of their roles.

4. Give managers the time limit for researching question 1 (ten minutes). Direct the IT support to begin the online research or pick up the printed materials for each team. Direct the administrative assistant to record information for the team using a table, checklist, or index cards.

5. Give a two-minute warning. Call "time." Tell reporters to first answer and then ask each member of the team question 2.

> **TIP**
>
> When setting up task-based activities, verify that students understand their roles using physical commands. For example: *If you report on your team's work, stand up* [reporter]. *If you keep the team on task, point to the clock* [manager]. *If you write the team's responses, raise your hand* [administrative assistant]. *If you help the team research, hold up your smartphone/tablet* [IT support].

D 1. Copy the sentence frames on the board.

2. Direct teams to help their administrative assistant use the sentence frames to record the team's findings. Direct the reporter to use the recorded information to report the team's findings to the class or another team.

Evaluation

10–15 minutes

TEST YOURSELF

1. Direct Partner A to read questions 1–4 from 1C on page 4 to Partner B. Partner B should close their book and write the answers in their notebook. When finished, students switch roles. Partner B reads questions 5–8 from 1C.

2. Direct both partners to open their books and check their spelling when they finish.

> **EXTENSION ACTIVITY**
> **Role-play**
>
> 1. Put students in pairs. Instruct them to write a short conversation between a learner and a teacher or guidance counselor.
>
> 2. Provide this structure on the board for pairs to follow:
>
> A: *Explain your personality and the way(s) that you like to learn.*
>
> B: *Identify the learning style.*
>
> A: *Ask what will help you remember better.*
>
> B: *Give A suggestions.*

LESSON 2 WRITING

Lesson Overview

MULTILEVEL OBJECTIVES

On- and Higher-level: Analyze, write, and edit a paragraph about a learning style

Pre-level: Read and write about learning styles

LANGUAGE FOCUS

Grammar: Simple present tense *(I remember things if my boss tells me about them.)*

Vocabulary: Learning-style vocabulary

For vocabulary support, see this **Oxford Picture Dictionary** topic: Succeeding in School, page 10

STRATEGY FOCUS

When writing, use examples to give the reader more information about your main idea.

READINESS CONNECTION

In this lesson, students analyze learning styles.

PACING

To compress this lesson: Assign the *Test Yourself* for homework.

To extend this lesson: Have students interview a partner and write a paragraph about his/her learning style. (See end of lesson.)

And/or have students complete **Workbook 4 page 3** and **Multilevel Activities 4 Unit 1 page 20**.

Lesson Notes

CORRELATIONS

CCRS: SL.1.B (d.) Explain their own ideas and understanding in light of the discussion.

SL.2.B Determine the main ideas and supporting details of a text read aloud or information presented in diverse media and formats, including visually, quantitatively, and orally.

SL.6.B Speak in complete sentences when appropriate to task and situation in order to provide requested detail or clarification

R.1.B Ask and answer such questions as who, what, where, when, why, and how to demonstrate understanding of key details in a text.

R.2.A Identify the main topic and retell key details of a text.

R.7.B Use information gained from illustrations and the words in a text to demonstrate understanding of the text.

R.8.B Describe how reasons support specific points the author makes in a text.

W.3.A Write narratives in which they recount two or more appropriately sequenced events, include some details regarding what happened, use temporal words to signal event order, and provide some sense of closure.

W.4.B Produce writing in which the development and organization are appropriate to task and purpose.

W.5.B With guidance and support from peers and others, develop and strengthen writing as needed by planning, revising and editing.

L.1.B (l.) Produce simple, compound and complex sentences.

L.2.B (d.) Use a comma to separate an introductory element form the rest of the sentence.

RF.4.B (a.) Read grade-level text with purpose and understanding.

ELPS: 2. An ELL can participate in level-appropriate oral and written exchanges of information, ideas, and analyses, in various social and academic contexts, responding to peer, audience, or reader comments and questions. 3. An ELL can speak and write about level-appropriate complex literary and informational texts and topics. 4. An ELL can construct level-appropriate oral and written claims and support them with reasoning and evidence.

Warm-up and Review
10–15 minutes (books closed)

Make signs that say *Auditory*, *Kinesthetic*, and *Visual*. Place them in different parts of the room and ask students to stand near the learning style they most identify with. Tell them to talk with their group members about why they identify with that learning style.

Introduction
5 minutes

1. Call on representatives from each group to share some information from their discussion.

2. State the objective: *Today we're going to write a paragraph about our learning styles.*

1 Prepare to write

Presentation
20–25 minutes

 Make a chart on the board and write *Auditory*, *Visual*, and *Kinesthetic* as the chart headers. Elicit answers to questions 1 and 2. Ask students which learning style each of their answers exemplifies and write them in the correct column. Point out that although one learning style may be dominant, most people use all of them at different times. Leave the chart on the board for students to refer to for their 2B writing assignment.

 1-04 1. Tell students they are going to read and listen to a man describing his learning style.

2. Direct students to read the paragraph silently. Check comprehension. Ask: *What three places does he talk about?* [work, home, and school] *What's his example of auditory learning at work?* [He doesn't remember information from emails, but he remembers things if his boss tells him.]

3. Play the audio. Have students read along silently.

4. Draw students' attention to the *Writer's Note*. Ask them to find *For example* in the paragraph. Point out that it begins a new sentence.

Guided Practice I
10 minutes

 1. Have students work independently to underline the answers to the questions in the model.

2. Point out the *Writer's Note* and ask students to annotate the information they underlined with the phrases "main idea," "examples of support," and "goal."

3. Ask students to compare their answers with a partner. Then check answers as a class.

Possible Answers
1. Carlos is an auditory learner. 2. He remembers things if his boss tells him about them; He prefers to watch the news on TV or listen on the radio; He likes to listen to interviews; He understands best when he hears new information and then talks about it. 3. His goal is to be a counselor for young people, so he wants to be a good listener. He is an auditory learner, and he learns by listening. Both his style and his goal involve good listening.

2 Plan and write

Guided Practice II
15–20 minutes

 1. Read the questions. Elicit students' answers.

2. Use students' responses to add new examples to the chart on the board from 1A.

B 1. Direct students to look back at the paragraph in 1B. Focus their attention on the structure of the paragraph. Ask them to look through the paragraph quickly and find the introductory phrases that the writer uses to show he is switching to a new topic. [At work, At home, In class]

2. Read through the paragraph template. Elicit ideas that could go in each sentence of the paragraph.

3. Check comprehension of the exercise. Ask: *Are you writing a list of answers to the questions, or are you writing a paragraph?* [a paragraph] *What's the difference?* [A paragraph has a main idea and examples to support the main idea. *Do you need a title?* [yes]

4. Have students work individually to write their paragraphs.

> **MULTILEVEL STRATEGIES**
>
> Adapt 2B to the level of your students.
>
> • **Pre-level** Work with these students to write a group paragraph. Read through the template. At each ellipsis, stop and elicit completions. If students have different learning styles, elicit appropriate completions for each and write them on the board (e.g., *I think I am an auditory learner / a visual learner. For example, I remember what the teacher says / I read*). Have students choose the completion that is appropriate for them. Have these learners copy the paragraph into their notebooks.
>
> • **Higher-level** Encourage these students to include an example of something they can do to strengthen a different skill. For example, elicit an example of something an auditory learner can do to strengthen their reading skills (listen to an audiotape while following the text in a book, or read an article aloud). Have students add one or two ideas of how they can improve their learning and review other learning styles.

3 Get feedback and revise

Guided Practice III
5 minutes

 Direct students to check their writing using the editing checklist. Tell them to read each item in the list and check their writing before moving on to the next item. Explain that students should not edit their writing at this stage. They should just use the checklist to check their work and mark any areas they want to revise.

Communicative Practice
15 minutes

B 1. Read the instructions aloud. Emphasize to students that they are responding to their partners' work, not correcting it.

2. Use the paragraph in 1B to model the exercise. *I think the sentence that says, "In class, I understand best when I hear new information from the teacher" gives a clear example. I'm not sure I understand the sentence…*

3. Direct students to exchange their paragraphs with a partner and follow the instructions.

 Allow students time to edit and revise their writing as necessary, using the editing checklist from 3A and their partner's feedback from 3B. If necessary, students could complete this task as homework.

> **TIP**
>
> After completing 3C, ask students to find new partners. Have them take turns reading their paragraphs aloud without the first sentence. Their partners should be able to identify the learning style.

Application and Evaluation
10 minutes

TEST YOURSELF

1. Review the instructions aloud. Assign a time limit (five minutes) and have students work independently.

2. Before collecting student work, invite two or three volunteers to share their sentences. Ask students to raise their hands if they wrote similar answers.

> **EXTENSION ACTIVITY**
>
> **Interview**
>
> 1. Put students in pairs.
>
> 2. Have students ask and answer questions about their learning styles and take notes on their partner's answers.
>
> 3. Have students write a paragraph about their partner's learning style.

LESSON 3 GRAMMAR

Lesson Overview

MULTILEVEL OBJECTIVES

On- and Higher-level: Use and listen for action and stative verbs to express feelings and opinions

Pre-level: Recognize action and stative verbs in statements

LANGUAGE FOCUS

Grammar: Simple present and present continuous with action and stative verbs (*She's working on a new painting.*)

Vocabulary: Personality and free-time activities

For vocabulary support, see this **Oxford Picture Dictionary** topic: Succeeding in School, page 10

STRATEGY FOCUS

Practice using stative verbs to describe feelings, knowledge, beliefs, and the senses.

READINESS CONNECTION

In this lesson, students work with others to create a chart.

PACING

To compress this lesson: Conduct 2B and 2C as whole-class activities.

To extend this lesson: Have students play a game with action and stative verbs. (See end of lesson.)

And/or have students complete **Workbook 4 pages 4–5**, **Multilevel Activities 4 Unit 1 pages 21–22,** and **Multilevel Grammar Exercises 4 Unit 1**.

Lesson Notes

CORRELATIONS

CCRS: SL.1.B (d.) Explain their own ideas and understanding in light of the discussion.

SL.2.B Determine the main ideas and supporting details of a text read aloud or information presented in diverse media and formats, including visually, quantitatively, and orally.

SL.6.B Speak in complete sentences when appropriate to task and situation in order to provide requested detail or clarification.

R.1.B Ask and answer such questions as who, what, where, when, why, and how to demonstrate understanding of key details in a text.

L.1.B (b.) Explain the function of nouns, pronouns, verbs, adjectives, and adverbs in general and their functions in particular sentences. (h.) Form and use the simple verb tenses. (l.) Produce simple, compound and complex sentences.

L.1.C (c.) Form and use the progressive verb tenses. (f.) Use verb tense to convey various times, sequences, states, and conditions.

RF.4.B (a.) Read grade-level text with purpose and understanding.

ELPS: 1. An ELL can construct meaning from oral presentations and literary and informational text through level-appropriate listening, reading, and viewing. 2. An ELL can participate in level-appropriate oral and written exchanges of information, ideas, and analyses, in various social and academic contexts, responding to peer, audience, or reader comments and questions. 10. An ELL can demonstrate command of the conventions of standard English to communicate in level-appropriate speech and writing.

Warm-up and Review
10–15 minutes (books closed)

Review the concepts of *visual*, *auditory*, and *kinesthetic learners* by asking students to describe what each type of learner likes to do. As they provide examples, write the verb phrases on the board: *take notes, read books, draw pictures, fix things*.

Introduction
5–10 minutes

1. Point out that most (or all) of the words on the board are actions, or things that we physically do. Provide an example. Say: *I'm a visual learner. I like to read books. Liking is not an action, but reading is an action.*

2. State the objective: *Today we're going to use action and stative (non-action) verbs to talk about learning styles in the present tense.*

1 Use action verbs in the present

Presentation I
20–25 minutes

 1. Direct students to look at the picture and conversation. Ask: *What is the relationship between these people? What are they doing?* Establish that they are talking about someone else, the person who is painting in the picture.

2. Read the instructions aloud. Ask students to read the conversation silently and answer the questions.

3. Read the first question aloud. Call on a volunteer for the answer. Ask the volunteer where in the conversation they found the answer. Read the rest of the questions aloud, calling on a different volunteer for each answer. Ask students what *creative* means [using your imagination to come up with an idea or to make something].

Answers
1. She is Marco's sister. 2. She's working on a new painting./She's getting ready for an art show next month./She is in her studio. 3. No. 4. No.

 1. Demonstrate how to read the grammar chart. Read and have students repeat the sentences in the chart. Elicit the difference in meaning between simple present and present continuous. [Simple present refers to habitual activities; present continuous refers to activities happening now.]

2. Direct students to circle three simple present action verbs and underline two present continuous action verbs in the conversation in 1A. Point out that they should not include the verb *be*. Write the verbs on the board.

3. Directing students' attention to the conversation in 1A, ask: *Why are the two sentences in present continuous while all of the others are simple present?* [The other sentences talk about what Gina usually does. The two present continuous sentences describe what she is doing now.]

4. Pair students and direct them to read the chart aloud to each other. (One partner reads the left and the other reads the sentences on the right.) Then read the chart aloud as students follow along.

5. Assess students' understanding of the charts. Elicit negative and affirmative sentences in simple present and present continuous using the verbs.

Answers
Circled: paints, writes, plays Underlined: 's working, 's getting

Guided Practice I
15–20 minutes

1. Tell students they will collaborate to complete the description of the grammar point. Model collaboration by working with the class to complete the second sentence.

2. Pair students and have them work together to complete the description.

3. Project or write the completed definition on the board and have pairs verify the accuracy of their responses. Ask volunteers which sentences confused them and discuss.

Answers
action action present continuous

MULTILEVEL STRATEGIES
For 1C, seat same-level students together. • **Pre-level** While other students are completing 1C, ask pre-level students to copy the sentences from the chart in 1B. Tell them to use a different verb from the one in the chart. Give them time to copy the answers to 1C after they are written on the board.

Guided Practice II
5–10 minutes

1. Model the first item with the class.

2. Ask students to complete the sentences with the correct forms and then compare answers with a partner.

3. Ask students to read the completed sentences aloud. Elicit the clues that indicate which form should be used.

Answers	
1. works	3. is not working/isn't working
2. writes	4. are helping

MULTILEVEL STRATEGIES
For 1D, seat same-level students together. • **Higher-level** While other students are completing 1D, ask higher-level students to rewrite the sentences to use the other form and change appropriate context clues.

2 Learn stative verbs in the simple present

Presentation II
20–25 minutes

1. Introduce the new topic. *Now we're going to talk about stative verbs. These verbs describe states, or things like feelings, knowledge, beliefs, and the senses. They don't describe the things that we do.*

2. Read the instructions aloud. Direct students to read the sentences in the chart. Read and have students repeat the list of other stative verbs.

3. Elicit a sample sentence for each verb (e.g., *Everyone needs food and shelter.*).

4. Read the *Grammar Note*. Direct students to circle the correct words to complete the sentences and then compare answers with a partner. Ask volunteers to read the completed sentences aloud.

Answers	
1. love	4. am reading
2. watch	5. know
3. like	6. think

TIP
Students may question why *think* is on the list of stative verbs. Point out that when *think* means *believe* it is a stative verb. *Think* also can refer to the action of thinking, in which case it can be used in the present continuous. For example, *I am thinking about my mother. See* and *have* also have "action" meanings. *I'm seeing the doctor today. She's having a party.* In addition, stative verbs are sometimes used in the present continuous in informal spoken English. *I'm loving my new job. Wait! I'm remembering something!* Using the verb in a non-standard form makes it sound more active and emphatic.

Guided Practice III
10–15 minutes

1. Have students work with a partner to complete the conversation.

2. Call on two volunteers to read the conversation aloud. If volunteers read incorrect responses, elicit correct answers from the class.

3. Ask students to practice the conversation with their partners.

Answers	
remember	know
seem	don't understand
have	think

> **MULTILEVEL STRATEGIES**
>
> After 2B, provide more practice with stative verbs.
>
> • **Pre-level** While other students are writing a conversation, review simple-present tense with this group. Write *think, need,* and *hear* on the board. Ask students to write a negative and an affirmative third-person simple-present sentence with each verb. Use *own* as an example: *He owns that business. She doesn't own a car.* Have volunteers read their completed sentences aloud.
>
> • **On- and Higher-level** While you are working with pre-level students, ask these students to write an original conversation using four of the verbs from the chart and two action verbs. Have volunteers read their conversations aloud. Ask other students to identify the stative verbs.

C 1. Organize students into teams of three. Assign roles: manager, administrative assistant, and editor. Review responsibilities (Managers keep track of time, administrative assistants write the correct sentence on the board, editors consult charts and dictionaries as needed to confirm team edits). Demonstrate how to correct the sentence using the first example.

2. Have team members work together to correct the sentences. Circulate and monitor teamwork.

3. Project or have administrative assistants write the corrected sentences on the board and have teams check their work.

4. Address questions and any issues you noted during your observation.

> **Answers**
>
> 1. I **don't** own a car.
> 2. This answer **doesn't** seem right. Can you take a look?
> 3. **Do you understand** information better when you read it or when you hear it?
> 4. **I think** that most people believe that if they work hard, they can reach their goals.

> **TIP**
>
> After 2C, use stative verbs to practice expressing opinions in the third-person simple present. Put students in mixed-level groups. Tell each group to write three statements of opinion in the third person using stative verbs. *Seaweed tastes delicious. The flowers do not smell nice.* To increase the variety of statements, assign three verbs to each group. Have group members read the statements. If other students disagree, tell them to respond: *No, it doesn't! Yes, they do!*

3 Listen for action and stative verbs

Guided Practice IV
10–15 minutes

🔊 **1-05** 1. Say a couple of sentences about one of your students. *Carlos goes to the park every weekend. He plays soccer and eats a picnic lunch.* Ask the students whether you used action or stative verbs to talk about Carlos [action]. Say: *Now we're going to listen to sentences about different people. Decide whether the verbs are action or stative verbs.*

2. Play the audio. Direct students to read along silently without writing.

3. Replay the audio. Ask students to check the correct column and then compare answers with a partner.

4. Go over the answers as a class.

Answers	
1. stative	4. action
2. action	5. action
3. stative	6. stative

> **MULTILEVEL STRATEGIES**
>
> Replay the audio for 3 to allow pre-level students to catch up while you challenge on- and higher-level students.
>
> • **Pre-level** Have these students listen again to complete the chart.
>
> • **On- and Higher-level** Have these students write the verbs they hear.

4 Use action and stative verbs to express your opinions

Communicative Practice and Application
20–25 minutes

A 1. Read the questions aloud.

2. Ask students to think about and note their answers.

B Direct students to work with a partner to complete the questions.

C 1. Have pairs merge to form teams of four. Model the exercise by "joining" one of the pairs. Each pair takes a turn asking and answering questions while the class listens. Model creating a chart on the board and filling it in as the pairs ask and answer questions.

2. Check comprehension of the exercise. Ask: *Who asks questions?* [everyone] *Who answers questions?* [everyone]

3. Direct students to ask and answer questions from 4A and 4B in their teams and complete the chart.

4. Ask volunteers to share something interesting they learned about their classmates.

Evaluation
10–15 minutes

TEST YOURSELF

Ask students to write the sentences independently. Collect and correct their writing.

> **MULTILEVEL STRATEGIES**
>
> Target the *Test Yourself* to the level of your students.
>
> • **Pre-level** Allow these students to write six sentences about themselves only.
>
> • **Higher-level** Have these students write a paragraph in response to this prompt: *What are some similarities and differences in the way you and your partner feel about learning English?*

> **EXTENSION ACTIVITY**
> **Game**
>
> 1. Draw a 3x3 or 4x4 Bingo grid on the board. In the top left square, write _____ *loves to read*. In the square below that, write _____ *plays soccer*. Ask: *Who loves to read?* Write the name of a student who answers *yes* on the line. Repeat with *plays soccer*.
>
> 2. Ask students to make their own grids. In each square, instruct them to write a blank followed by an action or stative verb. Encourage them to use a different verb in each square. Circulate and monitor.
>
> 3. Review the objective for Bingo—making a line horizontally, vertically, or diagonally. When students have finished completing their grids, ask them to stand and walk around the room to ask and answer questions about the activities in the grid. They should write a different name on each line. Students call out "Bingo" when they complete a line. For greater challenge, suggest they complete the entire grid.

LESSON 4 EVERYDAY CONVERSATION

Lesson Overview

MULTILEVEL OBJECTIVES

On-, Pre-, and Higher-level: Express agreement and disagreement about education and listen for opinions

LANGUAGE FOCUS

Grammar: *Yes/no,* information, and *or* questions (*What does* visual *mean?*)

Vocabulary: *Agree, disagree, opinion, appropriate*

For vocabulary support, see this **Oxford Picture Dictionary** topic: Succeeding in School, page 10

STRATEGY FOCUS

Practice language to express an opinion.

READINESS CONNECTION

In this lesson, students listen activity for details.

PACING

To compress this lesson: Conduct *Discuss* as a whole class activity.

To extend this lesson: After completing 6B, have students complete a class chart on the board. (See end of lesson.)

And/or have students complete **Workbook 4 page 6** and **Multilevel Activities 4 Unit 1 page 23**.

Lesson Notes

CORRELATIONS

CCRS: SL.1.B (d.) Explain their own ideas and understanding in light of the discussion.

SL.1.C (c.) Pose and respond to specific questions by making comments that contribute to the discussion and elaborate on the remarks of others.

SL.2.B Determine the main ideas and supporting details of a text read aloud or information presented in diverse media and formats, including visually, quantitatively, and orally.

SL.4.B Report on a topic or text, tell a story, or recount an experience with appropriate facts and relevant, descriptive details, speaking clearly at an understandable pace.

SL.6.B Speak in complete sentences when appropriate to task and situation in order to provide requested detail or clarification.

R.1.B Ask and answer such questions as who, what, where, when, why, and how to demonstrate understanding of key details in a text.

R.2.A Identify the main topic and retell key details of a text.

R.6.B Identify the main purpose of a text, including what the author wants to answer, explain, or describe.

R.7.B Use information gained from illustrations and the words in a text to demonstrate understanding of the text.

L.1.A (k.) Understand and use question words (interrogatives).

L.1.B (l.) Produce simple, compound and complex sentences.

L.2.C (a.) Use correct capitalization. (e.) Use a comma to set off the words *yes* and *no*, to set off a tag question from the rest of the sentence, and to indicate direct address.

L.3.B (b.) Recognize and observe differences between the conventions of spoken and written standard English.

RF.2.A (g.) Isolate and pronounce initial, medial vowel, and final sounds (phonemes) in spoken single-syllable words.

RF.4.B (a.) Read grade-level text with purpose and understanding.

ELPS: 1. An ELL can construct meaning from oral presentations and literary and informational text through level-appropriate listening, reading, and viewing. 10. An ELL can demonstrate command of the conventions of standard English to communicate in level-appropriate speech and writing.

Warm-up and Review
10–15 minutes (books closed)

1. Write *How do you learn English?* on the board and elicit students' ideas about effective learning methods. Write their ideas on the board.

2. Ask: *Which methods have you tried? Which would you like to try?*

Introduction
5 minutes

1. Say: *You may think one of these is a good learning method, but your partner might not agree. We all have different opinions. It's important to know how to agree and disagree.*

2. State the objective: *Today we're going to learn how to express opinions about education.*

1 Learn ways to express opinions about education

Presentation I
10–20 minutes

A 🔊 1-06 1. Direct students to look at the picture. Ask: *Where are they? What are they doing? Are they having a serious conversation?*

2. Read the instructions aloud. Play the audio. Give students a minute to answer the question. Go over the answer as a class.

Possible Answers
Class sizes at their school, the best way to learn English

Guided Practice I
20–25 minutes

B 🔊 1-06 1. Read the instructions aloud. Read the questions aloud so students know what information to listen for. Play the audio again. Ask students to listen for the answers to each question.

2. Ask students to compare their answers with a partner. Circulate and monitor to ensure students understand the audio.

Answers
1. No, they don't. The man's opinion is that small classes are better for students. The woman likes large classes. Her opinion is that in a large class, you can meet lots of people.
2. No, they don't. The man's opinion is that watching TV is the best way to learn English. The woman's opinion is that talking and listening to people is better because there's real communication.

C 🔊 1-06 1. Read the instructions aloud. Explain that students are going to hear the audio one more time. They should write the words they hear to complete the sentences.

2. Play the audio. Call on volunteers to elicit the answers.

Answers
1. Maybe you're right
2. I'm not sure I agree
3. You have a point, but

2 Practice your pronunciation

Pronunciation Extension
10–15 minutes

A 🔊 1-07 1. Write: *letter, take, whistle,* and *education* on the board. Say the words and ask student to repeat them. Underline the letter *t* in each word. Ask: *Does t represent the same sound in each word?* Say: *Now we're going to focus on four different ways to pronounce* t.

2. Play the audio. Direct students to listen for the pronunciation of *t*.

3. Ask students to repeat the sentences in the chart.

B Have students work with a partner and write how they think the *t* is pronounced in the words.

Answers	
1. t	4. sh
2. t	5. d
3. t	6. NP

C 🔊 1-08 1. Play the audio. Have students listen and check their answers to 2B. Go over the answers as a class.

2. Ask students to take turns reading the words in 2B with a partner. Monitor and provide feedback.

3 Review *yes/no*, information, and *or* questions

Presentation and Guided Practice II
10–15 minutes

1. Introduce the new topic. Say: *Now we're going to review yes/no and or questions so we can talk about our opinions.*

2. Read the instructions aloud. Give students time to study the charts silently. Ask: *What are the first words in or questions?* [Do; Does]

3. Have students work with a partner to match the questions and answers. Call on volunteers to read the questions and answers aloud. Write the number-letter match on the board.

Answers
1. b   2. a   3. d   4. c

TIP
After 3, provide more practice with question formation. Have students work in pairs to create short opinion polls about a topic of interest to them. Tell each pair to write at least one *yes/no*, one information, and one *or* question. Monitor and provide feedback on the questions. Make a note of common errors and go over them with the class. Direct the pairs to walk around the classroom asking their questions. Call on volunteers to share any interesting information they learned about their classmates.

MULTILEVEL STRATEGIES

- **Higher-level** Direct these students to work in pairs to ask and answer the questions in 3 with their own ideas.

4 Building conversation skills

Guided Practice III
30–35 minutes

A Direct students to look at the picture and skim the conversation. Have them work with partners to identify the purpose of the conversation. Elicit responses and ask: *How do you know?* or *Why do you say that?* to encourage students to state their reasoning.

Possible Answers
The purpose of the conversation is to talk about opinions about teachers' salaries. The students are looking at a story/an article about teachers' salaries together and they don't agree.

B 🔊 1-09 1. Ask students to read the instructions and tell you what they are going to do [listen and respond to the question]. Play the audio and then elicit the answer to the question.

2. Ask students to read the conversation with a partner. Circulate and monitor pronunciation. Model and have students repeat difficult words or phrases.

3. Ask: *In what other situation could you use this conversation?* Point out a few phrases that are not specific to teaching. Ask volunteers to point out others.

Possible Answer
They disagree about teachers' salaries and about how difficult teaching is.

Communicative Practice and Application II
15–20 minutes

C 1. Pair students and have them read the instructions silently. Check their comprehension of the exercise. Ask: *What are the two roles?* [classmates] *Is the conversation about teachers' jobs?* [No, it's about comparing opinions on appropriate classroom behavior.]

2. Model and have students repeat the expressions in the *In Other Words* box. Explain that they should use these expressions in their conversations.

3. Draw a T-chart on the board. Label the left column *Classmate 1* and the right column *Classmate 2*. Elicit examples of what each person might say and make notes on the chart.

4. Set a time limit (three minutes). Have students act out the role-play. Call "time" and have students switch roles.

5. Ask three volunteer pairs to act out their role-play for the class. Tell students who are listening to take notes on the key phrases used and the reasons given.

MULTILEVEL STRATEGIES

For 4C, adapt the role-play to the level of your students.

• **Pre-level** Provide these students with a simplified role-play.

A: Do you think _____?
B: I don't know. Maybe, but I think _____.
A: Really? Don't you think _____?
B You have a point, but I think _____.
A: I'm not sure I agree. I think _____.

5 Focus on listening for details

Presentation and Guided Practice IV
20–25 minutes

A 1. Read the instructions aloud, and model a discussion with a volunteer. Ask: *Do you agree or disagree with the statement: The public schools in our area are doing an excellent job? Why or why not?*

2. Pair students and tell them to discuss their own answers to the question. Circulate and monitor.

B Direct students to read the sentences before they listen to the interview. Ask: *What kind of information will you be writing in the blanks?* Ask volunteers for predictions. If students struggle, start by offering your own prediction: *I think we will hear about issues in public schools.*

C 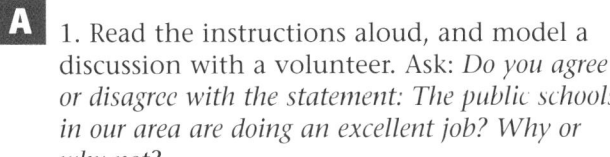 1. Play the audio. Ask students to listen and write the correct answers.

2. Pair students and have them compare answers. If a pair has different answers, have the class vote on the correct answer with a show of hands. Play the audio again if necessary to confirm answers.

Answers
1. Public Schools
2. too many
3. increase
4. security cameras
5. books and computers

6 Discuss

Communicative Practice and Application III
15–20 minutes

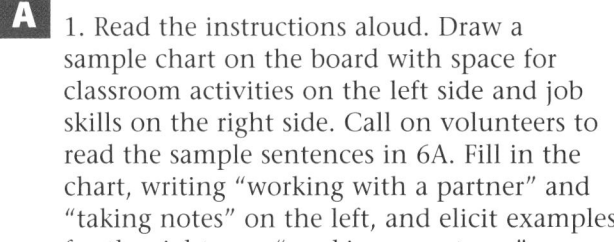

1. Read the instructions aloud. Draw a sample chart on the board with space for classroom activities on the left side and job skills on the right side. Call on volunteers to read the sample sentences in 6A. Fill in the chart, writing "working with a partner" and "taking notes" on the left, and elicit examples for the right: e.g, "working on a team" and "completing paperwork." Explain that students will make a chart like this one based on their own discussions.

2. Put students into teams of four and assign roles: reporter, manager, administrative assistant, and editor. Verify students' understanding of the roles: the reporter reports back to the class, the manager keeps track of time, the administrative assistant records information, and the editor checks grammar and spelling. Encourage students to use the phrases in the *Speaking Note* during their discussions.

3. Set a time limit for the discussions (ten minutes). Write a sentence frame. (*We think that ____ can help you practice ____ at work.*) on the board. Point out that this is similar to the sentence in 6B. Then circulate and monitor.

B Call "time." Have the teams work together to rewrite information from their chart to fit the sentence frame on the board. Editors will check grammar and spelling. Ask the reporter for each team to report the results of their team's discussion, using the sentence frame on the board.

Evaluation
5 minutes

TEST YOURSELF

1. Ask students to complete the checkboxes individually.

2. Tell students that you are going to read each of the items in the checklist aloud. If they are not at all confident with that skill, they should hold up a closed fist. If they are not very confident, they should hold up one finger. If they are somewhat confident, two fingers; confident, three fingers; very confident, four fingers. If they think they could teach the skill, they should hold up five fingers. Read each item in the checklist and identify students that may need further support.

TIP

For homework, you could ask students to write a sentence or two about what discussion skills they still need to work on or, if they are confident in all of the skills, what skill they are most proud of.

EXTENSION ACTIVITY

To extend 6B, draw a large blank chart on the board. As each reporter shares with the class, the administrative assistant from that group fills in the chart. If other teams came up with the same answers, they should not enter the information again.

LESSON 5 READING

Lesson Overview

MULTILEVEL OBJECTIVES

On-, Pre-, and Higher-level: Read about and discuss test anxiety

LANGUAGE FOCUS

Grammar: Simple-past and simple-present tense (*I took the driving test. I think children take too many tests.*); the suffix *-ize (vizualize)*

Vocabulary: *Challenge, college-entrance exam, faint, manageable*

For vocabulary support, see this **Oxford Picture Dictionary** topic: Succeeding in School, page 10

STRATEGY FOCUS

Bullets, or bullet points, help the writer list examples and help the reader find information.

READINESS CONNECTION

In this lesson, students locate and infer information about test anxiety.

PACING

To compress this lesson: Conduct the word study in 2A as a whole-class activity.

To extend this lesson: Have students debate the role of high schools in making students college-ready. (See end of lesson.)

And/or have students complete **Workbook 4 page 7** and **Multilevel Activities 4 Unit 1 pages 24–25**.

Lesson Notes

CORRELATIONS

CCRS: SL.1.B (b.) Follow agreed-upon rules for discussions. (c.) Ask questions to check understanding of information presented, stay on topic, and link their comments to the remarks of others. (d.) Explain their own ideas and understanding in light of the discussion.

SL.2.B Determine the main ideas and supporting details of a text read aloud or information presented in diverse media and formats, including visually, quantitatively, and orally.

R.1.B Ask and answer such questions as who, what, where, when, why, and how to demonstrate understanding of key details in a text.

R.2.A Identify the main topic and retell key details of a text.

R.5.B Know and use various text features to locate key facts or information in a text efficiently.

R.6.B Identify the main purpose of a text, including what the author wants to answer, explain, or describe.

R.7.C Interpret information presented visually, orally, or quantitatively and explain how the information contributes to an understanding of the text in which it appears.

R.8.B Describe how reasons support specific points the author makes in a text.

W.7.A Participate in shared research and writing projects.

L.1.B (l.) Produce simple, compound and complex sentences.

L.2.B (h.) Use conventional spelling for high-frequency and other studied words and for adding suffixes to base words.

L.4.B (e.) Use glossaries and beginning dictionaries, both print and digital, to determine or clarify the meaning of words and phrases.

RF.3.B (c.) Identify and know the meaning of the most common prefixes and derivational suffixes.

RF.4.B (a.) Read grade-level text with purpose and understanding.

ELPS: 1. An ELL can construct meaning from oral presentations and literary and informational text through level-appropriate listening, reading, and viewing. 3. An ELL can speak and write about level-appropriate complex literary and informational texts and topics. 8. An ELL can determine the meaning of words and phrases in oral presentation and literary and informational text.

Warm-up and Review
10–15 minutes (books closed)

Draw a happy face and sad face on the board as column heads. Elicit words that describe feelings and ask students which column they belong in. Write the words. If students run out of ideas, describe situations to elicit more "feeling" words. Ask: *How do you feel at the doctor's office? On a roller coaster? When you can't understand what someone is saying?*

Introduction
5 minutes

1. Add the word *anxiety* to the board. Tell students that it means extreme nervousness. If most of the words on the board are adjectives, point out that *anxious* is the adjective form of *anxiety*.

2. State the objective: *Today we're going to read and write about test anxiety.*

1 Read

Presentation
10–20 minutes

A Read the questions aloud. Use ideas from the *Introduction* to help guide discussion. Elicit advice from the class.

B Read the words and definitions. Elicit sample sentences for each word or supply them if the students can't come up with their own. Ask students how they think the words relate to the topic of *test anxiety*.

Pre-reading

C Read the instructions aloud and confirm that students understand where the "subheadings" and "bullets" are. Have students answer the question individually and then check answers with the class. If any students answer incorrectly, ask them to support their answer using the bulleted headings. Establish the correct answer.

Answer
b. The definition of test anxiety and possible solutions.

Guided Practice: While Reading
20–30 minutes

D 1. Ask students to read the article silently and answer the question.

2. Check answers with the class.

3. Check comprehension. Ask: *What tests are mentioned?* [a driving test, a test you take when you apply for a job, the GED® test, a college entrance exam] *When is test anxiety a problem?* [when it's so strong that it's difficult to study for or take a test] *Should you stay up late to study?* [no] *What should you do after the test?* [reward yourself]

Possible Answer
Test anxiety is feeling stressed before or during a test.

MULTILEVEL STRATEGIES

Adapt 1D to the level of your students.

- **Pre-level** Provide these students with a summary of the ideas in the reading. *Many people experience test anxiety. Test anxiety can cause headaches, nausea, and emotional symptoms. Test anxiety makes it difficult to focus and do well. You can control test anxiety. Take good care of yourself. Take breaks. Think positively. When you feel nervous, take deep breaths.* Direct students to read the summary while other students are reading 1D.

- **On- and Higher-level** Pair students and have them give a summary of the ideas in the reading. Have pairs join other pairs to compare their summaries.

Guided Practice: Rereading
10–15 minutes

E 1. Provide an opportunity for students to extract evidence from the text. Have students reread the article and underline any words or phrases that indicate whether the author is trying to encourage or discourage people who have test anxiety.

2. Pair students and tell them to compare the words they underlined and report anything they disagree on. Discuss and clarify as needed.

Possible Answers

The writer is trying to encourage people who have test anxiety.
It's normal to feel nervous before or during a test.
In fact, feeling a little stressed can help you focus and can even help you do well.
You did it!
You'll see: they help!

TIP

Have students go online to find out about other test-taking strategies. Decide which device(s) students will use and elicit search terms ("*test-taking strategies*" or "*managing test anxiety*").

F 1. Have students work individually to mark the correct answers. They should then write the line number(s) where they found the answer. Write the answers on the board.

2. Elicit and discuss any additional questions about the reading. You could introduce new questions for class discussion: *Have you ever had text anxiety? If so, how have you dealt with it? What are ways can people deal with this? In what other situations do people feel anxiety? Will the same tips work?*

Answers

1. c, line 15/a, line 17	3. c, lines 21–22
2. b, lines 18–19	4. c, lines 29–30

MULTILEVEL STRATEGIES

For 1F, work with pre-level students.

• **Pre-level** Ask these students *yes/no* and short-answer information questions about the reading [or the summary] while other students are completing 1F. *What are some symptoms of test anxiety?* [headaches, nausea, emotional symptoms] *How can you control test anxiety?* [take care of yourself, take breaks, think positively, take deep breaths] Have these students copy the answers to 1F from the board.

2 Word study

Guided Practice: Post-reading
10 minutes

A 1. Direct students to look at the chart and identify the topic [the suffix *-ize*]. Have students read the chart.

2. Read the first two sentences in the chart and the examples for *visualize* and *strategize*. Elicit sentences for the other words in the chart.

3. Have students repeat after you as you say each word with natural intonation, rhythm, and stress.

4. Direct students to complete the sentences and then compare answers with a partner. Read the correct answers and have students check their work.

Answers

1. characterize	3. immobilize
2. emphasize	4. minimize, maximize

 Direct students to work individually to write a sentence for each topic that includes the underlined word. Ask volunteers to write their sentences on the board. Have the rest of the class suggest grammar and spelling edits as needed.

3 Talk it over

Guided Practice
15–20 minutes

A Have students look at the graph and read the note. Point out that they need to use the information from the graph and the note to complete the sentences and answer the question. Set a time limit (ten minutes). Have students work in pairs to complete the task. Ask volunteers to share their answers with the class.

Answers

1. 38
2. 2005, 35
3. college-ready, 21
4. were college-prepared, enrolled in college
5. Data on how many students were college-ready from 1992 to 2013

Communicative Practice
20 minutes

 Read the questions aloud. Set a time limit (ten minutes). Pair students to answer the questions. Ask volunteers to share their ideas with the class.

Application

5–10 minutes

BRING IT TO LIFE

Ask students to use the library or the Internet to research how colleges in your area test new students for placement in classes. Suggest they search online for the school's website and then search on the website for "placement testing."

EXTENSION ACTIVITY

Debate

1. Set up a debate about question 4 in 3B.

2. After students have discussed the question, elicit arguments and write them on the board under *Yes* and *No*.

3. Choose eight students (two groups of four) to be the debaters. Tell one side they are going to argue in favor of high schools being responsible for making their students college-ready and the other that they are going to argue against it. Tell them to choose a role: 1, 2, 3, or 4. Number 1s will present the team's argument. Number 2s will respond to what the first team said. Number 3s will conclude. Number 4s will take notes and help teammates. Give students five minutes to talk with their teammates, choose their roles, and prepare their best arguments.

4. While the teams are preparing, explain to the rest of the class that they will be judges. Tell them they need to judge on how clear and convincing the arguments are, not on whether they agree or not.

5. Toss a coin to decide which team will go first. Have the Number 1s speak; then the Number 2s and Number 3s. Ask the class to choose a winning team. Applaud everyone for the effort.

AT WORK

Warm-up and Review
10–15 minutes (books closed)

Begin the lesson by asking students to describe situations they have experienced when they didn't understand something. Elicit ways they dealt with the situation.

Introduction
5 minutes

State the objective: *Today we're going to talk about what to do when you don't understand something in the workplace.* Ask why it's especially important to clarify things at work.

Presentation
5 minutes

 A 1-11 Read the instructions aloud. Play the audio. Give students a minute to think about the question. Elicit responses from the class.

Possible Answer
computer skills classes for employees

Guided Practice
10–15 minutes

B 1-11 Have students read the statements. Play the audio again. Direct students to listen and write *T* next to the true statements.

Answers			
1. T	2. F	3. T	4. T

 C 1-11 Read the instructions aloud. Elicit how an employee might show he or she didn't understand. Play the audio again, encouraging students to take notes in their notebooks. Set a time limit (five minutes) for students to discuss their answers with a partner. Circulate to monitor.

Possible Answers
He doesn't understand what the notice says/what is on the bulletin board.
He doesn't understand what "release time" means.

Presentation and Communicative Practice
10 minutes

 D 1. Direct students' attention to the *Do/Say* chart and ask them to identify the lesson's soft skill [letting someone know you don't understand]. Ask the class which column has examples of language [right] and which has examples of behaviors [left].

2. Say a phrase from the left and act it out. Say it again and have the class act it out with you. Say it a third time and have the class act it out for you. To confirm understanding, combine phrases: *Raise your hand and then point to what you don't understand.*

3. Model the sentence frames from the right using authentic intonation. Have students practice imitating your inflection.

4. Put students in teams of four and assign each team a question. Assign roles: reporter, manager, administrative assistant, and researcher. (Researchers will ask you questions on behalf of the team.) Verify understanding of the roles. Set a time limit (five minutes) and monitor.

5. Write sentence frames on the board that teams can use to summarize their response. *Our team discussed the following question: _____. We think _____ because _____.*

6. Call "time" and let reporters rehearse their report for one minute. Direct each reporter to present to three other teams.

Communicative Practice and Application
20–25 minutes

 E 1. Model the activity with a student. Say the first sentence. Elicit the question from the student. Point out that students should ask about the words in bold.

2. Direct students to work in pairs to take turns giving information and asking questions.

3. Invite volunteers to act out one of the situations.

F 1. Have pairs merge to form teams of four. Tell students that they are going to be discussing opportunities a company is offering employees.

2. Direct groups to brainstorm three opportunities. Each group should select a manager to run the meeting. The other three members take turns responding and asking for help to understand.

3. As students carry out their role-play, circulate and monitor. Provide global feedback once the activity ends.

TEAMWORK & LANGUAGE REVIEW

Lesson Overview

MULTILEVEL OBJECTIVES

On-, Pre-, and Higher-level: Expand upon and review unit grammar and life skills

LANGUAGE FOCUS

Grammar: Action and stative verbs (*I'm going to school. I need a new computer.*) Present tense questions (*Does the class start at 9:00?*)

Vocabulary: *Social, studying*

For vocabulary support, see this **Oxford Picture Dictionary** topic: Succeeding in School, page 10

READINESS CONNECTION

In this review, students determine how to talk with roommates about a problem.

PACING

To extend this review: Have students complete **Workbook 4 page 8**, **Multilevel Activities 4 Unit 1 page 26**, and **Multilevel Grammar Exercises 4 Unit 1**.

Lesson Notes

CORRELATIONS

CCRS: SL.1.B (a.) Come to discussions prepared, having read or studied required material; explicitly draw on that preparation and other information known about the topic to explore ideas under discussion. (b.) Follow agreed-upon rules for discussions. (c.) Ask questions to check understanding of information presented, stay on topic, and link their comments to the remarks of others. (d.) Explain their own ideas and understanding in light of the discussion.

SL.1.C (b.) Follow agreed-upon rules for discussions and carry out assigned roles.

SL.2.B Determine the main ideas and supporting details of a text read aloud or information presented in diverse media and formats, including visually, quantitatively, and orally.

R.1.B Ask and answer such questions as who, what, where, when, why, and how to demonstrate understanding of key details in a text.

R.2.A Identify the main topic and retell key details of a text.

L.1.A (k.) Understand and use question words (interrogatives).

L.1.B (l.) Produce simple, compound and complex sentences.

L.1.C (c.) Form and use the progressive verb tenses. (d.) Use modal auxiliaries to convey various conditions. (f.) Use verb tense to convey various times, sequences, states, and conditions.

RF.4.B (a.) Read grade-level text with purpose and understanding.

ELPS: 2. An ELL can participate in level-appropriate oral and written exchanges of information, ideas, and analyses, in various social and academic contexts, responding to peer, audience, or reader comments and questions. 5. An ELL can conduct research and evaluate and communicate findings to answer questions or solve problems. 10. An ELL can demonstrate command of the conventions of standard English to communicate in level-appropriate speech and writing.

Warm-up and Review
10–15 minutes (books closed)

1. Review *At Work* activity F.

2. Ask students to share the good, not-so-good, and interesting things that happened during the conversation. As students speak, write their responses in a chart on the board.

Introduction and Presentation
5 minutes

1. Pair students and direct them to look at the picture in their book. Ask them to describe what they see to their partner.

2. Ask volunteer pairs to share their ideas with the class.

Guided Practice
15–20 minutes

 1. Model the process for writing a question about the picture.

2. Set a time limit (five minutes). Have students work in teams to write the questions. Call on volunteers to read the completed questions aloud. Have students ask and answer with a partner.

MULTILEVEL STRATEGIES

For A, seat mixed-level students together.

- **Pre- level, On-, and Higher level** Assign pre-level students the role of administrative assistant and have them write the questions as on-level and higher-level students say them.

B Read the instructions aloud and have students work with their teams to decide who is having each conversation. Go over the answers as a class.

Possible Answers
Tom, Ana
Myra, Jan
Mia, Carlos
Maria, Pedro/Sima, Lia
Sima, Lia/Maria, Pedro

C Go over the first sentence. Direct students to work individually to read the rest of the sentences and find the stative and action verbs.

Answers
Circle: want, seem, need, know, have, love
Underline: go out, spend time, get, miss, change, is, am

D Have students work individually to complete the sentences. Ask volunteers to read the completed sentences aloud.

Answers
A: think; answers will vary
B: sounds; know; answers will vary
C: are holding
D: 'm catching
A: is driving

Communicative Practice
30–40 minutes

 1. Group students and assign roles: manager, director, editor, and actors. Explain that students are going to work with their teams to write a list of strategies for a particular person.

2. Read steps 2–5 of the activity aloud. Check comprehension of the task. *What is the first thing you should do?* [choose a person from the list] *What should you include in the list of strategies?* [a main idea and bullets]

3. Set a time limit (ten minutes) to complete the exercise. Circulate and answer any questions.

4. Have actors from each team read their team's suggestions to the class.

 1. Have students walk around the room to conduct the interviews. To get students moving, tell them to interview three people who were not in their team for E.

2. Set a time limit (five minutes) to complete the exercise.

3. Tell students to make a note of their classmates' answers but not to worry about writing complete sentences.

MULTILEVEL STRATEGIES

Adapt the mixer in F to the level of your students.

- **Pre-level** Allow these students to ask and answer without writing.
- **On- and Higher-level** Have these students ask two additional questions and write all answers.

G 1. Call on individuals to report what they learned about their classmates. Keep a running tally on the board for Exercise F question #3, marking how many students are mostly visual, mostly auditory, and mostly kinesthetic learners.

2. Use your tally for question 3 to create a pie chart on the board. Instruct students to copy the chart in their notebooks. Circulate and answer any questions.

PROBLEM SOLVING
10–15 minutes

A 1. Ask: *Can you study when other people in your house are watching TV or listening to music?* Tell students they will read a story about a woman who is having trouble studying. Direct students to read Rita's story silently.

2. Ask: *Are Rita's roommates students?* [No, they aren't.] *What do they like to do in the evening?* [They like to talk and play music.]

3. Play the audio and have students read along silently.

B Elicit answers to question 1. Have volunteers write answers to question 2 on the board until all of the class ideas have been put up.

Possible Answers
1. Rita has a lot of homework and she studies best when her apartment is quiet, but her roommates talk and play music so Rita can't concentrate. She doesn't know what to do about the situation.

Evaluation
20–25 minutes

To test students' understanding of the unit language and content, have them take the Unit 1 Test, available on the Teacher Resource Center.

UNIT 2 Breaking News

Unit Overview

This unit explores news and current events and expressing opinions with a range of employability skills and contextualizes past passive grammar structures.

KEY OBJECTIVES

Lesson 1	Identify types of news
Lesson 2	Identify types of information in a news story
Lesson 3	Use the past passive to describe an event
Lesson 4	Express agreement in a conversation
Lesson 5	Identify ways to support an opinion
At Work	Give your opinion at work
Teamwork & Language Review	Review unit language

UNIT FEATURES

Academic Vocabulary	device, generation, gender, injure, media, react, rely, remove, respond, source, survey, technology, traditional
Employability Skills	• Listen actively • Cooperate with others • Give your opinion in a group • Understand teamwork • Work with others • Communicate information • Differentiate between fact and opinion • Determine how to join in a discussion about current events

Resources	**Class Audio** CD1, Tracks 13–22
	Workbook Unit 2, pages 9–15
	Teacher Resource Center
	    Multilevel Activities 4 Unit 2
	    Multilevel Grammar Exercises 4 Unit 2
	    Unit 2 Test
	Oxford Picture Dictionary The Library, Entertainment

LESSON 1 VOCABULARY

Lesson Overview

MULTILEVEL OBJECTIVES

On-level: Identify different types of news and describe news preferences

Pre-level: Identify ways to get the news and use news vocabulary

Higher-level: Describe different types of news and explain news preferences

LANGUAGE FOCUS

Grammar: Simple-present tense (*I usually read the headlines.*)

Vocabulary: News sections and news words

For vocabulary support, see this **Oxford Picture Dictionary** topic: Entertainment, pages 242–243

READINESS CONNECTION

In this lesson, students work with others to communicate information about the news.

PACING

To compress this lesson: Conduct 2A as a whole-class activity.

To extend this lesson: Have students read headlines and practice categorizing the news. (See end of lesson.)

And/or have students complete **Workbook 4 page 9** and **Multilevel Activities 4 Unit 2 pages 28–29**.

Lesson Notes

CORRELATIONS

CCRS: SL.1.B (d.) Explain their own ideas and understanding in light of the discussion.

SL.2.B Determine the main ideas and supporting details of a text read aloud or information presented in diverse media and formats, including visually, quantitatively, and orally.

SL.4.B Report on a topic or text, tell a story, or recount an experience with appropriate facts and relevant, descriptive details, speaking clearly at an understandable pace.

SL.6.B Speak in complete sentences when appropriate to task and situation in order to provide requested detail or clarification.

R.1.B Ask and answer such questions as who, what, where, when, why, and how to demonstrate understanding of key details in a text.

R.4.B Determine the meaning of general academic and domain-specific words and phrases in a text relevant to a topic or subject area.

R.5.B Know and use various text features to locate key facts or information in a text efficiently.

R.7.C Interpret information presented visually, orally, or quantitatively and explain how the information contributes to an understanding of the text in which it appears.

L.1.B (l.) Produce simple, compound and complex sentences.

L.4.B (a.) Use sentence-level context as a clue to the meaning of a word or phrase. (e.) Use glossaries and beginning dictionaries, both print and digital, to determine or clarify the meaning of words and phrases.

RF.4.B (a.) Read grade-level text with purpose and understanding.

ELPS: 1. An ELL can construct meaning from oral presentations and literary and informational text through level-appropriate listening, reading, and viewing. 2. An ELL can participate in level-appropriate oral and written exchanges of information, ideas, and analyses, in various social and academic contexts, responding to peer, audience, or reader comments and questions. 3. An ELL can speak and write about level-appropriate complex literary and informational texts and topics. 5. An ELL can conduct research and evaluate and communicate findings to answer questions or solve problems. 8. An ELL can determine the meaning of words and phrases in oral presentation and literary and informational text.

Warm-up and Review
10–15 minutes (books closed)

Pass out different sections of a newspaper. Give students a couple of minutes to look through them. Ask students to look at the sections (not to read the articles). Then elicit what they found in their sections.

Introduction
5 minutes

1. Tell students which sections of the newspaper (or a news website) you usually read and why you like them.

2. State the objective: *Today we're going to learn vocabulary for talking about news sections and the news.*

1 Identify news sources

Presentation I
20–25 minutes

 1. Write *news* on the board, and ask: *How do you get the news?* Elicit students' answers and write them on the board.

2. Direct students to look at the web page of a news website. Ask: *What information do you see?* Elicit the words *sections* and *headlines*.

3. Check for understanding by asking students to look at the section *World News*. Ask: *What is the headline for this section?* Elicit examples.

4. Have students work in groups to answer the questions. Call on volunteers to provide answers.

Answers
1. World news, local news, entertainment, sports, opinion pieces, ads
2. Answers will vary.

 1-13 1. Direct students to read the questions. Then ask: *Where/In which section can you read opinions about the news?* [Editorial] Point out that 5 is written on the line next to question 1.

2. Have students write the correct number of the news section that answers the question. Have students compare their answers with a partner.

3. To prepare students for the listening, say: *Now we're going to hear two people discuss how they prefer to get their news and the news sections they like to read.* Ask students to listen and check their answers.

4. Play the audio so students can check their answers.

Answers	
1. 5	4. 4
2. 6	5. 2
3. 1	6. 3

MULTILEVEL STRATEGIES

Adapt 1B to the level of your students.

- **Pre-level** Have pre-level students sit together. Play the audio and pause every few lines to have students find answers to the questions.
- **Higher-level** Pair students and ask the question: *What news is most important to you?* Direct them to create a conversation using their own ideas.

 1-13 Read the instructions aloud. Play the audio again so students can answer the questions. Elicit the answers from the class.

Answers	
Wanda: newspaper	Stan: online news, radio

2 Learn more types of news

Presentation II
10–20 minutes

 1. Introduce the new topic: *Now we're going to talk about more types of news.* Direct students to look at the website. Ask: *What kind of website is this?*

2. Have students look at the website. Elicit and answer questions about unfamiliar vocabulary.

3. Have students work individually to match the words and definitions.

4. Call on volunteers to read the matching words and definitions aloud.

5. Ask questions to check for understanding. What are current events? [news about today] Where can you learn about conditions on the road? [traffic report]

Answers	
1. e	4. b
2. a	5. d
3. c	

Guided Practice I
10–15 minutes

 1. Model the conversation with a volunteer. Model it again using other information from 2A.

2. Set a time limit (three minutes). Direct students to practice with a partner.

3. Call on volunteers to present their version of the conversation for the class.

> **MULTILEVEL STRATEGIES**
>
> Adapt 2B to the level of your students.
>
> • **Pre- and On-level** Pair pre- and on-level students for 2B. Assign pre-level students part A for the first round and then have them switch roles.

Communicative Practice and Application
20–25 minutes

 1. Write the questions from 2C on the board. Model the activity with a volunteer. Write the answers to each question on the board.

2. Have students form teams of four and assign roles (manager, reporter, administrative assistant, researcher). Ask each member to take turns asking and answering the questions with three people not on their team. Set a time limit of five minutes.

3. Call "time." Have students return to their teams. Give managers a time limit of five minutes for members to share and tally their results.

> **TIP**
>
> When setting up task-based activities, verify that students understand their roles using physical commands. For example: *If you report on your team's work, stand up* [reporter]. *If you keep the team on task, point to the clock* [manager]. *If you write the team's responses, raise your hand* [administrative assistant]. *If you help with tallying the results, hold up your smartphone/tablet* [researcher].

 1. Copy the sentence frames on the board.

2. Direct teams to help their administrative assistant use the sentence frames to record the team's findings. Direct the reporter to use the recorded information to report the team's findings to the class or another team.

Evaluation
10–15 minutes

TEST YOURSELF

1. Direct Partner A to read questions 1–3 from 1B on page 20 to Partner B. Partner B should close their book and write the answers in their notebook. When finished, students switch roles. Partner B reads questions 4–6 from 1B.

2. Direct both partners to open their books and check their spelling when they finish.

> **EXTENSION ACTIVITY**
>
> **Categorize the News**
>
> 1. Pair students and provide them with several sections of a newspaper. (You can use the same sections from the *Warm-up*.) Tell each pair to copy or cut out two or three headlines from the paper.
>
> 2. Have the pairs exchange headlines. Then ask each pair to read the new headline aloud and to guess which section it came from. Alternatively, write the section titles on the board and have pairs tape their headlines in the correct place. Go over the answers as a class. Discuss new vocabulary.

LESSON 2 WRITING

Lesson Overview

MULTILEVEL OBJECTIVES

On- and Higher-level: Analyze, write, and edit a news story

Pre-level: Read and write a news story

LANGUAGE FOCUS

Grammar: Simple past tense (*They called the police.*)

Vocabulary: *Graffiti, responded, disagreement*

For vocabulary support, see this **Oxford Picture Dictionary** topic: Entertainment, pages 242–243

STRATEGY FOCUS

When you are writing, use adverbial time clauses to establish a sequence of events in the past.

READINESS CONNECTION

In this lesson, students communicate information by writing a news story.

PACING

To compress this lesson: Assign the *Test Yourself* for homework.

To extend this lesson: Watch a video clip from a recent news story and practice talking about past events. (See end of lesson.)

And/or have students complete **Workbook 4 page 10** and **Multilevel Activities 4 Unit 2 page 30**.

Lesson Notes

CORRELATIONS

CCRS: SL.1.B (d.) Explain their own ideas and understanding in light of the discussion.

SL.2.B Determine the main ideas and supporting details of a text read aloud or information presented in diverse media and formats, including visually, quantitatively, and orally.

R.1.B Ask and answer such questions as who, what, where, when, why, and how to demonstrate understanding of key details in a text.

R.2.A Identify the main topic and retell key details of a text.

R.5.A Know and use various text features to locate key facts or information in a text.

R.7.B Use information gained from illustrations and the words in a text to demonstrate understanding of the text.

W.2.A Write informative/explanatory texts in which they name a topic, supply some facts about the topic, and provide some sense of closure.

W.4.B Produce writing in which the development and organization are appropriate to task and purpose.

W.5.B With guidance and support from peers and others, develop and strengthen writing as needed by planning, revising and editing.

L.1.B (l.) Produce simple, compound and complex sentences.

L.2.B (b.) Capitalize appropriate words in titles. (d.) Use a comma to separate an introductory element form the rest of the sentence.

RF.4.B (a.) Read grade-level text with purpose and understanding.

ELPS: 1. An ELL can construct meaning from oral presentations and literary and informational text through level-appropriate listening, reading, and viewing. 3. An ELL can speak and write about level-appropriate complex literary and informational texts and topics. 6. An ELL can analyze and critique the arguments of others orally and in writing. 9. An ELL can create clear and coherent level-appropriate speech and text.

Warm-up and Review
10–15 minutes (books closed)

Bring in a picture or show a short video clip from a recent big news story. If you don't have a picture, write a "headline" on the board for the event. For example: *New President Elected. Hundreds Injured in Earthquake.* Ask questions (*who, what, why, where, when, how*) about the news story. As students answer, write the past-tense forms of the verbs they use on the board. Remind them that when they tell about an event, many of the verbs they use will be in the simple-past tense.

Introduction
5 minutes

1. Say: *If you answer the questions who, what, why, where, when, and how, you've probably covered the important information about any story.*

2. State the objective: *Today we're going to read and write news stories that answer these six questions.*

1 Prepare to write

Presentation
20–25 minutes

A 1. Build students' schema by asking questions about the picture. Ask: *What do you see in the picture?* [buildings, streets, people, cars, etc.] *Are the things in the picture mostly clean?* [yes] *What is not clean?* [the building on the right]

2. Give students one minute to tell a partner their responses to questions 1 and 2. Elicit answers from the class.

B 1. Tell students they are going to read and listen to a story about graffiti. Play the audio. Have students read along silently.

2. Elicit students' questions about vocabulary. Check comprehension. Ask: *Where does this happen?* [Lakeland] *Who put the graffiti on the building?* [teenagers] *Who is Mr. Suk?* [the building's owner]

3. Draw students' attention to the *Writer's Note*. Write the sentences from the note on the board. Elicit the adverbial time clauses in each sentence. Point out or elicit that when the time clause comes before the main clause, we use a comma. Elicit the sentence in the article that uses a time clause. [When angry neighbors saw them, they called the police.]

Guided Practice I
10 minutes

C 1. Have students work independently to answer the questions.

2. Have students compare answers with a partner. Go over the answers with the class.

Possible Answers
1. They were angry and they called the police. 2. Mr. Suk doesn't mind the graffiti. He thinks it is art. He doesn't agree with the neighbors. 3. The angry neighbors will probably attend the meeting. Mr. Suk might attend the meeting.

2 Plan and write

Guided Practice II
15–20 minutes

A 1. Read question 1 aloud. Elicit students' answers and write them on the board.

2. Choose one of the events on the board, and ask volunteers *who, what, where, when, why,* and *how* questions in order to elicit the story.

B 1. Direct students to look back at the article in 1B. Focus students' attention on the change from past tense in the first paragraph to present tense in the second paragraph. Elicit the reason for the change.

2. Read the questions for paragraph 1 aloud. Ask: *What tense will this paragraph be in?* [past] *Should you write the questions in your story?* [no, just the answers]

3. Read the question for paragraph 2 aloud. Point out that the question is in the past tense. Ask: *When should you use present tense when writing about reactions?* [when the event is still occurring or very recent]

4. Read the question for paragraph 3 aloud. Point out that the story will end with speculation about the future.

5. Draw students' attention to the headline and the beginning of the news story. Remind them to add a headline when they write. Have students work individually to write their stories.

> **TIP**
>
> Write examples of headlines on the board: *Police Called in Lakeland*; *Accident Injures Five*; *Flood Washes Away Bridge*. Ask: *Are these complete sentences?* [no] *What's missing?* [articles, some auxiliaries, some nouns] Explain that headlines use key words. They try to grab attention in as few words as possible.

> **MULTILEVEL STRATEGIES**
>
> Adapt 2B to the level of your students.
>
> • **Pre-level** Work with this group to write a story together. Elicit the answers to the questions and compose the story sentence by sentence.
>
> • **Higher-level** After these students finish, ask them to underline all of the verbs in their stories and discuss their verb-tense choices with a partner.

3 Get feedback and revise

Guided Practice III
5 minutes

A Direct students to check their writing using the editing checklist. Tell them to read each item in the list and check their papers before moving onto the next item. Explain that students should not edit their writing at this stage. They should just use the checklist to check their work and mark any areas they want to revise.

Communicative Practice
15 minutes

B 1. Read the instructions aloud. Emphasize to students that they are responding to their partners' work, not correcting it.

2. Use the news story in 1B to model the exercise. It answers the questions *who*, *what*, *when*, *where*, *why*, and *how*. [neighbors, disagree about graffiti, last night, an empty building in Lakeland, teenagers painted graffiti on an empty building, chief of police will hold a meeting]

3. Model step 2 with the class: *I'm not sure I understand the order of events...* Have students check each other's papers for clarity and for adverbial time clauses.

4. Direct students to exchange papers with a partner and follow the instructions.

C Allow students time to edit and revise their writing as necessary, using the editing checklist from 3A and their partner's feedback from 3B. If necessary, students could complete this task as homework.

> **TIP**
>
> After completing 3C, hold a "news meeting" in class. Ask for volunteers to come to the front of the room and read their stories. All non-volunteers are "editors." Ask the editors to listen and take notes. Tell them they need to rank the stories in order of importance. Have the editors come to a consensus about which story should be on the top of the front page or lead the TV broadcast.

Application and Evaluation
15 minutes

TEST YOURSELF

1. Review the instruction aloud. Ask students to share their ideas with the class. *What has happened at school recently? In your workplace? In your neighborhood?* Assign a time limit (15 minutes) and have students work independently. Give students notice when they have five minutes left.

2. Before collecting students' work, remind them to use the *editing checklist.* Collect and correct students' writing.

> **EXTENSION ACTIVITY**
>
> **Report the News**
>
> 1. Play a short video (two to three minutes) of a news event with the sound off. Use footage from television or the Internet or choose a scene from a movie—for example, a scene of robbers breaking into a bank.
>
> 2. Have students tell their partners about what they saw, including the answers to the *who, what, where, when, how,* and *why* questions. Tell them to invent the answers if necessary. Circulate and monitor.
>
> 3. Wrap up by eliciting and writing vocabulary that was necessary for telling the story.

LESSON 3 GRAMMAR

Lesson Overview

MULTILEVEL OBJECTIVES

On- and Higher-level: Use the past passive to discuss current events and listen for information in news stories

Pre-level: Identify the past passive in news stories

LANGUAGE FOCUS

Grammar: The past passive (*Drivers were surprised by the fog.*)

Vocabulary: *Injured, damaged, removed,*

For vocabulary support, see this **Oxford Picture Dictionary** topic: Entertainment, pages 242–243

READINESS CONNECTION

In this lesson, students cooperate with others to discuss news stories.

PACING

To compress this lesson: Conduct 1C as a whole-class activity.

To extend this lesson: Have students make headlines into past passive sentences. (See end of lesson.)

And/or have students complete **Workbook 4 pages 11–12**, **Multilevel Activities 4 Unit 2 pages 31–32**, and **Multilevel Grammar Exercises 4 Unit 2**.

Lesson Notes

CORRELATIONS

CCRS: SL.2.B Determine the main ideas and supporting details of a text read aloud or information presented in diverse media and formats, including visually, quantitatively, and orally.

R.1.B Ask and answer such questions as who, what, where, when, why, and how to demonstrate understanding of key details in a text.

R.5.A Know and use various text features to locate key facts or information in a text.

R.7.B Use information gained from illustrations and the words in a text to demonstrate understanding of the text.

L.1.D (g.) Form and use verbs in the active and passive voice.

L.2.B (b.) Capitalize appropriate words in titles.

RF.4.B (a.) Read grade-level text with purpose and understanding.

ELPS: 2. An ELL can participate in level-appropriate oral and written exchanges of information, ideas, and analyses, in various social and academic contexts, responding to peer, audience, or reader comments and questions. 3. An ELL can speak and write about level-appropriate complex literary and informational texts and topics. 7. An ELL can adapt language choices to purpose, task, and audience when speaking and writing. 9. An ELL can create clear and coherent level-appropriate speech and text. 10. An ELL can demonstrate command of the conventions of standard English to communicate in level-appropriate speech and writing.

Warm-up and Review
10–15 minutes (books closed)

Review past participles. Have students line up at the board in two teams. Direct one team member at a time to approach the board. Call out a verb in base form. The first person to correctly write the participle wins a point for the team. Allow team members to call out the answers to help their teammates at the board. Leave the participles on the board.

Introduction
5–10 minutes

1. Use the participles on the board to write several past-passive sentences that sound like news stories. *An election was held last night. Houses were damaged by the wind.*

2. State the objective: *Today we're going to learn how to use the past passive to describe events.*

1 Use the past passive

Presentation I
20–25 minutes

 1. Direct students to look at the photo in the article. Ask: *What happened?* [an accident; a highway crash with multiple cars]

2. Read the instructions aloud. Ask students to read the news story silently and answer the questions. Have students compare answers with a partner.

3. Read the first question aloud. Call on a volunteer for the answer. Ask the volunteer where in the article they found the answer. Read the rest of the questions aloud, calling on a different volunteer for each answer.

Answers
1. The police
2. No
3. Answers will vary.
4. No; Answers will vary.

 1. Demonstrate how to read the grammar chart.

2. Direct students to underline the five past passive verbs in the article in 1A. Write the sentences on the board. Have students compare answers with a partner.

3. Go over the answers with the class. Elicit the past passive verbs and underline them. As you elicit each answer, ask about the cause of each action. *Who closed the highway?* [the police] *Where were several people taken?* [to the hospital]

4. Assess students' understanding of the chart. Ask: *What was the accident caused by?* [the fog] *Who didn't take Min to the hospital?* [the paramedics] *Which is more important: Who was taken to the hospital or who took people to the hospital?* [who was taken]

Answers
was closed; were called; were taken; were removed; was reopened

Guided Practice I
20–25 minutes

 1. Tell students they will collaborate to complete the description of the grammar point. Model collaboration by working with the class to complete the first sentence. Encourage students to look at 1A and 1B to see which is more important, the action or the person who did it.

2. Pair students and have them work together to complete the description.

3. Project or write the completed definition on the board and have pairs verify the accuracy of their responses. Ask volunteers which sentences confused them and discuss.

Answers
more, know, say, clear

 Ask students to work individually to complete the sentences and then compare answers with a partner. Go over the answers as a class. Ask volunteers to write the answers on the board.

Answers	
1. was caused	4. was written
2. were injured	5. were taken
3. was reopened	

Guided Practice II
5–10 minutes

 1. Model the first item with the class. Show students how the object (*Highway 437*) moves into the subject position. Elicit the past passive form of *closed* [was closed].

2. Have students form teams of four and then work together to rewrite the sentences using *by* + nouns.

3. Ask volunteers to write the sentences on the board. Provide clarification or feedback to the whole class as needed.

Answers
1. After the accident, Highway 437 was closed by the police.
2. The injured people were taken to the hospital by paramedics.
3. The cars were removed from the highway by several tow trucks.
4. The photos we saw on the news were taken by traffic reporters in a helicopter.

> **TIP**
>
> For more practice with passive sentences, have students write passive riddles. Put the following sentence on the board as a model: *It was invented by Thomas Edison.* Ask students to guess what *it* is [the light bulb]. Group students and provide each group with a large sheet of paper. Have the groups write three to four passive sentences with "mystery" subjects. Write possible sentence beginnings on the board: *It was written... It was built... They were destroyed... It was conquered... It was performed... It was sung...* Post the papers and have the rest of the class guess the missing subjects.

2 Use past passive questions

Presentation II
20–25 minutes

A 1. Introduce the new topic: *Now we're going to ask questions with the past passive.*

2. Read the first *yes/no* question aloud. Call on a volunteer to give the answer. Ask: *What word comes first in a yes/no question in the past passive?* [was/were] Elicit the affirmative answers from the chart and then elicit the negative forms. [No, it wasn't.; No, they weren't.]

3. Write the information questions on the board. Elicit the form [question word + *was/were* + subject + past participle]. Ask the questions from the chart. Call on volunteers to give the answers in the chart. Say: *Sometimes we can give a short answer to information questions.* Elicit the short answers for the questions in the chart [An hour after the accident; To City Hospital].

4. Have students work in pairs to take turns asking and answering the questions in the chart.

Guided Practice III
10–15 minutes

B Ask students to work individually to complete the conversation and then compare their answers with a partner. Ask a volunteer pair to read their conversation aloud and write the answers on the board.

Answers
A: was caused
B: Was…hit
A: was hit
B: Were…hurt
A: was hit…wasn't hurt

> **MULTILEVEL STRATEGIES**
>
> Seat same-level students together for 2B.
>
> • **Pre-level** Work with these students to help them recognize the question and answer forms for past passive. Read each line aloud and call on a volunteer for the answer. Discuss the tense of each answer.
>
> • **On- and Higher-level** Direct these students to complete 2B and then practice the conversation with a partner. Have them write two or three original questions and answers about the article on page 24. Ask volunteers to read their questions and answers to the class.

> **TIP**
>
> For more practice with past-passive questions after 2B, post some of the news story pictures or headlines you have used during this unit. As a class, brainstorm questions about each story. Write the questions on the board.
>
> As an alternative practice, write news sections on the board: *Local, National, World, Health, Technology, Education, Traffic Report, Weather Forecast,* etc. Pair students and assign each pair one of the sections. Then have students write a passive "headline" under their pair's section on the board. Tell them to write about a real event if possible. Correct the "headlines" together. As a class, brainstorm past-passive questions about the headlines.

3 Listen for the past passive to determine the meaning

Guided Practice IV
10–15 minutes

🔊 **1-15** 1. Say: *Now we're going to listen to some statements about past events.*

2. Play the audio. Direct students to read along silently and point to the statement that has a similar meaning to the one they hear. Review the answer to number 1. Ask a volunteer what he or she heard.

3. Replay the audio. Stop after every statement and ask students to check the correct sentence.

4. Ask volunteers to read the correct answers aloud.

Answers	
1. b	3. b
2. a	4. b

> **MULTILEVEL STRATEGIES**
>
> Replay the audio for 3 to allow pre-level students to catch up while you challenge higher-level students.
>
> • **Pre- and On-level** Have these students listen again to choose the correct sentences.
>
> • **Higher-level** Direct these students to write the sentences they hear. When you have played all the sentences, ask volunteers to write them on the board. Compare the sentences on the board with their answers to 3.

4 Use the past passive to talk about real events

Communicative Practice and Application
20–25 minutes

 1. Read the instructions aloud. Ask: *What was built or damaged or closed or discovered recently?* Elicit an example of a recent news story that answers the question (e.g., A new stadium was built for the Olympics). Direct students to work independently to write headlines. Have students compare ideas in pairs.

2. Call on volunteers to share their headlines, correcting grammar as necessary. Establish the correct grammar for each sentence.

B Direct students to work with a partner to write two more news headlines using the past passive.

C 1. Have pairs merge to form teams of four. Model the exercise by "joining" one of the pairs. Each pair takes a turn asking and answering questions while the class listens.

2. Check comprehension of the exercise. Ask: *Who asks questions?* [everyone] *Who answers questions?* [everyone]

3. Ask volunteers to share one of the news headlines they heard from their team.

Evaluation
10–15 minutes

TEST YOURSELF

Ask students to write the sentences independently. Collect and correct their writing.

> **MULTILEVEL STRATEGIES**
>
> Target the *Test Yourself* to the level of your students.
>
> • **Pre-level** Ask these students to copy the following sentences and then reorder them in the correct sequence. *A waitress was carried out of the building by the firefighters. The neighbors called 911. A fire started in the kitchen of Sam's restaurant last night. The flames were seen by neighbors.* Ask students to identify whether the sentences are active or passive.
>
> • **Higher-level** Have students write a short paragraph in response to this prompt: *Describe a recent news event. Use at least three sentences in the past passive. Write three questions about your story for a partner to answer.* Have students who finish early read their paragraphs to a partner and ask the partner the three questions.

> **EXTENSION ACTIVITY**
> **Discussion**
>
> Distribute newspapers to pairs or small groups of students. Ask them to look for headlines that they can make into past-passive sentences. Have volunteers share their sentences with the class.

LESSON 4 EVERYDAY CONVERSATION

Lesson Overview

MULTILEVEL OBJECTIVES

On-, Pre-, and Higher-level: Give opinions about current events and listen for information in a news story

LANGUAGE FOCUS

Grammar: Reflexive pronouns *(Did you see it yourself?)*

Vocabulary: *Protesters, prohibited, makes sense, limit*

For vocabulary support, see this **Oxford Picture Dictionary** topic: Entertainment, pages 242–243

STRATEGY FOCUS

Practice using reflexive pronouns. Ask questions and restate information to check for understanding.

READINESS CONNECTION

In this lesson, students give opinions in a group and join in a discussion about current events.

PACING

To compress this lesson: Conduct *Discuss* as a whole-class activity.

To extend this lesson: After completing 6B, have students rank and discuss dangerous jobs. (See end of lesson.)

And/or have students complete **Workbook 4 page 13** and **Multilevel Activities 4 Unit 2 page 33**.

Lesson Notes

CORRELATIONS

CCRS: SL.1.B (a.) Come to discussions prepared, having read or studied required material; explicitly draw on that preparation and other information known about the topic to explore ideas under discussion. (b.) Follow agreed-upon rules for discussions. (c.) Ask questions to check understanding of information presented, stay on topic, and link their comments to the remarks of others. (d.) Explain their own ideas and understanding in light of the discussion.

SL.2.B Determine the main ideas and supporting details of a text read aloud or information presented in diverse media and formats, including visually, quantitatively, and orally.

SL.4.B Report on a topic or text, tell a story, or recount an experience with appropriate facts and relevant, descriptive details, speaking clearly at an understandable pace.

SL.6.B Speak in complete sentences when appropriate to task and situation in order to provide requested detail or clarification.

R.7.B Use information gained from illustrations and the words in a text to demonstrate understanding of the text.

L.1.B (d.) Use reflexive pronouns. (l.) Produce simple, compound and complex sentences.

L.3.B (b.) Recognize and observe differences between the conventions of spoken and written standard English.

RF.4.B (a.) Read grade-level text with purpose and understanding.

ELPS: 2. An ELL can participate in level-appropriate oral and written exchanges of information, ideas, and analyses, in various social and academic contexts, responding to peer, audience, or reader comments and questions. 4. An ELL can construct level-appropriate oral and written claims and support them with reasoning and evidence. 6. An ELL can analyze and critique the arguments of others orally and in writing. 7. An ELL can adapt language choices to purpose, task, and audience when speaking and writing. 9. An ELL can create clear and coherent level-appropriate speech and text. 10. An ELL can demonstrate command of the conventions of standard English to communicate in level-appropriate speech and writing.

Warm-up and Review
10–15 minutes (books closed)

Have students discuss *protests* using information they already know. Ask: *What is a protest? What do people do during a protest? What are some protests you know? What were people protesting?*

> **TIP**
> This topic may recall frightening memories for some students. Keep the discussion general and don't call on students to share their personal experiences unless they volunteer.

Introduction
5 minutes

1. Tell students that protests are common in the U.S., but they are usually nonviolent. Protests are an accepted way for groups of people to express their disagreement.

2. State the objective: *Today we're going to learn how to give our opinions about current events.*

1 Learn ways to talk about a current event

Presentation I
10–20 minutes

A 🔊 1-16 1. Direct students to look at the picture. Ask: *Does this protest look peaceful?*

2. Read the instructions aloud. Play the audio. Ask students to listen for the answer to the question: *What did the city want?*

3. Give students a few minutes to answer the question. Have students compare answers with a partner. Go over the answer as a class.

Answer
The city wanted to prohibit food trucks on the street.

Guided Practice I
20–25 minutes

B 1-16 1. Read the instructions aloud. Play the audio. Ask students to listen for the answers to each question.

2. Ask students to compare their answers with a partner. Circulate and monitor to ensure students understand the audio.

Possible Answers
1. The protesters wanted the city to allow the food trucks.
2. The traffic downtown was blocked for hours by the protest.
3. The speakers like the food trucks because the food is good and cheap, and it's important to support local businesses.

C 🔊 1-16 Read the instructions aloud. Explain that students are going to hear the audio one more time. They should write the words they hear to complete the sentences. Play the audio. Have students compare answers with a partner. Call on volunteers to elicit the answers.

Answers
1. So was I
2. I can understand that.

2 Practice your pronunciation

Pronunciation Extension
10–15 minutes

A 1-17 1. Write this exchange on the board: *A: There was a protest last night. B: Last week? A: No, last night.* Ask a volunteer to read part B and model the conversation for the class. Ask students which word you stressed in the last sentence [night]. Say: *Now we're going to focus on using stress to clarify meaning.*

2. Play the audio. Direct students to listen for the stressed words and underline them.

3. Ask what would happen if you didn't stress the words. [The listener might misunderstand again.]

Answers
A: The city wanted to prohibit food trucks.
B: <u>Limit</u> food trucks?
A: No, not limit food trucks, <u>prohibit</u> food trucks.

B After students finish reading, have them work with a partner to underline the words they think will be stressed.

Answers
1. A: The tree wasn't cut down.
B: It <u>was</u> cut down?
A: No, it <u>wasn't</u> cut down.
2. A: The protesters were very upset.
B: The <u>police</u> were upset?
A: No, the <u>protestors</u>.

C

🔊 **1-18** 1. Play the audio and have students check their work. Go over the answers as a class.

2. Have partners practice the conversations in 2A and 2B. Monitor and provide feedback.

TIP

Have students create an original conversation patterned after the ones in 2B. Have volunteers read their conversations to the class. Ask the class to identify the stressed words.

3 Learn reflexive pronouns

Presentation II and Guided Practice II
10–15 minutes

A
1. Draw your face on the board. Say: *I'm drawing myself.* Ask a male and a female volunteer to do the same. Say: *She's drawing herself. He's drawing himself.* Thank the students and say: *Thank you for drawing yourselves.* Have them sit down. Say: *They drew themselves.* Introduce the new topic: *Now we're going to learn about reflexive pronouns.*

2. Write on the board: *They drew themselves on the board.* Ask: *What is the verb?* [drew] *What is the subject of the verb?* [they] *What is the object?* [themselves] *Are the subject and object talking about different people or the same people?* [same]

3. Read the information in the chart aloud. Have students underline and repeat the reflexive pronouns. Elicit the answer to the question in the instructions.

Answers
Underline all *self* and *selves*

Guided Practice III
15–20 minutes

B
Have students work individually to complete the sentences with reflexive pronouns and then compare answers with a partner. Go over the answers as a class.

Answers	
1. yourself	3. yourselves
2. ourselves	4. herself

TIP

In 3B, point out that the expression in number 3 (*by* + reflexive pronoun) means "alone," "unaccompanied," or "without help." Have students practice the expression with several pronouns. *My daughter cooked dinner by _____. My father lives by _____.*

MULTILEVEL STRATEGIES

• **Pre-level** Allow pre-level students extra time to finish 3B while challenging on- and higher-level students.

• **On- and Higher-level** Have these students write two or three original sentences with reflexive pronouns while the pre-level students are finishing the exercise. Have volunteers put their sentences on the board.

4 Building conversation skills

Guided Practice IV
15–20 minutes

A
Direct students to look at the picture and skim the sample conversation. Have them work with partners to identify the purpose of the conversation. Elicit responses and ask: *How do you know?* or *Why do you say that?* to encourage students to state their reasoning.

Possible Answers
The purpose is to talk about a story on the news and opinions about the story. The news story is on TV, and they are talking about their opinions and their neighbors' opinions.

B
🔊 **1-19** 1. Ask students to read the instructions and tell you what they are going to do [listen and read and respond to the question]. Play the audio and then elicit the answer to the question.

2. Ask students to read the conversation with a partner. Circulate and monitor pronunciation. Model and have students repeat difficult words or phrases.

3. Ask: *In what other situation could you use this conversation?* Point out a few phrases that are not specific to the neighborhood issue of trees. Ask volunteers to point out others.

Possible Answer
She agrees with the neighbors; she is upset too.

Communicative Practice and Application I
15–20 minutes

C 1. Pair students and have them read the instructions silently. Check their comprehension of the exercise. Ask: *What are the two roles? What is the issue?*

2. Model and have students repeat the expressions in the *In Other Words* box. Explain that they should use these expressions in their conversations.

3. Draw a T-chart on the board. Label the left column *Friend 1* and the right column *Friend 2*. Elicit examples of what each person might say and make notes on the chart.

4. Set a time limit (three minutes). Have students act out the role-play. Call "time" and have students switch roles.

5. Ask three volunteer pairs to act out their role-play for the class. Tell students who are listening to make a simple table with four rows and two columns. Use the top row to label the columns: *Specific details* and *Expressions for agreement*. Have students take notes in the chart for each role-play.

> **MULTILEVEL STRATEGIES**
>
> For 4C, adapt the role-play to the level of your students.
>
> • **Pre-level** Provide these students with a simplified role-play.
>
> *Friend 1: Did you see the news? The city is planning to close the community center and people are upset.*
>
> *Friend 2: I can understand that. What did the mayor say?*
>
> *Friend 1: She said the building is in terrible shape and that's why the center needs to be closed.*
>
> *Friend 2: That's really too bad. Do you think the building could be repaired?*
>
> *Friend 1: That makes sense to me. I would help.*

2. Pair students and tell them to discuss their own answers to the question. Circulate and monitor.

B Direct students to read the sentences before they listen to the news report. Ask what kind of information they'll be writing in the blanks. Ask volunteers for predictions. If students struggle, start by offering your own prediction: *I think we will hear that a hurricane is expected to reach Florida on Wednesday.* Have students write their predictions in the chart.

C 🔊 1-20 1. Play the audio. Ask students to listen and complete the sentences.

2. Pair students and have them compare answers. If a pair has different answers, have the class vote on the correct answer with a show of hands.

Answers
1. hurricane
2. leave their homes
3. schools
4. food and water
5. asked to leave

> **MULTILEVEL STRATEGIES**
>
> Replay the news report to challenge on- and higher-level students while allowing pre-level students to catch up.
>
> • **Pre-level** Have these students listen again and complete the sentences.
>
> • **On- and Higher-level** Ask these students to listen for and write the past-passive verbs in the news report [were told, were opened, were asked]. The higher-level students may also notice the present passive [is expected] and the present continuous passive [are being brought].
>
> After you go over the answers to 5C, elicit the passive verbs and discuss their context.

5 Focus on listening for details

Presentation and Guided Practice
20–25 minutes

 1. Read the question aloud and model a discussion with a volunteer. Ask: *Do you think reporting the news can be a dangerous job? … Why? / Why not? … I agree because… / I disagree because…*

6 Discuss

Communicative Practice and Application II
15–20 minutes

A 1. Read the instructions aloud. List the three jobs on the board. Check comprehension. Ask: *If you think a reporter has a very dangerous job, what rating should you give it?*

2. Put students into teams of four and assign roles: reporter, manager, administrative assistant, and editor. Verify students' understanding of the roles. Encourage students to use the phrases in the *Speaking Note* during their discussions.

3. Set a time limit for the discussions (ten minutes). Write the sentence frame from 6B on the board. Then circulate and monitor.

B Call "time." Ask the reporter for each team to report the results of their team's discussion, using the sentence frame on the board.

Evaluation
5 minutes

TEST YOURSELF

1. Ask students to complete the checkboxes individually.

2. Tell students that you are going to read each of the items in the checklist aloud. If they are not at all confident with that skill, they should hold up a closed fist. If they are not very confident, they should hold up one finger. If they are somewhat confident, two fingers; confident, three fingers; very confident, four fingers. If they think they could teach the skill, they should hold up five fingers. Read each item in the checklist and identify students that may need further support.

> **TIP**
> For homework, you could ask students to write a sentence or two about what participation and discussion skills they still need to work on or, if they are confident in all of the skills, what skill they are most proud of.

> **EXTENSION ACTIVITY**
> To extend 6B, add other jobs to the board: *security guards, pilots/train engineers/boat captains, astronauts, doctors/nurses, farmers.* Ask students to rank all the jobs in order from least dangerous to most dangerous and give their reasons. Have students vote on the ranking.

LESSON 5 READING

Lesson Overview

MULTILEVEL OBJECTIVES

On-, Pre-, and Higher-level: Read about and discuss where people get the news

LANGUAGE FOCUS

Grammar: *I think* + noun clause (*I think [that] news reporters sometimes create news.*); the suffix *-ity (clarity)*

Vocabulary: *Rely on, figure, survey*

For vocabulary support, see this **Oxford Picture Dictionary** topic: Entertainment, pages 242–243

STRATEGY FOCUS

Use illustrations (charts, graphics, or cartoons) to understand material in the text that support the writer's point visually.

READINESS CONNECTION

In this lesson, students differentiate between fact and opinion.

PACING

To compress this lesson: Conduct the word study in 2B as a whole-class activity.

To extend this lesson: Have students play "Spot the Errors" in news stories. (See end of lesson.)

And/or have students complete **Workbook 4 page 14** and **Multilevel Activities 4 Unit 2 pages 34–35**.

Lesson Notes

CORRELATIONS

CCRS: SL.1.B (a.) Come to discussions prepared, having read or studied required material; explicitly draw on that preparation and other information known about the topic to explore ideas under discussion. (b.) Follow agreed-upon rules for discussions. (c.) Ask questions to check understanding of information presented, stay on topic, and link their comments to the remarks of others. (d.) Explain their own ideas and understanding in light of the discussion.

SL.2.B Determine the main ideas and supporting details of a text read aloud or information presented in diverse media and formats, including visually, quantitatively, and orally.

R.1.B Ask and answer such questions as who, what, where, when, why, and how to demonstrate understanding of key details in a text.

R.1.C Refer to details and examples in a text when explaining what the text says explicitly and when drawing inferences from the text.

R.2.A Identify the main topic and retell key details of a text.

R.5.A Know and use various text features to locate key facts or information in a text.

R.6.B Identify the main purpose of a text, including what the author wants to answer, explain, or describe.

R.7.C Interpret information presented visually, orally, or quantitatively and explain how the information contributes to an understanding of the text in which it appears.

R.8.B Describe how reasons support specific points the author makes in a text.

L.1.B (l.) Produce simple, compound and complex sentences.

L.2.B (h.) Use conventional spelling for high-frequency and other studied words and for adding suffixes to base words.

L.4.B (e.) Use glossaries and beginning dictionaries, both print and digital, to determine or clarify the meaning of words and phrases.

RF.3.B (c.) Identify and know the meaning of the most common prefixes and derivational suffixes.

RF.4.B (a.) Read grade-level text with purpose and understanding.

ELPS: 1. An ELL can construct meaning from oral presentations and literary and informational text through level-appropriate listening, reading, and viewing. 2. An ELL can participate in level-appropriate oral and written exchanges of information, ideas, and analyses, in various social and academic contexts, responding to peer, audience, or reader comments and questions. 3. An ELL can speak and write about level-appropriate complex literary and informational texts and topics. 4. An ELL can construct level-appropriate oral and written claims and support them with reasoning and evidence. 6. An ELL can analyze and critique the arguments of others orally and in writing. 8. An ELL can determine the meaning of words and phrases in oral presentation and literary and informational text.

Warm-up and Review
10–15 minutes (books closed)

Write *News Sources* on the board. Elicit the names of local newspapers and popular TV news shows and news websites. Write them on the board.

Introduction
5 minutes

1. Ask students for a show of hands about each name on the board. *Do you watch/read _____?* Tally the results on the board.

2. State the objective: *Today we're going to read about and discuss where people usually get their news.*

1 Read

Presentation
10–20 minutes

A Read the questions aloud. Ask volunteers to tell where they get the news and why they chose that source. Use the results of the tally on the board in the *Introduction* to answer question 2 with the class.

B Read the words and definitions. Elicit sample sentences for each word or supply them if the students can't. For example: *I rely on the TV news to tell me the weather forecast. I don't think the bookkeeper's figures are correct. I took an online survey about learning styles. It asked a lot of question about how I like to learn.*

Pre-reading

C Read the instructions aloud and confirm that students understand what scanning is [reading/looking at a text quickly to find certain kinds of information]. Have students answer the question individually and then check answers with the class. If any students answer incorrectly, ask them to support their answer using numerical information from the text. Establish the correct answer.

Answer
b. How people responded to a survey in 2014.

Guided Practice: While Reading
20–30 minutes

D 1. Ask students to read the article silently and answer the question. Have students compare answers with a partner.

2. Check answers with the class.

3. Check comprehension. Ask: *What is the survey about?* [where Americans get the news] *Who did they ask?* [1492 American adults] *How did results vary by age and gender?* [Younger adults and women are more likely to use social media as a news source and men are more likely to use cable news.]

4. Direct students to underline unfamiliar words they would like to know. Elicit the words and encourage other students to provide definitions or examples.

Answer
age, gender

> **MULTILEVEL STRATEGIES**
>
> Adapt 1D to the level of your students.
>
> • **Pre-level** Read the text aloud to these students as they follow along.
>
> • **On- and Higher-level** Pair students and have them read the article aloud to each other, taking turns to read each paragraph.

Guided Practice: Rereading
10–15 minutes

E 1. Read the instructions aloud. Play the audio and have students read along silently. Provide an opportunity for students to extract evidence from the text. Have students reread the article and underline any words or phrases that indicate the author's opinion.

2. Pair students and tell them to compare the words they underlined and report anything they disagree on. Discuss and clarify as needed.

Possible Answers
No, the writer doesn't express an opinion. The writer gives facts from a survey but doesn't give an opinion.

F 1. Have students work individually to answer the questions. They should then write the line number(s) where they found the answer. Write the answers on the board.

2. Elicit and discuss any additional questions about the article. You could introduce new questions for class discussion: *How have news habits changed over time? Why do you think people use a variety of sources?*

Possible Answers
1. The survey was about the devices and sources different people use to get the news. (lines 6–9)
2. newspaper, TV (lines 21–22)
3. younger adults (lines 26–27)
4. They don't trust news on social media. (lines 31–32)

MULTILEVEL STRATEGIES

Seat mixed-level students together for 1F.

Have on-level students find the line numbers in the article. Have higher-level students say the answers to the questions while pre-level students write down the answers.

2 Word study

Guided Practice: Post-reading
10 minutes

 1. Direct students to look at the chart and identify the topic [the suffix *–ity*]. Have students read the chart.

2. Read the first two sentences in the chart and the examples for *real* and *reality*. Elicit sentences for the other words in the chart.

3. Have students repeat after you as you say each word with natural intonation, rhythm, and stress.

4. Direct students to complete the sentences and then compare answers with a partner. Read the correct answers and have students check their work.

Answers
1. majority
2. ability
3. clarity
4. similarities
5. mobility

B Direct students to work individually to write a sentence for each topic that includes the underlined word. Have students compare sentences with a partner. Ask volunteers to write their sentences on the board. Have the rest of the class suggest grammar and spelling edits as needed.

3 Talk it over

Guided Practice
15–20 minutes

 Have students read the article and the *Reader's Note*. Point out that they need to use the information and the editorial cartoon from the article to complete the sentences. Set a time limit (ten minutes). Have students work in pairs to complete the task. Have pairs join another pair to check their answers. Ask volunteers to share their answers with the class.

Possible Answers
1. community members / citizen journalists
2. biased
3. The people in the cartoon may think that their news reporting is the same as a professional writer/photographer.
4. Answers will vary.

MULTILEVEL STRATEGIES

Seat same-level students together for 3A.

• **Pre-level** Read the article aloud with these students. Check comprehension by asking: *What is citizen journalism?* [when ordinary citizens write about and publish information about current events as they occur] *What has allowed citizen or grassroots journalism to develop?* [modern technology]

• **On- and Higher-level** Have students work in pairs to write three more questions based on the article. Then each pair joins another pair to ask and answer the questions.

Communicative Practice
20 minutes

B Read the questions aloud. Set a time limit (ten minutes). Allow students to think about the questions and discuss them in pairs. Ask volunteers to share their ideas with the class.

Application

5–10 minutes

BRING IT TO LIFE

Read the instructions aloud. Ask students to plan where they will get their article. Write the names of local papers, news magazines, and reputable Internet news addresses on the board. For students who will not be able to read a regular news article, provide adapted news articles from an ESL newspaper. (If you don't have a subscription to an ESL newspaper, such articles can be found online.)

EXTENSION ACTIVITY

Game

1. Put students in mixed-level groups. Direct each group to write a familiar news story that includes three wrong facts.

2. Have a reporter from each group read the news story aloud to the class. Have the class identify and correct the wrong information. *The hurricane didn't hit Wyoming. It hit Florida.*

AT WORK

Warm-up and Review
10–15 minutes (books closed)

Begin the lesson by writing several sentences on the board: *Supervisors should communicate through memos and emails. Meetings are the best way to communicate information at work. Everyone's opinion is equally important in the workplace.* Write *Agree* on one side of the board and *Disagree* on the other. Call several volunteers to the front of the class. Say the first statement and have volunteers position themselves according to how much they agree or disagree with it. Elicit ideas from the students. Repeat with other statements and volunteers.

Introduction
5 minutes

State the objective: *Today we're going to talk about giving opinions in a group or during a meeting.*

Presentation
5 minutes

 1-21 Read the instructions aloud. Play the audio. Give students a minute to think about the question. Elicit responses from the class.

Possible Answer
Information related to changes in the management team

Guided Practice
10–15 minutes

B **1-21** Read the statements aloud. Play the audio again. Direct students to listen and mark the statements true or false.

Answers	
1. F	4. F
2. T	5. F
3. T	

C **1-21** Read the instructions aloud. Play the audio again, encouraging students to take notes in their notebooks. Set a time limit (five minutes) for students to discuss the facts and opinions from the listening with a partner. Circulate to monitor.

Presentation and Communicative Practice
10 minutes

 1. Direct students' attention to the *Do/Say* chart and ask them to identify the lesson's soft skill [giving opinions]. Ask the class which column has examples of language [second and third] and which has examples of behaviors [first].

2. Say a phrase from the left and act it out. Say it again and have the class act it out with you. Say it a third time and have the class act it out for you. To confirm understanding, combine phrases: *Raise one hand a little and tilt your head a little to one side.*

3. Model the sentence frames from the right using authentic intonation. Have students practice imitating your inflection.

4. Put students in teams of four and assign each team a question. Assign roles: supervisor, manager, administrative assistant, and researcher. (Researchers will ask you questions on behalf of the team.) Verify understanding of the roles. Set a time limit (five minutes) and monitor.

5. Write sentence frames on the board that teams can use to summarize their response. *Our team discussed the following question: _____. We decided _____ because _____.*

6. Call "time" and let supervisors rehearse their report for one minute. Direct each supervisor to present to three other teams.

Communicative Practice and Application
20–25 minutes

E 1. Direct students to work in pairs to take turns reading the questions and expressing an opinion.

2. Invite volunteers to share their opinions.

 1. Have pairs merge to form teams of four. Tell students that they are going to be role-playing a staff meeting where they will express opinions.

2. Direct groups to come up with one thing a supervisor wants to tell the staff and one thing the supervisor wants the staff's opinion on. Each group should select a manager to run the meeting. The other three members can offer their opinions.

3. As students carry out the role-play, circulate and monitor. Provide global feedback once the activity ends.

TEAMWORK & LANGUAGE REVIEW

Lesson Overview

MULTILEVEL OBJECTIVES

On-, Pre-, and Higher-level: Expand upon and review unit grammar and life skills

LANGUAGE FOCUS

Grammar: Past passive (*The fire was put out quickly.*)

Vocabulary: Current events, local events, natural disasters, protests

For vocabulary support, see this **Oxford Picture Dictionary** topic: Entertainment, pages 242–243

READINESS CONNECTION

In this review, students work with others to solve a problem a person has with understanding the news.

PACING

To extend this review: Have students complete **Workbook 4 page 15**, **Multilevel Activities 4 Unit 2 page 36**, and **Multilevel Grammar Exercises 4 Unit 2**.

CORRELATIONS

CCRS: SL.1.B (a.) Come to discussions prepared, having read or studied required material; explicitly draw on that preparation and other information known about the topic to explore ideas under discussion. (b.) Follow agreed-upon rules for discussions. (c.) Ask questions to check understanding of information presented, stay on topic, and link their comments to the remarks of others. (d.) Explain their own ideas and understanding in light of the discussion.

SL.1.C (b.) Follow agreed-upon rules for discussions and carry out assigned roles.

SL.2.B Determine the main ideas and supporting details of a text read aloud or information presented in diverse media and formats, including visually, quantitatively, and orally.

R.1.B Ask and answer such questions as who, what, where, when, why, and how to demonstrate understanding of key details in a text.

R.2.A Identify the main topic and retell key details of a text.

Lesson Notes

W.2.A Write informative/explanatory texts in which they name a topic, supply some facts about the topic, and provide some sense of closure.

L.1.B (d.) Use reflexive pronouns. (l.) Produce simple, compound and complex sentences.

L.1.C (d.) Use modal auxiliaries to convey various conditions.

L.1.D (g.) Form and use verbs in the active and passive voice.

L.2.B (b.) Capitalize appropriate words in titles.

RF.4.B (a.) Read grade-level text with purpose and understanding.

ELPS: 2. An ELL can participate in level-appropriate oral and written exchanges of information, ideas, and analyses, in various social and academic contexts, responding to peer, audience, or reader comments and questions. 5. An ELL can conduct research and evaluate and communicate findings to answer questions or solve problems. 10. An ELL can demonstrate command of the conventions of standard English to communicate in level-appropriate speech and writing.

Warm-up and Review
10–15 minutes (books closed)

1. Review *At Work* activity F.

2. Ask students to share the good, not-so-good, and interesting things that happened during the role-play. As students speak, write their responses in a chart on the board.

Introduction and Presentation
5 minutes

1. Write one or two active-voice sentences on the board. *My mother cleaned the house yesterday. Someone threw trash onto the street again today.*

2. Ask volunteers to identify the verbs. Call on a volunteer to convert the sentences to passive voice. Discuss the *by* + noun phrase, which is not always necessary in the second sentence.

3. State the objective: *Today we're going to review using the past passive and reflexive pronouns to talk about the news.*

Guided Practice
15–20 minutes

A 1. Model the process for writing news headlines. Point to the first picture and read the example sentence.

2. Set a time limit (five minutes). Have students work with partners to complete the activity. Direct them to read their headlines together. Go over answers with the class.

B 1. Have students work individually to write answers to the questions. Then have students compare answers with a partner.

2. Have volunteers write the answers on the board.

3. Go over the answers with the class.

Possible Answers
1. Part of a national forest was destroyed by a fire.
2. The entire park was closed by the authorities.
3. The fire was put out by eight teams of firefighters.
4. 27 people were rescued by the emergency workers.
5. The area was re-opened by the officials the next week.

C 1. Have students work individually to complete the conversation. Then have students compare answers with a partner.

2. Have volunteers write the answers on the board.

3. Go over the answers with the class.

Answers
1. themselves
2. ourselves
3. yourself
4. myself

D Have volunteer pairs act out the conversation for the class.

Communicative Practice
30–40 minutes

E 1. Group students and assign roles: news writer, editorial writer, and editor. Explain that students are going to work with their teams to write a news story important to their communities right now.

2. Read steps 2–6 of the activity aloud. Check comprehension of the task. *What is the first thing you should do?* [choose a news story]

3. Set a time limit (ten minutes) to complete the exercise. Circulate and answer any questions.

4. Have editors from each team read their team's news story and editorial to another team.

F 1. Have students walk around the room to conduct the interviews. To get students moving, tell them to interview three people who were not in their team for E.

2. Set a time limit (five minutes) to complete the exercise.

3. Tell students to make a note of their classmates' answers but not to worry about writing complete sentences.

MULTILEVEL STRATEGIES
Adapt the mixer in F to the level of your students.
• **Pre- and On-level** Pair these students and have them interview other pairs together.
• **Higher-level** Have these students ask an additional question and write all answers.

G 1. Call on individuals to report what they learned about their classmates. Write important news events on the board as you hear them and keep a running tally of the number of students who mention them.

2. Use your tally for question 3 to create a bar graph on the board. Instruct students to draw bar graphs for the other important events in their notebooks. Circulate and answer any questions.

PROBLEM SOLVING
10–15 minutes

A 1. Ask: *Do you pay more or less attention to the news after learning English? Why?* Tell students they will read a story about a man who is having difficulty keeping up with the news. Direct students to read Anton's story silently.

2. Ask: *What did Anton do before he came to the U.S.?* [He always read the newspaper, watched the news, and he loved to talk about current events.] *What has changed?* [getting the news has become difficult]

3. Play the audio and have students read along silently.

B 1. Elicit answers to question 1. Brainstorm a list of strategies Anton could try and write them on the board.

2. Discuss the pros and cons of each strategy.

3. Pair students. Ask them to discuss their answers to question 3. Call on volunteers to share their opinions with the class.

Answers
1. Anton likes to follow the news and talk about the news with his friends, but it's hard for him to understand TV and radio news in English. He would like to be able to talk about the news with his co-workers.

Evaluation
20–25 minutes

To test students' understanding of the unit language and content, have them take the Unit 2 Test, available on the Teacher Resource Center.

UNIT 3 Going Places

Unit Overview

This unit explores transportation issues, including travel emergencies/problems, travel plans, and commuting, with a range of employability skills and contextualizes reported speech.

KEY OBJECTIVES

Lesson 1	Identify and discuss travel emergencies
Lesson 2	Identify communication issues and write an essay describing them
Lesson 3	Use reported speech to talk about personal, work, and academic experiences
Lesson 4	Make suggestions in the community or at work
Lesson 5	Identify and discuss transportation issues
At Work	Make suggestions at work
Teamwork & Language Review	Review unit language

UNIT FEATURES

Academic Vocabulary	*access, advocate, automated, availability, benefit, consumer, construction, convince, definitely, estimate, expand, generation, instruction, location, option, quotation, transportation, trend, vehicle*
Employability Skills	• Discuss the difference between *ask* and *tell* • Listen and decide on the solutions to problems and the consequences of the solutions • Identify ways to solve a scheduling conflict • Read issues and make suggestions • Decide how to allocate money • Listen actively • Work independently • Cooperate with others • Communicate verbally • Locate information

Resources	**Class Audio** CD1, Tracks 23–33
	Workbook Unit 3, pages 16–22
	Teacher Resource Center
	    Multilevel Activities 4 Unit 3
	    Multilevel Grammar Exercises 4 Unit 3
	    Unit 3 Test
	Oxford Picture Dictionary Parts of a Car, A Road Trip, Directions and Maps

LESSON 1 VOCABULARY

Lesson Overview

MULTILEVEL OBJECTIVES

On-level: Describe travel emergencies and give advice for travel problems

Pre-level: Identify travel emergencies and give advice for travel problems

Higher-level: Talk and write about travel emergencies and give advice for travel problems

LANGUAGE FOCUS

Grammar: Present tense (*He's locked out of the car.*)

Past tense (*I had a breakdown on the highway.*)

Vocabulary: Travel emergencies and travel problems

For vocabulary support, see these **Oxford Picture Dictionary** topics: Parts of a Car, pages 162–163; A Road Trip, pages 166–167

READINESS CONNECTION

In this lesson, students cooperate with others to discuss travel problems and emergencies.

PACING

To compress this lesson: Conduct 1B as a whole-class activity.

To extend this lesson: Have students role-play a travel emergency. (See end of lesson.)

And/or have students complete **Workbook 4 page 16** and **Multilevel Activities 4 Unit 3 pages 38–39**.

Lesson Notes

CORRELATIONS

CCRS: SL.1.B (d.) Explain their own ideas and understanding in light of the discussion.

SL.2.B Determine the main ideas and supporting details of a text read aloud or information presented in diverse media and formats, including visually, quantitatively, and orally.

SL.4.B Report on a topic or text, tell a story, or recount an experience with appropriate facts and relevant, descriptive details, speaking clearly at an understandable pace.

SL.6.B Speak in complete sentences when appropriate to task and situation in order to provide requested detail or clarification.

R.4.B Determine the meaning of general academic and domain-specific words and phrases in a text relevant to a topic or subject area.

R.7.B Use information gained from illustrations and the words in a text to demonstrate understanding of the text.

W.7.A Participate in shared research and writing projects.

L.1.B (l.) Produce simple, compound and complex sentences.

L.4.B (e.) Use glossaries and beginning dictionaries, both print and digital, to determine or clarify the meaning of words and phrases.

RF.4.B (a.) Read grade-level text with purpose and understanding.

ELPS: 1. An ELL can construct meaning from oral presentations and literary and informational text through level-appropriate listening, reading, and viewing. 2. An ELL can participate in level-appropriate oral and written exchanges of information, ideas, and analyses, in various social and academic contexts, responding to peer, audience, or reader comments and questions. 5. An ELL can conduct research and evaluate and communicate findings to answer questions or solve problems. 8. An ELL can determine the meaning of words and phrases in oral presentation and literary and informational text.

Warm-up and Review
10–15 minutes (books closed)

Show a picture of a car or draw a car on the board. Elicit the names of car parts (inside and out) and write them on the board.

Introduction
5 minutes

1. Point to different car parts listed on the board and ask students what can go wrong with them.

2. State the objective: *Today we're going to learn words for travel emergencies and problems.*

1 Identify vocabulary for travel emergencies

Presentation I
20–25 minutes

A Write *travel* on the board and have students brainstorm ways to travel and what they can take with them. Write their ideas on a large sheet of paper. Keep this list for the extension at the end of the lesson.

B 1. Direct students to look at the pictures. Elicit what is happening. Say each phrase in the box and have students repeat.

2. Have students work in pairs to complete the paragraphs. Have each pair join another pair to compare answers.

C 🔊 1-23 To prepare students for listening, say: *Now we're going to listen to these people talk about their car problems.* Play the audio and have students check their work. Go over the answers with the class.

Answers
1. had a breakdown
2. turned on the hazard lights
3. called the auto club
4. raise the hood
5. had a flat tire
6. changed the tire
7. put out safety triangles
8. send a tow truck
9. get directions

Guided Practice I
10–20 minutes

D 🔊 1-23 Have students copy the chart in their notebooks. Play the audio and have students work individually to take notes in the chart. Have students compare answers with a partner. Go over the answers with the class.

Possible Answers	
Emergency	Solutions
breakdown	hazard lights, call auto club, call a tow truck
flat tire	change the tire
bus breakdown	put out safety triangles, call dispatch, get a replacement bus

> **MULTILEVEL STRATEGIES**
>
> Adapt 1D to the level of your students.
>
> **Pre-level** Seat the pre-level students together. Copy the vocabulary list on the board and identify each as *emergency* or *solution*. Underline the key nouns in each phrase (e.g., *auto club, tire,* etc.).
>
> **On- and Higher-level** While you work with the pre-level students, pair other students to take turns saying an emergency and responding with a solution.
>
> A: *What do you do when you have a breakdown?*
> B: *Turn on the hazard lights.*

E 1. Have students work in a team to add travel emergencies and solutions to their charts. Elicit any words that teams did not know and write them on the board. Check with the class to see which of these words are known.

2. Direct students to look up any remaining unknown words in their dictionaries. Discuss those words in relation to the lesson.

2 Learn vocabulary for travel problems

Presentation II
10–20 minutes

A 1. Direct students to look at the pictures. Introduce the new topic: *Now we're going to talk about other problems you can have while you're traveling.*

2. Say and have students repeat the captions for each picture.

3. Ask students to work individually to match the pictures to the sentences. Go over the answers as a class.

4. Check comprehension. Say: *There are too many cars on the highway, so I'm ____.* [stuck in traffic] *I don't know where I am. I'm ____.* [lost]

Answers	
1. d	3. b
2. a	4. c

Guided Practice II
10–15 minutes

 1. Model the conversation with a volunteer. Model it again using different words from 2A.

2. Set a time limit (three minutes). Direct students to practice with a partner.

3. Call on volunteers to act out one of their conversations for the class.

MULTILEVEL STRATEGIES

Adapt 2B to the level of your students.

- **Pre- and On-level** Pair pre- and on-level students for 2B. Assign pre-level students part A for the first round and then have them switch roles.
- **Higher-level** Pair students and direct them to create a conversation based on their own ideas. Have students give another solution to the problem.

Communicative Practice and Application
20–25 minutes

 1. Write the questions from 2C on the board. Explain that students will work in teams to research and report on these questions. Ask: *Which question requires research?* [2] *Which search terms or questions can you use to find the information you need?* ["drivers" + carry in car; "emergency"] *What information will you scan for?* [objects, emergencies] *How will you record the information you find?* [table, checklist, index cards] Remind students to bookmark or record sites so they can find or cite them in the future.

2. Group students and assign roles: reporter, manager, administrative assistant, and IT support. Verify students' understanding of their roles.

3. Give managers the time limit for the task (ten minutes). Direct the administrative assistant to record information for the team using a table, checklist, or index cards. Have team members each survey their classmates on one of the questions.

4. Give a two-minute warning. Call "time." Tell managers to elicit the answers to each question. The administrative assistant will take notes.

TIP

When setting up task-based activities, verify that students understand their roles using physical commands. For example: *If you report on your team's work, stand up* [reporter]. *If you keep the team on task, point to the clock* [manager]. *If you write the team's responses, raise your hand* [administrative assistant]. *If you help the team research, hold up your smartphone/tablet* [IT support].

D 1. Copy the sentence frames on the board.

2. Direct teams to help their administrative assistant use the sentence frames to record the team's findings. Direct the reporter to use the recorded information to report the team's findings to the class or another team.

Evaluation
10–15 minutes

TEST YOURSELF

1. Direct Partner A to read prompts 1–4 from 1B on page 36 to Partner B. Partner B should close their book and write the vocabulary words in their notebook. When finished, students switch roles. Partner B reads prompts 5–9 from 1B.

2. Direct both partners to open their books and check their spelling when they finish.

EXTENSION ACTIVITY
Role-play

1. Put students in pairs. Instruct them to write a short conversation between someone who has a travel problem or emergency and someone who can give him/her advice.

2. Provide this structure on the board for pairs to follow:

A: *Express that you have a travel problem or emergency.*

B: *Ask about the problem.*

A: *Ask for advice.*

B: *Give advice.*

LESSON 2 WRITING

Lesson Overview

MULTILEVEL OBJECTIVES

On- and Higher-level: Analyze, write, and edit a story about using the phone

Pre-level: Read a story and write about using the phone

LANGUAGE FOCUS

Grammar: Past tense (*I didn't know that* hold *could mean* wait.)

Vocabulary: *Automated, quotation marks*

For vocabulary support, see this **Oxford Picture Dictionary** topic: Parts of a Car, pages 162–163

STRATEGY FOCUS

When you are repeating a speaker's words in writing, use a comma (,) and quotation marks (" ").

READINESS CONNECTION

In this lesson, students work independently to locate information in a story.

PACING

To compress this lesson: Assign the *Test Yourself* for homework.

To extend this lesson: Have students role-play a communication difficulty. (See end of lesson.)

And/or have students complete **Workbook 4 page 17** and **Multilevel Activities 4 Unit 3 page 40**.

Lesson Notes

CORRELATIONS

CCRS: SL.1.B (d.) Explain their own ideas and understanding in light of the discussion.

SL.2.B Determine the main ideas and supporting details of a text read aloud or information presented in diverse media and formats, including visually, quantitatively, and orally.

R.1.B Ask and answer such questions as who, what, where, when, why, and how to demonstrate understanding of key details in a text.

R.2.A Identify the main topic and retell key details of a text.

R.5.A Know and use various text features to locate key facts or information in a text.

R.7.B Use information gained from illustrations and the words in a text to demonstrate understanding of the text.

W.3.B Write narratives in which they recount a well-elaborated event or short sequence of events, include details to describe actions, thoughts, and feelings, use temporal words to signal event order, and provide a sense of closure.

W.4.B Produce writing in which the development and organization are appropriate to task and purpose.

W.5.B With guidance and support from peers and others, develop and strengthen writing as needed by planning, revising and editing.

L.1.B (l.) Produce simple, compound and complex sentences.

L.2.B (b.) Capitalize appropriate words in titles. (d.) Use a comma to separate an introductory element form the rest of the sentence. (e.) Use commas and quotation marks in dialogue.

RF.4.B (a.) Read grade-level text with purpose and understanding.

ELPS: 1. An ELL can construct meaning from oral presentations and literary and informational text through level-appropriate listening, reading, and viewing. 2. An ELL can participate in level-appropriate oral and written exchanges of information, ideas, and analyses, in various social and academic contexts, responding to peer, audience, or reader comments and questions. 3. An ELL can speak and write about level-appropriate complex literary and informational texts and topics. 5. An ELL can conduct research and evaluate and communicate findings to answer questions or solve problems.

Warm-up and Review
10–15 minutes (books closed)

Ask students to name places they call where they encounter automated message systems (banks, utility companies, credit-card companies, stores, schools, movie theaters, etc.). Write the places on the board. Discuss their experiences with these automated messages.

Introduction
5 minutes

1. Elicit and write typical recorded messages one might hear when calling the places on the board. *You have reached _____. This is the main menu. Press 1 for customer service.*

2. State the objective: *Today we're going to read and write about using the phone.*

1 Prepare to write

Presentation I
20–25 minutes

A 1. Direct students to look at the pictures. To build schema, ask: *What are the people in the pictures doing?* [The man is having trouble with his car and calling for help. The woman is calling someone and she is frustrated.]

2. Ask questions 1 and 2.

3. Write students' answers to question 1 on the board.

B 1. Introduce the story and its purpose: *Now we're going to read a story by Ahmed Bell. Ahmed is writing about the difficulty he had understanding phone conversations when he first came to the U.S.* Direct students to read the story silently.

2. Check comprehension. Ask: *What was his problem with the automated menu?* [He didn't understand which number to press.] *What did the person on the phone say that confused him?* [Can you hold?]

3. Play the audio. Have students read along silently.

4. Draw students' attention to the *Writer's Note*. Point out that quotation marks are only used when you repeat a speaker's exact words and commas are used after the speaker and the verb "said." *She said, "Can you hold?"*

Guided Practice I
10 minutes

C 1. Have students work independently to answer the questions in the story. Have students compare answers with a partner. Go over the answers with the class.

2. Have students take turns asking and answering the questions in pairs.

Possible Answers
1. It was difficult for him to use the phone.
2. He had trouble with the automated menu.
3. It meant "Can you wait?" or "Please wait."
4. Using the phone is much easier for him now.

MULTILEVEL STRATEGIES

Seat pre-level students together for 1C.

- **Pre-level** While other students are working on 1C, ask these students questions about the reading. *What was hard for Ahmed to use when he first came to the U.S.? What did Ahmed hear when he called the insurance company? What does "hold" mean on the phone? Can he understand phone messages now?* Give students time to copy the answers to 1C from the board.

2 Plan and write

Guided Practice II
15–20 minutes

A 1. Read the questions. Elicit students' answers.

2. Write some of the students' ideas on the board so they can refer to them during the writing assignment.

B 1. Direct students to look back at the story in 1B. Focus students' attention on the structure of the story. Elicit the topic of the first and second paragraphs. Point out the introductory sentence and the concluding sentence.

2. Point out the placement of the title and indentations in the example. Go over the connecting words and phrases in the box. Ask: *What tenses should you use in your story?*

3. Check comprehension of the exercise. Ask: *What are you writing about?* [a story about my experience communicating by phone] *What do you do with the first sentence of each paragraph?* [indent]

Lesson Plans 4   Unit 3   Lesson 2   Writing   61

4. Have students work individually to write their stories.

> **MULTILEVEL STRATEGIES**
>
> Adapt 2B to the level of your students.
>
> • **Pre-level** Direct these students to write one paragraph. Provide them with a topic sentence: *When I first came to the U.S., it was difficult to understand phone conversations.*
>
> • **Higher-level** Tell these students to include at least two examples of direct speech with commas and quotation marks. Have these students write three paragraphs.

3 Get feedback and revise

Guided Practice III
5 minutes

 Direct students to check their writing using the editing checklist. Tell them to read each item in the list and check their papers before moving onto the next item. Explain that students should not edit their writing at this stage. They should just use the checklist to check their work and mark any areas they want to revise.

Communicative Practice
15 minutes

 1. Read the instructions aloud. Emphasize to students that they are responding to their partners' work, not correcting it.

2. Use the story in 1B to model the exercise. *I think the sentence that says,* "I could understand people in person, but listening to people on the phone was a different story" *gives a good description of the situation.*

3. Direct students to exchange papers with a partner and follow the instructions.

C Allow students time to edit and revise their writing as necessary, using the editing checklist from 3A and their partner's feedback from 3B. If necessary, students could complete this task as homework.

> **TIP**
>
> After completing 3C, have students work in teams to identify common experiences in communicating by phone. Elicit ideas from each team and write them on the board. Ask students what strategies they use to address these issues.

Application and Evaluation
10 minutes

TEST YOURSELF

1. Review the instructions aloud. Assign a time limit (five minutes) and have students work independently.

2. Before collecting student work, invite two or three volunteers to share their sentences. Ask students to raise their hands if they wrote similar answers.

> **EXTENSION ACTIVITY**
>
> **Role-play**
>
> Role-play a communication difficulty. Put students in mixed-level groups. Tell each group to write a telephone conversation. Partner A's car just broke down and Partner B is a customer service representative at a company that provides emergency roadside assistance. Provide these sentence frames.
>
> *A: Hi. I'm calling to report…*
>
> *B: OK. I need some information. What is your…?*

LESSON 3 GRAMMAR

Lesson Overview

MULTILEVEL OBJECTIVES

On- and Higher-level: Use reported speech to write messages and listen for reported speech in statements about travel problems

Pre-level: Identify reported speech in statements about travel problems

LANGUAGE FOCUS

Grammar: Reported speech (*He said that he was lost.*)

Reported speech with *told* + noun or pronoun (*He told her he had a flat tire.*)

Vocabulary: *Lock out, breakdown, tow truck, emergency kit*

For vocabulary support, see these **Oxford Picture Dictionary** topics: Parts of a Car, pages 162–163; Directions and Maps, page 159

STRATEGY FOCUS

When you are repeating a speaker's words in writing, use a comma (,) and quotation marks (" ").

READINESS CONNECTION

In this lesson, students listen actively for reported speech.

PACING

To compress this lesson: Conduct 1B and 1C as whole-class activities.

To extend this lesson: Have students paraphrase a conversation. (See end of lesson.)

And/or have students complete **Workbook 4 pages 18–19**, **Multilevel Activities 4 Unit 3 pages 41–42**, and **Multilevel Grammar Exercises 4 Unit 3**.

Lesson Notes

CORRELATIONS

CCRS: SL.2.B Determine the main ideas and supporting details of a text read aloud or information presented in diverse media and formats, including visually, quantitatively, and orally.

L.1.B (g.) Form and use regular and irregular verbs. (h.) Form and use the simple verb tenses. (I.) Produce simple, compound and complex sentences.

L.1.C (c.) Form and use the progressive verb tenses. (f.) Use verb tense to convey various times, sequences, states, and conditions.

L.2.B (e.) Use commas and quotation marks in dialogue.

RF.4.B (a.) Read grade-level text with purpose and understanding.

ELPS: 3. An ELL can speak and write about level-appropriate complex literary and informational texts and topics. 7. An ELL can adapt language choices to purpose, task, and audience when speaking and writing. 10. An ELL can demonstrate command of the conventions of standard English to communicate in level-appropriate speech and writing.

Warm-up and Review
10–15 minutes (books closed)

Ask students to tell you about a time they had car trouble or a time they had a problem while traveling. Write their quotes on the board. *Tara said, "I got a flat tire." Kendra said, "I missed my flight."* Leave these sentences on the board.

Introduction
5–10 minutes

1. Circle the commas and the quotation marks in the sentences on the board. Say: *I use commas and quotation marks because I'm writing the exact words that the speakers used. Sometimes I want to report what you said, but I don't want to use the exact words.*

2. State the objective: *Today we're going to use reported speech to talk about travel problems.*

1 Learn reported speech

Presentation I
20–25 minutes

 1. Direct students to look at the pictures. Ask: *Where are the people in each of the pictures?* [on the road/in a car; in an office] *What is happening?* [The man is stuck in traffic and his co-workers are waiting for him.] *Who are the people in the picture on the right?* [Monty's co-workers]

2. Have two students read the speech bubbles aloud. Ask: *What does Monty say?* [I'm stuck in traffic.] *What does his co-worker tell the others?* [Monty called. He said he was stuck in traffic.]

B 1. Read the first quoted speech and reported speech sentences in the chart aloud. Have students repeat after you. Elicit the differences [punctuation marks, comma, tense]. Do the same for the rest of the sentences. Read the *Grammar Notes* aloud. Point out that quoted speech is also called direct speech, and reported speech is also called indirect speech.

2. Direct students to underline the reported speech in the conversation in 1A. Elicit the answer and write *He said he was stuck in traffic.* Elicit the differences between this reported speech and Monty's direct speech [pronouns, tense].

3. Assess students' understanding of the charts. Elicit the process of changing the direct speech sentences you wrote on the board during the *Warm-up* to reported speech. Ask: *Do I need the comma after* said? [no] *Do I need the quotation marks?* [no] *What do I change the subject to?* [he, she, or they]

Answer
He said he was stuck in traffic.

Guided Practice I
15–20 minutes

 1. Tell students they will collaborate to complete the description of the grammar point. Model collaboration by working with the class to complete the first sentence. Encourage students to look at 1A and 1B to confirm their ideas.

2. Pair students and have them work together to complete the description.

3. Project or write the completed definition on the board and have pairs verify the accuracy of their responses. Ask volunteers which sentences confused them and discuss.

Answers
quoted
quotation
talk about
simple past
past

Guided Practice II
5–10 minutes

 1. Read the instructions aloud. Direct students' attention to the first sentence. Elicit ideas from students. Complete this item as a class.

2. Ask students to work individually to complete the second sentence with reported speech and then check their answers with a partner.

3. Elicit more examples of students' phone calls and write them on the board (e.g., *Maria said, "I need to get gas;" Amir and Hamid said, "We forget the house number."*). Have students work in pairs to rewrite the sentences as reported speech.

4. Have volunteers write reported speech on the board. Provide clarification or feedback to the whole class as needed.

Answers
1. he was lost
2. they didn't know the address

MULTILEVEL STRATEGIES

For 1D, seat same-level students together.

- **Pre-level** While other students are completing 1D, work with these students. Ask them to identify the pronouns and verbs that need to be changed and go over the changes together.

- **On- and Higher-level** After these students finish 1D, ask them to write a quoted-speech sentence and change it into a reported-speech sentence. Ask volunteers to write their sentence pairs on the board.

> **TIP**
>
> After 1D, play a reported-speech "circle" game. Tell each student to write a short present-tense statement about a travel problem. Have students stand in a circle around the room. Have each student say his or her sentence aloud. (If you have a large class, allow students to work with a partner to write the sentence.) Tell students they need to try to remember who said what. Allow them to take notes.
>
> After everyone has spoken, call on individuals to report what one of their classmates said. *June said she was locked out of her car.* Remind them that with reported speech, it isn't necessary to use the exact words as long as the idea is the same.

2 Learn reported speech with *told* + noun or pronoun

Presentation II
20–25 minutes

1. Introduce the new topic: *Now we're going to learn reported speech with* told *plus noun or pronoun.* Ask: *What did I just say?* [Now, we're....] Say: *That's right. I told you we were going to learn reported speech....*

2. Read the sentences in the chart aloud. Elicit the form for reported speech with *said* and *told* and write them on the board: *Subject + said + (that) ....; Subject + told + object + (that) + ...* Ask: *What is the difference in form between sentences with* said *and* told? [*Told* is followed by an object.]

3. Read the *Grammar Notes* aloud. Confirm that object pronouns are not used after *said*.

4. Rewrite the sentences on the board from the *Warm-up* using *told*. For example: *Kendra told us that she missed her flight. Tara told the class that she got a flat tire.*

5. Ask students to work individually to complete the sentences and then compare answers with a partner. Call on volunteers to read the completed sentences aloud. Write the answers on the board.

Answers	
1. said	3. told
2. told	4. said

Guided Practice III
15–20 minutes

 Ask students to work individually to complete the reported speech sentences and then compare answers with a partner. Have a volunteer write the completed sentences on the board.

Answers
1. her that he needed the key to the closet
2. John that she was calling about the homework
3. his parents that he was taking driving lessons
4. us/my sister and me that she was locked out of her apartment

> **MULTILEVEL STRATEGIES**
>
> For 2B, seat same-level students together.
>
> • **Pre-level** Work with this group. Elicit the object pronouns and verb forms before students write each sentence.
>
> • **On- and Higher-level** Ask these students to write three to five additional reported-speech sentences using *told*. Ask volunteers to put their sentences on the board.

> **TIP**
>
> After 2A or 2B, put students in mixed-level groups of three to work on reported speech.
>
> 1. Tell each group to write a conversation with four short present-tense statements. Tell them not to include any questions. Ask the groups to choose one person as the "narrator." The narrator will tell about the conversation using reported speech.
>
> 2. Write a conversation on the board as an example. *John: We have a flat tire. Mary: That's OK. There's a spare in the trunk. I can change the tire. John: You always know how to solve a problem.* Ask two volunteers to read the parts of Mary and John. Then "report" their conversation to the class: *John said they had a flat tire. Mary told John there was a spare in the trunk...*
>
> 3. Assign a time limit (five minutes) for writing the conversation. Have two students from each group act out the conversation. Have the narrator tell about the conversation using reported speech. Encourage the narrator to use both *told* and *said*.

C 1. Elicit the importance of accuracy. Tell students they will be building their accuracy in this task.

2. Organize students into groups. Demonstrate how to correct the sentence using the first example.

3. Have team members work together to correct the sentences. Circulate and monitor teamwork.

4. Project or write the corrected sentences on the board and have teams check their work.

5. Address questions and any issues you noted during your observation.

Answers
1. He said that he was on Elk Road.
2. He said he was calling from a gas station
3. He told me that he had a flat tire.
4. He said he was going to be late.
5. He said he didn't want us to wait.
6. We told him we could wait/We said we could wait.

3 Listen for reported speech

Guided Practice IV
10–15 minutes

A 1. Say: *We're going to listen to different people talk about travel problems. You're going to listen and write reported speech. Write the missing words.*

2. Direct students' attention to the sentences. Ask them to predict the words that will complete the sentences.

3. Play the audio. Ask students to complete the sentences. If necessary, replay each sentence before moving on to the next one. Have students compare answers with a partner.

4. Ask volunteers to write the sentences on the board.

Answers
1. he was
2. she had
3. she was waiting
4. they were stuck
5. they were taking
6. told, said that
7. he wasn't going, his car was
8. she needed

> **MULTILEVEL STRATEGIES**
>
> Adapt 3A to the level of your students.
> • **Pre-level** Provide these students with the missing verbs in random order: *was waiting, wasn't going, were stuck, were taking, told, had, said, needed, was.* Have them use the words from the list as you play the audio.

B 1. Read the instructions aloud. Model the activity with a student. Put students in pairs to take turns asking and answering questions about the people in 3A.

2. Call on volunteers to talk about the people in 3A.

4 Use reported speech to talk about others' ideas

Communicative Practice and Application
20–25 minutes

A 1. Direct students to look at the photo. Ask what is happening in the picture.

2. Read the first question and have students repeat. Elicit some examples of ways to complete the question frames (e.g., *Do you have a new car?*). Have students work individually to complete the questions.

B Direct students to work with a partner to write two more questions.

C 1. Have students work in groups of three. Each group member takes a turn asking and answering questions. Have the group tell another group what their group members said.

2. Check comprehension of the exercise. Ask: *Who asks questions?* [everyone] *Who answers questions?* [everyone]

3. Ask volunteers to share something interesting they learned about their classmates using reported speech. Model the exercise by calling on several volunteers. Monitor and provide feedback on students' use of reported speech.

Evaluation

10–15 minutes

TEST YOURSELF

Ask students to write the sentences independently. Collect and correct their writing.

> **MULTILEVEL STRATEGIES**
>
> Target the *Test Yourself* to the level of your students.
>
> - **Pre-level** Provide sentence frames for these students to complete.
>
>   1. _____ (name) said that he/she preferred to _____.
>   2. _____ (name) said that he/she has a _____.
>   3. _____ (name) said that he/she was planning to _____.
>   4. _____ (name) told me that his/her favorite _____.
>
> - **Higher-level** Have these students write eight sentences about their classmates.

> **EXTENSION ACTIVITY**
>
> **Paraphrase a Conversation**
>
> Have students paraphrase a conversation. Play a short conversation from a movie, television show, or commercial. Ask students to report on the conversation to a partner.

LESSON 4 EVERYDAY CONVERSATION

Lesson Overview

MULTILEVEL OBJECTIVES

On-, Pre-, and Higher-level: Make travel plans and listen to phone messages

LANGUAGE FOCUS

Grammar: Reported speech with instructions (*Tomas said to check the tires.*)

Vocabulary: *Automated message system, attendant*

For vocabulary support, see this **Oxford Picture Dictionary** topic: A Road Trip, pages 166–167

STRATEGY FOCUS

Practice reported speech with instructions.

READINESS CONNECTION

In this lesson, students discuss the difference between *ask* and *tell*.

PACING

To compress this lesson: Conduct *Discuss* as a whole-class activity.

To extend this lesson: Have students report their discussions using reported speech. (See end of lesson.)

And/or have students complete **Workbook 4 page 20** and **Multilevel Activities 4 Unit 3 page 43**.

Lesson Notes

CORRELATIONS

CCRS: SL.1.B (b.) Follow agreed-upon rules for discussions. (c.) Ask questions to check understanding of information presented, stay on topic, and link their comments to the remarks of others. (d.) Explain their own ideas and understanding in light of the discussion.

SL.2.B Determine the main ideas and supporting details of a text read aloud or information presented in diverse media and formats, including visually, quantitatively, and orally.

SL.4.B Report on a topic or text, tell a story, or recount an experience with appropriate facts and relevant, descriptive details, speaking clearly at an understandable pace.

SL.6.B Speak in complete sentences when appropriate to task and situation in order to provide requested detail or clarification.

R.7.B Use information gained from illustrations and the words in a text to demonstrate understanding of the text.

L.1.B (g.) Form and use regular and irregular verbs. (h.) Form and use the simple verb tenses. (l.) Produce simple, compound and complex sentences.

L.1.C (c.) Form and use the progressive verb tenses. (d.) Use modal auxiliaries to convey various conditions. (f.) Use verb tense to convey various times, sequences, states, and conditions.

L.1.D (f.) Explain the function of verbals (gerunds, participles, infinitives) in general and their function in particular sentences.

RF.2.A (g.) Isolate and pronounce initial, medial vowel, and final sounds (phonemes) in spoken single-syllable words.

RF.4.B (a.) Read grade-level text with purpose and understanding.

ELPS: 1. An ELL can construct meaning from oral presentations and literary and informational text through level-appropriate listening, reading, and viewing. 2. An ELL can participate in level-appropriate oral and written exchanges of information, ideas, and analyses, in various social and academic contexts, responding to peer, audience, or reader comments and questions. 3. An ELL can speak and write about level-appropriate complex literary and informational texts and topics. 9. An ELL can create clear and coherent level-appropriate speech and text.

Warm-up and Review
10–15 minutes (books closed)

Show pictures of famous places in the U.S. and ask students to identify them. Find out who has visited the different places and whether anyone has plans to visit them in the future.

Introduction
5 minutes

1. Ask about each place that your students have been to or want to go to. *How would you get there? Where would you stay?*

2. State the objective: *Today we're going to learn to make travel plans.*

1 Learn ways to make travel plans

Presentation I
10–20 minutes

A 🔊 **1-26** 1. Direct students to look at the websites and ads. Ask: *What travel services are advertised?* [hotel, motel, airlines] *Did you ever call for motel or hotel reservations? Did you ever look at a hotel website?*

2. Read the instructions aloud. Play the audio. Give students a minute to answer the question. Go over the answer as a class.

Answer
The Seeta Airlines website

Guided Practice I
20–25 minutes

B 🔊 **1-26** 1. Read the instructions aloud. Play the audio. Ask students to listen for the answers to each question.

2. Ask students to compare their answers with a partner. Circulate and monitor to ensure students understand the audio. Check comprehension. Ask: *How long does Matthew have for a vacation?* [a week] *What are good things to see and do there?* [monuments and museums] *What is Matthew going to do for his cousin?* [cook dinner]

Possible Answers
1. He is asking for advice about traveling to Washington D.C.
2. He is planning to stay with his cousin.
3. Because Artie is from around Washington D.C.

C 🔊 **1-27** Read the instructions aloud. Explain that students are going to hear the audio one more time. They should write the words they hear to complete the sentences. Play the audio. Call on volunteers to elicit the answers.

Answers
1. if I were you
2. You might try
3. I'd

2 Practice your pronunciation

Pronunciation Extension
10–15 minutes

A 🔊 **1-28** 1. Write *He always tries to get his tickets on sale.* on the board. Say the sentence and ask students to repeat it. Underline each *s* and pronounce just those words so that students can hear the difference in the pronunciation of *s* [words with *s* sound: *tickets, sale*; words with *z* sound: *always, tries, his*]. Say: *Now we're going to focus on two pronunciations of the letter s.*

2. Play the audio. Direct students to listen for the *s* sounds.

3. Replay the audio and have students repeat the sentences.

B Have students work with a partner to predict how the words will be pronounced.

C 🔊 **1-29** Play the audio. Direct students to listen and check their work. Go over the answers as a class. Have students repeat the words.

Answers	
1. z	4. z
2. z	5. s
3. s	6. z

3 Use reported speech with instructions

Presentation II and Guided Practice II
10–15 minutes

 1. Introduce the new topic. *Now we're going to learn reported speech for giving instructions.*

2. Read the instructions aloud. Direct students to study the chart. Call on a volunteer to answer the question. Point out that we can use either *said* or *told* for reported instructions. The important note is that we use an infinitive after both. Elicit the forms: *subject + said + infinitive* and *subject + told + object + infinitive.* Ask: *What is an infinitive?* [*to* + verb]

3. Check comprehension of the chart. Write several "quotes" on the board, starting with the header *"My mother said,.."* Under that, write: *"Take sunscreen." "Wear comfortable shoes." "Don't forget to take pictures!"* Elicit and write the reported speech. *My mother told me to wear comfortable shoes.*

Answer
told

Guided Practice III
15–20 minutes

 1. Direct students to read the conversation between Pedro and Lois. Ask: *Who is going away? How does Pedro feel?*

2. Have students work individually to write the sentences in reported speech and then compare answers with a partner. Ask volunteers to write the sentences on the board.

Answers
1. Pedro told Lois to call him every day.
2. Lois told Pedro not to worry.
3. Pedro told Lois not to drive at night.
4. Lois told Pedro to relax.

MULTILEVEL STRATEGIES

For 3B, seat same-level students together.

• **Pre-level** Work with these students to complete the exercise as a group. Read each quote and elicit the necessary information for writing it in reported speech. *Who said "Don't worry"? Whom did she say it to? Should we use* said *or* told *in this case?* After you have worked through each sentence, have the group copy it into their books.

• **On- and Higher-level** While you are working with the pre-level students, tell these students to write three to five more things that Lois and Pedro might tell each other to do.

C 1. Ask students to use reported instructions to tell a partner about some good advice they have received about traveling or driving. Call on volunteers to share the advice with the class.

2. Read the questions aloud and have students repeat. Model the activity with a volunteer. Have the student ask you one of the questions and respond with your own information (e.g., *My friends often tell me to be on time.*).

3. Set a time limit (five minutes). Ask students to practice asking and answering the questions with several partners. Call on individuals to share their answers with the class.

MULTILEVEL STRATEGIES

Seat same-level students together for 3C.

• **Pre-level** Allow these students to focus on answering the questions with short answers rather than asking them.

• **Higher-level** Direct these students to read the questions aloud for their partners and provide complete answers.

4 Building conversation skills

Guided Practice IV
15–20 minutes

A Direct students to look at the picture and skim the conversation. Have them work with partners to identify the purpose of the conversation. Elicit responses and ask: *How do you know? Why do you say that?* Encourage students to state their reasoning.

Possible Answers
The purpose is to get advice and make suggestions about a trip. One co-worker is giving the other one advice.

B 🔊 1-30 1. Ask students to read the instructions and tell you what they are going to do [listen and read and respond to the questions]. Play the audio and then elicit the answers to the questions.

2. Ask students to read the conversation with a partner. Circulate and monitor pronunciation. Model and have students repeat difficult words or phrases.

3. Ask: *In what other situation could you use this conversation?* Point out a few phrases that are not specific to hotels. Ask volunteers to point out others.

Possible Answers
She appreciates the suggestions. She says, "That's a great suggestion; thanks."

Communicative Practice and Application I
15–20 minutes

C 1. Pair students and have them read the instructions silently. Check their comprehension of the exercise. Ask: *What is the relationship between the two speakers?* [co-workers] *What kind of information will one speaker give to the other?* [suggestions about visiting a new place]

2. Model and have students repeat the expressions in the *In Other Words* box. Explain that they should use these expressions in their conversations.

3. Draw a T-chart on the board. Label the left column *Co-worker 1* and the right column *Co-worker 2*. Elicit examples of what each person might say and make notes on the chart.

4. Set a time limit (three minutes). Have students act out the role-play. Call "time" and have students switch roles.

5. Ask three volunteer pairs to act out their role-play for the class. Tell students who are listening to make a simple table with four rows and two columns. Use the top row to label the columns: *Location* and *Suggestions*. Have students take notes in the chart for each role-play.

MULTILEVEL STRATEGIES
For 4C, adapt the role-play to the level of your students.
• **Pre-level** Ask these students to use the following for their conversation:
A: I want to go to _____ (name of city). Where should I stay?
B: How about _____?
A: What should I see? B: Why don't you _____?
• **Higher-level** Direct these students to talk about several places.

5 Focus on listening for details

Presentation and Guided Practice
20–25 minutes

A 1. Read the questions aloud and model a discussion with a volunteer. Ask: *Have you ever called a company or agency? What happened? I had to call my credit card company because there was a mistake in a charge on my bill. I wanted it removed. Were you successful? Yes,....*

2. Pair students and tell them to discuss their own answers to the questions. Circulate and monitor.

B Direct students to read the choices before they listen to the automated message. Ask what kind of information they'll be listening for. Ask volunteers for predictions. If students struggle, start by offering your own prediction: *I think we will hear about a hotel.*

C 🔊 1-31 1. Say: *We are going to listen to a motel automated message system. What do you think you can do on it?*

2. Play the audio. Have students check the things you can do on the system and write an *X* for the things you can't do. Have students compare answers with a partner. Elicit the answers.

Answers
Check: reserve a room, get information about jobs, find a nearby hotel, hear the message again
X: get room service, order a wedding cake

D 🔊 1-31 1. Direct students to read the sentences before listening.

2. Replay the audio and have students work individually to write the correct number or symbol.

3. Pair students and have them compare answers. If a pair has different answers, have the class vote on the correct answer with a show of hands.

Answers	
1. 3	4. #
2. 2	5. 4
3. 1	

> **MULTILEVEL STRATEGIES**
>
> For 5D, write the numbers 0, 1, 2, 3, 4, and # on the board and replay the automated phone message. Stop after each sentence.
>
> • **Pre-level** Write the key words on the board to help these students find the correct answer.
>
> • **On- and Higher-level** Elicit the key words from these students and write them on the board. *0. wait for the attendant, 1. make room reservations, 2. locate the Motel 212 nearest you, 3. reserve rooms for a conference, wedding, 4. employment information, # (pound key) hear the message again*

6 Discuss

Communicative Practice and Application II
15–20 minutes

A 1. Read the instructions aloud. Draw a sample chart on the board with three columns and two rows. The column headings should be: *little sister, supervisor, co-worker*. The row headings should be: *tell* and *ask*. Explain that students will make a chart like this one based on their discussion.

2. Put students into teams of four and assign roles: reporter, manager, administrative assistant, and editor. Verify students' understanding of the roles. [The reporter reports the results to the class, the manager keeps the group on time, the administrative assistant takes notes, and the editor makes corrections.]

3. Set a time limit for the discussions (ten minutes). Write the sentence frame from 6B on the board. Then circulate and monitor.

B Call "time." Ask the reporter for each team to report the results of their team's discussion, using the sentence frame in 6B.

> **EXTENSION ACTIVITY**
>
> To extend 6B, have students form pairs with people from another team. Have them report their team's discussion using reported speech (e.g., *Alain said that he told his little sister to clean her room*).

Evaluation
5 minutes

TEST YOURSELF

1. Ask students to complete the checkboxes individually.

2. Tell students that you are going to read each of the items in the checklist aloud. If they are not at all confident with that skill, they should hold up a closed fist. If they are not very confident, they should hold up one finger. If they are somewhat confident, two fingers; confident, three fingers; very confident, four fingers. If they think they could teach the skill, they should hold up five fingers. Read each item in the checklist and identify students that may need further support.

> **TIP**
>
> For homework, you could ask students to write a sentence or two about what discussion skills they still need to work on or, if they are confident in all of the skills, what skill they are most proud of.

LESSON 5 READING

Lesson Overview

MULTILEVEL OBJECTIVES

On-, Pre-, and Higher-level: Read about and discuss transportation and the sharing economy

LANGUAGE FOCUS

Grammar: The suffix -less (*A cell phone is useless if you forget to charge it.*)

Vocabulary: *Mobility reduction, wireless*

For vocabulary support, see this **Oxford Picture Dictionary** topic: Directions and Maps, page 159

STRATEGY FOCUS

Annotate a text to remember information and find details later.

READINESS CONNECTION

In this lesson, students read about transportation and make suggestions.

PACING

To compress this lesson: Conduct the word study in 2A as a whole-class activity.

To extend this lesson: Have students make predictions about transportation in 100 years. (See end of lesson.)

And/or have students complete **Workbook 4 page 21** and **Multilevel Activities 4 Unit 3 pages 44–45**.

Lesson Notes

CORRELATIONS

CCRS: SL.1.B (b.) Follow agreed-upon rules for discussions. (c.) Ask questions to check understanding of information presented, stay on topic, and link their comments to the remarks of others. (d.) Explain their own ideas and understanding in light of the discussion.

R.1.B Ask and answer such questions as who, what, where, when, why, and how to demonstrate understanding of key details in a text.

R.1.C Refer to details and examples in a text when explaining what the text says explicitly and when drawing inferences from the text.

R.2.A Identify the main topic and retell key details of a text.

R.5.A Know and use various text features to locate key facts or information in a text.

R.7.C Interpret information presented visually, orally, or quantitatively and explain how the information contributes to an understanding of the text in which it appears.

L.1.B (l.) Produce simple, compound and complex sentences.

L.2.B (h.) Use conventional spelling for high-frequency and other studied words and for adding suffixes to base words.

L.4.B (e.) Use glossaries and beginning dictionaries, both print and digital, to determine or clarify the meaning of words and phrases.

RF.3.B (c.) Identify and know the meaning of the most common prefixes and derivational suffixes.

RF.4.B (a.) Read grade-level text with purpose and understanding.

ELPS: 1. An ELL can construct meaning from oral presentations and literary and informational text through level-appropriate listening, reading, and viewing. 2. An ELL can participate in level-appropriate oral and written exchanges of information, ideas, and analyses, in various social and academic contexts, responding to peer, audience, or reader comments and questions. 9. An ELL can create clear and coherent level-appropriate speech and text.

Warm-up and Review
10–15 minutes (books closed)

Draw an "idea map" on the board. Write *Everyday transportation* in the center circle. Ask students to brainstorm words they associate with commuting to work or school. Categorize their words on the board into branches for individual cars, public transportation, and non-motorized options.

Introduction
5 minutes

1. Use students' ideas from the *Warm-up* to talk about things that have changed in the last one hundred years.

2. State the objective: *Today we're going to read about and discuss transportation in the 21st Century.*

1 Read

Presentation
10–20 minutes

A Read the questions aloud. Use ideas from the *Introduction* to help guide discussion. Ask: *How is taking the bus or subway different today than 20 or 30 years ago? What are some new ways people get to school or work?*

B Read the words and definitions. Elicit sample sentences for each word or supply them if the students can't. Ask students to identify the forms of transportation that are on the board from the *Warm-up* (personal cars, subway, bus, bikes, etc.). Elicit other forms of transportation.

Pre-reading

C 1. Read the instructions aloud and confirm that students remember what it means to scan (look quickly for something specific, in this case numbers).

2. Direct students' attention to the *Reader's Note*. Have students scan for and circle the numbers in the text.

3. Have students mark the statements true or false individually and then compare answers with a partner. Check answers as a class. If any students answer incorrectly, ask them to support their answer using numerical information from the text. Establish the correct answers.

Answers	
1. F	2. T

Guided Practice: While Reading
20–30 minutes

D 1. Ask students to read the article silently and answer the question. Then have them compare answers with a partner.

2. Check the answer with the class.

3. Check comprehension. Ask: *What are some changes that allow users to access transportation today?* [rapid growth in smartphone ownership, Internet access, and social networking] *What is carsharing?* [a service that allows people to use cars they don't own] *What are the benefits of these new services?* [greater use of public transportation and a reduction of the number of vehicles owned] Have students annotate the text when they find the answers.

Answer
They are all enabled by technology.

MULTILEVEL STRATEGIES

Adapt 1D to the level of your students.
- **Pre-level** Read the text aloud to these students as they follow along.
- **On- and Higher-level** Pair students and have them read the article aloud to each other, taking turns to read each paragraph.

Guided Practice: Rereading
10–15 minutes

E 1. Provide an opportunity for students to extract evidence from the text. Have students reread the article and underline any words or phrases that indicate the writer's suggestions.

2. Pair students and tell them to compare the words they underlined and report anything they disagree on. Discuss and clarify as needed.

Answers
The writer offers a suggestion. <u>Governments should think carefully about the community's needs before beginning major highway projects.</u>

TIP

Have students go online to find out about these transportation services in your area. Decide which device(s) students will use and elicit search terms ("car-sharing," "bike-sharing," + your city).

F 1. Have students work individually to choose the words that describe the relationship between the concepts. They should then write the line number(s) where they found the answer. Have students compare answers with a partner. Write the answers on the board.

2. Elicit and discuss any additional questions about the reading. You could introduce new questions for class discussion: *Have you used the services mentioned in the article? Why or why not? What might be some reasons why people don't use these services?*

Answers
1. is possible because of (lines 17–19)
2. when they have (lines 14–16)
3. because of (lines 3–5)
4. after (lines 24–29)
5. because (lines 36–38)

MULTILEVEL STRATEGIES

For 1F, work with pre-level students.

• **Pre-level** Ask these students *yes/no* and short-answer information questions about the reading while other students are completing 1F. *Are Americans driving more or less?* [less] *What is the service called when you give a ride to someone else?* [ridesharing] Have these students copy the answers to 1F from the board.

2 Word study

Guided Practice: Post-reading
10 minutes

A 1. Direct students to look at the chart and identify the topic [the suffix *-less*]. Have students read the chart.

2. Read the first two words and definitions in the chart. Elicit an example of something that is *wireless* and something that is *useless*. Have students work with a partner to think of examples for *harmless* and *speechless*.

3. Have students repeat after you as you say each word with natural intonation, rhythm, and stress.

4. Direct students to complete the sentences and then compare answers with a partner. Read the correct answers and have students check their work.

Answers
1. useless
2. Wireless
3. speechless
4. harmless

B Direct students to work individually to write a sentence for each topic that includes the underlined word. Have students compare sentences with a partner. Ask volunteers to write their sentences on the board. Have the rest of the class suggest grammar and spelling edits as needed.

3 Talk it over

Guided Practice
15–20 minutes

A Have students look at the graph and read the note. Point out that they need to use the information from the graph and the note to complete the sentences and answer the question. Set a time limit (ten minutes). Have students work in pairs to complete the task. Ask volunteers to share their answers with the class.

Answers
1. decreased
2. 20th
3. 45, 64
4. increased
5. increase
6. Answer will depend on the current year; current year minus 2000.

Communicative Practice
20 minutes

B 1. Read the questions aloud. Set a time limit (ten minutes). Have students discuss the questions in pairs.

2. Ask volunteers to share their ideas with the class.

Application
5–10 minutes

BRING IT TO LIFE

Ask students to brainstorm a list of suggestions to make transportation better in your area. Ask volunteers to share their ideas. Have the class choose one of the ideas and brainstorm a plan for putting it into action.

EXTENSION ACTIVITY

Discussion

1. Write several topics related to the transportation on the board: *personal vehicles, public transportation, transportation sharing programs.*

2. Put students into groups. Remind students that during the introduction they talked about how transportation is today compared to 100 years ago. Tell them that now they're going to think about 100 years in the future. Ask the groups to come up with predictions for each of the topics. Tell them to write sentences with *will* and the suffix *-less. In the future, personal vehicles will be useless.*

3. Have a reporter from each group share the group's ideas with the class.

AT WORK

Warm-up and Review
10–15 minutes (books closed)

Begin the lesson by telling students you have to plan a big meeting for all the faculty. Brainstorm a list of things to prepare.

Introduction
5 minutes

State the objective: *Today we're going to talk about planning a meeting.*

Presentation
5 minutes

A Read the instructions aloud. Play the audio. Give students a minute to think about the question. Elicit responses from the class.

Possible Answer
They are discussing planning for a staff meeting tomorrow.

Guided Practice
10–15 minutes

B Play the audio again. Direct students to listen for each issue and put a check next to any that they hear mentioned. Have students compare answers with a partner. Go over the answers with the class.

Answers
Check: number of chairs getting a different room giving something to people who come how to get cash to buy food

C Read the instructions aloud. Play the audio again, encouraging students to take notes in their notebooks. Set a time limit (five minutes) for students to discuss their answers with a partner. Circulate to monitor.

Possible Answers
Suggestion: look for a bigger room Consequence: people won't know where to go Suggestion: bring in more chairs Consequence: have to bring in chairs tomorrow Suggestion: make copies of the new procedures for everyone Consequence: might be a lot of paper Suggestion: go out tomorrow to get doughnuts and coffee Consequence: won't have much time

Presentation and Communicative Practice
10 minutes

D 1. Direct students' attention to the *Do/Say* chart and ask them to identify the lesson's soft skill [making suggestions]. Ask the class which column has examples of language [right] and which has examples of behaviors [left].

2. Say a phrase from the left and act it out. Say it again and have the class act it out with you. Say it a third time and have the class act it out for you. To confirm understanding, combine phrases: *Make eye contact and lean toward me.*

3. Model the question and sentence frames from the right using authentic intonation. Have students practice imitating your inflection.

4. Put students in teams of four and assign each team a question. Assign roles: reporter, manager, administrative assistant, and researcher. (Researchers will ask you questions on behalf of the team.) Verify understanding of the roles. Set a time limit (five minutes) and monitor.

5. Write sentence frames on the board that teams can use to summarize their response. *Our team discussed the following question:_____. We decided _____ because_____.*

6. Call "time" and let reporters rehearse their report for one minute. Direct each reporter to present to three other teams.

Communicative Practice and Application
20–25 minutes

E 1. Direct students to work in pairs to come up with suggestions to resolve each issue.

2. Invite volunteers to share their suggestions.

F 1. Have pairs merge to form teams of four. Tell students that they are going to be role-playing planning an event at work.

2. Direct groups to come up with three issues and suggest three solutions. Each group should select a manager to run the meeting. The other three members should each choose an issue to bring up.

3. As students carry out the role-play, circulate and monitor. Provide global feedback once the activity ends.

TEAMWORK & LANGUAGE REVIEW

Lesson Overview

MULTILEVEL OBJECTIVES

On-, Pre-, and Higher-level: Expand upon and review unit grammar and life skills

LANGUAGE FOCUS

Grammar: Reported speech (*Maya said that there were two injured people.*)

Vocabulary: Travel and transportation

For vocabulary support, see this **Oxford Picture Dictionary** topic: A Road Trip, pages 166–167

READINESS CONNECTION

In this review, students listen and decide on the solutions to a problem and the consequences of the solutions.

PACING

To extend this review: Have students complete **Workbook 4 page 22**, **Multilevel Activities 4 Unit 3 page 46**, and **Multilevel Grammar Exercises 4 Unit 3**.

Lesson Notes

CORRELATIONS

CCRS: SL.1.B (a.) Come to discussions prepared, having read or studied required material; explicitly draw on that preparation and other information known about the topic to explore ideas under discussion. (b.) Follow agreed-upon rules for discussions. (c.) Ask questions to check understanding of information presented, stay on topic, and link their comments to the remarks of others. (d.) Explain their own ideas and understanding in light of the discussion.

SL.1.C (b.) Follow agreed-upon rules for discussions and carry out assigned roles.

SL.2.B Determine the main ideas and supporting details of a text read aloud or information presented in diverse media and formats, including visually, quantitatively, and orally.

SL.4.B Report on a topic or text, tell a story, or recount an experience with appropriate facts and relevant, descriptive details, speaking clearly at an understandable pace.

R.1.B Ask and answer such questions as who, what, where, when, why, and how to demonstrate understanding of key details in a text.

R.2.A Identify the main topic and retell key details of a text.

L.1.B (l.) Produce simple, compound and complex sentences.

L.1.C (d.) Use modal auxiliaries to convey various conditions.

L.1.D (f.) Explain the function of verbals (gerunds, participles, infinitives) in general and their function in particular sentences.

L.2.B (e.) Use commas and quotation marks in dialogue.

RF.4.B (a.) Read grade-level text with purpose and understanding.

ELPS: 1. An ELL can construct meaning from oral presentations and literary and informational text through level-appropriate listening, reading, and viewing. 2. An ELL can participate in level-appropriate oral and written exchanges of information, ideas, and analyses, in various social and academic contexts, responding to peer, audience, or reader comments and questions. 9. An ELL can create clear and coherent level-appropriate speech and text.

Warm-up and Review
10–15 minutes (books closed)

1. Review *At Work* activity F.

2. Ask students to share the good, not-so-good, and interesting things that happened during the role-play. As students speak, write their responses in a chart on the board.

Introduction and Presentation
5 minutes

1. Pair students and direct them to look at the picture in their book. Ask them to describe what they see to their partner.

2. Ask volunteer pairs to share their ideas with the class.

Guided Practice
15–20 minutes

A 1. Model the process for changing the reported speech to quoted speech. Write *Maya:* on the board. Elicit the words she says. [I've been in a car accident. My name is Maya.] Review the changes in verb forms and pronouns.

2. Direct students' attention to the report. Ask: *How many lines does Maya have?* [four] *How many lines does the operator have?* [Note: the operator will answer the phone, making it three.] Write the alternating names on the board.

3. Set a time limit (five minutes). Have students work with partners to complete the conversation.

4. Ask volunteers to write the conversation on the board. Elicit any variations (e.g., *My leg is hurting badly./My leg hurts badly.*).

5. Have students practice the conversation in pairs.

B 1. Direct students' attention to the picture. Ask: *Who do you see? Who is Saul? Who is the woman on the stretcher? Who is Lidia?*

2. Have students form teams of four: manager, administrative assistant, editor, and reporter. The manager facilitates and keeps track of time, the administrative assistant records the sentences, the editor checks spelling and grammar, and the reporter reads sentences to the class.

3. Set a time limit of ten minutes. Circulate and provide help as needed.

4. Give a two-minute warning. At the end of ten minutes, call "time." Call on reporters to read a sentence to the class. Have volunteers write the sentences on the board.

5. Elicit additions, variations, and edits from the class.

Possible Answers
1. Lidia told Saul not to move the patient too much. 2. Lidia asked Maya if she had any allergies. 3. Saul told Ana to stay calm. 4. Ana told Saul that her leg hurt. 5. Maya told Lidia that she had an allergy to penicillin.

C 1. Direct students' attention to the model. Elicit the pronoun changes. [*Hospital dispatcher=he, him; Saul and Ana = them, they*]

2. Direct students to work with their teams to write sentences. Set a time limit of five minutes.

3. Ask volunteers to write the answers on the board.

Answers
1. He asked them to tell him the number of people they were transporting. 2. He told her to stay calm. 3. Lidia asked her if she had any allergies. 4. She told him not to move the patient too much.

Communicative Practice
30–40 minutes

D 1. Group students and assign roles: manager, director, and actors. Explain that students are going to work with their teams to to write a conversation between a travel agent and a customer.

2. Read steps 2–4 of the activity aloud. Check comprehension of the task. *What is the first thing you should do?* [choose a type of vacation spot from the list] *What will the director do?* [gives directions for the task] *What will the new actors do?* [say the conversation aloud]

3. Set a time limit (ten minutes) to complete the exercise. Have managers keep their team on task and manage time. Circulate and answer any questions.

E 1. Have students walk around the room to conduct the interviews. To get students moving, tell them to interview three people who were not in their team for D.

2. Set a time limit (five minutes) to complete the exercise.

3. Tell students to make a note of their classmates' answers but not to worry about writing complete sentences.

MULTILEVEL STRATEGIES
Adapt the mixer in E to the level of your students. • **Pre-and On-level** Pair these students and have them interview other pairs together. • **Higher-level** Have these students ask an additional question and write all answers.

F 1. Call on individuals to report what they learned about their classmates. Keep a running tally on the board for each question, listing each thing students mention that travelers should take on a trip.

2. Have students use your tally for question 3 to create bar graphs in their notebooks. Circulate and answer any questions.

PROBLEM SOLVING
15–20 minutes

A 1. Ask: *Would you drive your car on a long trip?* Tell students they will read a story about a man who is deciding whether or not to drive to another city. Direct students to read Kofi's story silently.

2. Ask: *How much is the airfare?* [$400 roundtrip] *How old is the car?* [more than ten years old] *How much are new tires?* [about $500] *How much does Kofi have in the bank?* [$800]

3. Play the audio and have students read along silently.

B 1. Elicit answers to question 1. Have volunteers write answers to question 2 on the board until all of the class ideas have been put up.

2. Have the class vote on Kofi's best course of action.

Possible Answers
1. Kofi has to travel for a job interview. Airfare is expensive, but Kofi's car needs new tires. Tires cost more than the airfare and would take most of the money Kofi has in the bank.

Evaluation
20–25 minutes

To test students' understanding of the unit language and content, have them take the Unit 3 Test, available on the Teacher Resource Center.

UNIT 4 Get the Job

Unit Overview

This unit explores career planning, applying for jobs, and interviewing with a range of employability skills and contextualizes past perfect grammar structures.

KEY OBJECTIVES	
Lesson 1	Identify career planning resources
Lesson 2	Write a cover letter email to apply for a job
Lesson 3	Use the past perfect to describe work experience
Lesson 4	Use the simple past, the past perfect, and the present perfect to talk about work and academic experience
Lesson 5	Identify ways to plan a career path
At Work	Show a willingness to learn at work
Teamwork & Language Review	Review unit language

UNIT FEATURES	
Academic Vocabulary	*assessment, assistant, contact, coordinator, identified, license, medical, negative, occupation, professional, projection, registration, reliable, research, resources, sector, technical*
Employability Skills	• Decide whether you agree or disagree with statements about jobs • Discuss good and bad things to do at a job interview • Determine what steps you need to do to look for a job • Understand teamwork • Communicate information • Work with others • Communicate verbally • Speak so others can understand
Resources	**Class Audio** CD1, Tracks 34–44 **Workbook** Unit 4, pages 23–29 **Teacher Resource Center** 　Multilevel Activities 4 Unit 4 　Multilevel Grammar Exercises 4 Unit 4 　Unit 4 Test **Oxford Picture Dictionary** Job Skills, Office Skills, Career Planning, Job Search, Interview Skills

LESSON 1 VOCABULARY

Lesson Overview

MULTILEVEL OBJECTIVES

On-level: Describe and talk about career planning and job training opportunities

Pre-level: Identify and describe career planning and job training opportunities

Higher-level: Talk and write about career planning and job training

LANGUAGE FOCUS

Grammar: Should and could (She should go to the career planning center. You could talk to your boss.)

Vocabulary: Career planning and job training vocabulary

For vocabulary support, see these **Oxford Picture Dictionary** topics: Job Skills, page 176; Career Planning, pages 174–175; Job Search, pages 168–169

READINESS CONNECTION

In this lesson, students understand teamwork by conducting research about job training or career planning services.

PACING

To compress this lesson: Conduct 2A as a whole-class activity.

To extend this lesson: Have students look at job ads and discuss the requirements for the job. (See end of lesson.)

And/or have students complete **Workbook 4 page 23** and **Multilevel Activities 4 Unit 4 pages 48–49**.

Lesson Notes

CORRELATIONS

CCRS: SL.1.B (d.) Explain their own ideas and understanding in light of the discussion.

SL.2.B Determine the main ideas and supporting details of a text read aloud or information presented in diverse media and formats, including visually, quantitatively, and orally.

SL.4.B Report on a topic or text, tell a story, or recount an experience with appropriate facts and relevant, descriptive details, speaking clearly at an understandable pace.

SL.6.B Speak in complete sentences when appropriate to task and situation in order to provide requested detail or clarification.

R.1.B Ask and answer such questions as who, what, where, when, why, and how to demonstrate understanding of key details in a text.

R.4.B Determine the meaning of general academic and domain-specific words and phrases in a text relevant to a topic or subject area.

R.5.B Know and use various text features to locate key facts or information in a text efficiently.

R.7.C Interpret information presented visually, orally, or quantitatively and explain how the information contributes to an understanding of the text in which it appears.

W.7.A Participate in shared research and writing projects.

L.1.B (l.) Produce simple, compound and complex sentences.

L.4.B (a.) Use sentence-level context as a clue to the meaning of a word or phrase. (e.) Use glossaries and beginning dictionaries, both print and digital, to determine or clarify the meaning of words and phrases.

RF.4.B (a.) Read grade-level text with purpose and understanding.

ELPS: 2. An ELL can participate in level-appropriate oral and written exchanges of information, ideas, and analyses, in various social and academic contexts, responding to peer, audience, or reader comments and questions. 5. An ELL can conduct research and evaluate and communicate findings to answer questions or solve problems. 8. An ELL can determine the meaning of words and phrases in oral presentation and literary and informational text.

Warm-up and Review
10–15 minutes (books closed)

Write *Good Jobs* on the board. Ask students to name what they would consider to be good jobs. Write them on the board.

Introduction
5 minutes

1. Ask for a show of hands. *How many people would like to have one of these jobs on the board? How many people know how to plan for getting the job they want?*

2. State the objective: *Today we're going to learn career planning and job training vocabulary.*

1 Identify career planning vocabulary

Presentation I
20–25 minutes

A Write *Ways to Get a Job* on the board. Have students work in pairs or small groups to brainstorm ideas. Call on volunteers to write their ideas on the board. Continue until all the ideas have been listed.

B 1. Direct students to look at the guide. Read the instructions aloud.

2. Have students work individually to check the steps they have done. Then ask students to discuss their answers with a partner.

3. Have volunteers present the steps they have done. Have the class vote on what they think is the best advice.

Guided Practice I
10–15 minutes

C 1. Direct students' attention to the words and definitions. Read each aloud and have students repeat. Model the first item with the class. Have students find *career counselor* in the guide. Ask: *What do you think a career counselor does? What clues in the guide can tell you this?*

2. Have students work individually to match the words and definitions and then compare answers with a partner.

Answers	
1. a	4. d
2. f	5. e
3. b	6. c

D 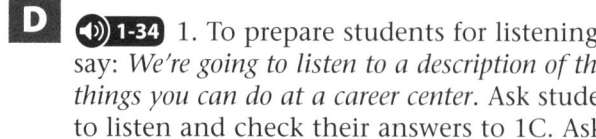 1. To prepare students for listening, say: *We're going to listen to a description of the things you can do at a career center.* Ask students to listen and check their answers to 1C. Ask students to circle the items in 1C that don't match the listening passage. Elicit those items and play them again, focusing on clues to meaning.

2. Replay the audio and challenge students to listen for additional information about each of the career center's services. Call on volunteers to share what they heard.

2 Learn more about career planning

Presentation II
10–20 minutes

A 1. Direct students to look at the website. Introduce the new topic: *Now we're going to read more about career training.*

2. Read the instructions aloud. Ask students to look at the boldfaced headings. Say and have students repeat the phrases.

3. Teach critical vocabulary: *advance* [move up or forward], *employability skills* [skills that help you get a job]. Ask students to work with a partner to complete the sentences. Ask volunteers to read the completed sentences aloud. Write the answers on the board.

Answers
1. on-the-job training
2. internship
3. apprenticeship
4. job skills workshop
5. online course

MULTILEVEL STRATEGIES
For 2A, use mixed-level pairs.
• **Pre-level** Ask these students to read the incomplete sentences aloud to their partners and write the correct answers.
• **On- and Higher-level** Ask these students to supply the missing words.

Guided Practice II
10–15 minutes

 1. Model the conversation with a volunteer. Model it again using other information from 2A.

2. Set a time limit (three minutes). Direct students to practice with a partner.

3. Call on volunteers to present their version of the conversation for the class.

> **MULTILEVEL STRATEGIES**
>
> Adapt 2B to the level of your students.
>
> • **Pre- and On-level** Pair pre- and on-level students for 2B. Assign pre-level students part A for the first round and then have them switch roles.
>
> • **Higher-level** Pair students and have them ask and answer questions about other information on the website.

Communicative Practice and Application
20–25 minutes

 1. If students will use the Internet for this task, establish what device(s) they'll use: a class computer, tablets, or smartphones. Alternatively, print information from the Internet before class and distribute to groups.

2. Write the questions from 2C on the board. Explain that students will work in teams to research and report on these questions. Ask: *Which question requires research?* [1] *Which search terms or questions can you use to find the information you need?* ["job training" + your city; "career planning services" + your city] *What information will you scan for?* [names; addresses of services; lists of services] *How will you record the information you find?* [table, checklist, index cards] Remind students to bookmark or record sites so they can find or cite them in the future.

3. Group students and assign roles: manager, administrative assistant, reporter, and IT support. Verify students' understanding of their roles.

4. Give managers the time limit for researching question 1 (ten minutes). Direct the IT support to begin the online research or pick up the printed materials for each team. Direct the administrative assistant to record information for the team using a table, checklist, or index cards.

5. Give a two-minute warning. Call "time." Tell reporters to first answer and then ask each member of the team the other questions.

> **TIP**
>
> When setting up task-based activities, verify that students understand their roles using physical commands. For example: *If you report on your team's work, stand up* [reporter]. *If you keep the team on task, point to the clock* [manager]. *If you write the team's responses, raise your hand* [administrative assistant]. *If you help the team research, hold up your smartphone/tablet* [IT support].

 1. Copy the sentence frames on the board.

2. Direct teams to help their administrative assistants use the sentence frames to record the team's findings. Direct the reporter to use the recorded information to report the team's findings to the class or another team.

Evaluation
10–15 minutes

TEST YOURSELF

1. Direct Partner A to read prompts 1–3 from 1C on page 52 to Partner B. Partner B should close their book and write the answers in their notebooks. When finished, students switch roles. Partner B reads questions 4–6 from 1C.

2. Direct both partners to open their books and check their spelling when they finish.

> **EXTENSION ACTIVITY**
>
> **Job Ads**
>
> 1. Put students in groups. Pass out job ads cut from the newspaper or printed off the Internet or have students look at ads on their smartphones or tablets. Tell the groups to look for the five ads they think are the most interesting.
>
> 2. Ask a reporter from each group to present the group's ads to the class. Tell them to share any job training or experience requirements that are mentioned in the ads. Have students discuss any career planning they can do to get the jobs.

LESSON 2 WRITING

Lesson Overview

MULTILEVEL OBJECTIVES

On- and Higher-level: Analyze, write, and edit a cover letter email

Pre-level: Read a cover letter email and write about job experience

LANGUAGE FOCUS

Grammar: Simple present, present perfect, and present continuous (*I am reliable. I have attached my resume. I am writing in response to your job listing.*)

Vocabulary: *Sincerely*

For vocabulary support, see these **Oxford Picture Dictionary** topics: Job Skills, page 176; Office Skills, page 177; Job Search, pages 168–169

STRATEGY FOCUS

When you are writing a cover letter email, include information that is not in your resume.

READINESS CONNECTION

In this lesson, students communicate information in writing to get a job.

PACING

To compress this lesson: Assign the *Test Yourself* for homework.

To extend this lesson: Hold a job fair. Have students take on the roles of job candidates and employers. (See end of lesson.)

And/or have students complete **Workbook 4 page 24** and **Multilevel Activities 4 Unit 4 page 50**.

Lesson Notes

CORRELATIONS

CCRS: SL.1.B (d.) Explain their own ideas and understanding in light of the discussion.

SL.2.B Determine the main ideas and supporting details of a text read aloud or information presented in diverse media and formats, including visually, quantitatively, and orally.

R.1.B Ask and answer such questions as who, what, where, when, why, and how to demonstrate understanding of key details in a text.

R.2.A Identify the main topic and retell key details of a text.

R.5.A Know and use various text features to locate key facts or information in a text.

W.2.A Write informative/explanatory texts in which they name a topic, supply some facts about the topic, and provide some sense of closure.

W.4.B Produce writing in which the development and organization are appropriate to task and purpose.

W.5.B With guidance and support from peers and others, develop and strengthen writing as needed by planning, revising and editing.

W.6.B With guidance and support, use technology to produce and publish writing (using keyboarding skills) as well as to interact and collaborate with others.

L.1.B (l.) Produce simple, compound and complex sentences.

L.2.B (c.) Use commas in greetings and closings of letters. (d.) Use a comma to separate an introductory element form the rest of the sentence.

L.2.C (a.) Use correct capitalization. (c.) Use punctuation to separate items in a series.

RF.4.B (a.) Read grade-level text with purpose and understanding.

ELPS: 1. An ELL can construct meaning from oral presentations and literary and informational text through level-appropriate listening, reading, and viewing. 2. An ELL can participate in level-appropriate oral and written exchanges of information, ideas, and analyses, in various social and academic contexts, responding to peer, audience, or reader comments and questions. 3. An ELL can speak and write about level-appropriate complex literary and informational texts and topics.

Warm-up and Review
10–15 minutes (books closed)

Write *Positive Adjectives* on the board. Have the students brainstorm adjectives that they might use to describe themselves in a cover letter: *reliable, dependable, organized, hardworking, enthusiastic, motivated*. Call on volunteers to give you an example of how they demonstrate such behaviors.

Introduction
5 minutes

1. Say: *When you apply for a new job, you need to sell yourself or make yourself look good to employers. One opportunity you have for this is in the cover letter email.*

2. State the objective: *Today we'll learn how to write a cover letter email.*

1 Prepare to write

Presentation
20–25 minutes

 1. Build students' schema by asking questions about the email. Ask: *What does Re mean?* [regarding] *Why is it helpful to include a subject of an email?* [to help the person know what the email is about]

2. Give students time to read and think about the questions. Elicit responses from the class.

Possible Answers
1. He is writing to her to apply for a job.
2. She is a supervisor at a store.

 1-35 1. Introduce the model email and its purpose: *You're going to read an email from a job applicant to someone who is probably in human resources at a store. As you read, look for the purpose of the email: why is he writing?* Have students read the email silently.

2. Check comprehension. Ask: *What job is he writing about?* [customer service representative] *What does Luis talk about in the second paragraph?* [his skills, experience, and qualities] *Is the email formal or informal?* [formal] *How do you know?* [it includes formal language – "Dear," "Sincerely"]

3. Play the audio. Ask students to number the paragraphs as they read along.

Guided Practice I
10 minutes

 1. Read the instructions aloud. Have students read the statements. Have students work independently to mark the sentences *true, false,* or *no information*.

2. Have students compare answers with a partner. Write the answers on the board. Ask students to correct the false statements.

3. Point out the *Writer's Note* and ask: *What information do you think is in the email that is not on the resume? What information might you include in a cover letter that is not on a resume?*

Answers	
1. T	4. T
2. NI	5. NI
3. F	

 Read the instructions. Have students work individually to answer the questions and then compare answers with a partner. Elicit answers from the class.

Answers
1. He is sending his resume.
2. He has two years' experience as a cashier and he has completed a training class in customer skills; he has excellent computer skills and he is fluent in English and Spanish.
3. He wants Ms. Porter to meet with him.

MULTILEVEL STRATEGIES

For 1D, seat pre-level students together.

- **Pre-level** While other students are working on 1D, ask these students questions about the reading. *Did Luis send his resume with the letter? Does he have sales experience? How are his computer skills? What does Luis want to do with Ms. Porter so he can learn more about the position?* Give students time to copy the answers to 1D from the board.

2 Plan and write

Guided Practice II
15–20 minutes

 1. Direct students to look at the job listings.

2. Give students time to read and think about the questions. Elicit their answers. Write other jobs they would like to apply for on the board.

1. Direct students to look back at the cover letter email in 1B. Focus students' attention on the verb tenses in the letter. Ask them to look through the letter quickly and underline the one present-continuous [am writing] and three present-perfect verbs [have attached, have completed, have listed]. Elicit the reason for those tense choices and discuss any questions.

2. Read through the letter template. Elicit ideas that could go in each paragraph. Have students write their cover letter emails individually.

3. Check comprehension of the exercise. Ask: *How many paragraphs do you need to write?* [three] *How can you introduce each paragraph?* [I am writing…I believe…I would like…]

4. Have students work individually to write their emails.

> **MULTILEVEL STRATEGIES**
>
> Adapt 2B to the level of your students.
>
> • **Pre-level** Tell these students to refer to the model in 1B for formatting their contact information and the addressee's information. Provide a skeleton letter to help them write the body.
>
> *I am writing in response to your job listing for a_____. I have attached my resume.*
>
> *I have _____ experience as a _____.*
>
> *I have _____ skills. I am _____.*
>
> *I would like to meet with you. Thank you for considering me for this position.*
>
> *Sincerely yours,*
>
> _____

3 Get feedback and revise

Guided Practice III
5 minutes

A Direct students to check their writing using the editing checklist. Tell them to read each item in the list and check their papers before moving onto the next item. Explain that students should not edit their writing at this stage. They should just use the checklist to check their work and mark any areas they want to revise.

Communicative Practice
15 minutes

 1. Read the instructions aloud. Emphasize to students that they are responding to their partners' work, not correcting it.

2. Use the letter in 1B to model the exercise. *I think the sentence that says, "My computer skills are excellent, and I am fluent in English and Spanish" shows that Luis is a good candidate. I'm not sure I understand the sentence…*

3. Direct students to exchange papers with a partner and follow the instructions.

C Allow students time to edit and revise their writing as necessary, using the editing checklist from 3A and their partner's feedback from 3B. If necessary, students could complete this task as homework.

> **EXTENSION ACTIVITY**
>
> **Job Fair**
>
> Hold a "job fair" in class. Ask for volunteers to come to the front of the room and describe their skills and experience. All non-volunteers are "employers." Ask the employers to listen and take notes. Tell them they need to select candidates for certain jobs. Have the employers discuss which applicants they would like to interview and why.

Application and Evaluation
10 minutes

TEST YOURSELF

1. Review the instructions aloud. Assign a time limit (five minutes) and have students work independently.

2. Before collecting student work, invite two or three volunteers to share their sentences. Ask students to raise their hands if they wrote similar answers.

LESSON 3 GRAMMAR

Lesson Overview

MULTILEVEL OBJECTIVES

On- and Higher-level: Use the past perfect in sentences about applying for jobs and life experience and listen for information about life experience

Pre-level: Identify the past perfect in sentences about applying for jobs and life experience and use past participles

LANGUAGE FOCUS

Grammar: Past perfect (*He hadn't planned any questions before he arrived. Had you sent a resume before you called?*)

Vocabulary: Job search

For vocabulary support, see these **Oxford Picture Dictionary** topics: Career Planning, pages 174–175; Job Search, pages 168–169

READINESS CONNECTION

In this lesson, students speak using the past perfect so others can understand.

PACING

To compress this lesson: Conduct 2A and 2B as whole-class activities.

To extend this lesson: Have students practice the past perfect in questions and answers. (See end of lesson.)

And/or have students complete **Workbook 4 pages 25–26**, **Multilevel Activities 4 Unit 4 pages 51–52**, and **Multilevel Grammar Exercises 4 Unit 4**.

Lesson Notes

CORRELATIONS

CCRS: SL.2.B Determine the main ideas and supporting details of a text read aloud or information presented in diverse media and formats, including visually, quantitatively, and orally.

R.1.B Ask and answer such questions as who, what, where, when, why, and how to demonstrate understanding of key details in a text.

L.1.B (e.) Form and use the past tense of frequently occurring irregular verbs. (l.) Produce simple, compound and complex sentences.

L.1.C (e.) Form and use the perfect verb tenses.

L.2.C (a.) Use correct capitalization. (d.) Use a comma to separate and introductory element from the rest of the sentence.

RF.4.B (a.) Read grade-level text with purpose and understanding.

ELPS: 7. An ELL can adapt language choices to purpose, task, and audience when speaking and writing. 9. An ELL can create clear and coherent level-appropriate speech and text. 10. An ELL can demonstrate command of the conventions of standard English to communicate in level-appropriate speech and writing.

Warm-up and Review
10–15 minutes (books closed)

Write these sentences on the board out of order: *She was called in for an interview. She wrote a cover letter. She got the job. She sent it to the company with her resume. Maria saw a job ad in the newspaper. She dressed carefully for the interview.* Ask volunteers to rewrite the sentences in the correct order. Leave the sentences on the board.

Introduction
5–10 minutes

1. Elicit the tense of the story on the board. Say: *We tell stories in the simple past when we are telling them in sequence. First Maria saw the ad; then she wrote the cover letter; then she sent it to the company. But sometimes we want to put two ideas together, so we use the verb tense to show the sequence of events.* Write on the board: *Maria wrote a cover letter for a job she had seen in the paper.* Underline *had seen*. Say: *This tells us that she saw the ad before she wrote the letter. This tense is called the past perfect.*

2. State the objective: *Today we're going to use the past perfect to talk about applying for jobs.*

1 Learn the past perfect

Presentation I
20–25 minutes

A 1. Direct students to look at the picture and story. Ask: *Who are these people? What are they doing?* [Luis and Ms. Porter from the store, she's interviewing him]

2. Read the instructions aloud. Ask students to read the story silently and answer the questions.

3. Read the first question aloud. Call on a volunteer for the answer. Ask the volunteer where in the story they found the answer. Read the rest of the questions aloud, calling on a different volunteer for each answer.

Answers
1. He did some research about the company and he completed the application online. 2. He planned some questions to ask in the interview. 3. He wrote Ms. Porter a thank-you email. 4. She read Luis' cover letter and resume; she called him about an interview.

B 1. Demonstrate how to read the grammar chart.

2. Direct students to underline the past perfect verbs in the story in 1A. Write the sentences on the board.

3. Ask: *How do you know that Luis had done research before he arrived for the interview?* [the use of past perfect, *had done*]

4. Read the *Grammar Note* aloud. Discuss the meaning of each past-perfect verb in the story. Say: *Ms. Porter had read Luis's resume before what?* [before she called him about an interview] *Luis had found information about the company before what?* [before he arrived at the interview]

5. Assess students' understanding of the chart. Draw a timeline on the board like the one in the book. Replace the two actions with: *Luis sent the email to Ms. Porter. Luis did research about the company.* Elicit a sentence using the past perfect. [Luis had sent the email to Ms. Porter before he did research about the company.] Use the sentences from the *Warm-up* to elicit more past-perfect verbs. *They called (Maria) in for an interview because she had ____. She felt good at the interview because she had ____.*

Answers
Underlined: had read, had already done, had completed, hadn't planned

Guided Practice I
15–20 minutes

 1. Tell students they will collaborate to complete the description of the grammar point. Model collaboration by working with the class to complete the first sentence. Encourage students to look at 1A and 1B to see if the past perfect is used for the first or second event.

2. Pair students and have them work together to complete the description.

3. Project or write the completed description on the board and have pairs verify the accuracy of their responses. Ask volunteers which sentences confused them and discuss.

Answers
past perfect, simple past, earlier, later

90 Unit 4 Lesson 3 Grammar

> **MULTILEVEL STRATEGIES**
>
> For 1C, seat mixed-level students together.
>
> • **Pre-, On- and Higher-level** Assign pre-level students the role of administrative assistant, on-level students the role of manager, and higher-level students the role of researcher. The administrative assistant fills in the blanks according to the team's decisions, the manager reads the description and manages the team's discussion, and the researcher looks up the definition of the grammar point online or checks against an answer key to verify the team's answers.

Guided Practice II
5–10 minutes

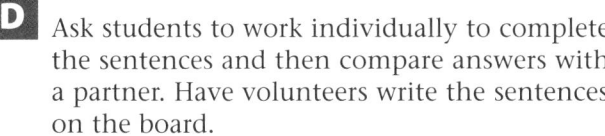 Ask students to work individually to complete the sentences and then compare answers with a partner. Have volunteers write the sentences on the board.

Answers
1. she had read
2. had not called
3. had not looked
4. had researched
5. had given

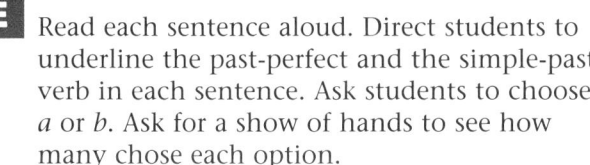 Read each sentence aloud. Direct students to underline the past-perfect and the simple-past verb in each sentence. Ask students to choose *a* or *b*. Ask for a show of hands to see how many chose each option.

Answers		
1. b	2. a	3. b

> **MULTILEVEL STRATEGIES**
>
> After 1E, provide more practice with the past perfect.
>
> • **Pre-level** Provide these students with a series of sentences containing a simple-past and a past-perfect verb. Ask them to underline the verbs and label them as *1* or *2* to indicate which action happened first. *1. By the time she got home, the manager had called her twice. 2. He applied for a job he had learned about at the career center. 3. She felt qualified for the job because she had worked at a restaurant. 4. He was ready for the questions because he had prepared. 5. She hadn't slept much the night before she went to the interview.* Go over the answers together.
>
> • **On- and Higher-level** Provide these students with pictures of people or have them look through magazines. Tell them to write sentences about what was happening at the time of the picture and what they imagine had happened before. (*She was sad because she hadn't done well on the interview.*)

2 Learn past perfect questions

Presentation II
20–25 minutes

  1. Introduce the new topic: *Now we're going to ask and answer questions in the past perfect.*

2. Read and have students repeat the questions and answers. Point out the simple-past verbs in the chart. Emphasize that the past perfect is used to talk about something that happened before another event in the past (the event in the simple past).

3. Check students' understanding of form. Ask: *What word is first in yes/no questions?* [had] Elicit the form: *Had* + subject + past participle. Then elicit the form for information questions: *Wh-* word + *had* + subject + past participle. Write the forms on the board.

4. Have students identify the verb that is used in short answers.

Answer
had

B Ask students to work with a partner to complete the sentences. Call on volunteer pairs to read the questions and answers aloud. Write the answers on the board.

Answers
1. had you looked at
2. Had Pietro finished
3. had they seen
4. had she gone
5. Had you worked

TIP

After 2B, have students practice short answers in different tenses. Ask questions and call on different students to answer. *Do you have a job? Did you work last year? Have you ever gone on a job interview? Would you like to find a job? Had you ever studied past perfect before we began this lesson?*

MULTILEVEL STRATEGIES

Use mixed-level pairs for 2B.

• **Pre-level** Ask these students to read the complete question or answer (the one without the blank) aloud to their partners.

• **On- and Higher-level** Ask these students to read the incomplete question or answer and to supply the completion.

3 Listen for the past perfect to determine the meaning

Guided Practice IV
10–15 minutes

A 1. Ask: *Had you studied English before you came to the U.S.?* Say: *Now we're going to listen to a man named Mopati talk about things he had done in his country before he came to the U.S.*

2. Direct students to read the sentences before they listen to the audio. Play the audio.

3. Replay the audio. Ask students to circle the correct words. Have students compare answers with a partner. Go over the answers as a class.

Answers	
1. big city	4. Spanish
2. small town	5. businessman
3. French	6. teacher

B 1. Read the instructions aloud. Model the conversation with a volunteer. Then ask: *Had Mopati lived in a small town before he came to the U.S.?* [No, he hadn't.]

2. Have students work in pairs to take turns asking and answering questions using the past perfect. Call on volunteers to perform their conversations for the class.

Answers
1. Before Mopati came to the U.S., where had he always lived?
He had always lived in a big city.
2. Where does he live now?
Now he lives in a small town.
3. What had Mopati studied before he came to the U.S.?
He had studied French.
4. What is he studying now?
He is studying Spanish.
5. Before he came to the U.S., what had he always wanted to be?
He had always wanted to be a businessman.
6. What does he want to be now?
He wants to be a teacher.

4 Use the past perfect to talk about your life experience

Communicative Practice and Application
20–25 minutes

A Direct students to work independently to complete the questions and then compare answers with a partner. Go over the answers with the class.

Answers
1. had never done
2. had never seen
3. had never heard

B Direct students to work with a partner to write two more questions using the past perfect.

C 1. Have pairs merge to form teams of four. Model the exercise by "joining" one of the pairs. Each pair takes a turn asking and answering questions while the class listens.

2. Check comprehension of the exercise. Ask: *Who asks questions?* [everyone] *Who answers questions?* [everyone]

3. Ask volunteers to share something interesting they learned about their classmates. Discuss the students' ideas as a class. Elicit several completions for this sentence: *Most students had never _____ before they came to the U.S.*

> **TIP**
>
> Have students practice with more sentences with *Before* + past perfect. Put up several ideas to help them get started. *Before I met my best friend, I had never _____. Before I had studied English, I had never _____. Before I started my job, I had never _____. Before I moved to the house I live in now, I had never _____.* Tell students to use the ideas on the board or their own ideas. Call on volunteers to share their sentences with the class.

Evaluation
10–15 minutes

TEST YOURSELF

Ask students to write the sentences independently. Collect and correct their writing.

> **MULTILEVEL STRATEGIES**
>
> Target the *Test Yourself* to the level of your students.
>
> • **Pre-level** Provide sentence frames for these students to complete. *Before ____ (name) came to the U.S., he/she had never _____. Before ____ (name) started this class, he/she had never heard of the word _____.*
>
> • **Higher-level** Ask these students to write four sentences about their partners and four sentences about themselves.

> **EXTENSION ACTIVITY**
> **Discussion**
>
> Provide more practice with the past perfect.
>
> 1. Write the following questions on the board: *1. Why was he nervous at the interview? 2. Why did he get fired? 3. Why did she celebrate after the interview? 4. Why didn't he pass the class? 5. Why couldn't she answer the questions?*
>
> 2. Direct students to work with a partner to write answers to the questions using the past perfect and *because*. *He was nervous at the interview because he had arrived late.*

LESSON 4 EVERYDAY CONVERSATION

Lesson Overview

MULTILEVEL OBJECTIVES

On-, Pre-, and Higher-level: Interview for a job and listen for details

LANGUAGE FOCUS

Grammar: Simple past, past perfect, and present perfect (*He got the job. He hadn't worked before. He has learned a lot.*)

Vocabulary: Applicant, responsibilities, contribute, stock clerk

For vocabulary support, see these **Oxford Picture Dictionary** topics: Job Skills, page 176; Office Skills, page 177; Interview Skills, page 179

STRATEGY FOCUS

Use language to encourage a team member or a group.

READINESS CONNECTION

In this lesson, students discuss good and bad things to do at a job interview.

PACING

To compress this lesson: Conduct *Discuss* as a whole-class activity.

To extend this lesson: Have students discuss the top three things people should and shouldn't do during interviews. (See end of lesson.)

And/or have students complete **Workbook 4 page 27** and **Multilevel Activities 4 Unit 4 page 53**.

Lesson Notes

CORRELATIONS

CCRS: SL.1.B (a.) Come to discussions prepared, having read or studied required material; explicitly draw on that preparation and other information known about the topic to explore ideas under discussion. (b.) Follow agreed-upon rules for discussions. (c.) Ask questions to check understanding of information presented, stay on topic, and link their comments to the remarks of others. (d.) Explain their own ideas and understanding in light of the discussion.

SL.2.B Determine the main ideas and supporting details of a text read aloud or information presented in diverse media and formats, including visually, quantitatively, and orally.

SL.4.B Report on a topic or text, tell a story, or recount an experience with appropriate facts and relevant, descriptive details, speaking clearly at an understandable pace.

SL.6.B Speak in complete sentences when appropriate to task and situation in order to provide requested detail or clarification.

R.1.B Ask and answer such questions as who, what, where, when, why, and how to demonstrate understanding of key details in a text.

R.7.B Use information gained from illustrations and the words in a text to demonstrate understanding of the text.

L.1.B (e.) Form and use the past tense of frequently occurring irregular verbs. (g.) Form and use regular and irregular verbs. (l.) Produce simple, compound and complex sentences.

L.1.C (d.) Use modal auxiliaries to convey various conditions. (e.) Form and use the perfect verb tenses.

L.3.B (a.) Choose words and phrases for effect.

RF.4.B (a.) Read grade-level text with purpose and understanding.

ELPS: 1. An ELL can construct meaning from oral presentations and literary and informational text through level-appropriate listening, reading, and viewing. 2. An ELL can participate in level-appropriate oral and written exchanges of information, ideas, and analyses, in various social and academic contexts, responding to peer, audience, or reader comments and questions. 9. An ELL can create clear and coherent level-appropriate speech and text. 10. An ELL can demonstrate command of the conventions of standard English to communicate in level-appropriate speech and writing.

Warm-up and Review
10–15 minutes (books closed)

Write *Job Interview* on the board. Ask students what advice they would give to someone going on a job interview. Write their ideas on the board in categories: *Dress, Behavior, Preparation.*

Introduction
5 minutes

1. Say: *All of these things are important, but of course, the most important part is what you actually say to the interviewer. What questions will he or she ask and how will you answer?*

2. State the objective: *Today we'll learn how to respond to job-interview questions.*

1 Learn ways to respond to interview questions

Presentation I
10–20 minutes

 1. Direct students to look at the pictures. Ask students to predict which woman will have a better job interview. Elicit reasons for their predictions.

2. Play the audio. Give students a minute to read and think about the question. Go over the answers as a class.

Answers
Ms. Adams'

Guided Practice I
20–25 minutes

 1. Read the instructions and questions aloud. Play the audio. Ask students to listen for the answers to each question.

2. Ask students to compare their answers with a partner. Circulate and monitor to ensure students understand the audio.

Possible Answers
1. Ms. Jones uses less formal language; she says "You mean?" and "Like" and short answers. She doesn't try to give the interviewer more information about herself. Ms. Adams uses more formal language; she says "Do you mean?" instead of "You mean?" and she shows that she is interested in the position.
2. Ms. Adams. He asks her more questions and he says that she has some of the experience he is looking for. He asks her about her long-term goals.

 1. Read the instructions aloud. Explain that students are going to hear the audio one more time. They should write the words they hear to complete the sentences. Play the audio. Have students compare answers with a partner. Call on volunteers to elicit the answers.

2. Have students work in pairs to practice the conversations. Circulate and monitor pronunciation. Model and have students repeat difficult words or phrases.

Answers	
1. You mean	3. Do you mean
2. Like	4. Is that

2 Practice your pronunciation

Pronunciation Extension
10–15 minutes

A 1-39 1. Write *A: Tell me about your first English class. B: My first English class* on the board. Direct a volunteer to say sentence A. Reply, saying sentence B with falling intonation, as if you were reading a book title. Have a different volunteer say sentence A. Respond with rising intonation to indicate a check of understanding. Ask students which version was a question. Write the question mark at the end of the sentence and repeat the rising intonation. Say: *Now we're going to focus on using rising intonation to check understanding.*

2. Play the audio. Direct students to listen for the rising intonation.

3. Replay the audio and ask students to repeat sentence B.

B Direct students to practice the conversations with a partner. Monitor and provide feedback on rising intonation.

C 🔊 1-40 Play the audio again. Have students check their pronunciation in 2B. Call on volunteers to read the conversations aloud. Provide feedback.

> **TIP**
>
> Have students practice producing their own comprehension checks. Write questions on the board. *1. Where did you work before you came here? 2. Where did you study before? 3. What will you do when you finish school? 4. Have you studied English for very long? 5. Do you study every day?* Tell students to take turns asking these questions with a partner and responding with a check for understanding.

3 Compare the simple past, past perfect, and present perfect

Presentation II and Guided Practice II
10–15 minutes

 1. Introduce the new topic. *Now we're going to contrast the simple past, the past perfect, and the present perfect. We'll use all of these tenses to talk about work.*

2. Read the sentences in the chart aloud. Elicit the form for each tense and write them on the board:

Simple past: Subject + simple past

Past perfect: Subject + *had(n't)* + past participle

Present perfect: Subject + *has(n't)/have(n't)* + past participle

Review the tenses by asking questions about the chart: *What time expressions indicate simple past?* [in 2014, from 2013 to 2016] *Which indicate past perfect?* [before, when] *When do we use past perfect?* [for the first of two past events] *What time cues tell us to use present perfect?* [since] *What other words do you think tell us to use present perfect?* [already, yet, ever, never]

3. Check comprehension of the chart. Ask: *When did Sam get his first job in the hospital?* [in 2014] *Did he take a training class before that?* [yes[*Does he still work at the hospital?* [yes] *Is he still learning English?* [yes]

4. Direct students to work individually to mark the sentences *true* or *false* and then compare answers with a partner. Go over the answers as a class.

Answers	
1. F	4. F
2. F	5. T
3. F	

> **TIP**
>
> Have students make a timeline of the events in the chart. Ask: *What is the first time mentioned in the chart?* [2014] *Did anything happen before that?* [Yes, he had already taken a training class.] Students can use the timeline to help them with the task in 3A.

Guided Practice III
15–20 minutes

B 1. Have students work individually to circle the verbs in the sentences and then compare their answers with a partner. Go over the answers as a class.

2. Set a time limit (five minutes). Ask students to practice asking and answering the questions with several partners. Call on individuals to share their answers with the class.

Answers		
1. have	2. Had	3. didn't

> **MULTILEVEL STRATEGIES**
>
> Seat mixed-level students together for 3B.
>
> • **Pre-level** Allow these students to focus on answering the questions with short answers rather than asking them.
>
> • **Higher-level** Direct these students to read the questions aloud for their partners and provide complete answers.

4 Building conversation skills

Guided Practice IV
15–20 minutes

 Direct students to look at the picture and skim the conversation. Have them work with partners to identify the purpose of the conversation. Elicit responses and ask: *How do you know? Why do you say that?* Encourage students to state their reasoning.

> **Possible Answers**
>
> The conversation is a job interview. The purpose is for the interviewer to learn about Luis' experience and skills and for Luis to describe himself and say how he is qualified for the job.

B 🔊 **1-41** 1. Ask students to read the instructions and tell you what they are going to do [listen and read and respond to the question]. Play the audio and then elicit the answer to the question.

2. Ask students to read the conversation with a partner. Circulate and monitor pronunciation. Model and have students repeat difficult words or phrases.

3. Ask: *In what other situations could you use this conversation?* Point out a few phrases that are not specific to working with customers. Ask volunteers to point out others.

Possible Answers
Luis has worked as a cashier and a stock clerk. He completed a customer skills training class. He says that he is a good team player and does his best to contribute.

Communicative Practice and Application I
15–20 minutes

C 1. Pair students and have them read the instructions silently. Check their comprehension of the exercise. Ask: *What are the two roles? Where do you think the conversation takes place?*

2. Model and have students repeat the expressions in the *In Other Words* box. Explain that they should use these expressions in their conversations.

3. Draw a T-chart on the board. Label the left column *Interviewer* and the right column *Applicant*. Elicit examples of what each person might say and make notes on the chart.

4. Set a time limit (three minutes). Have students act out the role-play. Call "time" and have students switch roles.

5. Ask three volunteer pairs to act out their role-play for the class. Tell students who are listening to make a simple table with four rows and three columns. Use the top row to label the columns: *Experience*, *Training*, and *Skills*. Have students take notes in the chart for each role-play.

> **MULTILEVEL STRATEGIES**
>
> For 4C, adapt the role-play to the level of your students.
>
> • **Pre-level** Have students work in mixed level pairs. Direct pre-level students to ask the questions in 4B. Their partners can answer with different information.

5 Focus on listening for details

Presentation and Guided Practice
20–25 minutes

A Read the statement aloud and model a discussion with a volunteer. Say: *I think it's a good idea to have a resume, even if you aren't looking for a job. Do you agree?... Why? / Why not? ... I agree because... / I disagree because...*

B Direct students to look at picture. Ask: *What do you think she's working on?*

C 🔊 **1-42** 1. Direct students to read the sentences before listening.

2. Play the audio and have students work individually to circle the correct words. Have them compare answers with a partner. Go over the answers as a class. Write them on the board.

Answers	
1. hasn't	3. class
2. present	4. her country

> **MULTILEVEL STRATEGIES**
>
> Adapt 5C to the level of your students.
>
> • **Pre-level** While other students are completing 5C, write questions on the board for these students to answer. *Has Hanna finished her training class? What does Hanna need to write after the month? Does she need to write the name of her English class or the name of her teacher? Where did she graduate from high school?* Call on volunteers for the answers. Allow these students to copy the answers to 5C from the board.

6 Discuss

Communicative Practice and Application II
15–20 minutes

A 1. Read the instructions aloud. Draw a sample chart on the board with space for things you should do in a job interview on one side and things you shouldn't do on the other. Elicit an example of each and write it under the correct heading.

2. Have volunteers read the sample conversation. Go over the *Speaking Note*.

3. Put students into teams of four and assign roles: supervisor, manager, administrative assistant, and editor. Verify students'

understanding of the roles. Encourage students to use the phrases in the *Speaking Note* during their discussions.

4. Set a time limit for the discussions (ten minutes). Write the sentence frame from 6B on the board. Then circulate and monitor.

 Call "time." Ask the supervisor for each team to report the results of their team's discussion, using the sentence frame on the board.

> **EXTENSION ACTIVITY**
>
> To extend 6B, draw a large blank chart on the board. As each supervisor shares with the class, the administrative assistant from that group fills in the chart. If other teams came up with the same answers, they should not enter the information again. Have students discuss the top three things that people should and shouldn't do during interviews.

Evaluation
5 minutes

TEST YOURSELF

1. Ask students to complete the checkboxes individually.

2. Tell students that you are going to read each of the items in the checklist aloud. If they are not at all confident with that skill, they should hold up a closed fist. If they are not very confident, they should hold up one finger. If they are somewhat confident, two fingers; confident, three fingers; very confident, four fingers. If they think they could teach the skill, they should hold up five fingers. Read each item in the checklist and identify students that may need further support.

> **TIP**
>
> For homework, you could ask students to write a sentence or two about what discussion skills they still need to work on or, if they are confident in all of the skills, what skill they are most proud of.

LESSON 5 READING

Lesson Overview

MULTILEVEL OBJECTIVES

On-, Pre-, and Higher-level: Read about and discuss career planning

LANGUAGE FOCUS

Grammar: The suffixes -er and -ee (*An employer employs an employee.*)

Vocabulary: *Field, variety, wages*

For vocabulary support, see these **Oxford Picture Dictionary** topics: Career Planning, pages 174–175; Job Search, pages 168–169

STRATEGY FOCUS

The title or caption of a chart often includes important information the reader needs to interpret the chart correctly.

READINESS CONNECTION

In this lesson, students determine what steps they need to do to look for a job.

PACING

To compress this lesson: Conduct the word study in 2A as a whole-class activity.

To extend this lesson: Have students use action verbs. (See end of lesson.)

And/or have students complete **Workbook 4 pages 28** and **Multilevel Activities 4 Unit 4 pages 54–55**.

Lesson Notes

CORRELATIONS

CCRS: SL.1.B (a.) Come to discussions prepared, having read or studied required material; explicitly draw on that preparation and other information known about the topic to explore ideas under discussion. (b.) Follow agreed-upon rules for discussions. (c.) Ask questions to check understanding of information presented, stay on topic, and link their comments to the remarks of others. (d.) Explain their own ideas and understanding in light of the discussion.

SL.6.B Speak in complete sentences when appropriate to task and situation in order to provide requested detail or clarification.

R.1.B Ask and answer such questions as who, what, where, when, why, and how to demonstrate understanding of key details in a text.

R.1.C Refer to details and examples in a text when explaining what the text says explicitly and when drawing inferences from the text.

R.2.A Identify the main topic and retell key details of a text.

R.5.B Know and use various text features to locate key facts or information in a text efficiently.

R.7.C Interpret information presented visually, orally, or quantitatively and explain how the information contributes to an understanding of the text in which it appears.

W.8.B Recall information from experiences or gather information from print and digital sources; take brief notes on sources and sort evidence into provided categories.

L.1.B (l.) Produce simple, compound and complex sentences.

L.2.B (h.) Use conventional spelling for high-frequency and other studied words and for adding suffixes to base words.

L.4.B (e.) Use glossaries and beginning dictionaries, both print and digital, to determine or clarify the meaning of words and phrases.

RF.3.B (c.) Identify and know the meaning of the most common prefixes and derivational suffixes.

RF.4.B (a.) Read grade-level text with purpose and understanding.

ELPS: 1. An ELL can construct meaning from oral presentations and literary and informational text through level-appropriate listening, reading, and viewing. 2. An ELL can participate in level-appropriate oral and written exchanges of information, ideas, and analyses, in various social and academic contexts, responding to peer, audience, or reader comments and questions. 3. An ELL can speak and write about level-appropriate complex literary and informational texts and topics. 4. An ELL can construct level-appropriate oral and written claims and support them with reasoning and evidence. 8. An ELL can determine the meaning of words and phrases in oral presentation and literary and informational text.

Warm-up and Review
10–15 minutes (books closed)

Write *Skills* on the board and elicit examples. Encourage students to think of interpersonal skills as well as work skills.

Introduction
5 minutes

1. Say: *Everybody has skills whether they have had job experience or not. Some skills come from job training or education, but some you learn in your life outside of work. Knowing what skills you have is the first step in planning a career.*

2. State the objective: *Today we're going to read and write about career planning.*

1 Read

Presentation
10–20 minutes

A Read the questions aloud. Use ideas from the *Introduction* to help guide discussion.

B Read the words and definitions. Elicit sample sentences for each word or supply them if the students can't. Ask students to identify fields that are hiring more people and fields that are losing jobs.

Pre-reading

C Read the instructions aloud and confirm that students understand what *skim* means [to read quickly to get the gist, or main point of the text]. Have students answer the question individually and then compare answers with a partner. Check answers with the class. If any of the students answer incorrectly, ask them to support their answer using the information from the first and last paragraphs. Establish the correct answer.

Answer
c. How to go from a job to a career

Guided Practice: While Reading
20–30 minutes

D 1. Ask students to read the article silently and answer the question. Have them compare answers with a partner.

2. Check answers with the class.

3. Check comprehension. Ask: *Is finding a career quick and easy?* [No, it takes time and effort.] *What should you do first when you are exploring careers?* [learn about yourself]

Possible Answer
You can learn about careers and the education and training you need for them.

> **MULTILEVEL STRATEGIES**
>
> Adapt 1D to the level of your students.
>
> • **Pre-level** Read the text aloud to these students as they follow along.
>
> • **On- and Higher-level** Pair students and have them read the website content aloud to each other, taking turns to read each paragraph.

Guided Practice: Rereading
10–15 minutes

E 1. Provide an opportunity for students to extract evidence from the text. Have students reread the article and take notes in the graphic organizer on the information.

2. Pair students and tell them to compare their charts and report anything they disagree on. Discuss and clarify as needed.

Possible Answers
To learn about yourself:
1. take an interest inventory
2. take a skills assessment
3. do these assessments on your own
To research careers:
1. use the CareerOneStop website
2. speak to a career counselor
To set goals:
1. think about where you want to be in 1 year and in 5 years
2. figure out steps you need to take to get there

 1. Confirm that student remember what *scan* means [to look quickly for specific information]. Ask students what words they should scan for to find the answer to 1 [career, occupation, field]. Have students work individually to circle the correct words and then compare answers with a partner. Go over the answers as a class.

2. Elicit and discuss any additional questions about the reading. You could introduce new questions for class discussion: *What is a skills assessment? Have you taken one? Where can you find them?*

> **Answers**
> 1. An occupation
> 2. life skill
> 3. grow
> 4. hundreds

> **MULTILEVEL STRATEGIES**
>
> For 1F, work with pre-level students.
>
> • **Pre-level** Ask these students *yes/no* and short-answer information questions about the reading while other students are completing 1F. *Can an interest inventory help you learn about yourself?* [yes] *Is using a computer a soft or hard skill?* [hard] *What about working on a team?* [soft] *How many careers are on the government website?* [more than 900]

2 Word study

Guided Practice: Post-reading
10 minutes

 1. Direct students to look at the chart and identify the topic (the suffixes *–er* and *-ee*). Read the information on the suffixes aloud. Read the example sentence aloud.

2. Have students repeat after you as you say each word with natural intonation, rhythm, and stress.

3. Direct students to complete the sentences and then compare answers with a partner. Read the correct answers and have students check their work.

> **Answers**
> 1. employee, employer
> 2. trainer, trainees
> 3. payee, payer

B Direct students to work individually to write a sentence for each topic that includes the underlined word. Ask volunteers to write their sentences on the board. Have the rest of the class suggest grammar and spelling edits as needed.

> **MULTILEVEL STRATEGIES**
>
> For 2B, seat pre-level students together.
>
> • **Pre-level** Direct these students to copy the words from the chart into their notebooks with a definition. Allow them to look in their dictionaries if necessary.

3 Talk it over

Guided Practice
15–20 minutes

 1. Have students look at the graph and read the note. Point out that they need to use the information from the graph and the note to complete the sentences and answer the question. Have students read the *Reader's Note* and then check students' understanding of the graph. Ask: *What is the employment change for the health care and social assistance sector?* [3,794,800]

2. Have students work in pairs to complete the task. Set a time limit (ten minutes). Ask volunteers to share their answers with the class.

> **Answers**
> 1. 2024
> 2. service providing
> 3. health care
> 4. manufacturing
> 5. health care and social assistance
> 6. workers' age

Communicative Practice
20 minutes

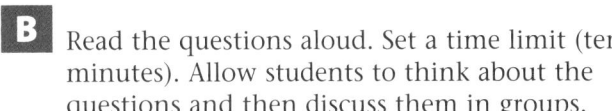 Read the questions aloud. Set a time limit (ten minutes). Allow students to think about the questions and then discuss them in groups.

 Ask volunteers to share their ideas with the class.

Application
5–10 minutes

BRING IT TO LIFE

Talk to students about career-interest inventories and skills surveys. Explain that interest inventories will ask about what kinds of activities you like to do and skill surveys will ask about what you know how to do.

> **EXTENSION ACTIVITY**
>
> **Action Verbs**
>
> 1. Tell students that career counselors often recommend that people use action verbs in their resumes and cover letters. Write these words on the board: *design, develop, create, build, maintain, prepare, supply, transport.*
>
> 2. As a class, brainstorm sentences using these verbs that might appear in a cover letter or resume. Encourage students to use their own experience.

AT WORK

Warm-up and Review
10–15 minutes (books closed)

Begin the lesson by talking about something you would like to learn to help you in your job or career. Elicit from the class how you can go about learning it.

Introduction
5 minutes

State the objective: *Today we're going to talk about learning at work.*

Presentation
5 minutes

A **1-43** Read the instructions aloud. Play the audio. Give students a minute to think about the question. Elicit responses from the class.

Answers
Larry, an employee, and Ms. Lopez, a supervisor

Guided Practice
10–15 minutes

B **1-43** Have students read the sentences. Play the audio again. Direct students to listen and mark the sentences *true* or *false* and then compare answers with a partner. Go over the answers with the class.

Answers	
1. F	3. T
2. T	4. T

C **1-43** Read the instructions aloud. Play the audio again, encouraging students to take notes in their notebooks. Set a time limit (five minutes) for students to discuss their answers with a partner. Circulate to monitor.

Possible Answers
He says, "I am always interested in the chance to learn something new.", "Can you tell me a little bit more about it?", "That sounds really interesting.", "I would be very interested.", and "Thank you so much; I am really interested …so I really appreciate the opportunity."

TIP
Play the audio again and have students take notes on how Ms. Lopez offers Larry an opportunity to take the supervisory training. Elicit phrases and write them on the board: *I wanted to talk to you about something that's coming up. It's an opportunity that I think might be right for you. Are you familiar with the professional development office? I think you are a good candidate. I think it's a good fit for you.* Leave the phrases on the board for students to use in Exercise E.

Presentation and Communicative Practice
10 minutes

D 1. Direct students' attention to the *Do/Say* chart and ask them to identify the lesson's soft skill [expressing a willingness to learn]. Ask the class which column has examples of language [right] and which has examples of behaviors [left].

2. Say a phrase from the left and confirm understanding. Ask: *What does it mean to be well-informed?* [know a lot about something] *What does it mean to volunteer for something at work?* [let your supervisor know you're willing to take on a new task or responsibility without extra pay]

3. Model the sentence frames from the right using authentic intonation. Have students practice imitating your inflection.

4. Put students in teams of four and assign each team a question. Assign roles: supervisor, manager, administrative assistant, and researcher. (Researchers will ask you questions on behalf of the team.) Verify understanding of the roles. Set a time limit (five minutes) and monitor.

5. Write sentence frames on the board that teams can use to summarize their response. *Our team discussed the following question:_____. We decided ____ because____.*

6. Call "time" and let supervisors rehearse their report for one minute. Direct each supervisor to present to three other teams.

Communicative Practice and Application
20–25 minutes

E 1. Model the first situation with a volunteer. Offer the student supervisory training using phrases from the board. Elicit appropriate responses to show a willingness to learn. Direct students to work in pairs to take turns offering and responding to offers.

2. Invite volunteers to act out their conversations for the class.

F 1. Have pairs merge to form teams of four. Read the instructions aloud. Confirm understanding of the task: *What will the group do first?* [make a list of opportunities] *What will the supervisor do?* [offer opportunities] *What will the other team members do?* [take turns responding to the supervisor]

2. Each group should select a supervisor to hold meetings with each "employee." The other three members should each take turns responding. The "employees" who are listening should take notes on the opportunity and the expressions the employee uses to indicate willingness to learn.

3. As students carry out the role-play, circulate and monitor. Have students provide feedback to each other in their teams. Then provide global feedback once the activity ends.

TEAMWORK & LANGUAGE REVIEW

Lesson Overview

MULTILEVEL OBJECTIVES

On-, Pre-, and Higher-level: Expand upon and review unit grammar and life skills

LANGUAGE FOCUS

Grammar: Past perfect (*He had already accepted another job when she called him.*)

Vocabulary: Career preparation vocabulary

For vocabulary support, see these **Oxford Picture Dictionary** topics: Job Skills, page 176; Office Skills, page 177; Career Planning, pages 174–175

READINESS CONNECTION

In this review, students practice team writing, data analysis, and problem solving skills.

PACING

To extend this review: Have students complete **Workbook 4 page 29**, **Multilevel Activities 4 Unit 4 page 56**, and **Multilevel Grammar Exercises 4 Unit 4**.

Lesson Notes

CORRELATIONS

CCRS: SL.1.B (a.) Come to discussions prepared, having read or studied required material; explicitly draw on that preparation and other information known about the topic to explore ideas under discussion. (b.) Follow agreed-upon rules for discussions. (c.) Ask questions to check understanding of information presented, stay on topic, and link their comments to the remarks of others. (d.) Explain their own ideas and understanding in light of the discussion.

SL.1.C (b.) Follow agreed-upon rules for discussions and carry out assigned roles.

SL.2.B Determine the main ideas and supporting details of a text read aloud or information presented in diverse media and formats, including visually, quantitatively, and orally.

SL.4.B Report on a topic or text, tell a story, or recount an experience with appropriate facts and relevant, descriptive details, speaking clearly at an understandable pace.

R.1.B Ask and answer such questions as who, what, where, when, why, and how to demonstrate understanding of key details in a text.

R.2.A Identify the main topic and retell key details of a text.

R.7.B Use information gained from illustrations and the words in a text to demonstrate understanding of the text.

L.1.B (l.) Produce simple, compound and complex sentences.

L.1.C (d.) Use modal auxiliaries to convey various conditions. (e.) Form and use the perfect verb tenses.

RF.4.B (a.) Read grade-level text with purpose and understanding.

ELPS: 1. An ELL can construct meaning from oral presentations and literary and informational text through level-appropriate listening, reading, and viewing. 2. An ELL can participate in level-appropriate oral and written exchanges of information, ideas, and analyses, in various social and academic contexts, responding to peer, audience, or reader comments and questions. 5. An ELL can conduct research and evaluate and communicate findings to answer questions or solve problems. 9. An ELL can create clear and coherent level-appropriate speech and text.

Warm-up and Review
10–15 minutes (books closed)

1. Review *At Work* activity F.

2. Ask students to share the good, not-so-good, and interesting things that happened during the role-play. As students speak, write their responses in a chart on the board.

Introduction and Presentation
5 minutes

1. Write these sentences on the board: *Mei applied for three jobs. She finally got an interview.* Ask students: *What happened first?* Underline *applied* and connect the two sentences with *before*. Say: *How can I make it clear that Mei applied for the jobs first and then she got the interview?* [change *applied* to *had applied*; Mei had applied for three jobs before she got an interview.]

2. State the objective: *Today we're going to review the past perfect in order to talk about career preparation.*

Guided Practice
15–20 minutes

A
1. Direct students to look at the pictures. Elicit what is happening in each picture.

2. Have students look at the timeline. Check comprehension. Ask: *What happened in 1990?* [Al arrived in the U.S.]

3. Have students work in groups to create a timeline using the six events shown in the pictures. Tell students they will be making up the actual dates and years.

4. Have volunteers from each group write their timeline on the board.

5. Have the class discuss any similarities or differences in the timelines.

B
1. Have students work in pairs to write at least six past perfect questions about Al's career path.

2. Have pairs join other pairs to form teams of four. Have team members compare their questions.

C
1. Model the conversation with a volunteer.

2. Have the teams of four take turns asking and answering questions from B.

3. Circulate and monitor as necessary. Provide feedback and correction.

D
1. Have students work in teams to complete the paragraph about Irene's career path.

2. Go over answers as a class.

Answers
1. had
2. thought
3. had worked
4. has learned
5. had
6. believed
7. has thought

Communicative Practice
30–40 minutes

E
1. Group students and assign roles: manager, writer, editor, presenter. Have students work with different people than they did in the previous activities. Explain that students are going to work with their teams to write a story about someone on a career path.

2. Read steps 2–4 of the activity aloud. Check comprehension of the task. *What is the first thing you should do?* [think of a career path] *Can you write about Al or Irene?* [no]

3. Set a time limit (ten minutes) to complete the exercise. Circulate and answer any questions.

4. Have presenters from each team read their team's story to another team.

> **TIP**
> Have students brainstorm as a class or in their teams a variety of career paths or desirable jobs (e.g., manufacturing line supervisor, construction person, chef, etc.). Once they have a list, they can choose the career path that will be best for E.

F
1. Have students walk around the room to conduct the interviews. To get students moving, tell them to interview three people who were not in their team for E.

2. Set a time limit (five minutes) to complete the exercise.

3. Tell students to make a note of their classmates' answers but not to worry about writing complete sentences. They should write down each type of career training in answer to question 1 (e.g., certificate program, university degree, on-the-job training, etc.) and keep a tally of responses.

> **MULTILEVEL STRATEGIES**
> Adapt the mixer in F to the level of your students.
> - **Pre- and On-level** Pair these students and have them interview other pairs together.
> - **Higher-level** Have these students ask an additional question and write all answers.

G
1. Call on individuals to report what they learned about their classmates. Keep a running tally on the board for the responses to question 1.

2. Use your tally for question 1 to create a chart on the board for one answer. Instruct students to indicate all responses on a chart in their notebooks. Circulate and answer any questions. Then ask volunteers to complete the chart on the board.

PROBLEM SOLVING
10–15 minutes

A 1. Ask: *Would you like to find a job? If you have a job, would you like a different job from the one you have now?* Tell students they will read a story about a woman who wants a new job. Direct students to read Jin's story silently.

2. Ask: *Where does she work? How long has she worked there? What are her skills? What kind of job would she like? Does she have skills and training for accounting?*

3. Play the audio and have students read along silently.

B 1. Elicit answers to question 1. Have students work in groups to list possible actions Jin could take and discuss possible consequences of each.

2. Call on volunteers to share their ideas. Write the ideas on the board. Have students vote on which action Jin should take first.

Possible Answers
1. Jin works in her family's restaurant. She has learned a lot but she is thinking about her future. She would like to be an accountant. She doesn't know how to look for a job in the U.S. because she has only worked in her family's business.

Evaluation
20–25 minutes

To test students' understanding of the unit language and content, have them take the Unit 4 Test, available on the Teacher Resource Center.

UNIT 5 Safe and Sound

Unit Overview

This unit explores safety and emergencies at work, in the community, and at home and contextualizes modals and other structures for necessity and prohibition.

	KEY OBJECTIVES
Lesson 1	Identify safety hazards and use safety warnings
Lesson 2	Make an outline for a safety plan
Lesson 3	Use *have to, have got to* and *must*, to discuss what to do in an emergency
Lesson 4	Use *should have* to give an opinion about the past
Lesson 5	Identify facts and opinions about safety at home and at work
At Work	Ask for clarification at work
Teamwork & Language Review	Review unit language

	UNIT FEATURES
Academic Vocabulary	*data, equipment, injuries, instructions, quotation, survey, vary*
Employability Skills	• Understand teamwork • Work with others • Locate information • Communicate information • Communicate verbally • Listen actively • Analyze information • Think critically • Choose solutions to workplace safety issues and emergencies • Determine what makes a job safe or unsafe • Decide how to talk about a safety issue at work

Resources	**Class Audio** CD2, Tracks 02–12
	Workbook Unit 5, pages 30–36
	Teacher Resource Center
	   Multilevel Activities 4 Unit 5
	   Multilevel Grammar Exercises 4 Unit 5
	   Unit 5 Test
	Oxford Picture Dictionary Public Safety, Emergencies and Natural Disasters, Emergency Procedures, Jobs and Occupations, Job Safety

LESSON 1 VOCABULARY

Lesson Overview

MULTILEVEL OBJECTIVES

On-level: Describe and talk about safety hazards, warnings, and precautions

Pre-level: Identify safety hazards, warnings, and precautions

Higher-level: Talk and write about safety hazards, warnings, and precautions

LANGUAGE FOCUS

Grammar: Imperative (*Be alert.*)

Vocabulary: Safety hazard, warning, and precaution vocabulary

For vocabulary support, see these **Oxford Picture Dictionary** topics: Public Safety, page 146; Job Safety, page 197

READINESS CONNECTION

In this lesson, students understand teamwork by conducting research on safety hazards.

PACING

To compress this lesson: Conduct 1C as a whole-class activity.

To extend this lesson: Have students write safety advice. (See end of lesson.)

And/or have students complete **Workbook 4 page 30** and **Multilevel Activities 4 Unit 5 pages 58–59**.

Lesson Notes

CORRELATIONS

CCRS: SL.1.B (d.) Explain their own ideas and understanding in light of the discussion.

SL.4.B Report on a topic or text, tell a story, or recount an experience with appropriate facts and relevant, descriptive details, speaking clearly at an understandable pace.

SL.6.B Speak in complete sentences when appropriate to task and situation in order to provide requested detail or clarification.

R.1.B Ask and answer such questions as who, what, where, when, why, and how to demonstrate understanding of key details in a text.

R.4.B Determine the meaning of general academic and domain-specific words and phrases in a text relevant to a topic or subject area.

R.5.B Know and use various text features to locate key facts or information in a text efficiently.

R.7.B Use information gained from illustrations and the words in a text to demonstrate understanding of the text.

W.7.A Participate in shared research and writing projects.

L.1.B (l.) Produce simple, compound and complex sentences.

L.4.B (a.) Use sentence-level context as a clue to the meaning of a word or phrase. (e.) Use glossaries and beginning dictionaries, both print and digital, to determine or clarify the meaning of words and phrases.

RF.4.B (a.) Read grade-level text with purpose and understanding.

ELPS: 1. An ELL can construct meaning from oral presentations and literary and informational text through level-appropriate listening, reading, and viewing. 5. An ELL can conduct research and evaluate and communicate findings to answer questions or solve problems. 9. An ELL can create clear and coherent level-appropriate speech and text.

Warm-up and Review
10–15 minutes (books closed)

Write *At Home* and *At Work* on the board. Ask students to name things that can cause accidents or injuries in each place. Write their ideas in the correct column.

Introduction
5 minutes

1. Say: *Anything that can cause an injury or an accident is a safety hazard.*

2. State the objective: *Today we're going to learn words for safety hazards and warnings and we'll talk about safety procedures.*

Identify safety hazards and warnings

Presentation I
20–25 minutes

 1. Direct students to look at the picture. Ask: *Have you ever worked in a place like this?* Elicit the realia (signs, labels) students can read and copy. Write the words and phrases on the board (*poisonous fumes, restricted area, broken ladder, frayed cord, flammable, danger, radioactive, corrosive chemicals, caution, slippery floor, damaged equipment area*). Say each word or phrase and have students repeat.

2. Teach critical vocabulary in the picture (*label, barrel, drain*).

3. Have students work in groups to answer the questions. Set a time limit (three minutes).

4. Call "time." Elicit answers from the class.

B 1. Read the instructions aloud. Direct students' attention to the notice below the picture. Ask: *Which words are in bold?* [authorized, caution]

2. Direct students to work individually to identify the words in the notice or the picture that provide context clues for the target vocabulary. Then have them compare ideas with a partner.

3. Elicit context clues by asking questions about each target word or phrase, e.g., *How can tell you what* frayed *means?* [the picture of the cord on the fan: it's broken or torn] *Do you think a frayed cord is safe to use?* [No, you should be careful.]

Guided Practice I
10–20 minutes

C 🔊 **2-02** 1. Read the instructions aloud. Direct students to look at the model. Ask: *What are fumes?* [something you can breathe or smell] *If something is poisonous, what does it do?* [makes you sick or kills you] *What words in the sentence help you find the right answer?* [*dangerous* and *breathe*]

2. Have students work individually to complete the sentences and then compare answers with a partner.

3. Prepare students to listen by saying, *Now we're going to listen to a woman describe the hazards in her workplace. While you listen, check your work in 1C.* Ask students to circle the items in 1C that don't match the listening passage. Elicit those items and play them again, focusing on clues to meaning in the 1C sentences. Ask volunteers to write the sentences on the board.

4. Direct students to look up any remaining unknown words in their dictionaries. Discuss those words in relation to the lesson.

Answers
1. poisonous fumes
2. flammable
3. restricted area
4. frayed cord
5. radioactive
6. Corrosive chemicals
7. slippery
8. broken ladder

 1. Read the questions aloud. Pair students to answer the questions.

2. Write *safety* and *warning signs* on the board and elicit students' answers to questions 1 and 2. Point out any safety or warning signs that you have in your classroom—for example, warnings on the fire extinguisher.

2 Learn about safety precautions

Presentation II
10–20 minutes

 1. Direct students to look at the poster. Introduce the new topic: *Now we're going to talk about things you can do to prevent accidents, or safety procedures.*

2. Read the instructions aloud and direct students to read the poster silently. Elicit questions about vocabulary. Check comprehension. Ask: *Which safety rule am I following if I report a burglary?* [report suspicious activities immediately] *What does suspicious mean?* [you don't trust it, it might be dangerous] *What are some things that you think are suspicious?*

3. Have students work individually to match the safety rule with the example and then compare answers with a partner. Go over the answers as a class.

Answers	
1. c	3. b
2. d	4. a

Guided Practice II
10–15 minutes

B 1. Model the conversation with a volunteer. Model it again using other information from 2A.

2. Set a time limit (three minutes). Direct students to practice with a partner.

3. Call on volunteers to present their version of the conversation for the class.

> **MULTILEVEL STRATEGIES**
>
> Adapt 2B to the level of your students.
>
> • **Pre- and On-level** Pair pre- and on-level students for 2B. Assign pre-level students part A for the first round and then have them switch roles.
>
> • **Higher-level** Pair students and direct them to create conversations that use different examples.

Communicative Practice and Application
20–25 minutes

C 1. If students will use the Internet for this task, establish what device(s) they'll use: a class computer, tablets, or smartphones. Alternatively, print information from the Internet before class and distribute to groups.

2. Write the questions from 2C on the board. Explain that students will work in teams to research and report on these questions. Ask: *Which question could require research?* [2] *Which search terms or questions can you use to find the information you need?* ["hazards" or "prevent accidents" + "at home"/"at school"/"at work"] *How will you record the information you find?* [table, checklist, index cards] Remind students to bookmark or record sites so they can find or cite them in the future.

3. Group students and assign roles: manager, administrative assistant, IT support, and reporter. Verify students' understanding of their roles.

4. Give managers the time limit for researching question 2 (ten minutes). Direct the IT support to begin the online research or pick up the printed materials for each team. Direct the administrative assistant to record information for the team using a table, checklist, or index cards.

5. Give a two-minute warning. Call "time." Tell reporters to report the answers for the first question and then ask each member of the team question 2.

6. Make a two-column chart with the headings *Hazard* and *Prevention*. As students mention hazards, write them in the chart and elicit the safety precautions associated with them.

> **TIP**
>
> After 2C, have your students look at real warning labels. You can find warning labels on cleaning products, toys, and electronic equipment; in appliance manuals; and on the Internet (type *warning label* into an image search engine). Write short warning-label sentences on the board or make a transparency or photocopies of a longer label. Discuss the meaning of the sentences. Go over unknown vocabulary with students.

D 1. Copy the sentence frames on the board.

2. Direct teams to help their administrative assistant use the sentence frames to record the team's findings. Direct the reporter to use the recorded information to report the team's findings to the class or another team.

Evaluation
10–15 minutes

TEST YOURSELF

1. Direct Partner A to read the prompts from 1–4 from 1C on page 68 to Partner B. Partner B should close their book and write the answers in their notebook. When finished, students switch roles. Partner B reads prompts 5–8 from 1C.

2. Direct both partners to open their books and check their spelling when they finish.

> **MULTILEVEL STRATEGIES**
>
> Target the *Test Yourself* to the level of your students.
>
> • **Pre-level** Provide these students with a list of words and phrases to choose from.
>
> • **Higher-level** Direct these students to write sentences using each word or phrase.

> **EXTENSION ACTIVITY**
>
> **Write Safety Advice**
>
> Put students in groups. Provide each group with a common item that could cause a safety problem. Cover any warning labels on the items. If you don't have actual items, give each group the name of an item that would contain a warning: light bulb, a pair of scissors, box of matches, bottle of cleaning fluid, electrical cord. Have the groups write safety advice for their items. Have a reporter from each group share the group's advice.

LESSON 2 WRITING

Lesson Overview

MULTILEVEL OBJECTIVES

On- and Higher-level: Analyze, write, and edit an emergency plan

Pre-level: Read and write about emergency preparedness

LANGUAGE FOCUS

Grammar: Imperative (*Stay indoors.*)

Vocabulary: Emergencies and natural disasters

For vocabulary support, see these **Oxford Picture Dictionary** topics: Public Safety, page 146; Emergencies and Natural Disasters, pages 148–149; Emergency Procedures, pages 150–151

STRATEGY FOCUS

When you are making an outline, use phrases or short sentences.

READINESS CONNECTION

In this lesson, students think critically to write a safety plan.

PACING

To compress this lesson: Assign the *Test Yourself* for homework.

To extend this lesson: Present emergency plans to the class. (See end of lesson.)

And/or have students complete **Workbook 4 page 31** and **Multilevel Activities 4 Unit 5 page 60**.

Lesson Notes

CORRELATIONS

CCRS: SL.1.B (d.) Explain their own ideas and understanding in light of the discussion.

SL.2.B Determine the main ideas and supporting details of a text read aloud or information presented in diverse media and formats, including visually, quantitatively, and orally.

R.1.B Ask and answer such questions as who, what, where, when, why, and how to demonstrate understanding of key details in a text.

R.5.B Know and use various text features to locate key facts or information in a text efficiently.

W.2.A Write informative/explanatory texts in which they name a topic, supply some facts about the topic, and provide some sense of closure.

W.4.B Produce writing in which the development and organization are appropriate to task and purpose.

W.5.B With guidance and support from peers and others, develop and strengthen writing as needed by planning, revising and editing.

L.1.B (l.) Produce simple, compound and complex sentences.

L.2.C (a.) Use correct capitalization.

RF.4.B (a.) Read grade-level text with purpose and understanding.

ELPS: 1. An ELL can construct meaning from oral presentations and literary and informational text through level-appropriate listening, reading, and viewing. 2. An ELL can participate in level-appropriate oral and written exchanges of information, ideas, and analyses, in various social and academic contexts, responding to peer, audience, or reader comments and questions. 10. An ELL can demonstrate command of the conventions of standard English to communicate in level-appropriate speech and writing.

Warm-up and Review
10–15 minutes (books closed)

Ask students if they know of any weather emergencies or natural disasters. Write them on the board. Elicit a description of each type of disaster.

> **TIP**
> Some students enjoy talking about this topic, but others may be reminded of unpleasant experiences. Be sure to address questions to the class at large and only call on volunteers to answer.

Introduction
5 minutes

1. Say: *For every emergency, we need to think of three things: how to prepare for (or prevent) it, what to do when it happens, and what to do afterwards.*

2. State the objective: *Today we're going to read and write an emergency plan.*

1 Prepare to write

Presentation I
20–25 minutes

A 1. Build students' schema by asking questions about the words in the *Need help?* box. Say each word and have students repeat. Elicit a description of each one. Check comprehension by asking questions: *Which word refers to a big snowstorm? If there is a lot of rain and the streets are full of water, what is that called?*

2. Give students one minute to tell a partner their responses to questions 1 and 2. Elicit responses from the class.

B 1. Tell students they are going to read a family's plan for what to do before, during, and after a hurricane. Ask them to guess what they might read in the plan.

2. Direct students to read the plan silently. Check comprehension. Ask: *What supplies do they already have for their emergency kit?* [canned food, can opener, blankets, radio] *What do they need to buy?* [batteries, first-aid kit, bottled water, flashlights] *Why do you think they need these things? What information do they need?* [learn evacuation routes, identify emergency contact person]

3. Play the audio. Ask students to read along.

4. Draw students' attention to the *Writer's Note*. Elicit several words from the emergency plan that would normally have an article.

> **MULTILEVEL STRATEGIES**
> Adapt 1B to the level of your students.
> • **Pre-level** Write vocabulary and definitions on the board to help these students understand the reading. *Supplies*: things that are necessary; *Evacuation*: leaving a dangerous place; *Route*: the way to go.
> • **On- and Higher-level** Have students work in pairs to write three questions about the emergency plan and then join another pair to ask and answer the questions.

Guided Practice I
10 minutes

C Have students work independently to mark the statements *T* (true), *F* (false), or *NI* (no information) and then compare answers with a partner. Write the answers on the board.

Answers	
1. F	3. T
2. T	4. NI

> **TIP**
> Take advantage of this lesson to go over your school's safety and fire-evacuation plan with your students.

2 Plan and write

Guided Practice II
15–20 minutes

A 1. Read the questions. Elicit students' answers.

2. List the emergencies on the board and write students' preparation ideas under each one.

B 1. Direct students to look back at the outline in 1B. Focus students' attention on the imperative sentences in the outline. Ask them to underline the first word in the sentences that begin with a verb. Elicit the form of the verb [the base form] and point out how each sentence has the same structure.

2. Read the questions for each part of the outline aloud and elicit possible answers.

3. Check comprehension of the exercise. Ask: *How many parts does your outline need?* [three] *What should each part cover?* [part 1—before, part 2—during, part 3—after] *Do you need to write long sentences?* [no]

4. Have students work individually to write their emergency plans.

MULTILEVEL STRATEGIES

Adapt 2B to the level of your students.

• **Pre-level** Work with this group to create an outline together. Choose an emergency and brainstorm together for each part of the outline.

TIP

Use this lesson as an opportunity to play an emergency plan video to the class. There are videos from safety experts and organizations online. Choose a video that has a speaker or speakers who are skilled at speaking about safety. Expand on the activity by having students write a "thank-you note" to the speaker about something important they learned.

EXTENSION ACTIVITY
Presentation

After 3C, form groups of three. If possible, group students according to which emergency they wrote their plans for. Have each group present the three most important ideas from each part of the outline to the class.

3 Get feedback and revise

Guided Practice III
5 minutes

A Direct students to check their writing using the editing checklist. Tell them to read each item in the list and check their papers before moving onto the next item. Explain that students should not edit their writing at this stage. They should just use the checklist to check their work and mark any areas they want to revise.

Communicative Practice
15 minutes

B 1. Read the instructions aloud. Emphasize to students that they are responding to their partners' work, not correcting it.

2. Use the emergency plan in 1B to model the exercise. *The plan to buy batteries and bottled water before the storm is a really good idea. The difference between what to do before the storm and during the storm is very clear. I'm not sure I understand what to do after the storm.*

3. Direct students to exchange papers with a partner and follow the instructions.

C Allow students time to edit and revise their writing as necessary, using the editing checklist from 3A and their partner's feedback from 3B. If necessary, students could complete this task as homework.

Application and Evaluation
10 minutes

TEST YOURSELF

1. Review the instructions aloud. Assign a time limit (five minutes) and have students work independently.

2. Before collecting students' work, invite two or three volunteers to share their sentences. Ask students to raise their hands if they wrote similar answers.

LESSON 3 GRAMMAR

Lesson Overview

MULTILEVEL OBJECTIVES

On-, Pre-, and Higher-level: Use *have to, have got to,* and *must* to discuss necessity and prohibition and listen to emergencies

LANGUAGE FOCUS

Grammar: Modals of necessity and prohibition (*You have to wear a hard hat.*)

Vocabulary: Safety

For vocabulary support, see these **Oxford Picture Dictionary** topics: Public Safety, page 146; Emergencies and Natural Disasters, pages 148–149; Emergency Procedures, pages 150–151

STRATEGY FOCUS

Use *had to* to express necessity in the past.

READINESS CONNECTION

In this lesson, students work with others to ask about life experiences.

PACING

To compress this lesson: Conduct 1B and 1C as whole-class activities.

To extend this lesson: Have students create a home safety survey and pool their results. (See end of lesson.)

And/or have students complete **Workbook 4 pages 32–33**, **Multilevel Activities 4 Unit 5 pages 61–62**, and **Multilevel Grammar Exercises 4 Unit 5**.

Lesson Notes

CORRELATIONS

CCRS: SL.2.B Determine the main ideas and supporting details of a text read aloud or information presented in diverse media and formats, including visually, quantitatively, and orally.

R.1.B Ask and answer such questions as who, what, where, when, why, and how to demonstrate understanding of key details in a text.

R.5.B Know and use various text features to locate key facts or information in a text efficiently.

L.1.B (l.) Produce simple, compound and complex sentences.

L.1.B (e.) Form and use the past tense of frequently occurring irregular verbs. (l.) Produce simple, compound and complex sentences.

L.1.C (d.) Use modal auxiliaries to convey various conditions.

L.2.C (a.) Use correct capitalization. (d.) Use a comma to separate and introductory element from the rest of the sentence.

RF.4.B (a.) Read grade-level text with purpose and understanding.

ELPS: 1. An ELL can construct meaning from oral presentations and literary and informational text through level-appropriate listening, reading, and viewing. 2. An ELL can participate in level-appropriate oral and written exchanges of information, ideas, and analyses, in various social and academic contexts, responding to peer, audience, or reader comments and questions. 7. An ELL can adapt language choices to purpose, task, and audience when speaking and writing. 9. An ELL can create clear and coherent level-appropriate speech and text. 10. An ELL can demonstrate command of the conventions of standard English to communicate in level-appropriate speech and writing.

Warm-up and Review
10–15 minutes (books closed)

Write potentially dangerous situations on the board. *Swimming in the Ocean, Going Camping in the Mountains, Driving, Crossing the Street.* Ask volunteers to come to the board and write safety warnings under the appropriate situations. *Don't swim too far. Bring a flashlight. Don't speed. Look both ways.* Leave these sentences on the board.

Introduction
5–10 minutes

1. Say: *When we say* Don't swim too far! *we are giving a warning or strong advice. We can also say* You must not swim here. *to express prohibition.*

2. State the objective: *Today we're going to talk about necessity and prohibition in order to discuss what to do in an emergency.*

1 Use *have to, not have to, have got to, must,* and *must not*

Presentation I
20–25 minutes

A 1. Direct students to look at the picture. Ask: *What is this?* [a news article] *Who do you think is in the picture? What do you think he is talking about?*

2. Read the instructions aloud. Direct students to read the article to find the answers to the questions. Have students compare answers with a partner. Call on a different volunteer for each answer.

Answers
1. Mayor Sam Andreas
2. The mayor says that people have to worry about a major earthquake in Silton Bay.
3. He thinks that people may believe that they are safe from earthquakes.

 1. Demonstrate how to read the grammar chart. Read each sentence aloud and have students repeat them after you.

2. Direct students to underline the examples of *have to, have got to, must,* and *must not* in 1A. Write the sentences on the board.

3. Ask: *Are these sentences giving advice or are they stronger?* [They're stronger.] *What form of the main verb follows these words?* [the base or simple form with no ending] Say: *A storm is coming in tonight, but it's not going to be too bad.* Have students choose the sentence that is better for the situation: *1. We don't need to evacuate. 2. We must not evacuate.* [1] *Tomorrow a terrible blizzard is coming and the roads will be covered with three feet of snow.* Have students choose the sentence that is better for the situation: *1. You don't need to drive. 2. We must not drive.* [2]

4. Focus on form. Write three sentence frames on the board: *I _____ buy supplies. I _____ _____ buy supplies. I _____ _____ _____ buy supplies.* Elicit the words to complete these three sentences about what you need to do [*must, have to, have got to*].

5. Assess students' understanding of the chart. Ask them to change the imperative sentences on the board from the *Warm-up* into sentences with *have to, have got to, must,* and *must not*.

Answers
Underlined:
Para 1: don't have to
Para 2: has to, has to, must, We've all got to
Para 3: must not

C Have students work in pairs to complete the sentences about necessity and prohibition. Go over the answers with the class.

Answers
has, does not have, Have got to, must not, necessary

Guided Practice I
15–20 minutes

D Ask students to work individually to complete the sentences and then compare answers with a partner. Ask volunteers to write the answers on the board.

Answers	
1. must not	4. must not
2. don't have to	5. must not
3. doesn't have to	6. don't have to

2 Use *have to* and *must* in the past

Presentation II
20–25 minutes

 1. Introduce the new topic. Say: *You have to do your homework.* Ask: *Is this sentence about the past, present, or future?* [present or future] Say: *You had to do your homework last night.* Ask: *Is this sentence about the past, present, or future?* [past]

2. Read and have students repeat the sentences in the chart. Draw students' attention to the verbs in the past sentences and the *Grammar Note*. Ask: *How do we express necessity in the past?* [with *had to*] *Can we use* must *or* have got to *in the past?* [no]

3. Check understanding of the chart. Have students work in pairs to rewrite the sentences in the left column in the past tense. Ask volunteers to write them on the board.

4. Direct students to circle the correct words to complete the sentences. Ask volunteers to read the completed sentences aloud.

Answers
1. had to
2. didn't have to
3. have to
4. had to
5. must
6. has got to

Guided Practice II
10–15 minutes

 1. Read the instructions aloud. Model the activity with a volunteer. Read Part A's lines and show students how to use the information from the *Need help?* box.

2. Pair students and have them talk about their experiences. Monitor and provide feedback as needed.

3. Ask volunteers to tell the class about their partner's experiences.

MULTILEVEL STRATEGIES

For 1D, use mixed-level pairs.

- **Pre-level** Direct these students to listen to their partners read the completed sentences aloud. Tell them to read the sentences back to their partners when they finish the exercise in order to check their answers.

- **On- and Higher-level** Have these students read the sentences to their partners, filling in the missing words as they go. Tell them to listen to their partners read the sentences back and check their work.

 Read each statement aloud. Refer students to the chart in 1B for the answers. Have students compare ideas with a partner. Ask for a show of hands to see which choice students made for each item. Write the answers on the board.

Answers	
1. P	4. N
2. N	5. P
3. NN	

TIP

Provide more practice with *have to, have got to*, and *must*. Write down a number of dangerous situations on pieces of paper. *The stove is on fire. You just heard a tornado warning. It looks like someone is drowning. Someone is choking. You run out of gas on the freeway. You see a car accident.* Make enough so that you can give every student one sentence. Tell students to walk around the room talking to different partners. Partner A reads the situation. Partner B tells about something you *must, must not*, and *don't have to* do in that situation. Then have students switch roles. When they finish, each student moves to find a new partner.

Once students are comfortable with *have to, have got to*, and *must*, contrast those modals with *should*, which expresses advice rather than necessity. Write another set of situations on the board. *I'm going downtown at night. I'm going roller-skating for the first time. I'm going to the desert. I'm going to the mountains. My baby just learned to walk. My house is going to be empty for a week. I'm going to have a barbecue. I'm going to the beach. I'm going to ride a motorcycle.* Direct students to tell you what you should do in each situation. Ask if there are also things you *must* and *must not* do.

MULTILEVEL STRATEGIES

Seat same-level students together for 2B.

- **Pre-level** Write complete conversations on the board and have them practice and then switch roles.

A: *When you were a child, did you have to walk to school?*

B: *Yes, I did. What about you?*

A: *I didn't have to walk to school, but I had to walk to soccer practice.*

- **On- and Higher-level** Have them write two or three original questions and practice in pairs. Ask volunteers to read their questions and answers to the class.

TIP

After 2B, provide more practice with *had to* and *didn't have to*. Write a list of questions on the board and direct students to take turns asking a partner the questions and answering in complete sentences. *1. What did you have to do before you came to school today? 2. What did you have to do last weekend? 3. What did you have to do to enroll in this class? 4. What did you have to do last night?* After students have discussed what they had to do, direct them to go back and talk about things they didn't have to do in each situation and to explain why. *I didn't have to put gas in my car before I came to school today because I got gas yesterday.*

3 Listen for the verb to determine the meaning

Guided Practice III
10–15 minutes

🔊 **2-04** 1. Say: *Now we're going to listen to some emergency situations.*

2. Play the audio. Direct students to read along silently without writing.

3. Replay the audio. Ask students to choose the sentence with the same meaning and then compare answers with a partner.

4. Ask for a show of hands to find out how students answered. Settle disagreements by replaying segments as necessary.

5. Check comprehension. Elicit the emergency in each item [electrical fire, tornado, tornado, hurricane, three big storms, storm].

Answers

1. a	4. a
2. b	5. b
3. a	6. a

MULTILEVEL STRATEGIES

Replay the audio for 3 to allow pre-level students to catch up while you challenge on- and higher-level students.

- **Pre-level** Have these students listen again to complete the exercise.
- **On- and Higher-level** Have these students close their books and write two of the sentences they hear.

EXTENSION ACTIVITY
Survey

After 3, have students create a home-safety survey.

1. Put students in groups. Tell them to work together to create a survey with five *yes/no* questions about home safety. *Do you have a fire extinguisher?* Tell each group member to copy the questions.

2. Have students ask their survey questions of students from other groups. Encourage them to move around and talk to different people, but tell them not to answer the same survey question twice.

3. Have the original groups reconvene and pool their results. Ask a reporter to share the group's results with the class. *Six out of ten people have a fire extinguisher at home.*

4 Use *have to* to talk about your life experience

Communicative Practice and Application
20–25 minutes

 1. Direct students' attention to the photo. Ask: *Where is this? Do you think it is in the U.S.? Why or why not?* Direct students to work independently to complete the questions and then compare ideas with a partner.

2. Call on volunteers to share their sentences, correcting grammar as necessary. Establish the correct time expressions [1 and 3 use either *in your country* or *before you came here*; 2 and 4 use either *now* or *in the U.S.*]

B Direct students to work with a partner to write two more questions using *have to*.

C 1. Have pairs merge to form teams of four. Model the exercise by "joining" one of the pairs. Each pair takes a turn asking and answering questions while the class listens.

2. Check comprehension of the exercise. Ask: *Who asks questions?* [everyone] *Who answers questions?* [everyone]

3. Ask volunteers to share something interesting they learned about their classmates.

Evaluation
10–15 minutes

TEST YOURSELF

Ask students to write the sentences independently. Collect and correct their writing.

MULTILEVEL STRATEGIES

Target the *Test Yourself* to the level of your students.

- **Pre-level** Allow these students to write three sentences. Provide these sentence frames for them to complete: _____ *(name of student)* didn't have to _____ in his/her country, but now he/she has to _____. _____ *(name of student)* had to _____ before he/she came to the U.S., but now he/she doesn't have to _____. _____ *(name of student)* had to _____ in his/her country, but in the U.S., he/she doesn't have to _____.

LESSON 4 EVERYDAY CONVERSATION

Lesson Overview

MULTILEVEL OBJECTIVES

On-, Pre-, and Higher-level: Report unsafe conditions and listen for job information

LANGUAGE FOCUS

Grammar: *Should have (You should have locked the door.)*

Vocabulary: *restricted, protective, occupation*

For vocabulary support, see these **Oxford Picture Dictionary** topics: Emergency Procedures, pages 150–151; Jobs and Occupations, pages 170–173; Job Safety, page 197

STRATEGY FOCUS

Practice language to understand other points of view.

READINESS CONNECTION

In this lesson, students listen actively and determine what makes a job safe or unsafe.

PACING

To compress this lesson: Conduct *Discuss* as a whole-class activity.

To extend this lesson: After completing 6B, have students write a letter to report a hazard. (See end of lesson.)

And/or have students complete **Workbook 4 page 34** and **Multilevel Activities 4 Unit 5 page 63**.

Lesson Notes

CORRELATIONS

CCRS: SL.1.B (a.) Come to discussions prepared, having read or studied required material; explicitly draw on that preparation and other information known about the topic to explore ideas under discussion. (b.) Follow agreed-upon rules for discussions. (c.) Ask questions to check understanding of information presented, stay on topic, and link their comments to the remarks of others. (d.) Explain their own ideas and understanding in light of the discussion.

SL.2.B Determine the main ideas and supporting details of a text read aloud or information presented in diverse media and formats, including visually, quantitatively, and orally.

SL.4.B Report on a topic or text, tell a story, or recount an experience with appropriate facts and relevant, descriptive details, speaking clearly at an understandable pace.

SL.6.B Speak in complete sentences when appropriate to task and situation in order to provide requested detail or clarification.

R.1.B Ask and answer such questions as who, what, where, when, why, and how to demonstrate understanding of key details in a text.

R.2.A Identify the main topic and retell key details of a text.

R.6.B Identify the main purpose of a text, including what the author wants to answer, explain, or describe.

R.7.B Use information gained from illustrations and the words in a text to demonstrate understanding of the text.

L.1.B (e.) Form and use the past tense of frequently occurring irregular verbs. (g.) Form and use regular and irregular verbs. (l.) Produce simple, compound and complex sentences.

L.1.C (d.) Use modal auxiliaries to convey various conditions.

L.1.D (f.) Explain the function of verbals (gerunds, participles, infinitives) in general and their function in particular sentences.

RF.4.B (a.) Read grade-level text with purpose and understanding.

ELPS: 1. An ELL can construct meaning from oral presentations and literary and informational text through level-appropriate listening, reading, and viewing. 2. An ELL can participate in level-appropriate oral and written exchanges of information, ideas, and analyses, in various social and academic contexts, responding to peer, audience, or reader comments and questions. 9. An ELL can create clear and coherent level-appropriate speech and text. 10. An ELL can demonstrate command of the conventions of standard English to communicate in level-appropriate speech and writing.

Warm-up and Review
10–15 minutes (books closed)

Write *Mistakes We Made* on a large sheet of paper. Write a list of safety-related mistakes that you have made in the past. *I left the oven on when I went to work. I didn't unplug the iron. She left her door unlocked.* Ask students to tell you about mistakes they have made in the past and write them on the board.

Introduction
5 minutes

1. Say: *If we make these mistakes at home, we have to take care of them. But if we see safety problems at work or on public property, we have to report them.*

2. State the objective: *Today we'll learn to report safety problems and listen for information about safety problems at work.*

1 Learn ways to report unsafe conditions

Presentation I
10–20 minutes

 A 2-05 1. Direct students to look at the picture. Ask: *Where are they?* [a warehouse] *What do you see?* [oil barrels, pipes, an exit door] *What are they wearing?* [hard hats, coveralls]

2. Play the audio. Tell students to discuss the question with a partner. Elicit the answer.

Answer
He is a supervisor.

Guided Practice I
20–25 minutes

 B 2-05 1. Read the instructions aloud. Have students read the questions. Play the audio. Ask students to listen for the answers to each question.

2. Ask students to compare their answers with a partner. Circulate and monitor to ensure students understand the audio.

Answers
1. She reported that there were flammable chemicals too close to the furnace. They were not in the restricted area; they were out in the open on the floor.
2. She reported that there was an oil spill in one corner. One of the containers was leaking.
3. Yes, he did. He said, "Thanks for letting me know." and "Thanks for bringing those items to my attention."

 C 2-06 Read the instructions aloud. Explain that students are going to hear the audio one more time. They should write the words they hear to complete the sentences. Play the audio. Have students compare answers with a partner. Call on volunteers to elicit the answers.

Answers
1. I want to report
2. I noticed
3. I think

2 Practice your pronunciation

Pronunciation Extension
10–15 minutes

A 2-07 1. Say: *You are going to listen to a conversation with words that use –ough.* Have students find the words in the conversation.

2. Play the audio as students read the conversation silently. Ask: *Does –ough have the same sound in each word?* [no]

B 2-07 1. Write on the board: *He's still coughing even though he bought cough syrup.* Say the sentence and ask students to repeat it. Underline and pronounce the words with *ough*. Say: *Do these words sound the same or different?* [different] *Now we're going to focus on different pronunciations of* ough.

2. Play the audio. Direct students to listen for the pronunciation of *ough*.

3. Have students match the words with the same sounds. Go over the answers as a class.

Answers	
1. b	3. a
2. d	4. c

C 🔊 2-08 1. Play the audio and have students read along silently.

2. Have partners take turns reading both roles in the conversation. Monitor and provide feedback on pronunciation of the *ough* words.

3 Use *should have*

Presentation II and Guided Practice II
25–30 minutes

A 1. Introduce the new topic: *In the conversation in 1B, the employer says,* The maintenance crew should have put them in the locked area. *Did they put the chemicals in a locked area?* [no]

2. Read the sentences in the chart and the *Grammar Note* aloud. Ask about the meaning of each sentence. *Did you put the boxes in the storeroom?* [no] *Where are the boxes?* [in the hall] *Did he listen to his manager?* [no] *Did he forget the boxes?* [yes]

3. Check comprehension. Ask: *When we use* should have *to give advice, are we talking about the present or the past?* [past] *Are we talking about something we did right or something we did wrong?* [wrong] *We use* should have *to talk about things we wish we could change but we can't.*

4. Use the sentences from the *Warm-up* and demonstrate how to talk about them with *should have*. *I shouldn't have left the oven on. I should have unplugged the iron. She shouldn't have left her door unlocked.*

Answer
The boxes are in the hall.

B Have students work individually to write the answers. Have students compare their answers with a partner. Go over the answers as a class.

Answers
1. You should have reported the problem.
2. We/You shouldn't have gone into the restricted area.
3. They should have worn protective gloves.
4. She shouldn't have used a lamp with a frayed cord.

MULTILEVEL STRATEGIES

Adapt 3B to the level of your students.
- **Pre-level** Provide these students with present-tense versions of the advice in the activity and ask them to fill in an appropriate modal.

2. We _____ go into restricted areas.
3. They _____ wear protective gloves.
4. She _____ buy a new electrical cord.

C 1. Model the activity. Tell the class about a mistake you made at school and what you should have done.

2. Set a time limit (five minutes). Ask students to practice asking and answering the questions with several partners. Call on individuals to share their answers with the class.

4 Building conversation skills

Guided Practice III
15–20 minutes

A Direct students to look at the picture. Ask: *Who do you see? What is her job? Who is she talking to? What do you think she is talking about?* Have students skim the conversation. Have them work with partners to identify the purpose of the conversation. Elicit responses and ask: *How do you know?* or *Why do you say that?* to encourage students to state their reasoning.

Possible Answers
The purpose is to report two problems at the bus station. The driver/The employee is pointing to something and she looks worried. She says, "I want to report something suspicious."

B 🔊 2-09 1. Ask students to read the instructions and tell you what they are going to do [listen and read and respond to the question]. Play the audio and then elicit the answer to the question.

2. Ask students to read the conversation with a partner. Circulate and monitor pronunciation. Model and have students repeat difficult words or phrases.

3. Ask: *In what other situation could you use this conversation?* Point out a few phrases that are not specific to buses and packages. Ask volunteers to point out others.

Possible Answer
A package, because it has been there for a while and there is no one near it.

Communicative Practice and Application I
15–20 minutes

C 1. Pair students and have them read the instructions silently. Check their comprehension of the exercise. Ask: *What are the two roles?* [park visitor and park employee] *Is the conversation at a bus station?* [No, it's at a park.]

2. Model and have students repeat the expressions in the *In Other Words* box. Explain that they should use these expressions in their conversations.

3. Draw a T-chart on the board. Label the left column *Park visitor* and the right column *Park employee*. Elicit examples of what each person might say and make notes on the chart.

4. Set a time limit (three minutes). Have students act out the role-play. Call "time" and have students switch roles.

5. Ask three volunteer pairs to act out their role-play for the class. Tell students who are listening to make a table with four rows and two columns. Use the top row to label the columns: *safety hazards* and *solutions*. Have students take notes in the chart for each role-play.

MULTILEVEL STRATEGIES

For 4C, adapt the role-play to the level of your students.

- **Pre-level** Provide these students with a simplified role-play.

Park visitor: I want to report a problem. There's _____.

Park employee: OK, thanks for letting me know. I'll _____.

5 Focus on listening for details

Presentation and Guided Practice
20–25 minutes

A 1. Read the instructions aloud. Ask: *What kind of hazards do people in each occupation face?*

2. Pair students and tell them to discuss their own answers to the question. Circulate and monitor.

B Direct students to look at the photo. Ask: *Who do you see?* [two people] *What is their job?* [news reporters] Direct students to read the sentences in 5D before they listen to the interview. Ask what kind of information they'll be writing in the blanks [numbers]. Ask volunteers for predictions. If students struggle, start by offering your own prediction: *I think we will hear that people working in education had 100 injuries or illnesses for every 10,000 workers.*

C 1. Play the audio. Ask students to listen and check the occupation that is NOT mentioned.

2. Pair students and have them compare answers. Then go over answers as a class.

Answer
nurses

D 1. Play the audio. Ask students to listen and complete the sentences.

2. Pair students and have them compare answers. If a pair has different answers, have the class vote on the correct answer with a show of hands.

3. Ask: *Which statistic(s) did you find surprising?*

Answers	
1. 59	4. lowest
2. 300	5. 6
3. 12	

6 Discuss

Communicative Practice and Application II
15–20 minutes

 1. Read the instructions aloud. Draw a sample chart on the board with space for occupations on one side and possible hazards on the other. Call on volunteers to read the sample sentences in 6A. Fill in the chart, writing "nursing" on the left and listing reasons on the right. Explain that students will make a chart like this one based on their own discussions. If you use IT support for this task, suggest students search for the name of the occupation online with the search terms "safety hazard" or "workplace hazard."

2. Put students into teams of four and assign roles: manager, administrative assistant, reporter, and IT support. Verify students' understanding of the roles (manager keeps the group on task and manages time, administrative assistant takes notes, IT support can research hazards online, and the reporter reports to the class). Encourage students to use the phrases in the *Speaking Note* during their discussions.

3. Set a time limit for the discussions (ten minutes). Write the sentence frame from 6B on the board. Then circulate and monitor.

 Call "time." Ask the reporter for each team to report the results of their team's discussion using the sentence frame on the board.

Evaluation
5 minutes

TEST YOURSELF

1. Ask students to complete the checkboxes individually.

2. Tell students that you are going to read each of the items in the checklist aloud. If they are not at all confident with that skill, they should hold up a closed fist. If they are not very confident, they should hold up one finger. If they are somewhat confident, two fingers; confident, three fingers; very confident, four fingers. If they think they could teach the skill, they should hold up five fingers. Read each item in the checklist and identify students that may need further support.

TIP

For homework, you could ask students to write a sentence or two about what discussion skills they still need to work on, or if they are confident in all of the skills, what skill they are most proud of.

EXTENSION ACTIVITY

Report a Safety Hazard

1. Tell students to imagine that their apartment building has a safety hazard that the landlord has not addressed. They need to tell the landlord about the problem.

2. Put students in multilevel pairs. Student A is the tenant and Student B is the landlord. Have Student A report the problem and Student B provide a solution.

LESSON 5 READING

Lesson Overview

MULTILEVEL OBJECTIVES

On-, Pre-, and Higher-level: Read about and discuss accidents and injuries

LANGUAGE FOCUS

Grammar: Nouns and adjectives (*He is cautious. You need to use caution.*); the suffix *-ous (cautious)*

Vocabulary: *Keep track of, sprain, strain, account for*

For vocabulary support, see these **Oxford Picture Dictionary** topics: Jobs and Occupations, pages 170–173; Job Safety, page 197

STRATEGY FOCUS

In this lesson, students distinguish between facts that support a point of view and opinions.

READINESS CONNECTION

In this lesson, students analyze information to discuss safety precautions.

PACING

To compress this lesson: Conduct the word study in 2A as a whole-class activity.

To extend this lesson: Have students use additional words that end with the suffix *-ous*. (See end of lesson.)

And/or have students complete **Workbook 4 page 35** and **Multilevel Activities 4 Unit 5 pages 64–65**.

Lesson Notes

CORRELATIONS

CCRS: SL.1.B (a.) Come to discussions prepared, having read or studied required material; explicitly draw on that preparation and other information known about the topic to explore ideas under discussion. (b.) Follow agreed-upon rules for discussions. (c.) Ask questions to check understanding of information presented, stay on topic, and link their comments to the remarks of others. (d.) Explain their own ideas and understanding in light of the discussion.

SL.2.B Determine the main ideas and supporting details of a text read aloud or information presented in diverse media and formats, including visually, quantitatively, and orally.

SL.6.B Speak in complete sentences when appropriate to task and situation in order to provide requested detail or clarification.

R.1.B Ask and answer such questions as who, what, where, when, why, and how to demonstrate understanding of key details in a text.

R.1.C Refer to details and examples in a text when explaining what the text says explicitly and when drawing inferences from the text.

R.2.B Determine the main idea of a text; recount the key details and explain how they support the main idea.

R.5.B Know and use various text features to locate key facts or information in a text efficiently.

R.6.B Identify the main purpose of a text, including what the author wants to answer, explain, or describe.

R.7.C Interpret information presented visually, orally, or quantitatively and explain how the information contributes to an understanding of the text in which it appears.

W.7.A Participate in shared research and writing projects.

L.1.B (l.) Produce simple, compound and complex sentences.

L.2.B (h.) Use conventional spelling for high-frequency and other studied words and for adding suffixes to base words.

L.4.B (e.) Use glossaries and beginning dictionaries, both print and digital, to determine or clarify the meaning of words and phrases.

RF.3.B (c.) Identify and know the meaning of the most common prefixes and derivational suffixes.

RF.4.B (a.) Read grade-level text with purpose and understanding.

ELPS: 1. An ELL can construct meaning from oral presentations and literary and informational text through level-appropriate listening, reading, and viewing. 2. An ELL can participate in level-appropriate oral and written exchanges of information, ideas, and analyses, in various social and academic contexts, responding to peer, audience, or reader comments and questions. 3. An ELL can speak and write about level-appropriate complex literary and informational texts and topics. 8. An ELL can determine the meaning of words and phrases in oral presentation and literary and informational text.

Warm-up and Review
10–15 minutes (books closed)

Review *symptoms* and *injuries*. Show pictures of injuries from *The Oxford Picture Dictionary* or another source. Ask volunteers to write the name of the injury or symptom on the board.

Introduction
5 minutes

1. Say: *Some of these injuries and symptoms occur because of an unsafe environment at work or at home.*

2. State the objective: *Today we're going to read and write about accidents at work and at home.*

1 Read

Presentation
10–20 minutes

A Read the questions aloud. Use ideas from the *Introduction* to help guide discussion.

B Read the words and definitions. Elicit sample sentences for each word or supply them if the students can't. Discuss students' experiences with sprains and strains.

Pre-reading
10–20 minutes

C Read the instructions aloud. Ask: *What should you look at when you preview a reading?* [titles, headings, visuals (charts, graphs, photos)] Have students answer the question individually and then check answers with the class. If any students answer incorrectly, ask them to support their answer. Establish the correct answer.

Answer
b. The U.S. Department of Labor and the Consumer Product Safety Commission

Guided Practice: While Reading
20–30 minutes

D 1. Direct students' attention to the *Reader's Note*. Write on the board: *Teaching is a dangerous occupation.* Elicit examples of facts that support this statement and advice and opinions about it. Write them on the board and distinguish between *fact* and *opinion*.

2. Ask students to read the article silently and answer the questions and then compare answers with a partner. Check answers with the class.

3. After students are finished reading, direct students to underline unfamiliar words they would like to know. Elicit the words and encourage other students to provide definitions or examples.

4. Check comprehension. Ask: *Who keeps track of the amount of time people take off from work?* [the U.S. Department of Labor] *What are the most common injuries?* [strains and sprains] *What are the most hazardous parts of the home?* [stairs and ramps] *What is one of the most dangerous activities?* [playing basketball]

Possible Answers
To tell readers about safety hazards at work and at home and to tell people to use safety precautions. Yes, because she gives information from experts to show why precautions are important.

> **MULTILEVEL STRATEGIES**
>
> Adapt 1D to the level of your students.
>
> • **Pre-level** Read the text aloud to these students as they follow along. Provide these students with a summary of the ideas in the reading. *Both the workplace and the home can be dangerous. Sprains and strains are the most common reasons people take time off from work. Stairs and ramps are dangerous parts of the home. One of the most dangerous activities is playing basketball. People can prevent accidents by following safety rules and using proper equipment.*
>
> Direct these students to read the summary while other students are reading 1D.
>
> • **On- and Higher-level** Pair students and have them read the article aloud to each other, taking turns to read each paragraph.

Guided Practice: Rereading
10–15 minutes

E 1. Provide an opportunity for students to extract opinion from the text. Have students reread the article and underline any words or phrases that indicate the author's point of view.

2. Pair students and tell them to compare the words they underlined and report anything they disagree on. Discuss and clarify as needed.

Answers
The first paragraph and the last paragraph. Underlines will vary.

TIP

Have students go online to find out more about hazards. Decide which device(s) students will use and elicit search terms ("home hazards").

F 1. Have students work individually to mark the answers *T* (true), *F* (false), and *NI* (no information). They should then write the line number(s) where they found the answer. Write the answers on the board.

2. Elicit and discuss any additional questions about the reading. You could introduce new questions for class discussion: *How can we prevent accidents at home? What role should the government have in accident prevention? What safety equipment do you have at home or in your workplace?*

Answers
1. NI
2. T (lines 16-17/graph)
3. F (lines 21-22)
4. T (lines 22-30)
5. NI

MULTILEVEL STRATEGIES

For 1F, work with pre-level students.

• **Pre-level** Ask students about the graph while other students are completing 1F. Elicit the numbers of injuries for each product. Have these students copy the answers to 1F from the board.

2 Word study

Guided Practice: Post-reading
10 minutes

A 1. Direct students to look at the chart and identify the topic (the suffix *-ous*). Have students read the chart.

2. Read the words in the chart aloud. Elicit and discuss any questions the students have about the noun and adjective forms. Say the words and have students repeat them.

3. Provide sample sentences to remind students of the different uses of nouns and adjectives. *You need to use caution. He is a cautious person. She didn't notice the danger. Those chemicals are dangerous. The garbage is a health hazard. Smoking is hazardous to your health.*

4. Direct students to work individually to circle the correct word to complete each sentence and then compare answers with a partner. Write the answers on the board.

Answers	
1. hazard	4. Hazardous
2. cautious; danger	5. various
3. dangerous	

B 1. Model the example. Write a sentence on the board using *disastrous* to describe a weather event. (*e.g. The blizzard in January was disastrous.*)

2. Have students write sentences individually and then compare sentences with a partner.

3. Ask volunteers to write their sentences on the board. Have the rest of the class suggest grammar and spelling edits as needed.

MULTILEVEL STRATEGIES

For 2B, seat pre-level students together.

• **Pre-level** Provide sentence frames:

1. _____ was disastrous.

2. I am always cautious when I _____.

3. I've seen continuous improvement in _____.

• **On- and Higher-level** Ask these students to write two sentences using the noun and the adjective form of one of the words in the box.

EXTENSION ACTIVITY

Writing Sentences

1. Write more *-ous* adjectives on the board: *religious, courageous, humorous, marvelous, mountainous, poisonous.*

2. Elicit the noun form of each word. As a class, brainstorm a sentence for both forms of each word.

3 Talk it over

Guided Practice
15–20 minutes

 Have students look at the graph. Point out that they need to use the information from the graph to complete the sentences and answer the question. Set a time limit (ten minutes). Have students work in pairs to complete the task and then compare answers with a partner. Ask volunteers to share their answers with the class.

Answers
1. 107
2. two
3. maids and housekeepers
4. landscaping and groundskeeping workers
5. workers in government jobs

Communicative Practice
20 minutes

 1. Read the questions aloud. Set a time limit (ten minutes).

2. Ask volunteers to share their ideas with the class.

Application
5–10 minutes

BRING IT TO LIFE

Ask students to search online. Suggest they search for "safety precautions" + "workplace," "home," and "school." Ask volunteers to share their ideas. Have the class choose the most important precaution for each location.

AT WORK

Warm-up and Review
10–15 minutes (books closed)

Write *Occupational Safety and Health Administration (OSHA)* on the board. Say: *This is an agency in the U.S government. What do you think it does?* Elicit ideas from students and write them on the board.

Introduction
5 minutes

State the objective: *Today we're going to learn about safety in the workplace and ways to ask for clarification when you don't hear or understand the speaker.*

Presentation
5 minutes

 2-11 Direct students' attention to the photo. Ask: *Why is he holding that sign? Have you ever asked about something you thought was unsafe? Why or why not?* Read the instructions aloud. Play the audio. Give students a minute to think about the question and compare answers with a partner. Elicit responses from the class.

Possible Answers
Worker safety and rights

Guided Practice
10–15 minutes

 2-11 Direct students' attention to the list of safety laws. Ask: *Who has to follow safety laws?* [employers and workers] Play the audio again. Direct students to listen to the description and complete the laws.

Possible Answers
1. safe workplace
2. equipment
3. chemicals
4. language they understand
5. safety
6. don't have to

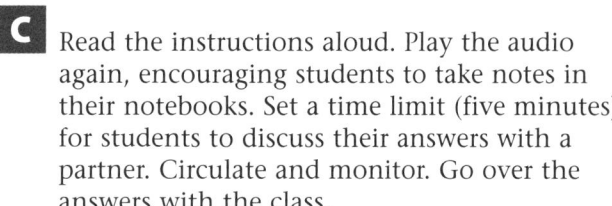 Read the instructions aloud. Play the audio again, encouraging students to take notes in their notebooks. Set a time limit (five minutes) for students to discuss their answers with a partner. Circulate and monitor. Go over the answers with the class.

Presentation and Communicative Practice
10 minutes

 1. Direct students' attention to the *Do/Say* chart and ask them to identify the lesson's soft skill [getting clarification]. Ask the class which column has examples of language [right] and which has examples of behaviors [left].

2. Say a phrase from the left and act it out. Say it again and have the class act it out with you. Say it a third time and have the class act it out for you. To confirm understanding, combine phrases: *Make eye contact and raise your hand.*

3. Model the sentence frames from the right using authentic intonation. Have students practice imitating your inflection.

4. Put students in teams of four and assign each team a question. Assign roles: manager, administrative assistant, reporter, and researcher. (Researchers will ask you questions on behalf of the team.) Verify understanding of the roles. Set a time limit (five minutes) and monitor.

5. Write sentence frames on the board that teams can use to summarize their responses. *Our team discussed the following question: _____. We decided _____ because_____.*

6. Call "time" and let reporters rehearse their report for one minute. Direct each reporter to present to two other teams.

Communicative Practice and Application
20–25 minutes

 1. Model the activity with a volunteer. Point out that in A's first line, he or she says a word that doesn't make sense but sounds like something that does. In A's second line, the speaker should speak clearly. Direct students to work in pairs to take turns reading sentences with nonsense words and asking for clarification.

2. Invite volunteers to role-play for the class.

TIP

Have students make a list of important vocabulary and key points from the unit, including this lesson. They can use the terms in sentences with their partners.

The most dangerous parts of the house are stairs and ramps.

Could you repeat that slowly?

F 1. Have pairs merge to form teams of four. Tell students that they are going to be role-playing a staff conversation where they will talk about OSHA laws and what they mean.

2. Have each team member take responsibility for one law. (Two laws will be covered by two people each.)

3. As students carry out the role-play, circulate and monitor. Provide global feedback once the activity ends.

TEAMWORK & LANGUAGE REVIEW

Lesson Overview

MULTILEVEL OBJECTIVES

On-, Pre-, and Higher-level: Expand upon and review unit grammar and life skills

LANGUAGE FOCUS

Grammar: Necessity and prohibition in the present and past *(You have to see a doctor. You shouldn't have lifted that box.)*

Vocabulary: Safety

For vocabulary support, see these **Oxford Picture Dictionary** topics: Public Safety, page 146; Emergencies and Natural Disasters, pages 148–149; Emergency Procedures, pages 150–151; Job Safety, page 197

READINESS CONNECTION

In this review, students choose solutions to workplace safety issues and emergencies.

PACING

To extend this review: Have students complete **Workbook 4 page 36**, **Multilevel Activities 4 Unit 5 page 66**, and **Multilevel Grammar Exercises 4 Unit 5**.

Lesson Notes

CORRELATIONS

CCRS: SL.1.B (a.) Come to discussions prepared, having read or studied required material; explicitly draw on that preparation and other information known about the topic to explore ideas under discussion. (b.) Follow agreed-upon rules for discussions. (c.) Ask questions to check understanding of information presented, stay on topic, and link their comments to the remarks of others. (d.) Explain their own ideas and understanding in light of the discussion.

SL.1.C (b.) Follow agreed-upon rules for discussions and carry out assigned roles.

SL.2.B Determine the main ideas and supporting details of a text read aloud or information presented in diverse media and formats, including visually, quantitatively, and orally.

SL.4.B Report on a topic or text, tell a story, or recount an experience with appropriate facts and relevant, descriptive details, speaking clearly at an understandable pace.

R.1.B Ask and answer such questions as who, what, where, when, why, and how to demonstrate understanding of key details in a text.

R.2.A Identify the main topic and retell key details of a text.

R.7.B Use information gained from illustrations and the words in a text to demonstrate understanding of the text.

W.3.A Write narratives in which they recount two or more appropriately sequenced events, include some details regarding what happened, use temporal words to signal event order, and provide some sense of closure.

L.1.B (l.) Produce simple, compound and complex sentences.

L.1.C (d.) Use modal auxiliaries to convey various conditions.

L.1.D (f.) Explain the function of verbals (gerunds, participles, infinitives) in general and their function in particular sentences.

L.4.B (a.) Use sentence-level context as a clue to the meaning of a word or phrase.

RF.4.B (a.) Read grade-level text with purpose and understanding.

ELPS: 2. An ELL can participate in level-appropriate oral and written exchanges of information, ideas, and analyses, in various social and academic contexts, responding to peer, audience, or reader comments and questions. 3. An ELL can speak and write about level-appropriate complex literary and informational texts and topics. 9. An ELL can create clear and coherent level-appropriate speech and text. 10. An ELL can demonstrate command of the conventions of standard English to communicate in level-appropriate speech and writing.

Warm-up and Review
10–15 minutes (books closed)

1. Review *At Work* activity F.

2. Ask students to share the good, not-so-good, and interesting things that happened during the role-play. As students speak, write their responses in a chart on the board.

Introduction and Presentation
5 minutes

1. Pair students and direct them to look at the picture in their book. Ask them to describe what they see to their partner. Elicit all the safety hazards.

2. Ask volunteer pairs to share their ideas with the class.

3. State the objective: *Today we're going to review what we've studied in this unit to talk about safety.*

Guided Practice
15–20 minutes

A 1. Review the past of *should*. Write sentences on the board. *I tripped over my daughter's toy. Maya got shocked when she plugged in the frayed electrical cord. Roberto cut his foot when he walked outside barefoot.* Say: *These things already happened. How can we use* should *to talk about the past?* Elicit a sentence with *should have* or *shouldn't have* for each situation and write it on the board.

2. Direct students to look at the picture and the captions. Have them work in groups of three or four to write at least six sentences about the construction site. Ask volunteers to write their sentences on the board.

B Have students continue to work in their teams to circle the correct answer. Call on volunteers for the answers.

Answers	
1. a	4. b
2. b	5. a
3. b	6. a

C 1. Have students work in pairs to write a sentence about something in the picture. Assign half the students to write a sentence with *must* or *must not* and the others with *have* or *don't have to*.

2. Ask volunteers to write their sentences on the board. Correct and provide feedback on each sentence as a class. Then work with the class to put the sentences in order to write a paragraph.

Communicative Practice
30–40 minutes

D 1. Group students and assign roles: manager, director, actors. Explain that students are going to work with their teams to write a conversation about a family emergency plan.

2. Read steps 2–5 of the activity aloud. Check comprehension of the task. *What is the first thing you should do?* [choose a problem from the list] *What do you need to include in your plan?* [what you have to do, what you don't have to do, what you must not do]

3. Set a time limit (ten minutes) to complete the activity. Circulate and answer any questions.

4. Have actors present the plan to the class.

E 1. Have students walk around the room to conduct the interviews. To get students moving, tell them to interview three people who were not in their team for D.

2. Set a time limit (five minutes) to complete the exercise.

3. Tell students to make a note of their classmates' answers but not to worry about writing complete sentences.

> **MULTILEVEL STRATEGIES**
>
> Adapt the mixer in E to the level of your students.
>
> - **Pre-and On-level** Pair these students and have them interview other pairs together.
> - **Higher-level** Have these students ask an additional question and write all answers.

F Call on individuals to report the responses from their classmates. Write a list of answers to question 3 on the board.

PROBLEM SOLVING
10–15 minutes

A 1. Ask: *If you noticed a safety problem at work, would you be afraid to tell your boss?* Tell students they will read a story about a man who sees a safety problem at work. Direct students to read Mario's story silently.

2. Ask: *Are the employees trained in safety?* [yes] *Is the factory a dangerous place?* [no] *What is the safety problem?* [Some of the emergency exits are locked.] Play the audio and have students read along silently.

B Elicit answers to question 1. Have volunteers write answers to question 2 on the board until all of the class ideas have been put up. Put students into groups of three or four. Have them vote on Mario's best course of action.

Possible Answer
1. Mario is worried because some of the emergency exits at his workplace are locked, even though that is very unsafe. He doesn't know if he should report the unsafe practice/ how to report the unsafe practice.

TIP
Pair students. Ask them to write a short letter giving advice to Mario. Call on volunteers to read their letters to the class.

Evaluation
20–25 minutes

To test students' understanding of the unit language and content, have them take the Unit 5 Test, available on the Teacher Resource Center.

UNIT 6 Getting Ahead

Unit Overview

This unit explores interpersonal skills, employees' skills and responsibilities with a range of employability skills and contextualizes adjective clause structures.

KEY OBJECTIVES

Lesson 1	Identify interpersonal skills and personal qualities
Lesson 2	Write an email to report on progress and ask for feedback
Lesson 3	Use adjective clauses to describe employees' skills and responsibilities
Lesson 4	Ask for information
Lesson 5	Identify main idea and supporting details
At Work	Listen actively at work
Teamwork & Language Review	Review unit language

UNIT FEATURES

Academic Vocabulary	attribute, automatic, benefit, clarification, conflict, contact, define, demonstrate, diverse, emphasis, ethic, evaluation, finalize, flexible, inflexible, initiative, input, participant, quote, reliable, resolve, respond, scheduling, technical, unreliable
Employability Skills	• Understand teamwork • Work with others • Locate information • Communicate information • Communicate verbally • Listen actively • Analyze information • Think critically • Solve problems • Determine which skills are most important in business • Decide how to successfully manage several different employees

Resources	**Class Audio** CD2, Tracks 13–22
	Workbook Unit 6, pages 37–43
	Teacher Resource Center
	   Multilevel Activities 4 Unit 6
	   Multilevel Grammar Exercises 4 Unit 6
	   Unit 6 Test
	Oxford Picture Dictionary The Workplace, Career Planning, Job Skills

LESSON 1 VOCABULARY

Lesson Overview

MULTILEVEL OBJECTIVES

On-level: Describe and talk about interpersonal skills and personal qualities

Pre-level: Identify and describe interpersonal skills and personal qualities

Higher-level: Talk and write about interpersonal skills and personal qualities

LANGUAGE FOCUS

Grammar: Adjectives (*She is very reliable.*)

Vocabulary: Interpersonal skills and personal qualities

For vocabulary support for pre-level students, see these **Oxford Picture Dictionary** topics: The Workplace, pages 182–183; Job Skills, page 176

READINESS CONNECTION

In this lesson, students understand teamwork by conducting research on interpersonal skills and personal qualities.

PACING

To compress this lesson: Conduct 1D as a whole-class activity.

To extend this lesson: Have students complete a self-evaluation. (See end of lesson.)

And/or have students complete **Workbook 4 page 37** and **Multilevel Activities 4 Unit 6 pages 68–69**.

Lesson Notes

CORRELATIONS

CCRS: SL.1.B (b.) Follow agreed-upon rules for discussions. (c.) Ask questions to check understanding of information presented, stay on topic, and link their comments to the remarks of others. (d.) Explain their own ideas and understanding in light of the discussion.

SL.2.B Determine the main ideas and supporting details of a text read aloud or information presented in diverse media and formats, including visually, quantitatively, and orally.

SL.4.B Report on a topic or text, tell a story, or recount an experience with appropriate facts and relevant, descriptive details, speaking clearly at an understandable pace.

SL.6.B Speak in complete sentences when appropriate to task and situation in order to provide requested detail or clarification.

R.1.B Ask and answer such questions as who, what, where, when, why, and how to demonstrate understanding of key details in a text.

R.4.B Determine the meaning of general academic and domain-specific words and phrases in a text relevant to a topic or subject area.

R.5.B Know and use various text features to locate key facts or information in a text efficiently.

W.7.A Participate in shared research and writing projects.

L.1.B (l.) Produce simple, compound and complex sentences.

L.4.B (a.) Use sentence-level context as a clue to the meaning of a word or phrase. (e.) Use glossaries and beginning dictionaries, both print and digital, to determine or clarify the meaning of words and phrases.

RF.4.B (a.) Read grade-level text with purpose and understanding.

ELPS: 1. An ELL can construct meaning from oral presentations and literary and informational text through level-appropriate listening, reading, and viewing. 2. An ELL can participate in level-appropriate oral and written exchanges of information, ideas, and analyses, in various social and academic contexts, responding to peer, audience, or reader comments and questions. 3. An ELL can speak and write about level-appropriate complex literary and informational texts and topics. 5. An ELL can conduct research and evaluate and communicate findings to answer questions or solve problems. 8. An ELL can determine the meaning of words and phrases in oral presentation and literary and informational text.

Warm-up and Review
10–15 minutes (books closed)

Write several job locations on the board. *Restaurant, Factory, Hospital, School, Office.* Elicit the job titles of different people who work in each location and write them in the correct category.

Introduction
5 minutes

1. Ask students to name people at each job site who work together. For example: *Waiters interact with bussers, cooks, cashiers, and customers.* Ask if any of the jobs don't require working with people.

2. State the objective: *Today we're going to talk about the interpersonal skills and qualities you need to succeed on the job.*

1 Identify interpersonal skills

Presentation I
20–25 minutes

1. Read the instructions aloud. Elicit or explain the difference between hard and soft skills. Ask: *What are hard skills?* [specific teachable skills that can be measured, such as using a computer or speaking Spanish] *What are soft skills?* ["people" or interpersonal skills that are harder to measure] As a class, brainstorm soft skills they have learned about. Write students' ideas on the board.

2. Model the activity. Say: *I think asking for clarification is easier than other skills in English because you can learn specific phrases.* Pair students to identify soft skills that are easier and harder to do in English. Remind them to state and discuss their reasons. Ask volunteers to state their ideas and give reasons. Add reasons next to the appropriate skill on the board.

B 1. Copy the first two rows of the chart onto the board.

2. Model the task by "thinking aloud" about the first skill in the chart and marking the first column appropriately. Work with a volunteer to demonstrate completing the last two columns.

3. Direct students to review the vocabulary independently, marking the first column of the chart in their books.

4. Pair students and ask them to complete the last two columns of the chart together.

1. Elicit any words that pairs did not know and write them on the board. Check with the class to see which of these words are known.

2. Direct students to look up any remaining unknown words in their dictionaries. Discuss those words in relation to the lesson.

(Note: 1D and 1E will confirm students' understanding of the target vocabulary.)

Guided Practice I
10–20 minutes

D 1. Direct students to look at the model. Then read sentence 2 aloud. If students struggle to answer, ask them to look at the key words in the sentence. Ask if there are any words in the sentence that are similar to the vocabulary from 1B. Elicit the answer.

2. Set a time limit (five minutes). Direct students to complete the activity individually and then check their answers in pairs. Do not check the answers as a class yet.

Answers	
1. b	5. a
2. e	6. f
3. g	7. d
4. c	8. h

E 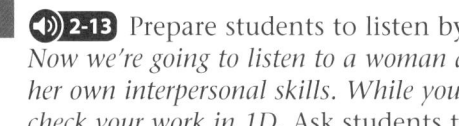 Prepare students to listen by saying, *Now we're going to listen to a woman describe her own interpersonal skills. While you listen, check your work in 1D.* Ask students to circle the items in 1D that don't match the listening passage. Elicit those items and play them again, focusing on clues to meaning in the 1D sentences.

2 Learn about personal qualities

Presentation II
10–20 minutes

1. Introduce the new topic: *Now we're going to talk about personal qualities.* Direct students to look at the picture and form. Ask: *Who do you see?* [supervisor and employee] *What do you think they are talking about?* [evaluation]

2. Direct students to read the evaluation silently.

3. Ask: *In which column can you find words that describe an employee?* [the first column] Read the personal-quality words aloud and have students repeat them.

4. Check comprehension. Ask: *What do you call someone who never lies?* [honest] *What do you call someone who is always on time and completes all of his or her work?* [reliable] *What do you call someone who can work well with everyone and listens to different ideas?* [tolerant]

5. Have students work individually to complete the sentences and then compare answers with a partner. Go over the answers as a class.

Answers	
1. reliable	4. independent
2. honest	5. responsible
3. flexible	6. tolerant

Guided Practice II
10–15 minutes

 1. Model the conversation with a volunteer. Model it again using other information from 2A.

2. Set a time limit (three minutes). Direct students to practice with a partner.

3. Call on volunteers to present their version of the conversation for the class.

Possible Answers
The supervisor thinks that Ayana is always reliable. She is on time and completes all her work. He thinks she is responsible; she works well without supervision. He says that she needs to be more flexible. Sometimes she has difficulty making changes. He says she is honest. She tells the truth and follows company rules. He says she does her best work on a team but she also can be independent and work alone. He says she is tolerant. She works well with everyone and listens to everyone's ideas.

MULTILEVEL STRATEGIES

Adapt 2B to the level of your students.

• **Pre- and On-level** Pair pre- and on-level students for 2B. Provide these students with sentence frames for the conversation:

A: What is Ayana like?

B: She is _____.

A: What does she need to work on?

B: She sometimes _____.

Assign pre-level students part A for the first round and then have them switch roles.

• **Higher-level** Pair students and have them brainstorm other personal quality words for their conversation.

Communicative Practice and Application
20–25 minutes

 1. Write the questions from 2C on the board. Explain that students will work in teams to research and report on these questions. Say: *Each student will survey three other students who are not on their team.*

2. Draw a chart on the board with four columns and four rows. The top row has these headings: *Name, On a team, In a family, In a class.* Model the task by asking a volunteer both questions and writing the information in the chart.

3. Group students and assign roles: reporter, manager, administrative assistant, and researcher. Verify students' understanding of their roles.

4. Give managers a time limit for surveying other students (five minutes) and a time limit for sharing information with the team (five minutes). Direct the researcher to look up any unfamiliar words for interpersonal skills and personal qualities that team members mention. Direct the administrative assistant to record information for the team using a chart like the one on the board. After five minutes, remind students to rejoin their teams and share information from the survey.

5. Give a two-minute warning. Call "time."

TIP
When setting up task-based activities, verify that students understand their roles using physical commands. For example: *If you report on your team's work, stand up* [reporter]. *If you keep the team on task, point to the clock* [manager]. *If you write the team's responses, raise your hand* [administrative assistant]. *If you help the team research, hold up your smartphone/tablet* [researcher].

D 1. Copy the sentence frames on the board.

2. Direct teams to help their administrative assistant use the sentence frames to record the team's findings. Direct the reporter to use the recorded information to report the team's findings to the class or another team.

3. Write *In a Family* and *In a Class* on the board. Elicit the qualities students chose as most important and write them in each category. Elicit examples of how a person demonstrates those qualities.

Evaluation

10–15 minutes

TEST YOURSELF

1. Direct Partner A to read prompts 1–4 from 1D on page 84 to Partner B. Partner B should close their book and write the answers in their notebooks. When finished, students switch roles. Partner B reads prompts 5–8 from 1D.

2. Direct both partners to open their books and check their spelling when they finish.

> **EXTENSION ACTIVITY**
>
> **Self-evaluation**
>
> Have students complete a self-evaluation.
>
> 1. Copy the chart in 2A on the board. Change the title to *Student Evaluation for* _____ and leave the *Rating* and *Comments* columns blank.
>
> 2. Direct students to copy the chart and complete it with ratings and comments about themselves as students. Allow but do not require them to share their self-evaluations with you.

LESSON 2 WRITING

Lesson Overview

MULTILEVEL OBJECTIVES

On- and Higher-level: Analyze, write, and edit an email to report on progress

Pre-level: Read and write an email about progress

LANGUAGE FOCUS

Grammar: Present, present perfect, present perfect continuous tenses (*I appreciate your feedback. Three of the assistants have been trained. I have also been working on our scheduling system.*)

Vocabulary: *Update, procedures, input, initiative, feedback*

For vocabulary support, see this **Oxford Picture Dictionary** topic: The Workplace, pages 182–183

STRATEGY FOCUS

When you write a workplace memo, include *To, From,* and *Re:* lines. Don't indent.

READINESS CONNECTION

In this lesson, students communicate information by writing a progress report.

PACING

To compress this lesson: Assign the *Test Yourself* for homework.

To extend this lesson: Have students role-play an in-person progress report. (See end of lesson.)

And/or have students complete **Workbook 4 page 38** and **Multilevel Activities 4 Unit 6 page 70**.

Lesson Notes

CORRELATIONS

CCRS: SL.1.B (d.) Explain their own ideas and understanding in light of the discussion.

SL.2.B Determine the main ideas and supporting details of a text read aloud or information presented in diverse media and formats, including visually, quantitatively, and orally.

R.1.B Ask and answer such questions as who, what, where, when, why, and how to demonstrate understanding of key details in a text.

R.2.A Identify the main topic and retell key details of a text.

R.5.A Know and use various text features to locate key facts or information in a text.

W.2.B (a.) Introduce a topic and group related information together; include illustrations when useful to aiding comprehension. (b.) Develop the topic with facts, definitions, and details. (c.) Use linking words and phrases to connect ideas within categories of information. (d.) Provide a concluding statement or section.

W.4.B Produce writing in which the development and organization are appropriate to task and purpose.

W.5.B With guidance and support from peers and others, develop and strengthen writing as needed by planning, revising and editing.

L.1.B (l.) Produce simple, compound and complex sentences.

L.1.C (c.) Form and use the progressive verb tenses. (d.) Use modal auxiliaries to convey various conditions. (e.) Form and use the perfect verb tenses. (f.) Use verb tense to convey various times, sequences, states, and conditions.

L.2.C (a.) Use correct capitalization. (g.) Use a comma before a coordinating conjunction in a compound sentence.

RF.4.B (a.) Read grade-level text with purpose and understanding.

ELPS: 2. An ELL can participate in level-appropriate oral and written exchanges of information, ideas, and analyses, in various social and academic contexts, responding to peer, audience, or reader comments and questions. 3. An ELL can speak and write about level-appropriate complex literary and informational texts and topics. 4. An ELL can construct level-appropriate oral and written claims and support them with reasoning and evidence. 6. An ELL can analyze and critique the arguments of others orally and in writing. 7. An ELL can adapt language choices to purpose, task, and audience when speaking and writing.

Warm-up and Review
10–15 minutes (books closed)

Write *Progress Report* on the board. Ask students if they have ever made one or had one sent to them. If so, elicit what the progress report described and included. Point out that a progress report will include things that are completed, in progress, or not completed.

Introduction
5 minutes

1. Refer to the *Warm-up* activity. Ask: *Who gives progress reports and why? Who gets a progress report?*

2. State the objective: *Today we're going to read and write a progress report.*

1 Prepare to write

Presentation
20–25 minutes

A 1. Direct students' attention to the memo. Read the directions. Build students' schema by asking questions about the memo. Ask: *Is this writing formal or informal?* [formal] *How do you know?* [To: Mr. Roberts, uses formal expressions such as *I would like*] Point out the *Writer's Note*. Check comprehension: *Does this memo include* To, From, *and* Re (subject) *lines*? [yes] Have students say the words that come after each line.

2. Give students two minutes to tell a partner their responses to questions 1 and 2. Elicit responses from the class.

B 1. Introduce the model memo: *You're going to read a memo from an employee to a supervisor.* Explain or elicit unfamiliar vocabulary: *update, procedures, input, initiative, feedback*. Have students read the memo silently.

2. Check comprehension. Ask: *What kind of job does Ayana have?* [She works in a medical office.] *What three office procedures does she write about?* [using software for making patient appointments, scheduling system for medical assistants, updating system for entering patient information into medical records]

3. Play the audio. Ask students to number the paragraphs as they read along.

Guided Practice I
10 minutes

C Have students work independently to answer the questions. Have them underline the information that gives the answer in the memo. Then have students compare answers with a partner. Go over the answers as a class.

Possible Answers
1. Ayana is writing this memo because she wants to update Mr. Roberts on her progress with new office procedures. 2. She has finished training three of the medical assistants to use the new software for making patient appointments online. She still has to train the part-time weekend assistants. 3. She is proposing to work on updating the system for entering patient information into medical records. 4. She is asking for the supervisor's feedback, and she is asking him to let her know if he has any questions because she wants to be sure her idea is alright before she starts working on it.

2 Plan and write

Guided Practice II
15–20 minutes

A 1. Brainstorm topics your class has worked on and write them on the board. For each, elicit examples of things they have done or progress they have made.

2. Read question 2. Ask volunteers to identify things they still need to do.

B Read through the memo template. Elicit ideas that could go in each paragraph. Have students write their memos individually.

MULTILEVEL STRATEGIES
Adapt 2B to the level of your students. • **Pre-level** Work with these students to write a group memo. Read through the template. At each ellipsis, stop and elicit completions. Decide as a group what to write. Have these learners copy the group memo into their notebooks. • **On-** and **Higher-level** Encourage these students to include examples of what they have done outside of class to improve their English skills.

3 Get feedback and revise

Guided Practice III
5 minutes

 Direct students to check their writing using the editing checklist. Tell them to read each item in the list and check their papers before moving onto the next item. Explain that students should not edit their writing at this stage. They should just use the checklist to check their work and mark any areas they want to revise.

Communicative Practice
15 minutes

 1. Read the instructions aloud. Emphasize to students that they are responding to their partners' work, not correcting it.

2. Use the memo in 1B to model the exercise. *I think your second paragraph explains your progress well. Your offer to take the initiative was very clear.*

3. Direct students to exchange memos with a partner and follow the instructions.

C Allow students time to edit and revise their writing as necessary, using the editing checklist from 3A and their partner's feedback from 3B. If necessary, students could complete this task as homework.

> **TIP**
> After completing 3C, hold a class discussion to decide what topics students want to make more progress on. Elicit ideas for how they can do this inside and outside of class.

Application and Evaluation
10 minutes

TEST YOURSELF

1. Review the instructions aloud. Assign a time limit (five minutes) and have students work independently.

2. Before collecting student work, invite two or three volunteers to share their sentences. Ask students to raise their hands if they wrote similar answers.

> **EXTENSION ACTIVITY**
> **Role-play**
> Have students work in pairs to role-play an in-person progress report. One role is the student and the other a tutor. The student will give a progress report on his/her learning in class so far. The tutor will ask questions for more information and give suggestions. Then have students switch roles. Monitor and provide feedback. Ask volunteers to perform their role-plays for the class.

140   Unit 6   Lesson 2   Writing   Lesson Plans 4

LESSON 3 GRAMMAR

Lesson Overview

MULTILEVEL OBJECTIVES

On- and Higher-level: Use adjective clauses to talk about job applicants and listen for information

Pre-level: Identify adjective clauses in sentences about job applicants and listen for information

LANGUAGE FOCUS

Grammar: Adjective clauses (*Please greet the customers who sit at your tables.*)

Vocabulary: Interpersonal skills and job qualifications

For vocabulary support, see these **Oxford Picture Dictionary** topics: The Workplace, pages 182–183; Career Planning, pages 174–175; Job Skills, page 176

STRATEGY FOCUS

Students practice using adjective clauses to give more information.

READINESS CONNECTION

In this lesson, students communicate information using adjective clauses.

PACING

To compress this lesson: Conduct 2A and 2B as whole-class activities.

To extend this lesson: Have students talk about their job preferences using adjective clauses. (See end of lesson.)

And/or have students complete **Workbook 4 pages 39–40, Multilevel Activities 4 Unit 6 pages 71–72,** and **Multilevel Grammar Exercises 4 Unit 6**.

Lesson Notes

CORRELATIONS

CCRS: SL.1.B (d.) Explain their own ideas and understanding in light of the discussion.

SL.2.B Determine the main ideas and supporting details of a text read aloud or information presented in diverse media and formats, including visually, quantitatively, and orally.

SL.6.B Speak in complete sentences when appropriate to task and situation in order to provide requested detail or clarification.

R.1.B Ask and answer such questions as who, what, where, when, why, and how to demonstrate understanding of key details in a text.

L.1.B (e.) Form and use the past tense of frequently occurring irregular verbs. (l.) Produce simple, compound and complex sentences.

L.1.C (b.) Use relative pronouns (who, whose, whom, which, that) and relative adverbs (where, when, why).

L.2.C (a.) Use correct capitalization. (d.) Use a comma to separate and introductory element from the rest of the sentence.

RF.4.B (a.) Read grade-level text with purpose and understanding.

ELPS: 1. An ELL can construct meaning from oral presentations and literary and informational text through level-appropriate listening, reading, and viewing. 2. An ELL can participate in level-appropriate oral and written exchanges of information, ideas, and analyses, in various social and academic contexts, responding to peer, audience, or reader comments and questions. 3. An ELL can speak and write about level-appropriate complex literary and informational texts and topics.

Warm-up and Review
10–15 minutes (books closed)

Scramble the words in these sentences and write them on the board. *1A. Julie talks to the customers. 1B. The customers come to the front counter. 2A. Tom works with a team. 2B. The team designs catalogs. 3A. Tim spoke to the woman. 3B. The woman was interviewing new employees.* Give students time to unscramble the sentences. Ask volunteers to write them on the board correctly.

Introduction
5–10 minutes

1. Say: *When we write short sentences, we have to repeat words. We can connect sentences so that we don't have to repeat the words. For sentence 1, we can say,* Julie talks to the customers who come to the front counter. *The connecting clause is called an adjective clause.*

2. State the objective: *Today we're going to use adjective clauses to talk about job experience and skills.*

1 Use adjective clauses

Presentation I
20–25 minutes

  1. Direct students to look at the picture. Ask: *Who are these people? Where are they?*

2. Read the instructions aloud. Ask students to read the conversation silently to find the answers to the questions and then compare answers with a partner. Go over the answers with the class.

Answers
1. one skill
2. making better eye contact with customers
3. the customers who sit at Alonso's tables

  1. Demonstrate how to read the grammar chart.

2. Direct students to underline the adjective clauses in the conversation in 1A. Go over the answers as a class.

3. Read the *Grammar Note* aloud. Ask students to identify the noun being described by the adjective clauses in the chart.

4. Read the chart through sentence by sentence. Then read it again and have students repeat after you.

5. Assess students' understanding of the chart. Direct students' attention to the adjective clause. Elicit the form of an adjective clause: *which/that/who + verb.* Explain that in some adjective clauses, the pronoun is the subject of the verb in the clause. Ask: *What pronouns can we use for things?* [which and that] *Which ones can we use for people?* [who or that]

6. Have students write the sentences in the chart as two separate sentences. *There is one skill. One skill needs work. Please greet the customers. The customers sit at your tables.* Elicit ways to join the sentences on the board from the *Warm-up*.

Answers
Underline: that needs work, who sit at your tables

Guided Practice I
15–20 minutes

  1. Tell students they will collaborate to complete the description of the grammar point. Model collaboration by working with the class to complete the first sentence. Encourage students to look at 1A and 1B for help with completing the description.

2. Pair students and have them work together to complete the description.

3. Project or write the completed definition on the board and have pairs verify the accuracy of their responses. Ask volunteers which sentences confused them and discuss.

Answers
noun, main, that, who

MULTILEVEL STRATEGIES

For 1C, seat mixed-level students together.

• **Pre- On- and Higher-level** Assign pre-level students the role of administrative assistant, on-level students the role of manager, and higher-level students the role of researcher. The administrative assistant fills in the blanks according to the team's decisions, the manager reads the description and manages the team's discussion, and the researcher looks up the definition of the grammar point online or checks against an answer key to verify the team's answers.

Guided Practice II
5–10 minutes

 1. Direct students' attention to the first pair of sentences. Ask: *Which word is repeated in both sentences?* [suggestion] Say: *The word that is repeated is the one the adjective clause will be about.*

2. Ask students to work individually to combine the sentences and then compare answers with a partner.

3. Ask volunteers to write the sentences on the board. Edit with the class.

Answers
1. The manager made a suggestion which helped Alonso. 2. Alonso has learned many skills which are important in his job. 3. He always remembers the customers who sit at his tables. 4. He is getting better at solving problems which happen in the kitchen.

MULTILEVEL STRATEGIES
For 1D, seat same-level students together. •**Pre-level** While other students are completing 1D, provide these students with the answers and ask them to underline the adjective clause and circle the noun it describes.

 1. Elicit the importance of accuracy. Tell students they will be building their accuracy in this task.

2. Organize students into groups. Demonstrate how to correct the sentence using the first example.

3. Have team members work together to correct the sentences. Circulate and monitor teamwork.

4. Project or write the corrected sentences on the board and have teams check their work.

Answers
1. Tyra's manager gave her feedback which/that helped her. 2. He wants her to work on managing conflict with some of the people who/that work with her. 3. Tyra is happy to work on a skill which/that will help her and her team. 4. Her manager knows that Tyra is tolerant of people who/that don't share her opinions.

2 Use adjective clauses inside main clauses

Presentation II
20–25 minutes

 1. Write this sentence on the board: *The secretary that gave me my application was very nice.* Ask students to identify the adjective clause and the noun it describes. Say: *Now we're going to learn about adjective clauses inside the main clause.* Point out that the adjective clauses on p. 88 describe the objects of verbs in the main clause. These adjective clauses describe the subjects of the main clause.

2. Read the sentences in the chart aloud. Ask students to read the main clauses independently and then read them with the adjective clauses. Elicit the form: subject + <u>who/that/which + verb + object</u> + verb + object. Underline the adjective clause.

4. Read the sentences in number 1 aloud. Ask: *What does* she *replace in the second sentence?* [the manager] Remind students to match pronouns to their nouns when combining sentences.

5. Direct students to work individually to write the rest of the sentences and then compare answers with a partner. Ask volunteers to write the sentences on the board.

Answers
1. The manager who/that had hired Alonso was very happy. 2. The suggestion which/that helped Alonso was about making eye contact. 3. The job opening which/that was listed at the career center was just filled. 4. The woman who/that was hired last week quit after two days.

MULTILEVEL STRATEGIES
Adapt 2A to the level of your students. •**Pre-level** Provide these students with the answers. Direct them to underline the adjective clause and circle the noun it describes. •**Higher-level** Direct students from this group who finish early to write an original sentence with an adjective clause inside the main clause. Have other students identify the clause and the noun it describes.

Guided Practice III
10–15 minutes

B Ask students to work individually to complete the sentences with their own ideas and then compare their opinions with a partner. Ask volunteers to write their sentences on the board.

> **MULTILEVEL STRATEGIES**
>
> Seat same-level students together for 2B.
>
> • **Pre-level** Work with these students to help them with adjective clauses. Write ideas to complete each sentence: *It provides health insurance. They always come on time. She listens well,* etc. Show students how to change these sentences into adjective clauses that will complete the sentences: *A company that provides health insurance is a good place to work.*
>
> • **On- and Higher-level** Direct these students to complete 2B with two of their own ideas for each item.

> **TIP**
>
> For more practice with adjective clauses after 2B, write this paragraph on the board: *Marta wanted the manager position _____. She called the number _____ and made an appointment. The man _____ was very nice. He told her to get a letter of recommendation from a supervisor _____. He asked her to choose a time _____ for an interview.*
>
> Write these adjective clauses as a list: 1. *that was announced in the company newsletter* 2. *that she spoke to* 3. *that was convenient for her* 4. *that she saw in the announcement* 5. *who she had worked with*
>
> Have students use the adjective clauses to complete the sentences [1, 4, 2, 5, 3]. To make the task more challenging, don't include the blanks in the paragraph and have students find the appropriate spots for the clauses.

3 Listen for adjective clauses to determine the meaning

Guided Practice IV
10–15 minutes

2-15 1. Say: *Now we're going to listen to questions and answers with an employer.* Tell students to read the sentences before listening.

2. Play the audio. Direct students to match the parts of the sentences and then compare sentences with a partner. Replay the audio. Ask students to check or complete their work.

3. Call on volunteers to read the completed sentences aloud.

Answers	
1. c	4. a
2. e	5. b
3. f	6. d

4 Use adjective clauses to talk about your opinions

Communicative Practice and Application
20–25 minutes

A Read the instructions aloud. Direct students to look at the list of applicants to find the answer to the question. Elicit the numbers of the applicants with hotel experience.

Answer
three

B 1. Direct students to work in teams to decide on an applicant to hire. Tell them to discuss the pros and cons of each applicant. Assign roles: manager, administrative assistant, and reporter. Have the manager keep the team on task and manage time. Have the administrative assistant make notes on the team's decision-making process.

2. Check comprehension of the exercise. Ask: *Should you discuss every applicant or just the one that seems best?* [every applicant]

C 1. Call on reporters to share their team's decision and their reasons with the class.

2. Try to come to a class consensus on the top two or three candidates and on the least desirable candidate.

> **TIP**
>
> For 4C, write the candidate numbers on the board and write *Pros* and *Cons* under each number. Ask volunteers to come to the board to write the pros and cons for each applicant. Base your class discussion on the information on the board.

Evaluation
10–15 minutes

TEST YOURSELF

Ask students to write the sentences independently. Collect and correct their writing.

MULTILEVEL STRATEGIES

Target the *Test Yourself* to the level of your students.

• **Pre-level** Provide sentence frames for these students to complete.

The woman who is a housekeeper here now is a good/bad candidate because _____.

The person who is currently a desk clerk is a good/bad candidate because _____.

The person who speaks five languages is a good/bad candidate because _____.

EXTENSION ACTIVITY
Discussion

Have students talk about their job preferences.

1. Put students in mixed-level groups. Write a series of sentence frames on the board:

I would like a job that _____. I'd like to have a boss that _____. I want to work in a place that _____. I want to be the kind of employee that _____. I'd like to have co-workers that _____.

2. Have each person in the group complete sentence 1 orally. When they get back to the first person in the group, have a different student start with sentence 2. Model the activity with one of the groups. Monitor and provide feedback.

LESSON 4 EVERYDAY CONVERSATION

Lesson Overview

MULTILEVEL OBJECTIVES

On-, Pre-, and Higher-level: Ask for information and listen for information in an automated phone message

LANGUAGE FOCUS

Grammar: Adjective clauses with *whose (She's the woman whose office is closest to the entrance.)*

Vocabulary: Payroll clerk, warehouse

For vocabulary support, see this **Oxford Picture Dictionary** topic: Job Skills, page 176

STRATEGY FOCUS

Practice using adjective clauses with *whose* to show who something belongs to.

READINESS CONNECTION

In this lesson, students listen actively and work with others to discuss interpersonal skills.

PACING

To compress this lesson: Conduct *Discuss* as a whole-class activity.

To extend this lesson: After completing 6B, have students complete a chart as a class. (See end of lesson.)

And/or have students complete **Workbook 4 page 41** and **Multilevel Activities 4 Unit 6 page 73**.

Lesson Notes

CORRELATIONS

CCRS: SL.1.B (a.) Come to discussions prepared, having read or studied required material; explicitly draw on that preparation and other information known about the topic to explore ideas under discussion. (b.) Follow agreed-upon rules for discussions. (c.) Ask questions to check understanding of information presented, stay on topic, and link their comments to the remarks of others. (d.) Explain their own ideas and understanding in light of the discussion.

SL.2.B Determine the main ideas and supporting details of a text read aloud or information presented in diverse media and formats, including visually, quantitatively, and orally.

SL.4.B Report on a topic or text, tell a story, or recount an experience with appropriate facts and relevant, descriptive details, speaking clearly at an understandable pace.

SL.6.B Speak in complete sentences when appropriate to task and situation in order to provide requested detail or clarification.

R.1.B Ask and answer such questions as who, what, where, when, why, and how to demonstrate understanding of key details in a text.

R.2.A Identify the main topic and retell key details of a text.

R.6.B Identify the main purpose of a text, including what the author wants to answer, explain, or describe.

R.7.B Use information gained from illustrations and the words in a text to demonstrate understanding of the text.

L.1.B (l.) Produce simple, compound and complex sentences.

L.1.C (b.) Use relative pronouns (who, whose, whom, which, that) and relative adverbs (where, when, why).

L.3.B (a.) Choose words and phrases for effect.

LRF.4.B (a.) Read grade-level text with purpose and understanding.

ELPS: 1. An ELL can construct meaning from oral presentations and literary and informational text through level-appropriate listening, reading, and viewing. 2. An ELL can participate in level-appropriate oral and written exchanges of information, ideas, and analyses, in various social and academic contexts, responding to peer, audience, or reader comments and questions. 3. An ELL can speak and write about level-appropriate complex literary and informational texts and topics. 9. An ELL can create clear and coherent level-appropriate speech and text. 10. An ELL can demonstrate command of the conventions of standard English to communicate in level-appropriate speech and writing.

Warm-up and Review
10–15 minutes (books closed)

Review question formation. Write *who, what, which, where, when, why, how,* and *whose* on the board. Call on volunteers to ask a question with one of the words. Challenge students not to use any verb that has already been used.

Introduction
5 minutes

1. Say: *These are the questions we use to ask for information. It is important to know how to ask for information. It is also important to know whom to ask for information.*

2. State the objective: *Today we're going to talk about getting information from the right people at work or school and getting information from an automated phone message.*

1 Learn ways to ask for information

Presentation I
10–20 minutes

 1. Direct students to look at the organizational chart. Ask: *What is an organizational chart?* [It shows people's jobs and responsibilities.] *How many people work at this company?* [six] *What is the job that is above all the others?* [General Manager] Read the job titles aloud and elicit the responsibilities of each person.

2. Play the audio. Give students a minute to answer the questions and then compare answers with a partner. Go over the answers as a class.

Answers
Lilia should see the warehouse manager. Jamal should talk to Mr. Gupta.

Guided Practice I
20–25 minutes

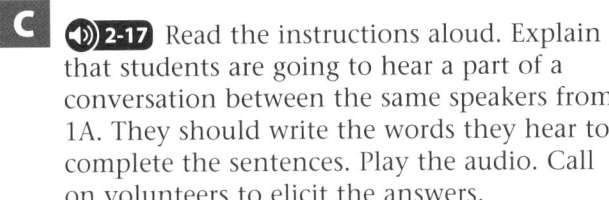 Read the instructions and the questions aloud. Play the audio again. Give students a few minutes to answer the questions and then compare answers with a partner. Go over the answers with the class.

Answers
1. The warehouse manager takes care of schedules.
2. Mr. Gupta wrote the memo.
3. Ernest is helpful. He knows a lot about the company.

 Read the instructions aloud. Explain that students are going to hear a part of a conversation between the same speakers from 1A. They should write the words they hear to complete the sentences. Play the audio. Call on volunteers to elicit the answers.

Answers
1. What's wrong
2. What's the matter
3. take you up there if you want

2 Practice your pronunciation

Pronunciation Extension
10–15 minutes

A 1. Ask several volunteers an obvious *yes/no* question. *Are you a student? Are you a doctor?* Write their *yes/no* answers on the board exactly as they say them. Read the *Speaking Note* aloud. Say: *There are different ways to say* yes *and* no *depending on how formal the situation is.*

2. Have students work with a partner to practice the conversations.

B 1. Play the audio. Have students check their pronunciation from 2A.

2. Ask students to take turns reading the sentences in 2A with a new partner. Monitor and provide feedback.

C 1. Model the questions and answers with a volunteer.

2. Direct students to practice with a partner. Have one partner ask all of the questions and the other partner answer. Tell them to switch roles when they finish.

3 Use adjective clauses with *whose*

Presentation II and Guided Practice II
10–15 minutes

 1. Write: *That's the man that I met in the office. She's the woman who helped me fill out my application.* Elicit the adjective clauses and the nouns they describe. Underline the clauses and circle the nouns.

2. Introduce the new topic. *Now we're going to look at another kind of adjective clause.* Read the instructions aloud. Direct students to read the sentences in the chart to find the answer. Read the *Grammar Note* aloud.

3. Check comprehension of the grammar in the chart. Ask: *Whose office is next to the cafe?* [Ms. Bell] *Whose son works here?* [Mr. and Mrs. Lopez's son]

Answer
They are the people whose son works here.

Guided Practice III
15–20 minutes

 1. Have students work with a partner to ask questions with *Who is…?* and to combine the sentences with *whose*. Model the conversation with a volunteer.

2. Call on volunteers to share their conversations with the class.

3. Set a time limit (five minutes). Ask students to practice asking and answering the questions with several partners. Call on individuals to share their answers with the class.

Answers
1. Who is Margaret? She's the team leader whose feedback is the most helpful. 2. Who is Mr. Edwards? He's the teacher whose class is really popular. 3. Who are Natasha and Jim? They are the employees whose wedding was this weekend. 4. Who is Julia? She is the student who lived in Italy last year 5. Who is Sima? She's the co-worker who always tries to help everyone.

MULTILEVEL STRATEGIES

After 3B, provide additional practice with adjective clauses. Use same-level pairs and target the practice to the level of your students.

- **Pre-level** Pair these students and provide them with sentences using adjective clauses with *whose*. Tell one partner to read the sentences and the other to ask the *who* question. *Alice is the _____ whose team is working on the new product. Karen is the _____ whose class is watching a movie.*

- **On- and Higher-level** Direct these students to write their own sentences using *whose* and have their partners ask the *who* question. Show some of the sentences you have written for pre-level students as an example.

After students have practiced with their partners, collect all of the sentences and call out some of them for the class to repeat.

---

4 Building conversation skills

Guided Practice IV
15–20 minutes

 Direct students to look at the picture. Ask: *Who do you see?* [two women/employees] *Where are they?* [in an office] *What are they looking at?* [a computer screen] Ask students to skim the conversation. Have them work with partners to identify the purpose of the conversation. Elicit responses and ask: *How do you know?* or *Why do you say that?* to encourage students to state their reasoning.

Possible Answer
The purpose is for one co-worker to offer to help another co-worker with a problem and for the second co-worker to ask for information to use to solve the problem.

 ◆) 2-19 1. Ask students to read the instructions and tell you what they are going to do [listen and read and respond to the question]. Play the audio and then elicit the answer to the question.

2. Elicit or explain unfamiliar words and phrases: *automatic deposit, payroll*. Ask students to read the conversation with a partner. Circulate and monitor pronunciation.

3. Ask: *In what other situations could you use this conversation?* [at school, in a store] Model and have students repeat difficult words or phrases. Point out a few phrases that are not specific to a payroll problem. Ask volunteers to point out others.

Possible Answer
She will look for a messy office with papers everywhere.

Communicative Practice and Application I
15–20 minutes

C 1. Pair students and have them read the instructions silently. Check their comprehension of the exercise. Ask: *What are the two roles?* [two classmates] *Is the conversation at work?* [No, it's in class.]

2. Model and have students repeat the expressions in the *In Other Words* box. Explain that they should use these expressions in their conversations.

3. Draw a T-chart on the board. Label the left column *Classmate 1* and the right column *Classmate 2*. Elicit examples of what each person might say and make notes on the chart. Encourage students to ask as many information questions as they can.

4. Set a time limit (three minutes). Have students act out the role-play. Call "time" and have students switch roles.

5. Ask three volunteer pairs to act out their role-play for the class. Tell students who are listening to take notes on the information requested and the answers.

MULTILEVEL STRATEGIES

For 4C, adapt the role-play to the level of your students.

• **Pre-level** Provide these students with a simplified role-play.

Classmate 1: My schedule is wrong. Who do I see about it?

Classmate 2: Go see Mr. Ang, the advisor. He takes care of schedule problems.

Classmate 1: How can I find him?

Classmate 2: His office is upstairs.

5 Focus on listening for details

Presentation and Guided Practice
20–25 minutes

A Read the instructions aloud and elicit ideas from the class.

B Direct students to look at the web page. Ask: *Whose website is this?* [Martinez Electronics] *Why is someone looking at the website?* [They want to contact the company.] *About what?* [a product or service] Ask students to make predictions about what they will hear.

C 🔊 2-20 1. Read the office names aloud and have students repeat. Elicit the function of each office.

2. Read the instructions and check comprehension of the exercise. Ask: *Are you going to write the extension number?* [no]

3. Play the audio. Have students number the departments in the order they hear them.

4. Pair students and have them compare answers. Elicit the answers from the class.

Answers
1. Sales and Service
2. Customer Service
3. Business Services
4. Warehouse
5. Human Resources
6. Main Office

D 🔊 2-20 1. Direct students to look at the directory before listening. Draw their attention to the sample answer.

2. Replay the audio and have students work individually to complete the directory and then compare answers with a partner. Go over the answers as a class.

Answers	
Office	**Extension**
Business Services	417
Customer Service	222
Human Resources	389
Main Office	565
Sales and Service	111
Warehouse	700

> **MULTILEVEL STRATEGIES**
>
> Replay the message in 5D to challenge on- and higher-level students while allowing pre-level students to catch up.
>
> - **Pre-level** Have these students listen again to complete the chart.
> - **On- and Higher-level** Ask these students to note the reason for choosing Sales and Service or Customer Service. After going over 5D, elicit the additional information.

6 Discuss

Communicative Practice and Application II
15–20 minutes

A 1. Read the instructions aloud. Draw a sample chart on the board with space for *Skills* on one side and *Actions* on the other. Direct students to read the sentence in 6B. Write "working on a team" under *Skills* and "asking for others' opinions" under *Actions*.

2. Put students into teams of four and assign roles: reporter, manager, administrative assistant, and editor. Verify students' understanding of the roles. The editor will check spelling and grammar. Encourage students to use the vocabulary for interpersonal skills and personal qualities during their discussions.

3. Set a time limit for the discussions (ten minutes). Write the sentence frame from 6B on the board. Then circulate and monitor.

B Call "time." Ask the reporter for each team to report the results of their team's discussion using the sentence frame on the board.

> **EXTENSION ACTIVITY**
>
> To extend 6B, draw a large blank chart on the board. As each reporter shares with the class, the administrative assistant from that group fills in the chart. If other teams came up with the same answers, they should not enter the information again.

Evaluation
5 minutes

TEST YOURSELF

1. Ask students to complete the checkboxes individually.

2. Tell students that you are going to read each of the items in the checklist aloud. If they are not at all confident with that skill, they should hold up a closed fist. If they are not very confident, they should hold up one finger. If they are somewhat confident, two fingers; confident, three fingers; very confident, four fingers. If they think they could teach the skill, they should hold up five fingers. Read each item in the checklist and identify students that may need further support.

> **TIP**
>
> For homework, you could ask students to write a sentence or two about what discussion skills they still need to work on or, if they are confident in all of the skills, what skill they are most proud of.

LESSON 5 READING

Lesson Overview

MULTILEVEL OBJECTIVES
On-, Pre-, and Higher-level: Read about and discuss skills training

LANGUAGE FOCUS
Grammar: Adjectives (*She's irresponsible.*)

Vocabulary: The prefixes *dis-*, *in-*, and *un-*; *diverse*, *enthusiastic*, *pay off*

For vocabulary support, see these **Oxford Picture Dictionary** topics: Career Planning, pages 174–175; Job Skills, page 176

STRATEGY FOCUS
Identify the main idea and supporting details in an article.

READINESS CONNECTION
In this lesson, students determine which skills are most important in business.

PACING
To compress this lesson: Conduct the word study in 2A as a whole-class activity.

To extend this lesson: Practice additional adjectives with the prefixes *in-*, *un-*, *ir-*, and *dis-*. (See end of lesson.)

And/or have students complete **Workbook 4 page 42** and **Multilevel Activities 4 Unit 6 pages 74–75**.

Lesson Notes

CORRELATIONS

CCRS: SL.1.B (a.) Come to discussions prepared, having read or studied required material; explicitly draw on that preparation and other information known about the topic to explore ideas under discussion. (b.) Follow agreed-upon rules for discussions. (c.) Ask questions to check understanding of information presented, stay on topic, and link their comments to the remarks of others. (d.) Explain their own ideas and understanding in light of the discussion.

SL.2.B Determine the main ideas and supporting details of a text read aloud or information presented in diverse media and formats, including visually, quantitatively, and orally.

SL.6.B Speak in complete sentences when appropriate to task and situation in order to provide requested detail or clarification.

R.1.B Ask and answer such questions as who, what, where, when, why, and how to demonstrate understanding of key details in a text.

R.1.C Refer to details and examples in a text when explaining what the text says explicitly and when drawing inferences from the text.

R.2.B Determine the main idea of a text; recount the key details and explain how they support the main idea.

R.5.B Know and use various text features to locate key facts or information in a text efficiently.

R.7.C Interpret information presented visually, orally, or quantitatively and explain how the information contributes to an understanding of the text in which it appears.

W.7.A Participate in shared research and writing projects.

L.1.B (l.) Produce simple, compound and complex sentences.

L.4.B (b.) Determine the meaning of the new word formed when a known prefix is added to a known word. (e.) Use glossaries and beginning dictionaries, both print and digital, to determine or clarify the meaning of words and phrases.

RF.3.B (c.) Identify and know the meaning of the most common prefixes and derivational suffixes.

RF.4.B (a.) Read grade-level text with purpose and understanding.

ELPS: 1. An ELL can construct meaning from oral presentations and literary and informational text through level-appropriate listening, reading, and viewing. 2. An ELL can participate in level-appropriate oral and written exchanges of information, ideas, and analyses, in various social and academic contexts, responding to peer, audience, or reader comments and questions. 3. An ELL can speak and write about level-appropriate complex literary and informational texts and topics. 8. An ELL can determine the meaning of words and phrases in oral presentation and literary and informational text.

Warm-up and Review
10–15 minutes (books closed)

Write *Shy, Outgoing, Honest, Reliable,* and *Funny* on the board. Elicit more examples of words that describe people's personalities. Write them on the board.

Introduction
5 minutes

1. Ask volunteers to come to the board and circle adjectives that describe positive employee traits. Ask if students think these attitudes or personality qualities are skills that can be learned.

2. State the objective: *Today we're going to read and discuss skills training.*

1 Read

Presentation
10–20 minutes

A Read the questions aloud. Elicit answers from the class. Make any associations you can between students' answers and the adjectives on the board from the *Warm-up. Outgoing people often have good people skills. Good team players are reliable.*

B Read the words and definitions. Elicit sample sentences from students using the words.

Pre-reading

C 1. Direct students to read the title of the article. Ask: *Does this mean people got money from the training?* [no] *What does it mean?* [that the skills training was successful] Direct students' attention to the *Reader's Note*. Read it aloud. Point out that the main idea is often in the first and last paragraphs of a text and the first or last sentences in a paragraph.

2. Read the instructions aloud. Have students answer the question individually and then check answers with a partner. Go over the answer with the class. If any students answer incorrectly, ask them to support their answer using information from the first sentence in each paragraph. Establish the correct answer.

Answer
c. Participants learned a number of valuable skills in the class.

Guided Practice: While Reading
20–30 minutes

D 1. Ask students to read the article silently and answer the question.

2. After students are finished reading, direct students to underline unfamiliar words they would like to know (e.g., *demonstrate, emphasis, diverse*). Elicit the words and encourage other students to provide definitions or examples. Note that *emphasis* is footnoted.

3. Check answers with the class.

4. Check students' comprehension. Ask: *Who is Sula Duarte?* [the center's director] *What is the training course about?* [helps people who are looking for work develop the skills they need] *How did the graduates feel about it?* [enthusiastic] *How many people were interviewed in the article?* [four]

Possible Answers
The center decided to offer this course because people need soft/essential/21st century skills in today's workplace. Participants who complete this program can demonstrate that they have the skills employers are looking for.

MULTILEVEL STRATEGIES

Adapt 1D to the level of your students.

• **Pre-level** Provide these students with a summary of the ideas in the reading. *Daniela, Musa, and Diego just graduated from a people-skills training class. Daniela learned about teamwork. Now she is more flexible and tolerant. Musa learned English skills that help him resolve conflicts at work, at home, and in the community. Diego learned about diverse groups of people. The next People Skills training class begins again in September.*

Direct these students to read the summary while other students are reading 1D.

• **On- and Higher-level** Pair students and have them read the article aloud to each other, taking turns to read each paragraph.

Guided Practice: Rereading
10–15 minutes

 1. Read the instructions aloud. Provide an opportunity for students to extract evidence from the text.

2. Have students reread the article and underline three supporting details. Ask students to compare answers with a partner.

3. Elicit students' answers.

Answers
Underlined: Now I know that when people work together, they actually get more work done. I needed to learn the right English to work in a group and manage conflict. Everything that we did in class is paying off. The skills I learned are helping me at work, in my community, and even at home. I've learned a lot about working with diverse groups of people.

TIP
Have students go online to find out about training classes in your area. Decide which device(s) students will use and elicit search terms ("workplace" + "training class" + your city).

 1. Have students work individually to mark the answers *T* (true), *F* (false), and *NI* (no information). They should then write the line number(s) where they found the answer. Write the answers on the board.

2. Elicit and discuss any additional questions about the reading. You could introduce new questions for class discussion: *Which of the skills do you think are the most useful? Which of the participants do you think will benefit the most? Why?*

Answers
1. T (lines 9–10) 2. NI 3. T (lines 22-24) 4. F (line 34) 5. F (lines 38–39)

MULTILEVEL STRATEGIES
For 1F, work with pre-level students.

• **Pre-level** Write questions on the board for these students to ask and answer while other students are completing 1F. Tell them to refer to their summaries.
1. What class did the three students take?
2. What did Daniela learn?
3. Where can Musa use his English skills to resolve conflicts?
4. What did Diego learn?

Call on volunteers for the answers. Have these students copy the answers to 1F from the board.

2 Word study

Guided Practice: Post-reading
10 minutes

 1. Direct students to look at the chart and identify the topic (the prefixes *dis-, in-, ir-* and *un-*). Have students read the chart.

2. Read the first two sentences in the chart and the examples for *irresponsible* and *disrespectul*. Elicit sentences for the other words in the chart.

3. Have students repeat after you as you say each word with natural intonation, rhythm, and stress.

4. Direct students to complete the sentences and then compare answers with a partner. Read the correct answers and have students check their work.

Answers
1. unreliable, responsible 2. inflexible, dishonest, irresponsible

B Direct students to work individually to write a sentence for each topic that includes the underlined word. Ask volunteers to write their sentences on the board. Have the rest of the class suggest grammar and spelling edits as needed.

> **EXTENSION ACTIVITY**
>
> **Writing Practice**
>
> After 2B, teach additional adjectives with the prefixes *in-, un-, ir-,* and *dis-*.
>
> 1. Write the following words on the board: *incompetent, intolerant, unqualified, unprofessional, irrational, disorganized, dissatisfied.* Elicit the positive form of the adjective and discuss both meanings.
>
> 2. As a class, write a sample sentence for the positive form of each word.
>
> 3. Have students work in pairs or groups to write a sample sentence for the negative form of each word. Ask volunteers to write their sentences on the board.

3 Talk it over

Guided Practice
15–20 minutes

A Have students look at the graph. Ask: *What does this graph show?* [attributes employers look for on a resume] *What is another word for* attribute? [quality or skill] *Which attribute do most employers look for?* [leadership] Point out that they need to use the information from the graph to complete the sentences and answer the questions. Set a time limit (ten minutes). Have students work in pairs to complete the task. Ask volunteers to share their answers with the class.

Answers
1. problem-solving skills
2. creativity
3. 3
4. 9th
5. Interpersonal skills, computer skills, friendly/outgoing personality, creativity
6. 160

Communicative Practice
20 minutes

B Read the questions aloud. Set a time limit (ten minutes). Allow students to think about the questions and rank the skills. Ask students to compare their answers with a partner.

C Ask volunteers to share their ideas with the class.

Application
5–10 minutes

BRING IT TO LIFE

Read the instruction aloud. Brainstorm search terms: *"diversity" + "skills," "diversity in the workplace,"* etc. Ask students to do online research to identify necessary skills. Put students in groups to share the skills they found. Elicit ideas from the class.

AT WORK

Warm-up and Review
10–15 minutes (books closed)

Begin the lesson by telling the students about a promotion you have received in the past. Describe the qualities or attributes that you think helped you get promoted. Make sure students know the noun and verb forms: *promotion, promote*. Ask students if they know anyone who has received a promotion and why they think he or she was promoted.

Introduction
5 minutes

State the objective: *Today we're going to talk about listening actively at work.*

Presentation
5 minutes

 2-21 Read the instructions aloud. Play the audio. Give students a minute to think about the question. Elicit responses from the class.

Possible Answer
They are discussing applicants for a warehouse manager position.

Guided Practice
10–15 minutes

 2-21 Play the audio again. Direct students to listen for each quality, skill, or experience and put a check next to any that they hear mentioned.

Possible Answers
Ana: responsible, quiet David: makes suggestions Tina: solves problems, had diversity training

 2-21 Read the instructions aloud. Ask: *What are some ways that people show preferences?* [They say it directly, they mention good qualities, they show it in their voices.] Play the audio again, encouraging students to take notes in their notebooks. Set a time limit (five minutes) for students to discuss their answers with a partner. Circulate and monitor.

Presentation and Communicative Practice
10 minutes

 1. Direct students' attention to the *Do/Say* chart and ask them to identify the lesson's soft skill [listening actively]. Ask the class which column has examples of language [right] and which has examples of behaviors [left].

2. Say a phrase from the left and act it out. Say it again and have the class act it out with you. Say it a third time and have the class act it out for you. To confirm understanding, combine phrases: *Lean forward and nod your head slowly.*

3. Model the language from the right using authentic intonation. Have students practice imitating your inflection.

4. Put students in teams of four and assign each team a question. Assign roles: reporter, manager, administrative assistant, and researcher. (Researchers will ask you questions on behalf of the team.) Verify understanding of the roles. Set a time limit (five minutes) and monitor.

5. Write sentence frames on the board that teams can use to summarize their response. *Our team discussed the following question:_____. We decided _____ because _____.*

6. Call "time" and let reporters rehearse their report for one minute. Direct each reporter to present to three other teams.

Communicative Practice and Application
20–25 minutes

 1. Direct students to work in pairs to talk about the employees in B.

2. Remind students to use the expressions and actions that show active listening. Circulate and monitor.

F 1. Have pairs merge to form teams of four. Tell students that they are going to be role-playing a supervisors' meeting where they will discuss three employees they are considering for promotion.

2. Direct groups to come up with descriptions of three different employees. Each group should select a manager to run the meeting. The other three members should each choose one of the employees to bring up.

3. As students carry out the role-play, circulate and monitor. Provide global feedback once the activity ends.

TEAMWORK & LANGUAGE REVIEW

Lesson Overview

MULTILEVEL OBJECTIVES

On-, Pre-, and Higher-level: Expand upon and review unit grammar and life skills

LANGUAGE FOCUS

Grammar: Adjective clauses (*I work at the company that makes those boxes.*)

Vocabulary: Job skills

For vocabulary support, see these **Oxford Picture Dictionary** topics: The Workplace, pages 182–183; Career Planning, pages 174–175; Job Skills, page 176

READINESS CONNECTION

In this review, students solve a problem at a workplace.

PACING

To extend this review: Have students complete **Workbook 4 page 43**, **Multilevel Activities 4 Unit 6 page 76**, and **Multilevel Grammar Exercises 4 Unit 6**.

Lesson Notes

CORRELATIONS

CCRS: SL.1.B (a.) Come to discussions prepared, having read or studied required material; explicitly draw on that preparation and other information known about the topic to explore ideas under discussion. (b.) Follow agreed-upon rules for discussions. (c.) Ask questions to check understanding of information presented, stay on topic, and link their comments to the remarks of others. (d.) Explain their own ideas and understanding in light of the discussion.

SL.1.C (b.) Follow agreed-upon rules for discussions and carry out assigned roles.

SL.2.B Determine the main ideas and supporting details of a text read aloud or information presented in diverse media and formats, including visually, quantitatively, and orally.

SL.4.B Report on a topic or text, tell a story, or recount an experience with appropriate facts and relevant, descriptive details, speaking clearly at an understandable pace.

R.1.B Ask and answer such questions as who, what, where, when, why, and how to demonstrate understanding of key details in a text.

R.2.A Identify the main topic and retell key details of a text.

R.7.B Use information gained from illustrations and the words in a text to demonstrate understanding of the text.

W.3.A Write narratives in which they recount two or more appropriately sequenced events, include some details regarding what happened, use temporal words to signal event order, and provide some sense of closure.

L.1.B (l.) Produce simple, compound and complex sentences.

L.1.C (b.) Use relative pronouns (who, whose, whom, which, that) and relative adverbs (where, when, why). (d.) Use modal auxiliaries to convey various conditions.

RF.4.B (a.) Read grade-level text with purpose and understanding.

ELPS: 2. An ELL can participate in level-appropriate oral and written exchanges of information, ideas, and analyses, in various social and academic contexts, responding to peer, audience, or reader comments and questions. 3. An ELL can speak and write about level-appropriate complex literary and informational texts and topics. 9. An ELL can create clear and coherent level-appropriate speech and text. 10. An ELL can demonstrate command of the conventions of standard English to communicate in level-appropriate speech and writing.

Warm-up and Review
10–15 minutes (books closed)

1. Review *At Work* activity F.

2. Ask students to share the good, not-so-good, and interesting things that happened during the role-play. As students speak, write their responses in a chart on the board.

Introduction and Presentation
5 minutes

1. Pair students and direct them to look at the picture in their book. Ask them to describe what they see to their partner.

2. Ask volunteer pairs to share their ideas with the class.

Guided Practice
15–20 minutes

A 1. Direct students' attention to the box. Make sure they understand the vocabulary. Check comprehension of the activity. Ask: *Who are the people in the picture?* [employees] *What are you doing with the words in the box?* [using the words to decide who the employees are]

2. Set a time limit (five minutes). Have students work in teams to complete the activity. Have volunteers share their questions and answers.

B Direct students' attention to the first pair of sentences. Elicit the noun that the adjective clause will describe [disagreements]. Have students work individually to complete the answers and then compare answers with their team members. Ask volunteers to write their sentences on the board.

Answers
1. Disagreements that/which aren't resolved can cause big problems on the job. 2. Mr. Freeman is the art therapist whose patients drew the pictures in the hall. 3. Emilio is good at giving feedback that/which helps employees. 4. The team that solved the problem won $100. 5. Sarah, whose background is engineering, helped the team win. 6. I like working with people who/that can resolve disagreements. 7. Sean is the physical therapy aide whose patients complained. 8. Mr. Diaz was the supervisor whose suggestions really helped me. 9. Mrs. Tanaka was the dietician whose meals were very creative. 10. Emilio supervises 10 employees who/that work well together.

MULTILEVEL STRATEGIES
For B, seat same-level students together. • **Pre-level** Provide these students with the adjective clauses and ask them to insert them in the right place in the sentence. (e.g., 2. *whose patients drew the pictures*) • **Higher-level** Have students from this group who finish the exercises early write two original sentences with an adjective clause (one with *whose*). Ask them to put their sentences on the board and have other students identify the adjective clauses.

C Direct students' attention to A. Say: *We're going to write a paragraph about the people in the picture.* Encourage students to use their imagination and vocabulary from the unit to add more details: *Ana is the one who works in the front office and doesn't have good people skills.*

Communicative Practice
30–40 minutes

D 1. Group students and assign roles: manager, writer, editor, presenter. Explain that students are going to work with their teams to write a paragraph about a person from the list.

2. Read steps 2–5 of the activity aloud. Check comprehension of the task. *What is the first thing you should do?* [choose a person from the list] *What will you identify?* [characteristics or attributes]

3. Set a time limit (ten minutes) to complete the exercise. Circulate and answer any questions.

4. Have presenters from each team read their team's paragraph to another team.

E 1. Have students walk around the room to conduct the interviews. To get students moving, tell them to interview three people who were not in their team for D.

2. Set a time limit (five minutes) to complete the exercise.

3. Tell students to make a note of their classmates' answers but not to worry about writing complete sentences.

MULTILEVEL STRATEGIES
Adapt the mixer in E to the level of your students. • **Pre-and On-level** Pair these students and have them interview other pairs together. • **Higher-level** Have these students ask an additional question and write all answers.

F 1. Call on individuals to report what they learned about their classmates. Keep a running tally on the board for question 2.

2. Ask students to use the tally for question 2 to create a bar graph in their notebooks. Circulate and answer any questions. Ask volunteers to complete one bar on the graph on the board.

PROBLEM SOLVING
10–15 minutes

A 1. Ask: *Did you ever work with a group that couldn't get along?* Tell students they will read a story about a woman who is trying to manage a difficult group. Direct students to read Lana's story silently.

2. Ask: *How many employees are on Lana's team?* [six] *What is happening with her group?* [They don't get along.]

3. Play the audio and have students read along silently.

B 1. Elicit answers to question 1. Have volunteers write answers to 2 on the board until all of the class ideas have been put up.

2. Put students into groups of three or four and have them discuss the pros and cons of each solution.

3. Pair students. Have them role-play a conversation between Lana and a friend. Have volunteers present their role-play to the class.

Possible Answer
1. Lana is a new team manager and her group isn't really a team. Some of them don't get along. She doesn't know what to do to help her group become a team.

Evaluation
20–25 minutes

To test students' understanding of the unit language and content, have them take the Unit 6 Test, available on the Teacher Resource Center.

UNIT 7
Making Ends Meet

Unit Overview

This unit explores personal financing and budgeting with a range of employability skills and contextualizes unreal conditional structures.

KEY OBJECTIVES

Lesson 1	Identify financial and budgeting opportunities and challenges
Lesson 2	Write a formal essay to agree or disagree with a prompt
Lesson 3	Use present unreal conditional statements to talk about obstacles and opportunities
Lesson 4	Negotiate and compromise on a budget
Lesson 5	Identify ways to reach financial goals
At Work	Build consensus at work
Teamwork & Language Review	Review unit language

UNIT FEATURES

Academic Vocabulary	*consensus, credit, economy, equivalent, evidence, financial, income, maximize, minimize, policy, respond, secure, variable*
Employability Skills	• Work independently • Understand teamwork • Work with others • Locate information • Communicate information • Communicate verbally • Listen actively • Analyze information • Understand budgets • Decide why it's important to save money • Decide how to talk to a friend about poor spending habits • Solve problems

Resources	**Class Audio** CD2, Tracks 23–33
	Workbook Unit 7, pages 44–50
	Teacher Resource Center
	   Multilevel Activities 4 Unit 7
	   Multilevel Grammar Exercises 4 Unit 7
	   Unit 7 Test
	Oxford Picture Dictionary The Bank, Money, Shopping, Finding a Home

LESSON 1 VOCABULARY

Lesson Overview

MULTILEVEL OBJECTIVES

On-level: Describe and talk about personal finance, banking, and budgeting

Pre-level: Identify and describe personal finance, banking, and budgeting

Higher-level: Talk and write about personal finance, banking, and budgeting

LANGUAGE FOCUS

Grammar: Past tense (*How much did they pay?*)

Vocabulary: Personal finance, banking, and budgeting

For vocabulary support, see these **Oxford Picture Dictionary** topics: Money, page 26; The Bank, page 134; Finding a Home, pages 48–49

READINESS CONNECTION

In this lesson, students understand teamwork by conducting research on budgets and financial literacy.

PACING

To compress this lesson: Conduct 2A as a whole-class activity.

To extend this lesson: Have students compare bank brochures. (See end of lesson.)

And/or have students complete **Workbook 4 page 44** and **Multilevel Activities 4 Unit 7 pages 78–79**.

Lesson Notes

CORRELATIONS

CCRS: SL.1.B (b.) Follow agreed-upon rules for discussions. (c.) Ask questions to check understanding of information presented, stay on topic, and link their comments to the remarks of others. (d.) Explain their own ideas and understanding in light of the discussion.

SL.2.B Determine the main ideas and supporting details of a text read aloud or information presented in diverse media and formats, including visually, quantitatively, and orally.

SL.4.B Report on a topic or text, tell a story, or recount an experience with appropriate facts and relevant, descriptive details, speaking clearly at an understandable pace.

SL.6.B Speak in complete sentences when appropriate to task and situation in order to provide requested detail or clarification.

R.1.B Ask and answer such questions as who, what, where, when, why, and how to demonstrate understanding of key details in a text.

R.4.B Determine the meaning of general academic and domain-specific words and phrases in a text relevant to a topic or subject area.

R.5.B Know and use various text features to locate key facts or information in a text efficiently.

W.7.A Participate in shared research and writing projects.

L.1.B (l.) Produce simple, compound and complex sentences.

L.4.B (a.) Use sentence-level context as a clue to the meaning of a word or phrase. (e.) Use glossaries and beginning dictionaries, both print and digital, to determine or clarify the meaning of words and phrases.

RF.4.B (a.) Read grade-level text with purpose and understanding.

ELPS: 1. An ELL can construct meaning from oral presentations and literary and informational text through level-appropriate listening, reading, and viewing. 2. An ELL can participate in level-appropriate oral and written exchanges of information, ideas, and analyses, in various social and academic contexts, responding to peer, audience, or reader comments and questions. 5. An ELL can conduct research and evaluate and communicate findings to answer questions or solve problems. 8. An ELL can determine the meaning of words and phrases in oral presentation and literary and informational text.

Warm-up and Review
10–15 minutes (books closed)

Write *Where does the money go?* on the board. Ask students what things they spend most of their money on. Write their ideas on the board.

Introduction
5 minutes

1. Ask students to rank the items on the board from the ones that generally cost the most to the ones that cost the least.

2. State the objective: *Today we're going to learn words for personal finance, banking, and budgeting.*

1 Identify vocabulary for personal finance and banking

Presentation I
20–25 minutes

 1. Direct students' attention to the picture. Build schema by asking questions: *Who do you see? What are they looking at?* [A couple is looking at a budget/list of assets and expenses, some flyers, and an insurance policy on the table.] *What is a personal budget?* [a list of income and expenses, usually for each month] Direct students' attention to the ad next to the picture. Ask: *What is the workshop about?* [financial literacy] *What do you think that is?* [knowing how to handle money]

2. Write *Banks* and *Credit Unions* and *Money Skills* on the board and elicit students' answers to questions 1 and 2. Note their ideas under the correct term.

Answers
1. Home loans, auto loans, financial literacy workshops
2. Answers will vary.

B 1. Read the instructions aloud. Model using context clues. Ask: *What is listed under "assets"?* [savings account, checking account, car value] *Are these things they have or things they owe?* [things they have] *So what are assets?* [things you have, things of value]

2. Ask students to figure out the meaning of the words and phrases in the flyer using context clues.

3. Pair students and ask them to compare ideas.

C 1. Ask students to work individually to complete the sentences and then compare answers with a partner.

2. To prepare students for listening, say: *We're going to listen to Roberto and Julia talk about their financial plans.* Ask students to listen and check their answers. Go over the answers with the class.

Answers
1. assets, debts
2. home loan
3. auto loan
4. interest rate

D 1. Read the instructions aloud. Play the audio again and have students listen for the answer. Elicit the answer from the class.

2. Check comprehension. Ask: *Who went to the financial literacy workshop?* [Julia] *Who went to the bank to get information?* [Roberto] *What insurance do they have?* [for the things in their apartment]

Answer
a home loan

Guided Practice I
10–20 minutes

E 1. Read the questions aloud and elicit one answer for each question.

2. Set a time limit (three minutes). Direct students to ask and answer questions with a partner.

3. Call on volunteers to share their answers with the class.

2 Learn about budgeting

Presentation II
10–20 minutes

A 1. Direct students to look at the budget plan. Build students' schema. Ask: *Who has a job?* [Julia and Roberto] *How much do they make each month together?* [$4,400] *How much do they spend every month including rent?* [$2,300] Introduce the new topic: *Now we're going to learn budgeting vocabulary.*

2. Read the items in the chart aloud. Elicit definitions of *mortgage* and *premium*. Ask for examples of miscellaneous items.

3. Ask students to work individually to match the words with their definitions.

4. Read and have students repeat the words. Call on volunteers to read the matching definitions.

5. Check comprehension. Ask: *Is your rent payment a fixed expense or a variable expense?* [fixed] *What do you call the money you pay for insurance?* [a premium]

Answers	
1. d	4. f
2. c	5. b
3. a	6. e

TIP
To help students with the pronunciation of the long words in the budget, write the words on the board. Elicit and mark the number of syllables and which syllable is stressed.

Guided Practice II
10–15 minutes

 1. Model the conversation with a volunteer. Model it again using other information from 2A.

2. Set a time limit (three minutes). Direct students to practice with a partner.

3. Call on volunteers to present their version of the conversation for the class.

MULTILEVEL STRATEGIES

Adapt 2B to the level of your students.

• **Pre- and On-level** Pair pre- and on-level students for 2B. Assign pre-level students part A for the first round and then have them switch roles.

• **Higher-level** Pair students and direct them to create three different questions based on the budget (e.g., *What are the fixed expenses?*).

Communicative Practice and Application
20–25 minutes

 1. If students will use the Internet for this task, establish what device(s) they'll use: a class computer, tablets, or smartphones. Alternatively, print information from the Internet before class and distribute to groups.

2. Write the questions from 2C on the board. Explain that students will work in teams to research and report on these questions. Ask: *Which question requires research?* [1 and 2]

Which search terms or questions can you use to find the information you need? ["benefits of household budgets"; "financial literacy"] *What information will you scan for?* [benefits, classes, resources] *How will you record the information you find?* [table, checklist, index cards] Remind students to bookmark or record sites so they can find or cite them in the future.

3. Group students and assign roles: reporter, manager, administrative assistant, and IT support. Verify students' understanding of their roles.

4. Give managers a time limit for researching questions 1 and 2 (15 minutes). Direct the IT support to begin the online research or pick up the printed materials for each team. Direct the administrative assistant to record information for the team using a table, checklist, or index cards.

5. Give a two-minute warning. Call "time." Tell reporters to answer the first question and then ask each member of the team question 2.

TIP
When setting up task-based activities, verify that students understand their roles using physical commands. For example: *If you report on your team's work, stand up* [reporter]. *If you keep the team on task, point to the clock* [manager]. *If you write the team's responses, raise your hand* [administrative assistant]. *If you help the team research, hold up your smartphone/tablet* [IT support].

D 1. Copy the sentence frames on the board.

2. Direct teams to help their administrative assistant use the sentence frames to record the team's findings. Direct the reporter to use the recorded information to report the team's findings to the class or another team.

Evaluation
10–15 minutes

TEST YOURSELF

1. Direct Partner A to read prompts 1–3 from 2A on page 101 to Partner B. Partner B should close their book and write the answers in their notebook. When finished, students switch roles. Partner B reads prompts 4–6 from 2A.

2. Direct both partners to open their books and check their spelling when they finish.

EXTENSION ACTIVITY

Comparing Bank Brochures

Have students compare bank brochures to see the different banking services provided to customers. Put students in mixed-level groups. Give each group brochures from two different banks. (You can pick these up at the banks or you can print them off the Internet. If you have access to computers in the class, you can do this together.) Direct each group to compare the two brochures by looking at types of accounts, fees, minimum balances, and interest rates. Ask a reporter from each group to share his/her group's findings.

LESSON 2 WRITING

Lesson Overview

MULTILEVEL OBJECTIVES

On- and Higher-level: Analyze, write, and edit an essay about money

Pre-level: Read and write an essay about money and write a paragraph about money

LANGUAGE FOCUS

Grammar: Can (Money can't buy happiness.)

Vocabulary: Essay, security, flexibility

For vocabulary support, see these **Oxford Picture Dictionary** topics: The Bank, page 134; Money, page 26

STRATEGY FOCUS

When writing formal essays, include several paragraphs and don't use the first person pronoun.

READINESS CONNECTION

In this lesson, students communicate information by writing an essay about money.

PACING

To compress this lesson: Assign the *Test Yourself* for homework.

To extend this lesson: Students have a discussion about money and culture. (See end of lesson.)

And/or have students complete **Workbook 4 page 45** and **Multilevel Activities 4 Unit 7 page 80**.

Lesson Notes

CORRELATIONS

CCRS: SL.1.B (d.) Explain their own ideas and understanding in light of the discussion.

R.1.B Ask and answer such questions as who, what, where, when, why, and how to demonstrate understanding of key details in a text.

R.2.A Identify the main topic and retell key details of a text.

R.5.A Know and use various text features to locate key facts or information in a text.

W.1.B (a.) Introduce the topic or text they are writing about, state an opinion, and create and organizational structure that lists reasons. (b.) Provide reasons that support the opinion. (c.) Use linking words and phrases to connect opinion and reasons.

W.4.B Produce writing in which the development and organization are appropriate to task and purpose.

W.5.B With guidance and support from peers and others, develop and strengthen writing as needed by planning, revising and editing.

L.1.B (l.) Produce simple, compound and complex sentences.

L.1.C (f.) Use verb tense to convey various times, sequences, states, and conditions.

L.2.C (a.) Use correct capitalization. (g.) Use a comma before a coordinating conjunction in a compound sentence.

L.5.B (b.) Identify real-life connections between words and their use.

L.6.B Use words and phrases acquired through conversations, reading and being read to, and responding to texts, including using adjectives and adverbs to describe.

RF.4.B (a.) Read grade-level text with purpose and understanding.

ELPS: 1. An ELL can construct meaning from oral presentations and literary and informational text through level-appropriate listening, reading, and viewing. 2. An ELL can participate in level-appropriate oral and written exchanges of information, ideas, and analyses, in various social and academic contexts, responding to peer, audience, or reader comments and questions. 3. An ELL can speak and write about level-appropriate complex literary and informational texts and topics. 6. An ELL can analyze and critique the arguments of others orally and in writing. 9. An ELL can create clear and coherent level-appropriate speech and text. 10. An ELL can demonstrate command of the conventions of standard English to communicate in level-appropriate speech and writing.

Warm-up and Review
10–15 minutes (books closed)

Write on the board: *Money doesn't grow on trees. Time is money. Money is the root of all evil.* Elicit and discuss the meaning of each expression.

Introduction
5 minutes

1. Ask students if they know of sayings about money in their first language. Ask how they would translate the sayings into English.

2. State the objective: *Today we're going to read and write an essay about money.*

1 Prepare to write

Presentation
20–25 minutes

A 1. Build students' schema by asking questions. Ask: *What is an essay prompt?* [It's a question or assignment that writers use to base an essay on.] *What is the title?* [Money Can't Buy Happiness] *How is that connected to the prompt?* [You have to tell why you agree or disagree with it.] *How long is the essay supposed to be?* [125 words or less]

2. Give students one minute to tell a partner their responses to questions 1 and 2. Elicit responses from the class.

B 1. Elicit the meaning of *essay*. Ask students when they might have to write an essay. [in classes, on some tests]

2. Direct students to read the essay silently. Check comprehension. Ask: *What does Edwin say money can buy?* [free time, security, flexibility] *What does he say it can't buy?* [happiness, time, friends, love]

3. Play the audio. Have students read along silently.

4. Draw students' attention to the *Writer's Note*. Have students identify the purpose of each paragraph. [1 introduces topic, 2 gives details, 3 summarizes] Point out that we use the expressions *I think...* and *In my opinion...* in speaking because they "soften" our statement of opinion but that they are not necessary in writing.

Guided Practice I
10 minutes

C 1. Have students work independently to answer the questions and then compare answers with a partner.

2. Elicit answers from the class.

Possible Answers
1. comfortable lives, free time, security, and flexibility
2. money
3. family, friends, good news, kind words, a happy event

MULTILEVEL STRATEGIES

For 1C, challenge on- and higher-level students while working with pre-level students.

•**On- and Higher-level** Write additional questions on the board for these students to answer after they finish 1C: *Look at the things Edwin says can bring happiness. What else can bring happiness? Did he leave out anything important that money can buy?* After volunteers have put up the answers to 1C, ask these students to share their ideas about the additional questions.

2 Plan and write

Guided Practice II
15–20 minutes

A Read the questions. Elicit students' answers. Write students' ideas about how people have changed the world with and without money on the board.

B 1. Read the prompt aloud. Tell students that 125 words is about half of a double-spaced typewritten (12-point font) page.

2. Direct students to look back at the essay in 1B. Focus students' attention on the first sentence of each paragraph. Point out that this sentence tells the reader what the rest of the paragraph will be about. Direct students to look at the last sentence of the first paragraph. Point out that this sentence signals a transition to the next paragraph.

3. Tell students that when they take a writing test, it's a good idea to quickly brainstorm some ideas before they begin writing. Brainstorm ideas for the essay as a class using the topic provided.

4. Check comprehension of the exercise. Ask: *How many words do you need to write?* [about 125] *What do you have to write about?* [agree or disagree with the statement] Have students work individually to write their essays.

> **MULTILEVEL STRATEGIES**
>
> Adapt 2B to the level of your students.
>
> •**Pre-level** Direct these students to write one paragraph. Tell them to write if they agree or disagree with the statement and write three or four reasons for their opinion.

3 Get feedback and revise

Guided Practice III
5 minutes

A Direct students to check their writing using the editing checklist. Tell them to read each item in the list and check their essays before moving onto the next item. Explain that students should not edit their writing at this stage. They should just use the checklist to check their work and mark any areas they want to revise.

Communicative Practice
15 minutes

B 1. Read the instructions aloud. Emphasize to students that they are responding to their partners' work, not correcting it.

2. Use the essay in 1B to model the exercise. *I think the sentence that says, "However, many of these people…" shows that you have thought about both sides of the question. I'm not sure I understand the sentence…*

3. Direct students to exchange papers with a partner and follow the instructions.

C Allow students time to edit and revise their writing as necessary, using the editing checklist from 3A and their partner's feedback from 3B. If necessary, students could complete this task as homework.

> **TIP**
>
> After completing 3C, hold a debate in class. Ask for volunteers to come to the front of the room and agree or disagree with the statement and give reasons. All non-volunteers are "audience members." Ask the audience members to listen and take notes. Tell them they need to evaluate the arguments and decide which side won the debate.

Application and Evaluation
10 minutes

TEST YOURSELF

1. Read the instructions aloud. Assign a time limit (five minutes) and have students work independently.

2. Before collecting students' work, invite two or three volunteers to share their sentences. Ask students to raise their hands if they wrote similar answers.

> **MULTILEVEL STRATEGIES**
>
> Adapt the *Test Yourself* to the level of your students.
>
> •**Pre-level** Direct these students to work together to write sentences.

> **EXTENSION ACTIVITY**
> **Discussion**
>
> Talk about money and culture. Write these questions on the board: *In the U.S. and in your native country, is it polite to talk about how much things cost? Can you ask someone how much money they earn? When you go out to dinner with friends, who pays? If you divide the bill, how do you divide it? Do you think American attitudes toward money are different from attitudes toward money in your native country? If so, how are they different?* Put students in groups of three and ask them to discuss the questions. Ask a reporter from each group to share the group's ideas with the class.

LESSON 3 GRAMMAR

Lesson Overview

MULTILEVEL OBJECTIVES

On- and Higher-level: Use the present unreal conditional to discuss financial needs and goals

Pre-level: Recognize the present unreal conditional in discussions of financial needs and goals

LANGUAGE FOCUS

Grammar: Present unreal conditional (*If I had enough money, I could go to college now.*)

Vocabulary: Finance and budgeting

For vocabulary support, see these **Oxford Picture Dictionary** topics: The Bank, page 134; Money, page 26; Shopping, page 27

READINESS CONNECTION

In this lesson, students work with others to discuss spending using present unreal conditionals.

PACING

To compress this lesson: Conduct 2A and 2B as whole-class activities.

To extend this lesson: Have students converse freely using unreal conditionals. (See end of lesson.)

And/or have students complete **Workbook 4 pages 46–47**, **Multilevel Activities 4 Unit 7 pages 81–82**, and **Multilevel Grammar Exercises 4 Unit 7**.

Lesson Notes

CORRELATIONS

CCRS: SL.2.B Determine the main ideas and supporting details of a text read aloud or information presented in diverse media and formats, including visually, quantitatively, and orally.

R.1.B Ask and answer such questions as who, what, where, when, why, and how to demonstrate understanding of key details in a text.

L.1.B (l.) Produce simple, compound and complex sentences.

L.1.D (h.) Form and use verbs in the indicative, imperative, interrogative, conditional and subjunctive mood. (j.) Explain the function of phrases and clauses in general and their function in specific sentences.

L.2.C (d.) Use a comma to separate and introductory element from the rest of the sentence.

RF.4.B (a.) Read grade-level text with purpose and understanding.

ELPS: 2. An ELL can participate in level-appropriate oral and written exchanges of information, ideas, and analyses, in various social and academic contexts, responding to peer, audience, or reader comments and questions. 3. An ELL can speak and write about level-appropriate complex literary and informational texts and topics. 7. An ELL can adapt language choices to purpose, task, and audience when speaking and writing. 9. An ELL can create clear and coherent level-appropriate speech and text.

Warm-up and Review
10–15 minutes (books closed)

Write three things on the board that you want to do but can't do right now: *Visit China, remodel my kitchen, write a book.* Say: *I want to _____, but I can't because _____.* Ask students for examples of things they want to do but can't do right now. Write them on the board.

Introduction
5–10 minutes

1. Write two sentences on the board about the things you want to do using the unreal conditional: *If I had money, I would visit China. If I had time, I would write a book.* Underline *had* in each sentence. Say: *I don't have time, and I don't have money. I use* if *with a past-tense verb to show that I am talking about something that isn't true at the moment or is impossible. This form is called the unreal conditional.*

2. State the objective: *Today we're going to use the present unreal conditional to discuss our financial needs and goals.*

1 Use present unreal conditional statements

Presentation I
20–25 minutes

1. Direct students to look at the picture and conversation. Ask: *Who are these people?* [two women who work in a store] *What are they doing?* [hanging up clothes] *What are they thinking about?* [going to a cafe and lunch]

2. Read the instructions aloud. Ask students to read the conversation silently and answer the questions.

3. Read the first question aloud. Call on a volunteer for the answer. Ask the volunteer where in the conversation they found the answer. Read the rest of the questions aloud, calling on a different volunteer for each answer.

Answers
1. She wants Molly to go out for lunch with her. 2. No, she can't. 3. About $40. 4. Because she is saving for college.

1. Demonstrate how to read the grammar chart. Read each sentence aloud and have students repeat.

2. Check comprehension. Ask: *Does Molly have enough money now to go to college?* [no] *Does she have to wait?* [yes] *Does Isabel eat in the cafe?* [yes] Direct students to underline the present unreal conditional statements in the conversation in 1A. Write the statements on the board.

3. Ask: *Are these statements about the past or the present?* [present] *Do they describe something real or possible?* [no]

4. Ask students to identify the forms of the verb used in each clause. Elicit the form and write it on the board:

If clause: *If* + subject + simple past verb

Main clause: subject + *could/would* + simple form verb

Go over the *Grammar Note*. Have volunteers change the order of the clauses in the chart.

5. Assess students' understanding of the chart. Elicit unreal conditional sentences to talk about their ideas from the *Warm-up* on the board.

Answers
<u>If I didn't eat in the cafe every day</u>, I'd save about $40 a week. <u>If I had enough money</u>, I'd start today.

Guided Practice I
15–20 minutes

C 1. Tell students they will collaborate to complete the description of the grammar point. Model collaboration by working with the class to complete the first sentence. Encourage students to look at 1A and 1B to see if the situations are true/not true or possible/not possible.

2. Pair students and have them work together to complete the description.

3. Project or write the completed definition on the board and have pairs verify the accuracy of their responses. Ask volunteers which sentences confused them and discuss.

Answers
not true, not possible, if, main, simple past

> **MULTILEVEL STRATEGIES**
>
> For 1C, seat mixed-level students together.
>
> • **Pre-, On-, and Higher-level** Assign pre-level students the role of administrative assistant, on-level students the role of manager, and higher-level students the role of researcher. The administrative assistant fills in the blanks according to the team's decisions, the manager reads the description and manages the team's discussion, and the researcher looks up the definition of the grammar point online or checks against an answer key to verify the team's answers.

Guided Practice II
5–10 minutes

 Ask students to work individually to complete the sentences and then compare answers with a partner. Ask volunteers to write the answers on the board.

Answers
1. would be, limited
2. took, would save
3. opened, would be
4. would save, brought

 1. Have students form teams of three: manager, writer, editor. Confirm understanding of roles (manager keeps time, writer writes the corrected sentence, editor checks sentence for grammar and spelling accuracy). Set a time limit of five minutes.

2. Read each sentence aloud. Elicit the correct form of the verb. Ask students to write the corrected sentence.

Answers
1. Sunny would spend less money if she shopped at less expensive stores.
2. If she did that, she would be able to pay back her loan more quickly.
3. She could start this weekend if she wanted to.

> **TIP**
>
> After 1E, play a "chain" game. Have students stand in a circle. Write *If I had a million dollars, I would travel around the world.* on the board. Underline the second clause and elicit a new sentence that uses that clause as the condition. *If I traveled around the world, I would stop in Spain. If I stopped in Spain, I would go to the beach.* Have students continue the chain until you've gone around the circle.

2 Use present unreal conditional questions

Presentation II
20–25 minutes

 1. Introduce the new topic: *Now we're going to ask questions using the unreal conditional.*

2. Read each question and answer aloud and have students repeat.

3. Read the first *yes/no* question in the chart aloud and write it on the board. Elicit the form: *Could/Would* + subject + simple verb + *if* + subject + simple past verb…? Underline *could*. Write the answer on the board and elicit the form: *Yes*, subject + *could/would… No,* + subject + *couldn't/wouldn't…* Check comprehension of the chart. Repeat the process with the information questions, eliciting the form: *Wh-* question word + *could/would* + subject + simple verb + *if* + subject + simple past verb…?

4. Check comprehension of the chart. Ask: *Does Molly have to work?* [Yes, she does.] *Does your son want a credit card?* [No, he doesn't.] *Can you live anywhere?* [No, I can't.] *Can we use contractions in answers beginning with* yes? [no]

5. Use the verbs from the *Warm-up* to check comprehension. Write *Could you go to China if you didn't have to work?* on the board. Elicit answers. Practice with more verbs and phrases from the *Warm-up*.

6. Direct students to circle the correct words to complete the sentences. Ask volunteers to read the completed sentences aloud.

Answers	
1. had	2. walked

Guided Practice III
10–15 minutes

 Have students work with a partner to complete the questions and answers. Tell them to take turns reading the completed questions and answers aloud.

Answers
1. didn't need, would…keep, would
2. had, would…drive, wouldn't
3. could…save, didn't shop, could save
4. would…do, wanted, would make

> **MULTILEVEL STRATEGIES**
>
> After 2B, have students work in mixed-level groups to practice conditionals.
>
> Write a series of simple-present sentences on the board. *1. I don't have money. I can't buy a car. 2. I don't have a car. I can't drive to school. 3. I don't have a job. I can't save money.*
>
> Connect two of the ideas with the future conditional and the present unreal conditional. *If I have money, I'll buy a car. If I had money, I would buy a car.* Elicit the difference in meaning between the two sentences. [The first is a future possibility; the second talks about a situation that is not true in the present.]
>
> Write a question with each of the structures. *Will you buy a car if you have money? Would you buy a car if you had money?*
>
> Give each group a large sheet of paper. Tell students to work with their groups to write conditional sentences—first using the ideas on the board and then using their own ideas.
>
> •**Pre-level** Have these students label each of their partners' sentences future or unreal.
>
> •**On-level** Have these students write the sentences.
>
> •**Higher-level** Have these students write the questions.
>
> Have a reporter from each group read the group's sentences and questions to the class. Correct them together.

3 Listen for the present unreal conditionals to determine the meaning

Guided Practice IV
10–15 minutes

🔊 **2-25** 1. Say: *Now we're going to listen to people talk about their financial situations.*

2. Play the audio. Direct students to read along silently without writing.

3. Replay the audio. Ask students to circle the correct statements and then compare answers with a partner.

4. Go over the answers as a class. Check comprehension. Ask: *Where do you think they are?* [in a social situation] *How do you know?* [They talk about money and use informal language.]

Answers
1. b
2. a
3. a
4. a

> **MULTILEVEL STRATEGIES**
>
> Replay the audio to allow pre-level students to catch up while you challenge on- and higher-level students.
>
> •**Pre-level** Have these students listen again to circle the correct statements.
>
> •**On- and Higher-level** Have these students write one or two of the sentences they hear.

4 Use the present unreal conditionals to talk about your ideas

Communicative Practice and Application
20–25 minutes

A 1. Direct students to work independently to complete the questions and then compare questions with a partner.

2. Call on volunteers to share their sentences, correcting grammar as necessary. Establish the correct answers for each sentence.

Answers
1. had, would you spend
2. would you do, had
3. could make, would you change

B Direct students to work with a partner to write two more questions using present unreal conditionals.

C 1. Have pairs merge to form teams of four. Model the exercise by "joining" one of the pairs. Each pair takes a turn asking and answering questions while the class listens.

2. Check comprehension of the exercise. Ask: *Who asks questions?* [everyone] *Who answers questions?* [everyone]

3. Ask volunteers to share something interesting they learned about their classmates.

> **MULTILEVEL STRATEGIES**
>
> After 4C, provide more practice with present unreal conditionals for all levels.
>
> • **Pre-level** Have these students use these sentence frames to write six sentences: *I would _____ if I _____. If you _____, could you _____? Where would you _____ if _____?*
>
> • **On-level** Have these students write one question with a present unreal conditional. Direct them to ask each other their questions and write their partners' short answers.
>
> • **Higher-level** Have these students write one question with an unreal conditional. Direct them to ask one follow-up information question for each *yes/no* question. Have them take notes on their partners' answers. Have volunteers from each group share their work with the class.

Evaluation
10–15 minutes

TEST YOURSELF

Ask students to write the sentences independently. Collect and correct their writing.

> **MULTILEVEL STRATEGIES**
>
> Target the *Test Yourself* to the level of your students.
>
> • **Pre-level** Provide sentence frames for these students to complete.
>
> *1. If (name) had $100 to spend on our class, she would _____.*
>
> *2. If (name) had $1,000 to spend on our school, he would _____.*
>
> *3. If (name) could make one change to our school, (name) would _____.*
>
> • **Higher-level** Have these students include an explanation of their choices.

> **EXTENSION ACTIVITY**
> **Discussion**
>
> Encourage free conversation with conditionals.
>
> 1. Write *What would you do if_____?* on the board. Elicit several endings for the question.
>
> 2. Direct students to walk around the room asking and answering different versions of the question.

LESSON 4 EVERYDAY CONVERSATION

Lesson Overview

MULTILEVEL OBJECTIVES

Pre-, On-, and Higher-level: Negotiate and compromise on a budget and listen for financial-planning information

LANGUAGE FOCUS

Grammar: Present unreal conditional with *be*

Vocabulary: *Negotiate, compromise,* financial-planning vocabulary

For vocabulary support, see these **Oxford Picture Dictionary** topics: The Bank, page 134; Money, page 26; Shopping, page 27

STRATEGY FOCUS

Practice asking for more detail.

READINESS CONNECTION

In this lesson, students listen actively and understand budgets.

PACING

To compress this lesson: Conduct *Discuss* as a whole-class activity.

To extend this lesson: Have students practice more with conditionals. (See end of lesson.)

And/or have students complete **Workbook 4 page 48** and **Multilevel Activities 4 Unit 7 page 83**.

Lesson Notes

CORRELATIONS

CCRS: SL.1.B (a.) Come to discussions prepared, having read or studied required material; explicitly draw on that preparation and other information known about the topic to explore ideas under discussion. (b.) Follow agreed-upon rules for discussions. (c.) Ask questions to check understanding of information presented, stay on topic, and link their comments to the remarks of others. (d.) Explain their own ideas and understanding in light of the discussion.

SL.2.B Determine the main ideas and supporting details of a text read aloud or information presented in diverse media and formats, including visually, quantitatively, and orally.

SL.4.B Report on a topic or text, tell a story, or recount an experience with appropriate facts and relevant, descriptive details, speaking clearly at an understandable pace.

SL.6.B Speak in complete sentences when appropriate to task and situation in order to provide requested detail or clarification.

R.1.B Ask and answer such questions as who, what, where, when, why, and how to demonstrate understanding of key details in a text.

R.2.A Identify the main topic and retell key details of a text.

R.6.B Identify the main purpose of a text, including what the author wants to answer, explain, or describe.

R.7.B Use information gained from illustrations and the words in a text to demonstrate understanding of the text.

L.1.B (l.) Produce simple, compound and complex sentences.

L.1.D (h.) Form and use verbs in the indicative, imperative, interrogative, conditional and subjunctive mood.

L.2.C (d.) Use a comma to separate and introductory element from the rest of the sentence.

L.3.B (b.) Recognize and observe differences between the conventions of spoken and written standard English.

L.6.B Use words and phrases acquired through conversations, reading and being read to, and responding to texts, including using adjectives and adverbs to describe.

RF.4.B (a.) Read grade-level text with purpose and understanding.

ELPS: 2. An ELL can participate in level-appropriate oral and written exchanges of information, ideas, and analyses, in various social and academic contexts, responding to peer, audience, or reader comments and questions. 4. An ELL can construct level-appropriate oral and written claims and support them with reasoning and evidence. 7. An ELL can adapt language choices to purpose, task, and audience when speaking and writing. 9. An ELL can create clear and coherent level-appropriate speech and text. 10. An ELL can demonstrate command of the conventions of standard English to communicate in level-appropriate speech and writing.

Warm-up and Review
10–15 minutes (books closed)

Write *Entertainment* on the board and elicit students' ideas for things they spend money on—for example, cable TV, movies, Internet, magazines, dancing, music downloads, restaurants, video games.

Introduction
5 minutes

1. Ask students if they think they spend a lot of money on entertainment. Point out that this is one area of the budget that people often cut when they need to save money.

2. State the objective: *Today we're going to learn to negotiate and compromise on a budget.*

1 Learn ways to negotiate and compromise on a budget

Presentation I
10–20 minutes

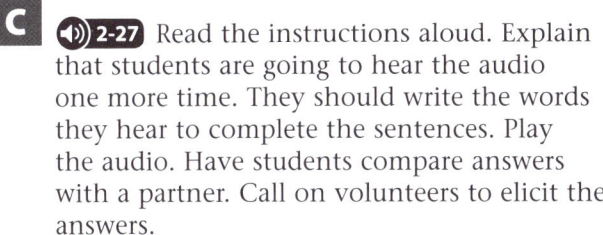

A 🔊 2-26 1. Direct students to look at the picture. Build students' schema by asking: *Who do you see?* [Julia and Roberto] *What is she thinking about?* [Roberto's coffee] *What is he thinking about?* [Julia's lunch] *What do you think they are talking about?* [spending money]

2. Read the instructions aloud. Play the audio. Give students a minute to answer the question. Go over the answer as a class.

Possible Answer
They are trying to buy a house.

Guided Practice I
20–25 minutes

 🔊 2-26 1. Read the instructions aloud. Have students read the questions. Play the audio. Ask students to listen for the answers to each question.

2. Ask students to compare their answers with a partner. Circulate and monitor to ensure students understand the audio.

Answers
1. $250
2. They spend $300 a month now. Julia suggests $200 and Roberto suggests $250 because he wants to be able to buy fresh fruits and vegetables. They compromise on $250.
3. Roberto agrees to stop buying coffee on the way to work. Julia agrees to stop buying lunch at work.
4. It means "We agree."

C 🔊 2-27 Read the instructions aloud. Explain that students are going to hear the audio one more time. They should write the words they hear to complete the sentences. Play the audio. Have students compare answers with a partner. Call on volunteers to elicit the answers.

Answers
1. How about if we made it
2. what if I made
3. how about if you

2 Practice your pronunciation

Pronunciation Extension
10–15 minutes

A 🔊 2-28 1. Write *If I were you, I'd study the vocabulary tonight.* on the board. Say the sentence and ask students to repeat it. Ask them to identify the pause. Say: *Now we're going to focus on pausing when we see a comma.*

2. Play the audio. Direct students to listen for the pauses.

B 🔊 2-29 1. Tell students to read each sentence and circle the comma. Have the students practice saying the sentences.

2. Play the audio. Tell students to listen and check the pauses.

C 🔊 2-29 Play the audio again. Ask students to take turns reading the sentences in 2B with a partner. Monitor and provide feedback.

3 Use present unreal conditionals with *be*

Presentation II and Guided Practice II
10–15 minutes

 1. Introduce the new topic: *Now we're going to talk about unreal conditionals using* be.

2. Direct students to look at the picture. Build students' schema by asking: *Where are they?* [car dealership] *Who do you see?* [a man and his son and a third person] Read the instructions aloud. Call on volunteers to answer the question.

3. Read the *Grammar Note* aloud. Write *If I were the president, I would____.* on the board. Provide your own completion. Call on volunteers and ask them to complete the sentence. Write their ideas on the board in the third person. *If (Ana) were the president, she would declare a few more holidays.*

Guided Practice III
15–20 minutes

 1. Have students work individually to complete the sentences with *were* or *weren't* and then compare answers with a partner. Go over the answers as a class. Ask volunteers to write the sentences on the board.

Answers	
1. were	3. weren't
2. weren't	4. were

> **MULTILEVEL STRATEGIES**
>
> Seat mixed-level students together for 3B.
>
> • **Pre-level** Focus on the meaning of the sentences. Elicit the real situation for each sentence. [The car isn't cheaper, the car is old, the salesman is listening, you are not Jason.] Explain that the unreal conditional expresses the opposite situation. Allow students to copy the answers from the board.
>
> • **Higher-level** Direct these students to write two more sentences using *were* or *weren't* to talk about Jason's situation using their own ideas.

4 Building conversation skills

Guided Practice IV
15–20 minutes

 Direct students to look at the picture. Build students' schema by asking: *Who do you see?* [three people, maybe landscapers] *What are they doing?* [landscaping, talking, using a wheelbarrow] Have students skim the conversation. Have them work with partners to identify the purpose of the conversation. Elicit responses and ask: *How do you know?* or *Why do you say that?* to encourage students to state their reasoning.

Possible Answer
The purpose of the conversation is to agree on how to do their work. They are looking at a plan together and discussing it, and they are giving their ideas about how they can get the work done.

B 🔊 **2-30** 1. Ask students to read the instructions and tell you what they are going to do [listen and read and respond to the question]. Play the audio and then elicit the answer to the question.

2. Ask students to read the conversation with a partner. Circulate and monitor pronunciation. Model and have students repeat difficult words or phrases.

3. Ask: *In what other situation could you use this conversation?* Point out a few phrases that are not specific to a landscaping job. Ask volunteers to point out others.

Answer
Because they need more help.

Communicative Practice and Application I
15–20 minutes

 1. Pair students and have them read the instructions silently. Check their comprehension of the exercise. Ask: *What are the two roles?* [manager and team leader] *What is the conversation about?* [moving boxes]

2. Model and have students repeat the expressions in the *In Other Words* box. Explain that they should use these expressions in their conversations.

3. Draw a T-chart on the board. Label the left column *Manager* and the right column *Team leader*. Elicit examples of what each person might say and make notes on the chart.

4. Set a time limit (three minutes). Have students act out the role-play. Call "time" and have students switch roles.

5. Ask three volunteer pairs to act out their role-play for the class. Tell students who are listening to make a simple table with four rows and two columns. Use the top row to label the columns: *Manager's suggestions* and *Team leader's suggestions*. Have students take notes in the chart for each role-play.

> **MULTILEVEL STRATEGIES**
>
> For 4C, adapt the role-play to the level of your students.
>
> • **Pre-level** Provide these students with sentence frames.
>
> A: We need to _____.
> B: I agree. Let's have _____ and then _____.
> A: What if we _____?
> B: OK; sounds good. But it would be better if _____.
> A: Great. It's a deal. _____.

5 Focus on listening for details

Presentation and Guided Practice
20–25 minutes

A 1. Read the question aloud and model a discussion with a volunteer. Ask: *What advice would you give a friend who wants to save money? … Why?*

2. Pair students and tell them to discuss their own answers to the question. Circulate and monitor.

B 🔊 **2-31** Have students predict what they will hear. If students struggle, start by offering your own prediction: *I think we will hear about someone who is having financial problems.* Play the audio. Elicit the answers to the questions.

> **Answers**
> 1. She is a credit counselor.
> 2. His problem is credit-card debt.

> **TIP**
>
> Use this focused listening exercise as a launching point for a discussion of credit-card debt. Ask: *Why do you think Mr. Moreno got into so much debt?* Discuss credit-card interest rates and ways that credit-card companies encourage people to go into debt—for example, offering no-interest for the first three months, offering cash loans, etc. Use credit-card advertisements for a lesson in "reading the fine print."

C 🔊 **2-31** 1. Direct students to read the sentences before they listen again.

2. Replay the audio and have students work individually to choose the correct answers and then compare answers with a partner. Take a tally of responses for each item and if students disagree on a response, replay the audio so they can check their answers.

Answers	
1. b	4. a
2. a	5. b
3. b	6. b

> **MULTILEVEL STRATEGIES**
>
> After 5C, replay the conversation to challenge on- and higher-level students while allowing pre-level students to catch up.
>
> •**Pre-level** Have these students listen again to go over their answers.
>
> •**On- and Higher-level** Write these questions on the board and tell these students to listen for the answers. *How much does Mr. Moreno spend on entertainment? How can he lower his energy costs and his phone bill?*

6 Discuss

Communicative Practice and Application II
15–20 minutes

A 1. Read the instructions aloud. Draw a sample chart on the board with space for ways to save money on one side and details/explanations on the other. Call on volunteers to read the sample sentences in 6A. Fill in the chart, writing *shopping at the farmer's market* on one side. Elicit details and explanations for the right [buy only what you want, only things in season]. Explain that students will make a chart like this one based on their own discussions.

2. Put students into teams of four and assign roles: reporter, manager, administrative assistant, and researcher. Verify students' understanding of the roles. Encourage students to use the phrases in the *Speaking Note* during their discussions.

3. Set a time limit for the discussions (ten minutes). Write the sentence frame from 6B on the board. Then circulate and monitor.

B Call "time." Ask the reporter for each team to report the results of their team's discussion, using the sentence frame on the board.

Evaluation
5 minutes

TEST YOURSELF

1. Ask students to complete the checkboxes individually.

2. Tell students that you are going to read each of the items in the checklist aloud. If they are not at all confident with that skill, they should hold up a closed fist. If they are not very confident, they should hold up one finger. If they are somewhat confident, two fingers; confident, three fingers; very confident, four fingers. If they think they could teach the skill, they should hold up five fingers. Read each item in the checklist and identify students that may need further support.

TIP

For homework, you could ask students to write a sentence or two about what discussion skills they still need to work on or, if they are confident in all of the skills, what skill they are most proud of.

EXTENSION ACTIVITY

Provide more practice with conditionals.

1. Put students in mixed-level groups. Give each group a large sheet of paper and tell them to write three to five *if* clauses for conditional sentences. Direct them to leave spaces for others to complete the sentences. Tell them not to repeat any ideas.

2. Have each group pass the paper to another group. Tell the groups to complete the sentences. Have a reporter from each group read the completed sentences aloud.

LESSON 5 READING

Lesson Overview

MULTILEVEL OBJECTIVES

On-, Pre-, and Higher-level: Read about and discuss financial planning

LANGUAGE FOCUS

Grammar: Simple past and present perfect (*My mother taught me about saving money. I have learned to limit my spending.*)

Vocabulary: *Advise, equivalent, intimidating, expenditures*

For vocabulary support, see these **Oxford Picture Dictionary** topics: The Bank, page 134; Money, page 26; Shopping, page 27

STRATEGY FOCUS

When writing, use evidence and reasons to support specific points you want to make.

READINESS CONNECTION

In this lesson, students decide why it is important to save money.

PACING

To compress this lesson: Conduct the word study in 2A as a whole-class activity.

To extend this lesson: Have students role-play a financial planner and customer. (See end of lesson.)

And/or have students complete **Workbook 4 page 49** and **Multilevel Activities 4 Unit 7 pages 84–85**.

Lesson Notes

CORRELATIONS

CCRS: SL.1.B (a.) Come to discussions prepared, having read or studied required material; explicitly draw on that preparation and other information known about the topic to explore ideas under discussion. (b.) Follow agreed-upon rules for discussions. (c.) Ask questions to check understanding of information presented, stay on topic, and link their comments to the remarks of others. (d.) Explain their own ideas and understanding in light of the discussion.

SL.2.B Determine the main ideas and supporting details of a text read aloud or information presented in diverse media and formats, including visually, quantitatively, and orally.

SL.6.B Speak in complete sentences when appropriate to task and situation in order to provide requested detail or clarification.

R.1.B Ask and answer such questions as who, what, where, when, why, and how to demonstrate understanding of key details in a text.

R.1.C Refer to details and examples in a text when explaining what the text says explicitly and when drawing inferences from the text.

R.2.B Determine the main idea of a text; recount the key details and explain how they support the main idea.

R.4.B Determine the meaning of general academic and domain-specific words and phrases in a text relevant to a topic or subject area.

R.5.B Know and use various text features to locate key facts or information in a text efficiently.

R.6.B Identify the main purpose of a text, including what the author wants to answer, explain, or describe.

R.7.C Interpret information presented visually, orally, or quantitatively and explain how the information contributes to an understanding of the text in which it appears.

W.8.B Recall information from experiences or gather information from print and digital sources; take brief notes on sources and sort evidence into provided categories.

L.1.B (l.) Produce simple, compound and complex sentences.

L.4.B (e.) Use glossaries and beginning dictionaries, both print and digital, to determine or clarify the meaning of words and phrases.

L.5.B (a.) Distinguish the literal and non-literal meanings of words and phrases in context.

RF.4.B (a.) Read grade-level text with purpose and understanding.

ELPS: 1. An ELL can construct meaning from oral presentations and literary and informational text through level-appropriate listening, reading, and viewing. 3. An ELL can speak and write about level-appropriate complex literary and informational texts and topics.

Warm-up and Review
10–15 minutes (books closed)

Tell students about something you are saving money for. Ask: *Are you saving for anything? What are you saving for? What are some things that people often save for?* Write their ideas on the board.

Introduction
5 minutes

1. Say: *Some of the things we want are too expensive for us to buy easily. In order to save for them, we have to have a plan.*

2. State the objective: *Today we're going to read about financial planning.*

1 Read

Presentation
10–20 minutes

A Read the questions aloud. Elicit ideas from the class.

B Read the words and definitions. Elicit sample sentences for each word or supply them if the students can't. Write the sentences on the board, providing help with the grammar.

Pre-reading

C 1. Read the instructions aloud and confirm that students understand where the "headings" are. Have students answer the question individually and then check answers with a partner. Go over the answer with the class. If any students answer incorrectly, ask them to support their answer using the headings. Establish the correct answer.

2. Read the *Reader's Note* aloud. Ask: *What should you look for when you evaluate the strength of a writer's position?* [arguments, reasoning, evidence]

Answer
The writer's purpose is to inform readers about ways to save money to reach goals.

Guided Practice: While Reading
20–30 minutes

D 1. Ask students to read the article silently and answer the question and then compare answers with a partner.

2. Check answers with the class.

3. Check comprehension. Ask: *Who does the writer talk about?* [her grandmother] *What is an example of a big-ticket item?* [a new home, a car] *What's the first step in financial planning?* [make a record of your income and expenses] *How much should you save?* [10 percent] *Why is it better to save your money in a bank?* [It earns interest.]

TIP
Have students go online to find out about interest rates at banks in your area. If you have access to the Internet in class, show students an online compound interest calculator. (You can find one by typing "compound interest calculator" into a search engine.) Students can plug in the current principal, annual addition, years to grow, and interest rate. The calculator will show them how much they can save over time.

MULTILEVEL STRATEGIES

Adapt 1D to the level of your students.

- **Pre-level** Provide these students with a summary of the ideas in the reading. *Financial planning means deciding how to use your money. The first step is to make a record of your income and expenses. Keep track of your spending for a month. Next, decide how much you can save. Ms. Ogun recommends saving ten percent of your take-home pay. It's a good idea to save your money in a bank. The chart shows you how much you make if you save one dollar a day in a bank with 2% interest. You should try to keep three to six months' living expenses in a savings account.*

Direct these students to read the summary while other students are reading 1D.

- **On- and Higher-level** Pair students and have them read the article aloud to each other, taking turns to read each paragraph.

Guided Practice: Rereading
10–15 minutes

E 1. Provide an opportunity for students to extract evidence from the text. Have students reread the article and underline the three points the writer wants to make. Suggest they highlight reasoning and evidence.

2. Pair students and tell them to compare the points they underlined and report anything they disagree on. Discuss and clarify as needed.

F 1. Have students work individually to complete the sentences and then compare answers with a partner. Write the answers on the board.

2. Elicit and discuss any additional questions about the reading. You could introduce new questions for class discussion: *Which suggestions do you think are the most helpful? Why do some people not use banks?*

Answers
1. economy
2. big-ticket; home/car/college tuition/retirement
3. take-home pay
4. interest
5. living expenses

2 Word study

Guided Practice: Post-reading
10 minutes

 1. Direct students to look at the chart and identify the topic (figurative language). Have students read the chart.

2. Say: *The literal meaning of "big-ticket item" is a large ticket. The figurative or non-literal meaning is a very expensive item.* Elicit the difference between literal and figurative. [Literal means exactly what it says and figurative has a meaning different than the literal meaning.]

3. Have students repeat after you as you say each phrase with natural intonation, rhythm, and stress.

4. Direct students to complete the sentences and then compare answers with a partner. Read the correct answers and have students check their work.

Answers
1. first step
2. big-ticket item
3. makes the world go around
4. a rainy day

> **TIP**
> Direct students to work individually to write a sentence for each phrase. Ask volunteers to write their sentences on the board. Have the rest of the class suggest grammar and spelling edits as needed.

 1. Read the instructions and questions aloud. Model the first item. Tell the class about a big-ticket item you would like to have and the steps you are taking to make that happen.

2. Have students work individually to answer the questions and then compare answers with a partner.

3. Elicit answers from the class. Call on volunteers to tell the class about one of their partner's answers.

3 Talk it over

Guided Practice
15–20 minutes

 1. Have students look at the pie chart and read the note. Point out that they need to use the information from the chart and the note to complete the sentences. Set a time limit (ten minutes). Have students work in pairs to complete the task. Ask volunteers to share their answers with the class.

2. Check comprehension of the pie chart and text. *What percent of food spending was spent at restaurants?* [5.1 percent] *What percent of spending is apparel?* [3.1 percent] *What rose faster than other prices in the U.S. economy from 2004 to 2013?* [retail food prices]

Answers	
1. housing	3. 64–65
2. education and reading	4. restaurants

Communicative Practice
20 minutes

 1. Read the questions aloud. Set a time limit (ten minutes). Allow students to think about the questions and then write their answers in the chart in their books or by drawing a new chart in their notebooks.

2. Have students interview two other students and write their answers in the chart.

 Ask volunteers to share their ideas with the class.

Application

5–10 minutes

BRING IT TO LIFE

Ask students to brainstorm ways their school could save money. Ask volunteers to share their ideas. Have the class choose one of the ideas and brainstorm a plan for putting it into action.

EXTENSION ACTIVITY

Role-play

Role-play a financial planner and customer.

1. Divide the class in half: A students and B students.

2. Tell the A students they are going to be financial planners and ask them to work with a partner to write five questions that they will ask their customers. They should ask about income and spending habits.

3. Tell the B students that they are the customers. They make plenty of money, but they have very bad spending habits and are in debt. Direct them to write down their (imaginary) income and living expenses. Tell them to think of excuses for their bad spending habits. *I have to eat in restaurants every day—I don't know how to cook!*

4. Have the A students meet with B students and ask their questions. The B students should respond with the information they have invented. Tell the A students to give advice.

5. Ask several volunteer pairs to perform their role-plays for the class.

AT WORK

Warm-up and Review
10–15 minutes (books closed)

Have students give ideas on the best ways to spend $100 on the classroom. Have the class vote on the best idea. Tell the class that another way to decide is to reach a consensus where everyone can agree on the decision.

Introduction
5 minutes

State the objective: *Today we're going to talk about building consensus.*

Presentation
5 minutes

 2-32 Read the instructions aloud. Play the audio. Give students a minute to think about the question. Elicit responses from the class.

Possible Answer
The man and woman are talking to a financial advisor about their small business/bakery and their ideas about expanding.

Guided Practice
10–15 minutes

B 2-32 Play the audio again. Direct students to listen for each problem and put a check next to any that they hear mentioned.

Answers
Check: they don't know how much money they have
they don't agree on expanding the business
they don't have a written budget

C 2-32 Read the instructions aloud. Play the audio again, encouraging students to take notes in their notebooks before they complete the sentences. Set a time limit (five minutes) for students to discuss their answers with a partner. Circulate and monitor.

Answers
1. a plan, a (written) budget
2. expand/open a second location
3. a. make a list of all of their monthly expenses
b. look at the Small Business Administration website
c. collect their financial paperwork
d. think about their (short-term and long-term) goals for their business

Presentation and Communicative Practice
10 minutes

 1. Direct students' attention to the *Do/Say* chart and ask them to identify the lesson's soft skill [building consensus]. Ask the class which column has examples of language [right] and which has examples of behaviors [left].

2. Say a phrase from the left and act it out. Say it again and have the class act it out with you. Say it a third time and have the class act it out for you. Ask: *How can you make sure you look at everyone equally?* Elicit ideas.

3. Model the sentence frames from the right using authentic intonation. Have students practice imitating your inflection.

4. Put students in teams of four and assign each team a question. Assign roles: reporter, manager, administrative assistant, and researcher. (Researchers will ask you questions on behalf of the team.) Verify understanding of the roles. Set a time limit (five minutes) and monitor.

5. Write sentence frames on the board that teams can use to summarize their response. *Our team discussed the following question:_____. We decided _____ because_____.*

6. Call "time" and let reporters rehearse their report for one minute. Direct each reporter to present to three other teams.

Communicative Practice and Application
20–25 minutes

E 1. Tell students that they are going to be role-playing a business partners' meeting where they will plan a company party. Read the instructions aloud. Ask volunteers to model the conversation.

2. Direct groups to come up with three advantages and three disadvantages. Each group should select a manager to run the meeting. The other three members should each choose an advantage and disadvantage to discuss.

3. As students carry out the role-play, circulate and monitor. Provide global feedback once the activity ends.

TEAMWORK & LANGUAGE REVIEW

Lesson Overview

MULTILEVEL OBJECTIVES

On-, Pre-, and Higher-level: Expand upon and review unit grammar and life skills

LANGUAGE FOCUS

Grammar: Present unreal conditionals (*If he saved every month, he would have money for emergencies.*)

Vocabulary: Financial-planning vocabulary

For vocabulary support, see these **Oxford Picture Dictionary** topics: The Bank, page 134; Money, page 26; Shopping, page 27

READINESS CONNECTION

In this review, students work together to solve a money problem.

PACING

To extend this review: Have students complete **Workbook 4 page 50, Multilevel Activities 4 Unit 7 page 86**, and **Multilevel Grammar Exercises 4 Unit 7**.

Lesson Notes

CORRELATIONS

CCRS: SL.1.B (a.) Come to discussions prepared, having read or studied required material; explicitly draw on that preparation and other information known about the topic to explore ideas under discussion. (b.) Follow agreed-upon rules for discussions. (c.) Ask questions to check understanding of information presented, stay on topic, and link their comments to the remarks of others. (d.) Explain their own ideas and understanding in light of the discussion.

SL.1.C (b.) Follow agreed-upon rules for discussions and carry out assigned roles.

SL.2.B Determine the main ideas and supporting details of a text read aloud or information presented in diverse media and formats, including visually, quantitatively, and orally.

SL.4.B Report on a topic or text, tell a story, or recount an experience with appropriate facts and relevant, descriptive details, speaking clearly at an understandable pace.

R.1.B Ask and answer such questions as who, what, where, when, why, and how to demonstrate understanding of key details in a text.

R.2.A Identify the main topic and retell key details of a text.

R.7.B Use information gained from illustrations and the words in a text to demonstrate understanding of the text.

L.1.B (l.) Produce simple, compound and complex sentences.

L.1.C (d.) Use modal auxiliaries to convey various conditions.

RF.4.B (a.) Read grade-level text with purpose and understanding.

ELPS: 1. An ELL can construct meaning from oral presentations and literary and informational text through level-appropriate listening, reading, and viewing. 2. An ELL can participate in level-appropriate oral and written exchanges of information, ideas, and analyses, in various social and academic contexts, responding to peer, audience, or reader comments and questions. 9. An ELL can create clear and coherent level-appropriate speech and text. 10. An ELL can demonstrate command of the conventions of standard English to communicate in level-appropriate speech and writing.

Warm-up and Review
10–15 minutes (books closed)

1. Review *At Work* activity E.

2. Ask students to share the good, not-so-good, and interesting things that happened during the role-play. As students speak, write their responses in a chart on the board.

Introduction and Presentation
5 minutes

1. Pair students and direct them to look at the picture in their book. Ask them to describe what they see to their partner.

2. Ask volunteer pairs to share their ideas with the class.

Guided Practice
15–20 minutes

 1. Read the instructions aloud. Put students in teams of four.

2. Set a time limit (five minutes). Have students work in teams to complete the activity. Ask volunteers to share their ideas with the class.

Answers			
1. a	2. b	3. a	4. a

 1. Have students look at the picture. Ask: *Who do you see?* [a couple, a bank employee] *Where are they?* [a bank]

2. Read the instructions aloud. Have students work in teams to complete the conversation.

3. Go over the answers with the class. Have students practice the conversation in their teams, rotating roles.

Answers	
1. you opened	10. (answers will vary)
2. I would give you	11. (answers will vary)
3. we put	12. you kept
4. (answers will vary)	13. (answers will vary)
5. (answers will vary)	14. would be free
6. would we have	15. we opened
7. (answers will vary)	16. would we get
8. you deposited	17. (answers will vary)
9. you would earn	

Communicative Practice
30–40 minutes

 1. Group students and assign roles: writer, editor, director, and actors. Explain that students are going to work with their teams to write and perform a role-play.

2. Read steps 2–4 of the activity aloud. Check comprehension of the task. *What is the first thing you should do?* [choose ideas from the list] *How many people are in the role-play?* [two]

3. Set a time limit (ten minutes) to complete the exercise. Have writers help write the role-play and the directors stage the role-play. Circulate and answer any questions.

4. Have actors from each team perform their role-play for the class. Have editors fix any errors from the performance.

D 1. Have students walk around the room to conduct the interviews. To get students moving, tell them to interview three people who were not in their team for C.

2. Set a time limit (five minutes) to complete the exercise.

3. Tell students to make a note of their classmates' answers but not to worry about writing complete sentences.

> **MULTILEVEL STRATEGIES**
>
> Adapt the mixer in D to the level of your students.
>
> • **Pre- and On-level** Pair these students and have them interview other pairs together.
>
> • **Higher-level** Have these students ask an additional question and write all answers.

 1. Call on individuals to report what they learned about their classmates. Keep a running tally on the board for each question, marking how many students are spenders vs. savers, motivations to save money, and best advice.

2. Use your tally for question 1 to create a pie chart as a class on the board.

PROBLEM SOLVING
10–15 minutes

A  1. Ask: *Do you have any friends with bad financial habits?* Tell students they will read a story about a woman who has a friend with money problems. Direct students to read Lula's story silently.

2. Ask: *What are Adele's bad habits?* [She buys expensive clothes, food, and gifts. She goes out to eat a lot.]

3. Play the audio and have students read along silently.

 1. Elicit answers to question 1.

2. Put students into groups of three or four. Ask each group to think of two or three possible solutions to Lula's problems and report them to the class. Ask a volunteer to write all possible solutions on the board.

3. Have students discuss the consequences of each idea. Call on volunteers to share their ideas with the class.

Possible Answer
Lula's best friend, Adele, isn't careful with her money. She spends a lot of money and Lula doesn't think she saves any money. Lula is worried about her.

Evaluation
20–25 minutes

To test students' understanding of the unit language and content, have them take the Unit 7 Test, available on the Teacher Resource Center.

UNIT 8 Satisfaction Guaranteed

Unit Overview

This unit explores shopping and purchase problems with a range of employability skills and contextualizes adjectives and adverbs.

KEY OBJECTIVES

Lesson 1	Identify shopping choices
Lesson 2	Write an email to complain about purchase problems
Lesson 3	Use adjectives ending in *-ed* and *-ing*
Lesson 4	Use *so* and *such* to describe items and experiences
Lesson 5	Identify agencies and organizations that inform and protect consumers
At Work	Help teammates participate at work
Teamwork & Language Review	Review unit language

UNIT FEATURES

Academic Vocabulary	*consumer, contract, evaluate, final, monitor, network, potentially, regulate*
Employability Skills	• Listen actively • Understand teamwork • Communicate information • Work with others • Cooperate with others • Convey information in writing • Interpret a pie chart and a note • Determine how to complain about a yard sale purchase

Resources	**Class Audio** CD2, Tracks 34–44
	Workbook Unit 8, pages 51–57
	Teacher Resource Center
	    Multilevel Activities 4 Unit 8
	    Multilevel Grammar Exercises 4 Unit 8
	    Unit 8 Test
	Oxford Picture Dictionary Shopping, Feelings

LESSON 1 VOCABULARY

Lesson Overview

MULTILEVEL OBJECTIVES

On-level: Describe and talk about shopping and problems with purchases

Pre-level: Identify shopping vocabulary and describe problems with purchases

Higher-level: Talk and write about shopping and problems with purchases

LANGUAGE FOCUS

Grammar: Adjectives (*It's faded.*)

Vocabulary: Shopping and problems with purchases

For vocabulary support, see this **Oxford Picture Dictionary** topic: Shopping, page 27

READINESS CONNECTION

In this lesson, students understand teamwork by conducting research on purchases.

PACING

To compress this lesson: Conduct 1D as a whole-class activity.

To extend this lesson: Have students write and role-play returning items. (See end of lesson.)

And/or have students complete **Workbook 4 page 51** and **Multilevel Activities 4 Unit 8 pages 88–89**.

Lesson Notes

CORRELATIONS

CCRS: SL.1.B (b.) Follow agreed-upon rules for discussions. (c.) Ask questions to check understanding of information presented, stay on topic, and link their comments to the remarks of others. (d.) Explain their own ideas and understanding in light of the discussion.

SL.2.B Determine the main ideas and supporting details of a text read aloud or information presented in diverse media and formats, including visually, quantitatively, and orally.

SL.4.B Report on a topic or text, tell a story, or recount an experience with appropriate facts and relevant, descriptive details, speaking clearly at an understandable pace.

SL.6.B Speak in complete sentences when appropriate to task and situation in order to provide requested detail or clarification.

R.4.B Determine the meaning of general academic and domain-specific words and phrases in a text relevant to a topic or subject area.

W.7.A Participate in shared research and writing projects.

L.1.B (l.) Produce simple, compound and complex sentences.

L.4.B (a.) Use sentence-level context as a clue to the meaning of a word or phrase. (e.) Use glossaries and beginning dictionaries, both print and digital, to determine or clarify the meaning of words and phrases.

L.6.B Use words and phrases acquired through conversations, reading and being read to, and responding to texts, including using adjectives and adverbs to describe.

RF.4.B (a.) Read grade-level text with purpose and understanding.

ELPS: 1. An ELL can construct meaning from oral presentations and literary and informational text through level-appropriate listening, reading, and viewing. 2. An ELL can participate in level-appropriate oral and written exchanges of information, ideas, and analyses, in various social and academic contexts, responding to peer, audience, or reader comments and questions. 5. An ELL can conduct research and evaluate and communicate findings to answer questions or solve problems. 7. An ELL can adapt language choices to purpose, task, and audience when speaking and writing. 8. An ELL can determine the meaning of words and phrases in oral presentation and literary and informational text.

Warm-up and Review
10–15 minutes (books closed)

Elicit items that students have returned to the store. Write the items on the board. Put them into categories—for example, household items and clothing.

Introduction
5 minutes

1. Ask volunteers to explain where they bought the items on the board and why they returned them.

2. State the objective: *Today we're going to learn words for shopping and describe problems with purchases.*

1 Identify shopping vocabulary

Presentation I
20–25 minutes

A 1. Elicit students' answers to question 1 and 2. Write their ideas for places and ways to shop on the board.

2. Ask volunteers to give their reasons for how they buy certain items.

B 1. Copy the first two rows of the chart onto the board.

2. Model the task by "thinking aloud" about the first word in the chart and marking the first column appropriately. Work with a volunteer to demonstrate completing the last two columns.

3. Direct students to review the vocabulary independently, marking the first column of the chart in their books.

4. Pair students and ask them to complete the last two columns of the chart together.

C 1. Elicit any words that pairs did not know and write them on the board. Check with the class to see which of these words are known.

2. Direct students to look up any remaining unknown words in their dictionaries. Discuss those words in relation to the lesson.

(Note: 1D and 1E will confirm students' understanding of the target vocabulary.)

Guided Practice I
10–20 minutes

D 1. Direct students to read through the list of questions silently. Then read question 2 aloud. If students struggle to answer, ask if there are any words in the question that are similar to the vocabulary from 1B. Elicit the answer.

2. Set a time limit (five minutes). Direct students to complete the activity individually, then check their answers in pairs. Do not check the answers as a class yet.

Answers	
1. f	5. d
2. g	6. b
3. h	7. e
4. c	8. a

E 🔊 2-34 1. Prepare students to listen by saying: *Now we're going to listen to a consumer reporter on TV give sales tips to viewers. While you listen, check your work in 1D.* Ask students to circle the items in 1D that don't match the listening passage. Elicit those items and play them again, focusing on clues to meaning in the 1D sentences.

2. Check comprehension. Write questions on the board for students to answer in pairs: *What is a word for shopper who likes to save money?* [thrifty] *Why do some things go on clearance?* [The store wants to get rid of them/get them out the door.] *What is one benefit to online shopping?* [You can shop 24 hours a day.] *What comes in the mail?* [a catalog] *What are some problems with shopping networks?* [not sure of the quality, may be expensive, high shipping costs] *What's another word for a tag sale?* [yard sale] Play the audio again if necessary. Go over the answers with the class.

2 Learn to describe purchase problems

Presentation II
10–20 minutes

A 1. Direct students to look at the picture. Elicit the names of the items in the cubbies. Introduce the new topic: *Now we're going to talk about problems with purchases.*

2. Discuss the words *defective merchandise* and *returns*. Read and have students repeat the words.

3. Ask students to work individually to complete the sentences and then compare answers with a partner. Call on volunteers to read the completed sentences aloud.

4. Check comprehension. Elicit examples of items that might become *faded, dented, scratched, stained,* or *torn*.

Answers	
1. faded	4. dented
2. scratched	5. torn
3. defective	6. stained

Guided Practice II
10–15 minutes

 1. Model the conversation with a volunteer. Model it again using other information from 2A.

2. Set a time limit (three minutes). Direct students to practice with a partner.

3. Call on volunteers to present their version of the conversation for the class.

> **MULTILEVEL STRATEGIES**
>
> Adapt 2B to the level of your students.
>
> • **Pre- and On-level** Pair pre- and on-level students for 2B. Assign pre-level students part B for the first round and then have them switch roles.
>
> • **Higher-level** Pair students and direct them to practice the conversation with different items.

Communicative Practice and Application
20–25 minutes

 1. If students will use the Internet for this task, establish what device(s) they'll use: a class computer, tablets, or smartphones. Alternatively, print information from the Internet before class and distribute to groups.

2. Write the questions from 2C on the board. Explain that students will work in teams to research and report on these questions. Ask: *Which question can you research online?* [both] *Which search terms or questions can you use to find the information you need?* ["buying in person", "buying in store", "buying online", "buying by phone"] *What information will you skim for?* [items, reasons] *How will you record the information you find?* [table, checklist, index cards] Remind students to bookmark or record sites so they can find or cite them in the future.

3. Group students and assign roles: reporter, manager, administrative assistant, and IT support. Verify students' understanding of their roles.

4. Give managers the time limit for researching question 1 (ten minutes). Direct the IT support to begin the online research or pick up the printed materials for each team. Direct the administrative assistant to record information for the team using a table, checklist, or index cards.

5. Give a two-minute warning. Call "time." Tell reporters to answer the first question and then ask each member of the team question 2.

> **TIP**
>
> When setting up task-based activities, verify that students understand their roles using physical commands. For example: *If you report on your team's work, stand up* [reporter]. *If you keep the team on task, point to the clock* [manager]. *If you write the team's responses, raise your hand* [administrative assistant]. *If you help the team research, hold up your smartphone/tablet* [IT support].

D 1. Copy the sentence frames on the board.

2. Direct teams to help their administrative assistant use the sentence frames to record the team's findings. Direct the reporter to use the recorded information to report the team's findings to the class or another team.

Evaluation
10–15 minutes

TEST YOURSELF

1. Direct Partner A to read questions 1–4 from 1D on page 116 to Partner B. Partner B should close their book and write the correct vocabulary words in their notebook. When finished, students switch roles. Partner B reads questions 5–8 from 1D.

2. Direct both partners to open their books and check their spelling when they finish.

> **EXTENSION ACTIVITY**
>
> **Role-play**
>
> 1. Put students in pairs. Ask them to role-play returning an item under the following circumstances. Write on the board: 1. *The item is defective.* 2. *The customer doesn't have a receipt.* 3. *The item can't be returned because it was on clearance.* 4. *The clerk thinks the customer damaged the item.*
>
> 2. Ask several pairs to perform their role-plays for the class. Discuss appropriate language to use in situations of conflict.

LESSON 2 WRITING

Lesson Overview

MULTILEVEL OBJECTIVES

On- and Higher-level: Analyze, write, and edit an email about a defective item

Pre-level: Read and write an email about a defective item

LANGUAGE FOCUS

Grammar: Past tense (*I ordered a shirt two weeks ago.*)

Vocabulary: Problems with purchases

For vocabulary support, see these **Oxford Picture Dictionary** topics: Shopping, page 27; Feelings, pages 42–43

STRATEGY FOCUS

When you are writing, use *first, second,* and *finally* to help the reader identify the important parts of your message.

READINESS CONNECTION

In this lesson, students convey information in an email about a problem with a purchase.

PACING

To compress this lesson: Assign the *Test Yourself* for homework.

To extend this lesson: Discuss services. (See end of lesson.)

And/or have students complete **Workbook 4 page 52** and **Multilevel Activities 4 Unit 8 page 90**.

Lesson Notes

CORRELATIONS

CCRS: SL.1.B (d.) Explain their own ideas and understanding in light of the discussion.

R.1.B Ask and answer such questions as who, what, where, when, why, and how to demonstrate understanding of key details in a text.

R.2.A Identify the main topic and retell key details of a text.

R.5.A Know and use various text features to locate key facts or information in a text.

W.2.B (a.) Introduce a topic and group related information together; include illustrations when useful to aiding comprehension. (b.) Develop the topic with facts, definitions, and details. (c.) Use linking words and phrases to connect ideas within categories of information. (d.) Provide a concluding statement or section.

W.4.B Produce writing in which the development and organization are appropriate to task and purpose.

W.5.B With guidance and support from peers and others, develop and strengthen writing as needed by planning, revising and editing.

L.1.B (l.) Produce simple, compound and complex sentences.

L.1.C (f.) Use verb tense to convey various times, sequences, states, and conditions.

L.2.C (a.) Use correct capitalization. (g.) Use a comma before a coordinating conjunction in a compound sentence.

L.6.B Acquire and use accurately level-appropriate conversational, general academic, and domain-specific words and phrases, including those that signal spatial and temporal relationships.

RF.4.B (a.) Read grade-level text with purpose and understanding.

ELPS: 1. An ELL can construct meaning from oral presentations and literary and informational text through level-appropriate listening, reading, and viewing. 2. An ELL can participate in level-appropriate oral and written exchanges of information, ideas, and analyses, in various social and academic contexts, responding to peer, audience, or reader comments and questions. 3. An ELL can speak and write about level-appropriate complex literary and informational texts and topics. 6. An ELL can analyze and critique the arguments of others orally and in writing. 9. An ELL can create clear and coherent level-appropriate speech and text. 10. An ELL can demonstrate command of the conventions of standard English to communicate in level-appropriate speech and writing.

Warm-up and Review
10–15 minutes (books closed)

Show pictures of the following items: a shirt, a pair of pants, a lamp, a TV. Ask students to identify the parts of each item (sleeve, waistband, seam, electrical cord, switch, screen, etc.). Have students brainstorm the specific problems that each item might have if it's defective.

Introduction
5 minutes

1. Tell students that sometimes when we want to return something, we can just go to the store, but sometimes we need to write the manufacturer. When we order things online, we might need to send an email.

2. State the objective: *Today we'll read and write an email about a problem with a purchase.*

1 Prepare to write

Presentation
20–25 minutes

 1. Build students' schema by asking questions about the email. Ask: *What does customer service do?* [handles complaints] *What kind of product do you think this is about?* [a kitchen appliance] *How can you find the email address if you want to write about a problem with the order?* [look on the website]

2. Give students a few minutes to tell a partner their responses to questions 1 and 2. Elicit responses from the class.

Answers
1. Answers will vary.
2. Bonnie Tate, to the customer service office at Stine Kitchens

B 1. Introduce the model email and its purpose: *You're going to read an email from a customer to the customer service department of a company. As you read, look for the purpose of the email: why is she writing?* Have students read the email silently.

2. Check comprehension. Ask: *Why doesn't she write to a specific person?* [She probably doesn't know the name.] *What product is she writing about?* [a coffee maker] *When did she order it?* [last week] *What is wrong with it?* [wrong color, the power cord is defective, did not receive mug]

3. Play the audio. Ask students to number the paragraphs as they read along.

4. Draw students' attention to the *Writer's Note*. Ask students to find the words *first*, *second*, and *finally* in the email.

Guided Practice I
10 minutes

C 1. Have students work independently to answer the questions about the email and then compare answers with a partner.

2. Go over the answers with the class. Ask: *Why does the writer use* first, second, *and* finally? [She describes three problems with the order.] Point out that using these words focuses attention on the number of points you are making.

3. As students answer number 3, write the organization of the email on the board: *1. what she bought and when she bought it; 2. the problems with the item; 3. what she wants the company to do about it.*

Possible Answers
1. She wanted to tell customer service why she was writing./She wanted the office to send the email to the correct employee.
2. She described her order and what happened and her feeling about it. She wanted to explain why she is writing to them.
3. She wrote about three problems. She organized the information with *First*, *Second*, and *Finally*.
4. She wants to exchange the coffee maker and she wants a free coffee mug.

MULTILEVEL STRATEGIES
Seat pre-level students together for 1C.
• **Pre-level** Work with this group. While other students are working with a partner, read the questions aloud. Help students locate the answer in the text and elicit an answer from the group.

2 Plan and write

Guided Practice II
15–20 minutes

A 1. Read the questions. Elicit students' answers. If students struggle with their answers, refer to the email in 1B and model. Ask: *What information does Bonnie include?* [order number, item number, problems, solution]

2. Write the items and problems that students mention on the board.

B 1. Read the instructions aloud. Check comprehension of the exercise. Ask: *Whom are you writing to?* [the customer service department of a company] *What's the purpose of your email?* [to describe a problem with a purchase]

2. Have students work individually to write an email using the model in 1B and the organizational structure on the board as models.

> **MULTILEVEL STRATEGIES**
>
> Adapt 2B to the level of your students.
>
> • **Pre-level** Provide sentence frames to help these students get started with their email.
> *Hello,*
> *I ordered a _____ (item number) on _____ (date). It came yesterday and I was very disappointed.*
> *First, _____. Second, _____. Finally, _____.*
> *I want to _____. Please reply by _____.*
> *Thank you,*
> *_____*

3 Get feedback and revise

Guided Practice III
5 minutes

A Direct students to check their writing using the editing checklist. Tell them to read each item in the list and check their papers before moving onto the next item. Explain that students should not edit their writing at this stage. They should just use the checklist to check their work and mark any areas they want to revise.

Communicative Practice
15 minutes

B 1. Read the instructions aloud. Emphasize to students that they are responding to their partners' work, not correcting it.

2. Use the email in 1B to model the exercise. *Your sentence, "I want to exchange the black coffee maker…" makes it very easy to understand what you are asking for. I'm not sure I understand the problem with the power cord.*

3. Direct students to exchange papers with a partner and follow the instructions.

C Allow students time to edit and revise their writing as necessary, using the editing checklist from 3A and their partner's feedback from 3B. If necessary, students could complete this task as homework.

> **TIP**
>
> After completing 3C, hold a "customer service meeting" in class. Ask for volunteers to come to the front of the room and explain their problems and what they want. All non-volunteers are "customer service representatives." Ask the representatives to listen and take notes. Tell them they need to prioritize the problems. Have the class come to a consensus about which problem they should deal with first.

Application and Evaluation
10 minutes

TEST YOURSELF

1. Read the instructions aloud. Assign a time limit (five minutes) and have students work independently.

2. Before collecting students' work, invite two or three volunteers to share their sentences. Ask students to raise their hands if they wrote similar answers.

> **EXTENSION ACTIVITY**
>
> **Discussion**
>
> Ask these questions: *Have you ever had to call the cable, telephone, electric, or other service company? What was the problem? What was the solution or outcome?* Encourage students to be as specific as possible and write their problems and solutions on the board.

LESSON 3 GRAMMAR

Lesson Overview

MULTILEVEL OBJECTIVES

On- and Higher-level: Use adjectives ending in -ed and -ing to complain or compliment and respond to a shopping survey

Pre-level: Recognize adjectives ending in -ed and -ing in complaints and compliments and respond to a shopping survey

LANGUAGE FOCUS

Grammar: Adjectives ending in -ed and -ing (*The movie was boring. He was bored.*)

Vocabulary: Adjectives to describe feelings and adverbs of degree

For vocabulary support, see this **Oxford Picture Dictionary** topic: Feelings, pages 42–43.

READINESS CONNECTION

In this lesson, students cooperate with others to use adjectives ending in -ed and -ing and adverbs of degree to talk about life experiences.

PACING

To compress this lesson: Conduct 2A and 2B as whole-class activities.

To extend this lesson: Have students complain about or recommend a recent experience. (See end of lesson.)

And/or have students complete **Workbook 4 pages 53–54**, **Multilevel Activities 4 Unit 8 pages 91–92**, and **Multilevel Grammar Exercises 4 Unit 8**.

Lesson Notes

CORRELATIONS

CCRS: SL.2.B Determine the main ideas and supporting details of a text read aloud or information presented in diverse media and formats, including visually, quantitatively, and orally.

R.1.B Ask and answer such questions as who, what, where, when, why, and how to demonstrate understanding of key details in a text.

R.4.B Determine the meaning of general academic and domain-specific words and phrases in a text relevant to a topic or subject area.

W.8.B Recall information from experiences or gather information from print and digital sources; take brief notes on sources and sort evidence into provided categories.

L.1.B (l.) Produce simple, compound and complex sentences.

L.1.D (b.) Explain the function of nouns, pronouns, verbs, adjectives, and adverbs in general and their functions in particular sentences.

L.4.B (a.) Use sentence-level context as a clue to the meaning of a word or phrase.

L.6.B Use words and phrases acquired through conversations, reading and being read to, and responding to texts, including using adjectives and adverbs to describe.

RF.4.B (a.) Read grade-level text with purpose and understanding.

ELPS: 2. An ELL can participate in level-appropriate oral and written exchanges of information, ideas, and analyses, in various social and academic contexts, responding to peer, audience, or reader comments and questions. 3. An ELL can speak and write about level-appropriate complex literary and informational texts and topics. 7. An ELL can adapt language choices to purpose, task, and audience when speaking and writing. 9. An ELL can create clear and coherent level-appropriate speech and text. 10. An ELL can demonstrate command of the conventions of standard English to communicate in level-appropriate speech and writing.

Warm-up and Review
10–15 minutes (books closed)

Make a chart on the board with three headers: *A Good Movie, A Bad Movie, How I felt* on the board. Ask volunteers to come to the board and write adjectives for each header.

Introduction
5–10 minutes

1. Circle any adjectives ending in *-ed/-ing* that the students have written on the board. Use the adjective and its opposite to form sentences. *The movie was boring. I was bored during that movie.*

2. State the objective: *Today we're going to use adjectives ending in -ed and -ing to talk about life experiences.*

1 Use adjectives ending in *-ed* and *-ing*

Presentation I
20–25 minutes

1. Direct students to look at the picture and conversation. Build students' schema by asking: *Who do you see?* [two teenaged boys] *What are they doing?* [playing a video game] *How do you think the boys feel?* [disappointed]

2. Read the questions. Ask students to read the conversation silently and answer the questions. Have them compare answers with a partner. Go over the answers with the class.

Answers
1. He dislikes it because it's not exciting. It's boring.
2. He thought it would be exciting.
3. He thinks it's boring.
4. No, we don't know.

1. Demonstrate how to read the grammar chart. Read each sentence in the chart aloud and have students repeat. Ask: *Which ending can be used to describe a person, but not a thing?* [*-ed*] *Which can describe something like a book or a soccer game?* [*-ing*] *Can -ing also describe a person?* [Yes, Jin is an interesting person.]

2. Read the *Grammar Note* aloud. Check comprehension. Ask: *Which ending do we use to describe something that causes a feeling?* [*-ing*] *Which ending describes a feeling?* [*-ed*]

3. Direct students to circle the examples of adjectives ending in *-ing* and *-ed* in the conversation in 1A. Write the examples on the board.

4. Ask: *How does Cho feel about the game?* [He's disappointed.] *Why is the game disappointing?* [It's boring, not exciting.]

5. Pair students and direct them to read the chart aloud to each other.

6. Assess students' understanding of the chart. Elicit the verb that forms the base of each adjective [*disappoint, bore*]. Elicit other adjectives that end in *-ing* and *-ed* and write them on the board.

Answers
Circle: disappointed, exciting, boring, interested

Guided Practice I
15–20 minutes

C

1. Tell students they will collaborate to complete the description of the grammar point. Model collaboration by working with the class to complete the first sentence. Encourage students to look at 1A and 1B to see which ending describes a person's feelings.

2. Pair students and have them work together to complete the description. Project or write the completed definition on the board and have pairs verify the accuracy of their responses. Ask volunteers which sentences confused them and discuss.

Answers
-ed, -ing, things, *-ed*, people

> **MULTILEVEL STRATEGIES**
>
> For 1C, seat mixed-level students together.
>
> • **Pre-, On-, and Higher-level** Assign pre-level students the role of administrative assistant, on-level students the role of manager, and higher-level students the role of researcher. The administrative assistant fills in the blanks according to the team's decisions, the manager reads the description and manages the team's discussion, and the researcher looks up the definition of the grammar point online or checks against an answer key to verify the team's answers.

Guided Practice II
15–20 minutes

 Ask students to work individually to circle the correct word to complete the sentences and then compare answers with a partner. Ask volunteers to write the answers on the board.

Answers	
1. bored	3. confusing
2. disappointed	4. exciting

TIP
Seat students in mixed-level groups. Give each group a newspaper entertainment section. Tell students to look at the movie ads and circle any participial adjectives that they can find. Go over the meaning of the adjectives.

E Read each statement aloud and ask students to raise their hands to indicate whether *a* or *b* is true.

Answers		
1. a	2. a	3. b

MULTILEVEL STRATEGIES
After 1E, provide more practice with participial adjectives. Write more participial adjectives on the board: *amusing, amused, embarrassing, embarrassed, frightening, frightened, frustrating, frustrated, relaxing, relaxed, satisfying, satisfied, tiring, tired,* etc.

- **Pre-level** Give these students one sentence frame. *I felt _____ because _____.* Ask them to complete the sentence using the following participial adjectives and their own ideas: *embarrassed, frightened, relaxed,* and *tired*.
- **On-level** Ask these students to use the adjectives provided to complete these sentences. *I felt _____ because _____. I thought the _____ was _____ because _____.*
- **Higher-level** Ask these students to write original sentences with as many of the adjectives provided as they can.

Have volunteers from all groups put their sentences on the board. Elicit whether the words are describing feelings or causes of feelings. Go over any words that no student chose to use in a sentence. Provide your own sample sentences to illustrate the meaning of those adjectives.

2 Use adverbs of degree

Presentation II
20–25 minutes

 1. Introduce the new topic. Ask individuals if they are tired or hungry until someone says yes. Say: *Are you very hungry or a little hungry?*

2. Say: Very *and* a little *are adverbs of degree. Now we're going to look at other adverbs of degree.* Read the sentences in the chart. Ask: *In which picture is the woman most confused?* [the one on the right] *In which picture is she the least confused?* [the one on the left] *Which adverb means the same as "very"?* [really]

3. Ask students to work individually to circle the correct adverb and then compare answers with a partner. Go over the answers as a class.

Answers	
1. really	3. very
2. extremely	4. a little

Guided Practice III
10–15 minutes

 Have students work individually to complete the sentences. Ask them to compare their ideas with a partner. Encourage the pairs to discuss each of the ideas by asking each other *why*.

TIP
After 2B, have students write group movie reviews. Elicit the names of famous movies that many of your students have seen. Write the names on the board and group students according to which movie they want to review. If you have students who haven't seen any of the movies, assign them to different groups and ask them to take on the role of recorder. Have each group write a short review for the movie. Encourage students to use adverbs of degree and adjectives in their reviews. Post the reviews around the class and have the groups circulate and read each other's reviews.

3 Listen for the adjectives to determine the meaning

Guided Practice IV
10–15 minutes

 1. Say: *Now we're going to listen to a customer interviewer. He will ask questions about your shopping experience. You need to choose an appropriate answer.* Have students look at the responses and make predictions.

2. Play the audio. Direct students to listen silently without writing.

3. Replay the audio. Ask students to choose the best response for each question.

4. Call on volunteers to read the correct responses aloud. Ask how many predicted the correct response. Elicit the reason for their prediction.

Answers	
1. a	4. b
2. a	5. a
3. b	6. b

MULTILEVEL STRATEGIES

Replay the audio for 3 to allow pre-level students to catch up while you challenge on- and higher-level students.

•**Pre-level** Have these students listen again to choose the correct response.

•**On- and Higher-level** Have these students take notes on each question. Elicit the gist of each question from a volunteer before you call on another student to read the answer.

4 Use adjectives ending in -*ed* and -*ing* and adverbs of degree to talk about your life experience

Communicative Practice and Application
20–25 minutes

A 1. Direct students to look at the picture. Ask: *Where are these people? How do they feel?*

2. Model the activity. Tell about a time when you did something really exciting.

3. Have students work independently to think about their experiences.

 Put students in pairs. Ask students to take turns describing their experiences.

C 1. Read the instructions aloud. Copy the chart on the board. Model the exercise by having a volunteer tell you about one of his or her experiences. Have the class tell you how to write the information in note form on the chart.

2. Have each pair join another pair. Tell them to make notes of each other's answers.

3. Check comprehension of the exercise. Ask: *Should you write everything your group members say?* [no] *What should you write down?* [information about exciting or interesting experiences] Set a time limit for the exercise (four minutes) and observe and take note of issues that arise.

4. Call on volunteers to share the experiences they found the most interesting.

Evaluation
10–15 minutes

TEST YOURSELF

Ask students to write the sentences independently. Collect and correct their writing.

MULTILEVEL STRATEGIES

Target the *Test Yourself* to the level of your students.

• **Higher-level** Have these students write a paragraph in response to this prompt: *How are your experiences and your group members' experiences different or similar?*

EXTENSION ACTIVITY

Complain or Recommend

1. Tell students to recommend or complain about a recent shopping experience or a recent restaurant experience—anything they feel strongly about. Elicit ideas and put them on the board.

2. Give students a couple of minutes to plan what they will say. Tell students to include how they felt and why. Have students include tips or recommendations.

3. Assign a time limit (five minutes). Have them circulate around the room and talk to several partners.

4. Call on volunteers to share some of the "good tips" they got from their classmates.

LESSON 4 EVERYDAY CONVERSATION

Lesson Overview

MULTILEVEL OBJECTIVES

On-, Pre-, and Higher-level: Report problems with services and listen for information about returning a product

LANGUAGE FOCUS

Grammar: So, such, such a/an + that (It's so expensive that we can't afford it. It's such a cheap store that you can afford anything there.)

Vocabulary: Shopping

For vocabulary support, see these **Oxford Picture Dictionary** topics: Shopping, page 27; Feelings, pages 42–43

STRATEGY FOCUS

Practice keeping a conversation on topic.

READINESS CONNECTION

In this lesson, students cooperate with others to discuss customer service.

PACING

To compress this lesson: Conduct *Discuss* as a whole-class activity.

To extend this lesson: After completing 6B, have students complete a chart as a class. (See end of lesson.)

And/or have students complete **Workbook 4 page 55** and **Multilevel Activities 4 Unit 8 page 93**.

Lesson Notes

CORRELATIONS

CCRS: SL.1.B (a.) Come to discussions prepared, having read or studied required material; explicitly draw on that preparation and other information known about the topic to explore ideas under discussion. (b.) Follow agreed-upon rules for discussions. (c.) Ask questions to check understanding of information presented, stay on topic, and link their comments to the remarks of others. (d.) Explain their own ideas and understanding in light of the discussion.

SL.2.B Determine the main ideas and supporting details of a text read aloud or information presented in diverse media and formats, including visually, quantitatively, and orally.

SL.4.B Report on a topic or text, tell a story, or recount an experience with appropriate facts and relevant, descriptive details, speaking clearly at an understandable pace.

SL.6.B Speak in complete sentences when appropriate to task and situation in order to provide requested detail or clarification.

R.1.B Ask and answer such questions as who, what, where, when, why, and how to demonstrate understanding of key details in a text.

R.2.A Identify the main topic and retell key details of a text.

R.6.B Identify the main purpose of a text, including what the author wants to answer, explain, or describe.

R.7.B Use information gained from illustrations and the words in a text to demonstrate understanding of the text.

L.1.B (b.) Explain the function of nouns, pronouns, verbs, adjectives, and adverbs in general and their functions in particular sentences. (l.) Produce simple, compound and complex sentences.

L.3.B (b.) Recognize and observe differences between the conventions of spoken and written standard English.

L.6.B Use words and phrases acquired through conversations, reading and being read to, and responding to texts, including using adjectives and adverbs to describe.

LRF.4.B (a.) Read grade-level text with purpose and understanding.

ELPS: 2. An ELL can participate in level-appropriate oral and written exchanges of information, ideas, and analyses, in various social and academic contexts, responding to peer, audience, or reader comments and questions. 4. An ELL can construct level-appropriate oral and written claims and support them with reasoning and evidence. 6. An ELL can analyze and critique the arguments of others orally and in writing. 7. An ELL can adapt language choices to purpose, task, and audience when speaking and writing. 9. An ELL can create clear and coherent level-appropriate speech and text. 10. An ELL can demonstrate command of the conventions of standard English to communicate in level-appropriate speech and writing.

Warm-up and Review
10–15 minutes (books closed)

Write *Services* on the board. Elicit the ones students use [Internet, cable, phone, streaming]. Ask students how they can lower costs of these services. Elicit ways that these services are different from utilities, such as electricity and water.

Introduction
5 minutes

1. Say: *Most companies allow customers to ask questions and report problems in several ways: through email, through online chat, or over the phone.*

2. State the objective: *Today we're going to learn ways to report problems with services.*

1 Learn ways to report problems with services

Presentation I
10–20 minutes

 1. Direct students to look at the picture. Build students' schema by asking: *What problems do you see?* [no cable or internet service] *How do you think the customer feels?* [upset, disappointed]

2. Read the instructions aloud. Play the audio. Give students a minute to answer the question and then compare answers with a partner. Go over the answer as a class.

Answer
Yesterday's bad weather caused the problem.

Guided Practice I
20–25 minutes

 1. Read the instructions and questions aloud. Play the audio. Ask students to listen for the answers to each question.

2. Ask students to compare their answers with a partner. Circulate and monitor to ensure students understand the audio.

Possible Answers
1. He's calling to report problems with his cable TV and Internet.
2. No, she doesn't.
3. She offers to tell him about the company's new calling plans.

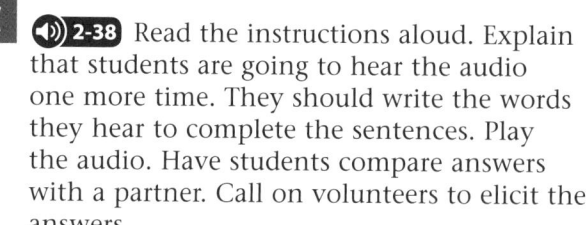 Read the instructions aloud. Explain that students are going to hear the audio one more time. They should write the words they hear to complete the sentences. Play the audio. Have students compare answers with a partner. Call on volunteers to elicit the answers.

Answers
1. I'm having some problems
2. nothing is working.
3. Do you know when it will be fixed

2 Practice your pronunciation

Pronunciation Extension
10–15 minutes

 1. Write on the board: *This is such an interesting book that I can't put it down.* Say the sentence and ask students to repeat it. Draw a linking line between the *ch* and the *a* in *such an* and the *t* and the *i* in *put it*. Repeat those phrases demonstrating the link. Say: *Now we're going to focus on linked consonants and vowels.*

2. Play the audio. Direct students to listen for the linking sounds.

B Play the audio. Have students work individually to draw a line between the linked consonants and vowels. Go over the answers as a class.

Answers	
Linked:	
1. your account	3. been out
2. Thank you	4. crews are

C Have students take turns reading the sentences with a partner. Monitor and provide feedback on pronunciation.

3 Use *So...that, such...that,* and *such a/an...that*

Presentation II and Guided Practice II
10–15 minutes

 1. Introduce the new topic by eliciting some of the *-ed/-ing* adjectives from the previous lesson. Use *so, such,* and *such a/an* in several sentences. _____ was such an exciting movie that I wanted to watch it again. But the tickets were so expensive that I decided to wait for it to be available online.

2. Say: *Now we're going to learn how to use* so *and* such. Have students look at the photo. Ask: *Where is she?* [a phone store] *What is she looking at?* [phones]

3. Tell students to read the information in the chart. Say each sentence and have students repeat. Elicit the forms and write them on the board: *Subject + verb + so + adjective/adverb + that ...* and *Subject + verb + such + (a/an) + noun + that....*

4. Have students look at the *Grammar Note*. Check comprehension. Ask: *What do we use these structures to show?* [a result] *Which do we use with an adjective or adverb?* [so] *Which do we use with an adjective and a count noun?* [such] Write *an easy test* on the board and elicit a sentence. Change it to *easy tests* and elicit another sentence. Write *so easy* and elicit a third sentence. Write students' sentences on the board.

5. Have students work individually to complete the sentences and then compare answers with a partner. Go over the answers as a class.

Answers	
1. so	3. such a
2. such a	4. such

Guided Practice III
15–20 minutes

 1. Have students work individually to answer the questions.

2. Set a time limit (five minutes). Ask students to practice asking and answering the questions with several partners. Call on individuals to share their answers with the class.

MULTILEVEL STRATEGIES

After 3B, provide more practice with *such* and *so* and target the practice to the level of your students.

- **Pre-level** Give these students additional sentences and ask them to create new sentences using *such* and *so*.
  1. *That book was interesting. I was surprised.*
  2. *The hotel was expensive. I decided not to stay there.*
- **On-level** Give these students this list of adjectives and ask them to create original sentences with *so* and *such*: *terrified, terrifying, tired, tiring, embarrassed, embarrassing.*
- **Higher-level** Give these students this list of adjectives and ask them to create original sentences with *so* and *such*: *encouraged, encouraging, overwhelming, overwhelmed, exhausting, exhausted*

Have volunteers from every group write one of their sentences on the board.

---

4 Building conversation skills

Guided Practice IV
15–20 minutes

 Direct students to look at the picture and skim the phone conversation. Ask: *What is the woman doing?* [talking on the phone and reading a sales announcement] Have them work with partners to identify the purpose of the phone call. Elicit responses and ask: *How do you know?* or *Why do you say that?* to encourage students to state their reasoning.

Possible Answers

The purpose of the call for the customer is to ask about buying a microwave. The purpose for the clerk is to help the customer/sell a microwave. The customer is looking at an ad for microwaves while she is on the phone.

B 🔊 2-41 1. Ask students to read the instructions and tell you what they are going to do [listen and read and respond to the question]. Play the audio and then elicit the answer to the question.

2. Ask students to read the conversation with a partner. Circulate and monitor pronunciation. Model and have students repeat difficult words or phrases.

3. Ask: *In what other situation could you use this conversation?* Point out a few phrases that are not specific to microwaves. Ask volunteers to point out others.

Answers
He apologizes because the microwave is sold out.

Communicative Practice and Application I
15–20 minutes

C 1. Pair students and have them read the instructions silently. Check their comprehension of the exercise. Ask: *What are the two roles?* [employee and customer] *Is the conversation in a store?* [no]

2. Model and have students repeat the expressions in the *In Other Words* box. Explain that they should use these expressions in their conversations.

3. Draw a T-chart on the board. Label the left column *Employee* and the right column *Customer*. Elicit examples of what each person might say and make notes on the chart.

4. Set a time limit (three minutes). Have students act out the role-play. Call "time" and have students switch roles.

5. Ask three volunteer pairs to act out their role-play for the class. Tell students who are listening to make a simple table with four rows and two columns. Use the top row to label the columns: *products* and *reasons unavailable*. Have students take notes in the chart for each role-play.

> **MULTILEVEL STRATEGIES**
>
> For 4C, adapt the role-play to the level of your students.
> • **Pre-level** Provide these students with a list of products and reasons to use in their role-plays.

5 Focus on listening for details

Presentation and Guided Practice
20–25 minutes

A Read the instructions and statement aloud. Pair students to discuss their opinions. Elicit ideas from volunteers.

B 1. Direct students to look at the picture. Ask: *How does the man feel?* [upset] *What do you think he wants?* [a new watch] Say: *Now you will hear a conversation between a customer and a customer service representative about a problem with a product.*

2. Direct students to read the sentences before listening and make predictions. Have them compare predictions with a partner.

C 2-42 Play the audio and have students work individually to circle the correct answers and then compare answers with a partner. Take a tally of responses for each item, and if students disagree on a response, replay the audio so they can check their answers.

Answers	
1. online	4. return
2. scratched	5. RA number
3. about three weeks ago	6. 14-603-4

> **MULTILEVEL STRATEGIES**
>
> Replay the conversation to challenge on- and higher-level students while allowing pre-level students to catch up.
> • **Pre-level** Have these students listen again to go over their answers.
> • **On- and Higher-level** Ask these students to listen for and write the sentence with *so...that*. [I'm so disappointed that I just want to return it.]

6 Discuss

Communicative Practice and Application II
15–20 minutes

A 1. Read the instructions aloud. Direct students' attention to the chart. Ask: *What skill can you use when the customer is somewhat disappointed?* [empathy] *What can you say to show empathy?* [I'm sorry, I apologize, unfortunately]

2. Brainstorm a list of people skills students know and write them on the board. Elicit examples of phrases that demonstrate each skill (e.g., clarifying – *Did you mean that....?*)

3. Put students into teams of four and assign roles: reporter, manager, administrative assistant, and editor. Verify students' understanding of the roles. Point out that the manager will also make sure that the conversation stays on topic. Encourage students to use the phrases in the *Speaking Note* during their discussions.

4. Set a time limit for the discussions (ten minutes). Write the sentence frame from 6B on the board. Then circulate and monitor.

B Call "time." Ask the reporters for each team to report the results of their team's discussion, using the sentence frame on the board.

> **EXTENSION ACTIVITY**
>
> To extend 6B, draw a large blank chart on the board. As each reporter shares with the class, the administrative assistant from that group fills in the chart. If other teams came up with the same answers, they should not enter the information again.

Evaluation
5 minutes

TEST YOURSELF

1. Ask students to complete the checkboxes individually.

2. Tell students that you are going to read each of the items in the checklist aloud. If they are not at all confident with that skill, they should hold up a closed fist. If they are not very confident, they should hold up one finger. If they are somewhat confident, two fingers; confident, three fingers; very confident, four fingers. If they think they could teach the skill, they should hold up five fingers. Read each item in the checklist and identify students that may need further support.

> **TIP**
>
> For homework, you could ask students to write a sentence or two about what discussion skills they still need to work on or, if they are confident in all of the skills, what skill they are most proud of.

LESSON 5 READING

Lesson Overview

MULTILEVEL OBJECTIVES

On-, Pre-, and Higher-level: Read about and discuss consumer rights

LANGUAGE FOCUS

Grammar: Adjectives *(These earrings are beautiful.)*

Vocabulary: *Consumer, beware, issue, policy, the public, recall, regulate*

For vocabulary support, see this **Oxford Picture Dictionary** topic: Shopping, page 27

STRATEGY FOCUS

In this lesson, students read sentences around new words to learn the meaning of new words.

READINESS CONNECTION

In this lesson, students interpret a pie chart and a note.

PACING

To compress this lesson: Conduct the word study in 2A as a whole-class activity.

To extend this lesson: Have students use consumer ratings to compare products. (See end of lesson.)

And/or have students complete **Workbook 4 page 56** and **Multilevel Activities 4 Unit 8 pages 94–95**.

Lesson Notes

CORRELATIONS

CCRS: SL.1.B (a.) Come to discussions prepared, having read or studied required material; explicitly draw on that preparation and other information known about the topic to explore ideas under discussion. (b.) Follow agreed-upon rules for discussions. (c.) Ask questions to check understanding of information presented, stay on topic, and link their comments to the remarks of others. (d.) Explain their own ideas and understanding in light of the discussion.

SL.6.B Speak in complete sentences when appropriate to task and situation in order to provide requested detail or clarification.

R.1.C Refer to details and examples in a text when explaining what the text says explicitly and when drawing inferences from the text.

R.2.B Determine the main idea of a text; recount the key details and explain how they support the main idea.

R.5.A Know and use various text features to locate key facts or information in a text.

R.4.B Determine the meaning of general academic and domain-specific words and phrases in a text relevant to a topic or subject area.

R.6.B Identify the main purpose of a text, including what the author wants to answer, explain, or describe.

R.7.C Interpret information presented visually, orally, or quantitatively and explain how the information contributes to an understanding of the text in which it appears.

W.7.A Participate in shared research and writing projects.

W.8.B Recall information from experiences or gather information from print and digital sources; take brief notes on sources and sort evidence into provided categories.

L.1.B (b.) Explain the function of nouns, pronouns, verbs, adjectives, and adverbs in general and their functions in particular sentences.

L.1.C (d.) Use modal auxiliaries to convey various conditions.

L.2.B (h.) Use conventional spelling for high-frequency and other studied words and for adding suffixes to base words.

L.4.B (e.) Use glossaries and beginning dictionaries, both print and digital, to determine or clarify the meaning of words and phrases.

L.6.B Use words and phrases acquired through conversations, reading and being read to, and responding to texts, including using adjectives and adverbs to describe.

RF.3.B (c.) Identify and know the meaning of the most common prefixes and derivational suffixes.

ELPS: 2. An ELL can participate in level-appropriate oral and written exchanges of information, ideas, and analyses, in various social and academic contexts, responding to peer, audience, or reader comments and questions. 3. An ELL can speak and write about level-appropriate complex literary and informational texts and topics. 4. An ELL can construct level-appropriate oral and written claims and support them with reasoning and evidence. 8. An ELL can determine the meaning of words and phrases in oral presentation and literary and informational text.

Warm-up and Review
10–15 minutes (books closed)

Find out what students know about consumer protection. Ask: *What would happen if a company were selling food that made people sick? Can companies lie in their advertisements?*

Introduction
5 minutes

1. Say: *A consumer is a person who uses a product. We are all consumers of many different products.*

2. State the objective: *Today we're going to read about and discuss consumer protection.*

1 Read

Presentation
10–20 minutes

A Read the questions aloud. Use ideas from the *Introduction* to help guide discussion.

B Read the words and definitions. Elicit sample sentences for each word or supply them if the students can't. Ask students to identify things that we issue [tickets, instructions]. Elicit examples of policies your school has. Ask: *What kinds of things do people often rate? Where can you find ratings?*

Pre-reading

 1. Read the instructions aloud. Have students answer the question individually and then check the answer with the class. If any students answer incorrectly, ask them to support their answer using the title of the article. Establish the correct answer.

2. Go over the *Reader's Note*. Write words that may be unfamiliar to students on the board: *beware, complicated, evaluate, monitor, regulate, industry*. Ask students to raise their hands as you say each one to indicate if they are unfamiliar with the word.

Answer
a. Organizations that protect consumers

Guided Practice: While Reading
20–30 minutes

D 1. Ask students to read the article silently and answer the question and then compare answers with a partner.

2. Check answers with the class.

3. Ask students to use the sentences around an unfamiliar word or phrase to guess meaning. Elicit ideas from the class for the words on the board.

4. Check comprehension. Ask: *How many organizations that protect consumers does the article mention?* [four] *What are they?* [Consumer Product Safety Commission, Federal Trade Commission, video game/movie industries, Consumer Reports] *Why is it difficult to evaluate many products?* [they are complicated] *What has declined since 1972?* [the rate of death and injuries caused by consumer products] *What kind of products does Consumer Reports test and compare?* [shampoos, insurance plans, cars, etc.]

Answers
the Consumer Product Safety Commission and the Federal Trade Commission

MULTILEVEL STRATEGIES

Adapt 1D to the level of your students.

• **Pre-level** Provide these students with a summary of the ideas in the reading. *There are several kinds of consumer protection in the U.S. 1. The Consumer Product Safety Commission protects the public from dangerous products. 2. The Federal Trade Commission makes sure that advertising, warranties, and labels are truthful. 3. The video game and movie industries put ratings on their products so that parents know which ones are OK for children. 4. Consumer Reports and other organizations compare products and report the results to their members.*

Direct these students to read the summary while other students are reading the article.

Guided Practice: Rereading
10–15 minutes

 1. Provide an opportunity for students to extract evidence from the text. Have students reread the article and underline any words or phrases that indicate the author's purpose.

2. Pair students and tell them to compare the words they underlined and report anything they disagree on. Discuss and clarify as needed.

Answers
The writer's main purpose is to inform readers about government agencies and private organizations that protect consumers. Underlines will vary.

> **TIP**
> Have students go online to find out about other consumer ratings. Decide which device(s) students will use and elicit search terms ("consumer ratings" and "product reviews").

F 1. Have students work in pairs to ask and answer the questions. They should then write the line number(s) where they found the answer. Go over the answers with the class.

2. Elicit and discuss any additional questions about the reading. You could introduce new questions for class discussion: *What kind of ratings do you pay attention to? Where do you look for ratings? Are there other products that you think should be regulated?*

Possible Answers
1. The CPSC works with consumer products like toys, power tools, and household chemicals.
2. A product recall is a rule that if a product is unsafe, customers can return it to be fixed or to get their money back.
3. The FTC is responsible for monitoring advertising to make sure it is truthful and regulating warranties.
4. They put ratings on their products to help parents decide which movies or games are OK for their children.
5. At www.consumerreports.org.

MULTILEVEL STRATEGIES

For 1F, used mixed-level pairs. Assign each student a role: Partner A or Partner B. Partner A asks questions 2, 3, and 5; Partner B asks 1 and 4.

•**Pre-level** Assign these students the role of Partner A. Tell them to use their summaries to answer the questions that Partner B asks.

2 Word study

Guided Practice: Post-reading
10 minutes

A 1. Direct students to look at the chart and identify the topic (the suffix *-ful*). Have students read the chart.

2. Read the first two sentences in the chart and the examples for *care, careful,* and *carefully.* Elicit sentences for the other words in the chart.

3. Have students repeat after you as you say each word with natural intonation, rhythm, and stress.

4. Direct students to complete the sentences and then compare answers with a partner. Read the correct answers and have students check their work.

Answers	
1. useful	4. carefully/truthfully
2. truthful	5. painful
3. helpful	6. hopeful

B Direct students to work individually to write a sentence for each topic that includes the underlined word. Ask volunteers to write their sentences on the board. Have the rest of the class suggest grammar and spelling edits as needed.

MULTILEVEL STRATEGIES

After 2B, seat same-level students together for more practice with nouns and *-ful* adjectives.

•**Pre-level** Ask these students to write five original sentences using *-ful* adjectives from the chart.

•**On- and Higher-level** Have these students write six sentences, two with an adjective form, two with a noun form, and two with the adverb form from the chart.

Ask volunteers from both groups to put their sentences on the board.

3 Talk it over

Guided Practice
15–20 minutes

 1. Have students look at the pie chart and read the note. Check comprehension. Ask: *What does the pie chart show?* [number of product recalls] *What do the different colors show?* [different items in the pie chart] Point out that they need to use the information from the graph and the note to complete the sentences.

2. Set a time limit (ten minutes). Have students work in pairs to complete the task. Ask volunteers to share their answers with the class.

Answers
1. 6
2. babies and kids/children
3. toys
4. ten
5. 25,333; 25,000

Communicative Practice
20 minutes

 1. Read the questions aloud. Set a time limit (ten minutes). Pair students to discuss the questions.

2. Ask volunteers to share their ideas with the class.

Application
5–10 minutes

BRING IT TO LIFE

Read the instructions aloud. Tell students that they can usually find a link to a store's return policy on the home page of its website.

EXTENSION ACTIVITY

Product Comparison

Look at Consumer Reports or another magazine or Internet site with reviews and ratings.

1. Show students several examples of rating scales. You can find these on the website or in a monthly magazine. Choose different products—for example, a car, a television, an appliance. Then look at the different criteria used for each item.

2. Put students in groups. Give each group a page of ratings so that they can compare products. Tell them to choose one of the items to buy. Ask a reporter from each group to explain which item his/her or group chose and why.

AT WORK

Warm-up and Review
10–15 minutes (books closed)

Write *Common Customer Complaints* on the board. Brainstorm with the class a list of what customers probably complain about in a store. Write the ideas on the board.

Introduction
5 minutes

State the objective: *Today we're going to talk about customer service.*

Presentation
5 minutes

 2-43 Read the instructions aloud. Play the audio. Give students a minute to think about the question. Elicit responses from the class.

Possible Answer
How to improve customer service

Guided Practice
10–15 minutes

 2-43 Play the audio again. Direct students to listen for each suggestion and put a check next to any that they hear mentioned.

Answers
know the store well
listen actively
summarize the customer's problem

 2-43 Read the instructions aloud. Play the audio again, encouraging students to take notes in their notebooks. Set a time limit (five minutes) for students to discuss their answers with a partner. Circulate and monitor.

Possible Answer
To talk about complaints about customer service and talk about solutions

Presentation and Communicative Practice
10 minutes

D 1. Direct students' attention to the *Do/Say* chart and ask them to identify the lesson's soft skill [help a teammate participate]. Ask the class which column has examples of language [right] and which has examples of behaviors [left].

2. Say a phrase from the left and act it out. Say it again and have the class act it out with you. Say it a third time and have the class act it out for you. To confirm understanding, combine phrases: *Look at me and hold your hand out (palm up).*

3. Model the sentence frames from the right using authentic intonation. Have students practice imitating your inflection.

4. Put students in teams of four and assign each team a question. Assign roles: reporter, manager, administrative assistant, and researcher. (Researchers will ask you questions on behalf of the team.) Verify understanding of the roles. Set a time limit (five minutes) and monitor.

5. Write sentence frames on the board that teams can use to summarize their response. *Our team discussed the following question:_____. We decided _____ because_____.*

6. Call "time" and let reporters rehearse their report for one minute. Direct each reporter to present to three other teams.

Communicative Practice and Application
20–25 minutes

E 1. Direct students to work in pairs to read the problems and make suggestions.

2. Invite volunteers to share their suggestions.

F 1. Have pairs merge to form teams of four. Tell students that they are going to be role-playing a staff meeting where they will suggest solutions to customer problems.

2. Direct groups to come up with three customer problems and three solutions. Each group should select a manager to run the meeting. The other three members should each choose a problem to bring up.

3. As students carry out the role-play, circulate and monitor. Provide global feedback once the activity ends.

TEAMWORK & LANGUAGE REVIEW

Lesson Overview

MULTILEVEL OBJECTIVES

On-, Pre-, and Higher-level: Expand upon and review unit grammar and life skills

LANGUAGE FOCUS

Grammar: Adjectives with -ed and -ing endings (*It's interesting.*) Adverbs of degree (*It's really interesting.*) Sentences with *so* and *such* (*It's so interesting that I want to see it again. It's such an interesting movie that I want to see it again.*)

Vocabulary: Shopping

For vocabulary support, see these **Oxford Picture Dictionary** topics: Shopping, page 27; Feelings, pages 42–43

READINESS CONNECTION

In this review, students determine how to complain about a yard sale purchase.

PACING

To extend this review: Have students complete **Workbook 4 page 57**, **Multilevel Activities 4 Unit 8 page 96**, and **Multilevel Grammar Exercises 4 Unit 8**.

Lesson Notes

CORRELATIONS

CCRS: SL.1.B (a.) Come to discussions prepared, having read or studied required material; explicitly draw on that preparation and other information known about the topic to explore ideas under discussion. (b.) Follow agreed-upon rules for discussions. (c.) Ask questions to check understanding of information presented, stay on topic, and link their comments to the remarks of others. (d.) Explain their own ideas and understanding in light of the discussion.

SL.1.C (b.) Follow agreed-upon rules for discussions and carry out assigned roles.

SL.2.B Determine the main ideas and supporting details of a text read aloud or information presented in diverse media and formats, including visually, quantitatively, and orally.

SL.4.B Report on a topic or text, tell a story, or recount an experience with appropriate facts and relevant, descriptive details, speaking clearly at an understandable pace.

R.1.B Ask and answer such questions as who, what, where, when, why, and how to demonstrate understanding of key details in a text.

R.2.A Identify the main topic and retell key details of a text.

R.7.B Use information gained from illustrations and the words in a text to demonstrate understanding of the text.

L.1.B (b.) Explain the function of nouns, pronouns, verbs, adjectives, and adverbs in general and their functions in particular sentences. (l.) Produce simple, compound and complex sentences.

L.1.C (d.) Use modal auxiliaries to convey various conditions.

L.6.B Use words and phrases acquired through conversations, reading and being read to, and responding to texts, including using adjectives and adverbs to describe.

RF.4.B (a.) Read grade-level text with purpose and understanding.

ELPS: 2. An ELL can participate in level-appropriate oral and written exchanges of information, ideas, and analyses, in various social and academic contexts, responding to peer, audience, or reader comments and questions. 4. An ELL can construct level-appropriate oral and written claims and support them with reasoning and evidence. 5. An ELL can conduct research and evaluate and communicate findings to answer questions or solve problems. 7. An ELL can adapt language choices to purpose, task, and audience when speaking and writing. 9. An ELL can create clear and coherent level-appropriate speech and text. 10. An ELL can demonstrate command of the conventions of standard English to communicate in level-appropriate speech and writing.

Warm-up and Review
10–15 minutes (books closed)

1. Review *At Work* activity F.

2. Ask students to share the good, not-so-good, and interesting things that happened during the role-play. As students speak, write their responses in a chart on the board.

Introduction and Presentation
5 minutes

1. Pair students and direct them to look at the picture in their book. Ask them to describe what they see to their partner.

2. Ask volunteer pairs to share their ideas with the class.

Guided Practice
15–20 minutes

  1. Model the process for completing the sentences in 1.

2. Set a time limit (five minutes). Have students work with partners to complete the activity and explain their answers. Go over answers with the class and elicit explanations.

Answers	
1. so, surprised	5. extremely, stained
2. very bored, interesting	6. really, confusing
3. pretty disappointed, so	7. such a, extremely
4. confusing	

B 1. Have students work in pairs to identify the speakers in A and give explanations.

2. Go over the answers with the class. Some students may have different answers. Ask students to explain why they answered the way they did.

C 1. Model the activity by reading the first sentence aloud. Have students work in pairs to answer the sentences.

2. Have pairs merge with another pair to compare their answers.

Answers	
1. such	4. so
2. such an	5. such a
3. so	

Communicative Practice
30–40 minutes

  1. Group students and assign roles: manager, director, editor, actors. Explain that students are going to work with their teams to write a conversation between a customer and a customer service representative.

2. Read steps 2–4 of the activity aloud. Check comprehension of the task. *What is the first thing you should do?* [choose a problem from the list] *What does each role do?* [managers keep track of time, directors encourage actors, actors rehearse and act out the scene, editors check grammar and vocabulary choice] *Who should write the conversation?* [everyone]

3. Set a time limit (ten minutes) to complete the exercise. Circulate and answer any questions.

4. Have actors act out the conversations for the class.

E 1. Have students walk around the room to conduct the interviews. To get students moving, tell them to interview three people who were not in their team for D.

2. Set a time limit (five minutes) to complete the exercise.

3. Tell students to make a note of their classmates' answers but not to worry about writing complete sentences.

> **MULTILEVEL STRATEGIES**
>
> Adapt the mixer in E to the level of your students.
>
> • **Pre-and On-level** Pair these students and have them interview other pairs together.
>
> • **Higher-level** Have these students ask an additional question and write all answers.

F 1. Call on individuals to report what they learned about their classmates. Keep a running tally on the board for the answers for #3, marking how many students would rather buy shoes at a thrift store, at a department store, or online.

2. Instruct students to draw graphs for question 3 in their notebooks. Circulate and answer any questions. Ask a volunteer to draw their graph on the board.

PROBLEM SOLVING
10–15 minutes

 1. Ask: *Do you ever shop at yard sales?* Tell students they will read a story about a woman who bought a vacuum cleaner at a yard sale. Direct students to read Lidia's story silently.

2. Ask: *What's wrong with the vacuum cleaner?* [It makes noise and doesn't clean well.] *How does Lidia feel?* [unhappy]

3. Play the audio and have students read along silently.

 1. Elicit answers to question 1.

2. Put students into groups of three or four. Ask each group to think of three or four possible solutions to Lidia's problem and report them to the class. Ask a volunteer to write all possible solutions on the board.

Answer
1. Lidia bought a vacuum cleaner at her neighbor's yard sale, but it doesn't work very well and she is unhappy that they didn't tell her about the problems it has.
2. Answers will vary.

Evaluation
20–25 minutes

To test students' understanding of the unit language and content, have them take the Unit 8 Test, available on the Teacher Resource Center.

UNIT 9 Take Care!

Unit Overview

This unit explores issues related to health care, including medical conditions, doctor's visits, and health insurance with a range of employability skills and contextualizes modals and other expressions for giving advice.

KEY OBJECTIVES

Lesson 1	Identify health and wellness practices
Lesson 2	Identify lifestyle issues and write a persuasive blog about them
Lesson 3	Give advice and strong advice
Lesson 4	Talk about changes to diet and exercise
Lesson 5	Identify health insurance options
At Work	Discuss safety at work
Teamwork & Language Review	Review unit language

UNIT FEATURES

Academic Vocabulary	*appropriate, available, confirm, define, detection, estimated, focused, injury, issue, maintain, medical, option, physical, portion*
Employability Skills	• Understand teamwork • Cooperate with others • Communicate information • Work with others • Communicate verbally • Understand graphs and tables • Solve problems • Analyze information • Determine the strongest advice • Determine the health precautions different kinds of workers should take • Analyze different types of medical insurance • Decide how to give advice on health to a loved one

Resources	**Class Audio** CD3, Tracks 02–13
	Workbook Unit 9, pages 58–64
	Teacher Resource Center
	    Multilevel Activities 4 Unit 9
	    Multilevel Grammar Exercises 4 Unit 9
	    Unit 9 Test
	Oxford Picture Dictionary Symptoms and Injuries, Illnesses and Medical Conditions, Taking Care of Your Health, Medical Care, A Hospital

LESSON 1 VOCABULARY

Lesson Overview

MULTILEVEL OBJECTIVES

On-level: Describe and talk about medical conditions and health history

Pre-level: Identify medical conditions and describe health history

Higher-level: Talk and write about health history using vocabulary for medical conditions

LANGUAGE FOCUS

Grammar: Present tense (*Early detection saves lives.*)

Vocabulary: Health history

For vocabulary support, see these **Oxford Picture Dictionary** topics: Illnesses and Medical Conditions, pages 112–113; Taking Care of Your Health, pages 116–117; Medical Care, page 111

READINESS CONNECTION

In this lesson, students work with others to conduct research on health.

PACING

To compress this lesson: Conduct 1C as a whole-class activity.

To extend this lesson: Have students identify vocabulary on a real medical history form. (See end of lesson.)

And/or have students complete **Workbook 4 page 58** and **Multilevel Activities 4 Unit 9 pages 98–99**.

Lesson Notes

CORRELATIONS

CCRS: SL.1.B (b.) Follow agreed-upon rules for discussions. (c.) Ask questions to check understanding of information presented, stay on topic, and link their comments to the remarks of others. (d.) Explain their own ideas and understanding in light of the discussion.

SL.2.B Determine the main ideas and supporting details of a text read aloud or information presented in diverse media and formats, including visually, quantitatively, and orally.

SL.4.B Report on a topic or text, tell a story, or recount an experience with appropriate facts and relevant, descriptive details, speaking clearly at an understandable pace.

SL.6.B Speak in complete sentences when appropriate to task and situation in order to provide requested detail or clarification.

R.1.B Ask and answer such questions as who, what, where, when, why, and how to demonstrate understanding of key details in a text.

R.4.B Determine the meaning of general academic and domain-specific words and phrases in a text relevant to a topic or subject area.

R.5.A Know and use various text features to locate key facts or information in a text.

W.7.A Participate in shared research and writing projects.

L.1.B (l.) Produce simple, compound and complex sentences.

L.4.B (a.) Use sentence-level context as a clue to the meaning of a word or phrase. (e.) Use glossaries and beginning dictionaries, both print and digital, to determine or clarify the meaning of words and phrases.

L.6.B Use words and phrases acquired through conversations, reading and being read to, and responding to texts, including using adjectives and adverbs to describe.

RF.4.B (a.) Read grade-level text with purpose and understanding.

ELPS: 1. An ELL can construct meaning from oral presentations and literary and informational text through level-appropriate listening, reading, and viewing. 2. An ELL can participate in level-appropriate oral and written exchanges of information, ideas, and analyses, in various social and academic contexts, responding to peer, audience, or reader comments and questions. 5. An ELL can conduct research and evaluate and communicate findings to answer questions or solve problems. 7. An ELL can adapt language choices to purpose, task, and audience when speaking and writing. 8. An ELL can determine the meaning of words and phrases in oral presentation and literary and informational text.

Warm-up and Review
10–15 minutes (books closed)

Write *Illnesses* on the board and elicit names of illnesses that students know. Write them on the board.

Introduction
5 minutes

1. Ask students which of the illnesses they think are serious. Ask which ones they would need to include on a medical history form.

2. State the objective: *Today we're going to learn how to talk about our medical history.*

1 Identify health history vocabulary

Presentation I
20–25 minutes

A 1. Write *things people do to stay healthy and live a long life* on the board and elicit one example from the whole class. Have students work together and brainstorm in a group. Make a list on the board of the words and phrases your students identify.

2. Have students identify the things they do the most. Elicit ideas and put a checkmark next to the activities students feel are essential to a healthy and long life, encouraging them to explain their reasons.

B 1. Direct students' attention to the article. Build students' schema by asking: *Who do you see in the photo?* [an old woman] *How does she look?* [happy and healthy] Make sure students understand what a *role model* is [someone who is a good example for others to follow].

2. Have students read the article. Have students work in pairs to answer the question.

3. Check comprehension. Ask: *Who is the article about?* [Althea Jones] *How old is she?* [101] *Who interviewed her?* [her friend Beatriz Garza] *What is the first reason she gives for her long life?* [heredity] *What other reasons does she give?* [taking care of your health, checkups, staying active, good nutrition/food]

C 1. Have students read the vocabulary in the left column. Instruct them to underline the phrases they find in the article. Point out that they can use the context, or words around the vocabulary, to guess meaning.

2. Pair students to match the words and definitions.

Answers	
1. d	5. e
2. a	6. b
3. f	7. c
4. g	

Guided Practice I
10–20 minutes

 🔊 **3-02** Prepare students to listen by saying, *Now we're going to listen to Althea's secrets for a long life. While you listen, check your work in 1C.* Ask students to circle the items in 1C that don't match the listening passage. Elicit those items and play them again, focusing on clues to meaning in the 1C sentences.

2 Learn vocabulary for medical conditions

Presentation II
10–20 minutes

 1. Direct students to look at the form on page 133. Elicit the name of the form and ask how many students have filled out something similar. Explain that there are a lot of medical conditions or problems listed on a medical history form and that they will learn some of these conditions.

2. Ask students to work individually to circle five problems or illnesses that Althea Jones has had.

3. Call on volunteers to read the medical conditions in the chart aloud and discuss their meanings. Have students repeat the words.

4. Check comprehension. Ask: *What's a word to describe a bad headache?* [severe] *What word describes a medical condition that lasts for a very long time and does not get better?* [chronic]

Answers
Circle: measles, chicken pox, allergic to penicillin, weakness in arms or legs, family history of heart disease

Guided Practice II
10–15 minutes

 Have students work with a partner to complete the paragraph. Go over the answers as a class.

Answers	
1. disease	4. severe
2. symptoms	5. chronic
3. weakness	6. allergic

TIP
If you have access to the Internet in class, have students look up a common illness or condition to find its symptoms. Put students in pairs and give each pair a condition to look up—for example, diabetes, high blood pressure, the flu, arthritis, ulcer, mumps, strep throat, measles. If students are interested in a particular condition, allow them to choose. Direct partners to find the main symptoms or warning signs and to share them with the class.

Communicative Practice and Application
20–25 minutes

 1. If students will use the Internet for this task, establish what device(s) they'll use: a class computer, tablets, or smartphones. Alternatively, print information from the Internet before class and distribute to groups.

2. Write the questions from 2C on the board. Explain that students will work in teams to research and report on these questions. Ask: *Which questions can you research online?* [all] *Which search terms or questions can you use to find the information you need?* ["heredity vs. lifestyle" + "health" and "advantages of screenings (or checkups)" and "protecting your health"] *How will you record the information you find?* [table, checklist, index cards] Remind students to bookmark or record sites so they can find or cite them in the future.

3. Group students and assign roles: reporter, manager, administrative assistant, and IT support. Verify students' understanding of their roles.

4. Give managers a time limit for researching the questions (ten minutes for offline research, 15 minutes for combined online and offline research). Direct the IT support to begin the online research or pick up the printed materials for each team. Direct the administrative assistant to record information for the team using a table, checklist, or index cards.

5. Give a two-minute warning. Call "time." Tell reporters to report on the team's responses to the questions and IT support to provide online search results.

TIP
When setting up task-based activities, verify that students understand their roles using physical commands. For example: *If you report on your team's work, stand up* [reporter]. *If you keep the team on task, point to the clock* [manager]. *If you write the team's responses, raise your hand* [administrative assistant]. *If you help the team research, hold up your smartphone/tablet* [IT support].

 1. Copy the sentence frames on the board.

2. Direct teams to help their administrative assistant use the sentence frames to record the team's findings. Direct the reporter to use the recorded information to report the team's findings to the class or another team.

Evaluation
10–15 minutes

TEST YOURSELF

1. Direct Partner A to read definitions 1–4 from 1C on page 132 to Partner B. Partner B should close their book and write the answers in their notebook. When finished, students switch roles. Partner B reads definitions 5–7 from 1C.

2. Direct both partners to open their books and check their spelling when they finish.

> **EXTENSION ACTIVITY**
> **Medical History Forms**
>
> Look at a real medical history form. Find a medical history form on the Internet and distribute copies or project a transparency of it. Ask students to identify vocabulary that they don't know.

LESSON 2 WRITING

Lesson Overview

MULTILEVEL OBJECTIVES

On- and Higher-level: Analyze, write, and edit a blog about healthy lifestyle changes

Pre-level: Read a blog and write about healthy lifestyles

LANGUAGE FOCUS

Grammar: Simple past, simple present, and present perfect tense (*I haven't blogged in a few weeks, so it's time to catch up. I got a surprise at my last physical.*)

Vocabulary: Healthy and unhealthy habits

For vocabulary support, see these **Oxford Picture Dictionary** topics: Illnesses and Medical Conditions, pages 112–113; Taking Care of Your Health, pages 116–117

STRATEGY FOCUS

When you are writing, use parentheses or explanations with *that is* or *that means* to define words or when you are using them in a special way.

READINESS CONNECTION

In this lesson, students analyze information from a blog post.

PACING

To compress this lesson: Assign the *Test Yourself* for homework.

To extend this lesson: Role-play a conversation about lifestyle changes. (See end of lesson.)

And/or have students complete **Workbook 4 page 59** and **Multilevel Activities 4 Unit 9 page 100**.

Lesson Notes

CORRELATIONS

CCRS: SL.1.B (d.) Explain their own ideas and understanding in light of the discussion.

R.1.B Ask and answer such questions as who, what, where, when, why, and how to demonstrate understanding of key details in a text.

R.2.A Identify the main topic and retell key details of a text.

R.5.A Know and use various text features to locate key facts or information in a text.

R.6.B Identify the main purpose of a text, including what the author wants to answer, explain, or describe.

W.2.B (a.) Introduce a topic and group related information together; include illustrations when useful to aiding comprehension. (b.) Develop the topic with facts, definitions, and details. (c.) Use linking words and phrases to connect ideas within categories of information. (d.) Provide a concluding statement or section.

W.4.B Produce writing in which the development and organization are appropriate to task and purpose.

W.5.B With guidance and support from peers and others, develop and strengthen writing as needed by planning, revising and editing.

W.8.B Recall information from experiences or gather information from print and digital sources; take brief notes on sources and sort evidence into provided categories.

L.1.B (k.) Use coordinating and subordinating conjunctions. (l.) Produce simple, compound and complex sentences.

L.1.C (f.) Use verb tense to convey various times, sequences, states, and conditions.

L.2.C (a.) Use correct capitalization. (g.) Use a comma before a coordinating conjunction in a compound sentence.

L.6.B Use words and phrases acquired through conversations, reading and being read to, and responding to texts, including using adjectives and adverbs to describe. Acquire and use accurately level-appropriate conversational, general academic, and domain-specific words and phrases, including those that signal spatial and temporal relationships.

RF.4.B (a.) Read grade-level text with purpose and understanding.

ELPS: 2. An ELL can participate in level-appropriate oral and written exchanges of information, ideas, and analyses, in various social and academic contexts, responding to peer, audience, or reader comments and questions. 10. An ELL can demonstrate command of the conventions of standard English to communicate in level-appropriate speech and writing.

Warm-up and Review
10–15 minutes (books closed)

1. Ask: *What are some unhealthy habits that people have?* List students' ideas on the board. Ask students to quantify how much or little of something makes it unhealthy. For example: *How much sugar and fat is unhealthy? How many cigarettes? How little exercise?*

2. Lead students in a discussion about advice, especially the cultural aspect of giving advice.

Introduction
5 minutes

1. Point out that some of the things on the board are not a problem if you do them occasionally but that doing them regularly is unhealthy.

2. State the objective: *Today we're going to read and write a persuasive blog post about lifestyle issues.*

1 Prepare to write

Presentation
20–25 minutes

A 1. Build students' schema by asking questions about the picture and the blog post. Ask: *Who is the writer?* [the woman in the photo] *What is she doing?* [jumping] *What is unusual about the woman?* [she has an artificial leg] *What do you think she writes about?* [adventure]

2. Give students one minute to tell a partner their responses to questions 1 and 2. Elicit responses from the class.

Answers
1. Informal; The writer uses *I* and begins with "Hi, friends."
2. She wants her readers to think about the importance of good health and make changes if they need to.

B 1. Introduce the model blog post: *You're going to read a blog post about lifestyle issues.* Have students read the blog post silently.

2. Check comprehension. Ask: *What place did she visit?* [Ellis Island] *What did the doctor tell her?* [Her blood sugar is too high.] *What health problem could she develop?* [diabetes] *What did she do?* [cut back on processed food and cut out sugar on weekdays]

3. Go over the *Writer's Note*. Play the audio. Ask students to underline the use of parentheses or explanations with *that is* or *that means* to define words.

Guided Practice I
10 minutes

C 1. Have students work independently to answer the questions and then compare answers with a partner.

2. Go over the answers with the class.

Answers
1. She is writing because she wants to tell people about herself and to encourage other people to pay attention to their health.
2. Get a checkup, be active, change their diet if they need to
3. Answers will vary.

MULTILEVEL STRATEGIES

For 1C, challenge higher-level students while working with pre-level students.

- **Higher-level** Have these students write a sentence about something they or someone they know has cut back on or cut out. Point out the use of a noun or gerund with these expressions. Remind students that they can also use *quit* or *stop* when talking about a habit and that those verbs are followed by gerunds.

2 Plan and write

Guided Practice II
15–20 minutes

A Read the instructions and questions aloud. Elicit answers. Write ideas on the board.

B 1. Read the instructions aloud. Direct students' attention to the template. Have them identify where Marisol includes these phrases in her post.

2. Have students write a blog post using the template and the blog post as models. They can use their notes and the ideas on the board.

> **MULTILEVEL STRATEGIES**
>
> Adapt 2B to the level of your students.
>
> - **Pre-level** Work with these students to write a group blog post. Read through the template. At each ellipsis, stop and elicit completions. Decide as a group what to write. Have these learners copy the group post into their notebooks.
> - **On-level** Encourage these students to include examples of lifestyle changes they made. Provide sentence frames: *I decided to cut back on…. I decided to…*
> - **Higher-level** Have these students give examples of lifestyle changes and advice on how to make lifestyle changes.

3 Get feedback and revise

Guided Practice III
5 minutes

A Direct students to check their writing using the editing checklist. Tell them to read each item in the list and check their papers before moving onto the next item. Explain that students should not edit their writing at this stage. They should just use the checklist to check their work and mark any areas they want to revise.

Communicative Practice
15 minutes

B 1. Read the instructions aloud. Emphasize to students that they are responding to their partners' work, not correcting it.

2. Use the blog post in 1B to model the exercise. *I think the sentence that says, "What you don't know CAN hurt you" is persuasive. I think when you say "Get out there and be active" you could be more specific.*

3. Direct students to exchange papers with a partner and follow the instructions.

C Allow students time to edit and revise their writing as necessary, using the editing checklist from 3A and their partner's feedback from 3B. If necessary, students could complete this task as homework.

> **TIP**
>
> After completing 3C, hold a "health fair" in class. Ask for volunteers to come to the front of the room and describe a health problem and appropriate lifestyle changes to make. All non-volunteers are "community members." Ask the community members to listen and take notes. Tell them they need to decide which lifestyle issues they want to prioritize in their community. Have them reach a consensus.

Application and Evaluation
10 minutes

TEST YOURSELF

1. Read the instructions aloud. Assign a time limit (five minutes) and have students work independently.

2. Before collecting student work, invite two or three volunteers to share their sentences. Ask students to raise their hands if they wrote similar answers.

> **EXTENSION ACTIVITY**
>
> **Role-play**
>
> Role-play a conversation about lifestyle changes.
>
> 1. Write a role-play scenario on the board.
> **Partner A:** You haven't felt well lately. Describe your problem to your partner.
> **Partner B:** You or someone you know had a similar problem in the past. Making a change in lifestyle or diet helped eliminate the problem. Tell your partner about it.
> **Partner A:** Thank your partner for the advice.
> 2. Have students practice the role-play with a partner. Call on volunteers to perform their role-play for the class.

LESSON 3 GRAMMAR

Lesson Overview

MULTILEVEL OBJECTIVES

On-, Pre- and Higher-level: Use modals to give advice and listen for health advice

LANGUAGE FOCUS

Grammar: Advice with *should, had better,* and *ought to* (*You should eat more healthy food. You shouldn't eat so much salt. You had better drink less coffee.*)

Vocabulary: Health ailments, conditions, health care

For vocabulary support, see these **Oxford Picture Dictionary** topics: Symptoms and Injuries, page 110; Illnesses and Medical Conditions, pages 112–113; Taking Care of Your Health, pages 116–117; Medical Care, page 111

READINESS CONNECTION

In this lesson, students determine the strongest advice.

PACING

To compress this lesson: Conduct 2A and 2B as whole-class activities.

To extend this lesson: Have students discuss mental health. (See end of lesson.)

And/or have students complete **Workbook 4 pages 60–61**, **Multilevel Activities 4 Unit 9 pages 101–102**, and **Multilevel Grammar Exercises 4 Unit 9**.

Lesson Notes

CORRELATIONS

CCRS: SL.1.B (d.) Explain their own ideas and understanding in light of the discussion.

SL.2.B Determine the main ideas and supporting details of a text read aloud or information presented in diverse media and formats, including visually, quantitatively, and orally.

R.1.B Ask and answer such questions as who, what, where, when, why, and how to demonstrate understanding of key details in a text.

W.8.B Recall information from experiences or gather information from print and digital sources; take brief notes on sources and sort evidence into provided categories.

L.1.B (l.) Produce simple, compound and complex sentences.

L.1.C (d.) Use modal auxiliaries to convey various conditions.

L.2.B (f.) Use an apostrophe to form contractions and frequently occurring possessives.

L.4.B (a.) Use sentence-level context as a clue to the meaning of a word or phrase.

L.6.B Use words and phrases acquired through conversations, reading and being read to, and responding to texts, including using adjectives and adverbs to describe.

RF.4.B (a.) Read grade-level text with purpose and understanding.

ELPS: 2. An ELL can participate in level-appropriate oral and written exchanges of information, ideas, and analyses, in various social and academic contexts, responding to peer, audience, or reader comments and questions. 3. An ELL can speak and write about level-appropriate complex literary and informational texts and topics. 7. An ELL can adapt language choices to purpose, task, and audience when speaking and writing. 9. An ELL can create clear and coherent level-appropriate speech and text. 10. An ELL can demonstrate command of the conventions of standard English to communicate in level-appropriate speech and writing.

Warm-up and Review
10–15 minutes (books closed)

1. Write *Give me some advice* on the board. Tell students that you have various problems and elicit their advice. *I can't sleep at night. I get a lot of colds. I get a lot of stomachaches. I get out of breath easily.* Note the language you want them to use on the board: *you should, you shouldn't, you'd better, you'd better not.* If they use imperatives, write the verb.

2. Elicit how students feel when they give/get advice and when it's OK to give advice.

Introduction
5–10 minutes

1. Say: *We have a lot of different ways of giving advice. Some of them are stronger than others.*

2. State the objective: *Today we're going to learn different ways to give advice about health.*

1 Use different forms of advice

Presentation I
20–25 minutes

1. Direct students to look at the pictures. Ask them to describe each patient and guess the problem [The man is overweight, maybe his stomach hurts; the woman is shaking and looks anxious; the girl looks sick.]

2. Read the questions. Ask students to read what the doctor says silently to find the answers. Call on individuals to share their answers.

Answers
1. He should cut back on junk food. He should start to exercise more.
2. She stays up late. She drinks a lot of coffee.
3. No, we don't.

1. Demonstrate how to read the grammar chart. Say each sentence and have students repeat. Ask: *What form of the verb follows the modals?* [simple form]

2. Direct students to circle the sentences in 1A that gives the strongest advice. Write it on the board.

3. Ask: *Which words indicate that the doctor is giving advice?* [should, ought to, shouldn't, had better, had better not]

4. Pair students and direct them to take turns reading the chart aloud to each other.

5. Assess students' understanding of the chart. Ask: *What is the negative form of* should? [shouldn't] *Of* had better? [had better not] *Of* ought to? [We don't use one] Refer to the problems on the board from the *Warm-up* and elicit advice using each form in the chart.

Answer
Circle: You'd better drink less coffee. You had better not go to school today.

Guided Practice I
15–20 minutes

1. Tell students they will collaborate to complete the description of the grammar point. Model collaboration by working with the class to complete the first sentence. Encourage students to look at 1A and 1B to complete the statements.

2. Pair students and have them work together to complete the description.

3. Project or write the completed definition on the board and have pairs verify the accuracy of their responses. Ask volunteers which sentences confused them and discuss.

Answers
give advice, the same, ought to, stronger, he had better

MULTILEVEL STRATEGIES
For 1C, seat mixed-level students together. • **Pre-, On-, and Higher-level** Assign pre-level students the role of administrative assistant, on-level students the role of manager, and higher-level students the role of researcher. The administrative assistant fills in the blanks according to the team's decisions, the manager reads the description and manages the team's discussion, and the researcher looks up the definition of the grammar point online or checks against an answer key to verify the team's answers.

Guided Practice II
5–10 minutes

 D Ask students to work individually to match the sentences and then compare answers with a partner. Tell them to take turns reading the matched sentences with a partner. Call on volunteers to read the matching sentences aloud.

Answers	
1. c	4. b
2. a	5. d
3. e	

MULTILEVEL STRATEGIES

For 1D, seat higher-level students together.

• **Higher-level** If these students finish before the others, have them work together in pairs to develop their own matching exercise. Tell them to write three or four statements and three or four pieces of advice to match those statements. Have them write their statements and pieces of advice out of order on the board. After you have gone over the 1D responses with the class, call on pre- and on-level students to match the sentences and advice written by the higher-level students.

 E 1. Have students form teams. Assign roles: manager, administrative assistant, and editor. The administrative assistant writes the corrected sentences according to the team's decisions, the manager keeps time and manages the team's discussion, and the editor looks up spelling or checks against an answer key to verify the team's answers.

2. Set a time limit of five minutes. Ask volunteers to write the correct sentences on the board.

Answers
1. You should be careful when you lift heavy boxes.
2. You ought to stay home from work if you can.
3. You had better go to the clinic to see the nurse.

2 Learn the difference between forms of advice

Presentation II
20–25 minutes

 A 1. Introduce the new topic. Write *You should eat more vegetables.* and *You'd better eat more vegetables.* on the board. Ask students which sentence is stronger. Point out that we often use *had better* when we want to imply a negative result. *You had better eat more vegetables or you're going to get sick.* Say: *Now we're going to look at other ways to give strong advice.*

2. Read the instructions and sentences in the chart aloud. Check comprehension. Ask: *Which words do we use for mild advice?* [should, ought to] *What kind of advice do we give with must?* [stronger advice] *Which expression is less formal?* [have got to]

3. Tell students to write two more sentences using the strongest types of advice. Call on volunteers to read their sentences aloud.

Guided Practice III
10–15 minutes

 B Ask students to work individually to categorize the advice and then compare answers with a partner. Go over the answers as a class.

Answers	
1. SR	3. SR
2. S	4. M

 C Have students work individually to write their advice and then compare answers with a partner. Elicit several pieces of advice for each situation. Discuss the strength of each piece of advice.

Possible Answers
1. You ought to go home.
2. You had better go see the nurse.
3. You should rest and drink fluids.
4. You have to see a doctor.

> **MULTILEVEL STRATEGIES**
>
> After 2C, provide more practice with modals for the pre- and on-level students while you challenge the higher-level students.
>
> Ask students to think about a mother whose first child is going off to college. Elicit advice the mother might give to her child. Direct students to put their pencils down and listen to one mother's advice. Read this paragraph aloud:
>
> *I know you'll have a lot of work to do, but you shouldn't drink too much coffee. You probably won't be eating very well, so you ought to take a vitamin every day. And you'd better not start staying out late with your friends because you have to call me every other day, and I'll know if you're up to no good!*
>
> Elicit advice that students remember from the paragraph, but don't write it on the board. Read the paragraph again. Seat students in groups and direct them to restate the mother's advice. Emphasize that it's not important to use her exact words; just to restate the same ideas. Then read the paragraph again. Give each group a large sheet of paper and ask students to write the mother's advice.
>
> • **On- and Pre-level** Have these students work together to write sentences restating the advice. *You shouldn't drink coffee.*
>
> • **Higher-level** Tell these students to reconstruct as much of the paragraph as they can remember.
>
> Put up the groups' sentences/paragraphs and go over them as a class. Are any important ideas missing? Compare the strength of the modals students used with the original paragraph. Explain *up to no good* if students misinterpreted or ignored it.

3 Listen for different forms of advice to determine the strength

Guided Practice IV
10–15 minutes

3-04 1. Say: *Now we're going to listen to people giving health advice. You need to decide whether Speaker A or Speaker B gives stronger advice.*

2. Play the audio. Direct students to listen silently without writing.

3. Replay the audio. Ask students to check the correct column in the chart.

4. Ask for a show of hands for each answer.

Answers	
1. Speaker A	4. Speaker A
2. Speaker B	5. Speaker B
3. Speaker B	6. Speaker A

> **MULTILEVEL STRATEGIES**
>
> Replay the audio for 3 to allow pre-level students to catch up while you challenge on- and higher-level students.
>
> • **Pre-level** Have these students listen again to complete the chart.
>
> • **On- and Higher-level** Have these students listen again and write the advice words they hear.

4 Use *should, had better, have to,* and *must* to talk about your opinions

Communicative Practice and Application
20–25 minutes

A 1. Direct students to look at the photo. Ask: *How does the woman feel?* [sick] *How do you know?* [She has a cold, she's blowing her nose.] *What should she do to feel better?* [drink juice, rest, etc.]

2. Read the instructions and questions aloud. Give students time to think about answers to the questions and take notes.

B Direct students to work with a partner to write two more questions.

C 1. Have pairs merge to form teams of four. Model the exercise by "joining" one of the pairs. Each pair takes a turn asking and answering questions while the class listens.

2. Check comprehension of the exercise. Ask: *Who asks questions?* [everyone] *Who answers questions?* [everyone]

3. Ask volunteers to share something interesting they learned from their classmates.

Evaluation
10–15 minutes

TEST YOURSELF

Ask students to write the sentences independently. Collect and correct their writing.

MULTILEVEL STRATEGIES

Target the *Test Yourself* to the level of your students.

- **Pre-level** Provide sentence frames for these students to complete.

1. (name) thinks that people should (advice) when they have a cold.

2. (name) thinks people ought to (advice) for their health.

3. (name) thinks people shouldn't (advice) to stay healthy.

4. (name) thinks someone who feels really sick had better (advice).

- **Higher-level** Have these students write a paragraph in response to this prompt: *Imagine your niece or nephew is away from home and isn't feeling well. What advice would you give him or her?*

EXTENSION ACTIVITY

Discussion

1. Write a series of statements on the board.

Occasionally, Ray feels sad for no reason.

Heejung often gets so frustrated that she yells at her children.

Keri cries every day.

Leo feels bored all of the time. He's not interested in anything.

2. Ask students what advice they would give these people. Ask which ones they think need professional help.

LESSON 4 EVERYDAY CONVERSATION

Lesson Overview

MULTILEVEL OBJECTIVES

Pre-, On-, and Higher-level: Ask and answer questions at a doctor's office and listen for medical information

LANGUAGE FOCUS

Grammar: Verb with gerunds and infinitives (*He quit smoking. He decided to cut back on salt.*)

Vocabulary: *Diabetes, prevention, shot, immunization, ointment, tetanus*

For vocabulary support, see these **Oxford Picture Dictionary** topics: Illnesses and Medical Conditions, pages 112–113; Taking Care of Your Health, pages 116–117; Medical Care, page 111; A Hospital, pages 122–123

STRATEGY FOCUS

Practice language to confirm information.

READINESS CONNECTION

In this lesson, students determine the health precautions different kinds of workers should take.

PACING

To compress this lesson: Conduct *Discuss* as a whole-class activity.

To extend this lesson: After completing 6B, have students write letters asking for advice. (See end of lesson.)

And/or have students complete **Workbook 4 page 62** and **Multilevel Activities 4 Unit 9 page 103**.

Lesson Notes

CORRELATIONS

CCRS: SL.1.B (a.) Come to discussions prepared, having read or studied required material; explicitly draw on that preparation and other information known about the topic to explore ideas under discussion. (b.) Follow agreed-upon rules for discussions. (c.) Ask questions to check understanding of information presented, stay on topic, and link their comments to the remarks of others. (d.) Explain their own ideas and understanding in light of the discussion.

SL.2.B Determine the main ideas and supporting details of a text read aloud or information presented in diverse media and formats, including visually, quantitatively, and orally.

SL.4.B Report on a topic or text, tell a story, or recount an experience with appropriate facts and relevant, descriptive details, speaking clearly at an understandable pace.

SL.6.B Speak in complete sentences when appropriate to task and situation in order to provide requested detail or clarification.

R.1.B Ask and answer such questions as who, what, where, when, why, and how to demonstrate understanding of key details in a text.

R.2.A Identify the main topic and retell key details of a text.

R.6.B Identify the main purpose of a text, including what the author wants to answer, explain, or describe.

R.7.B Use information gained from illustrations and the words in a text to demonstrate understanding of the text.

L.1.B (l.) Produce simple, compound and complex sentences.

L.1.C (d.) Use modal auxiliaries to convey various conditions. (f.) Use verb tense to convey various times, sequences, states, and conditions.

L.1.D (f.) Explain the function of verbals (gerunds, participles, infinitives) in general and their function in particular sentences.

RF.2.A (g.) Isolate and pronounce initial, medial vowel, and final sounds (phonemes) in spoken single-syllable words.

LRF.4.B (a.) Read grade-level text with purpose and understanding.

ELPS: 2. An ELL can participate in level-appropriate oral and written exchanges of information, ideas, and analyses, in various social and academic contexts, responding to peer, audience, or reader comments and questions. 4. An ELL can construct level-appropriate oral and written claims and support them with reasoning and evidence. 6. An ELL can analyze and critique the arguments of others orally and in writing. 7. An ELL can adapt language choices to purpose, task, and audience when speaking and writing. 9. An ELL can create clear and coherent level-appropriate speech and text. 10. An ELL can demonstrate command of the conventions of standard English to communicate in level-appropriate speech and writing.

Warm-up and Review
10–15 minutes (books closed)

Ask students how they feel about going to the doctor. *Do you go regularly or do you avoid going?* Find out if they go to an English-speaking doctor or if they go to a doctor who speaks their native language.

Introduction
5 minutes

1. Point out that even if the students' regular doctor speaks their native language, there are sometimes situations where we can't choose which doctor to see—for example, in the emergency room.

2. State the objective: *Today we're going to learn to talk to the doctor and listen for medical information.*

1 Learn ways to ask and answer questions at a medical visit

Presentation I
10–20 minutes

 3-05 1. Direct students to look at the picture. Build students' schema. Ask: *Who do you see?* [a patient and a doctor/physician's assistant] *What is the health-care worker doing?* [listening to the patient's heart/lungs] *Should patients ask questions when they get a physical?* [yes]

2. Write *set aside time for…* on the board and elicit what the expression means [to make or plan time to do something].

3. Read the instructions aloud. Play the audio. Give students a minute to answer the question. Go over the answer as a class.

Answer
She is there for a checkup.

Guided Practice I
20–25 minutes

 3-05 1. Read the instructions aloud. Play the audio. Ask students to listen for the answers to each question.

2. Ask students to compare their answers with a partner. Circulate and monitor to ensure students understand the audio.

Answers
1. She has a family history of heart trouble and her job is very stressful.
2. She is paying more attention to good nutrition, eating more dark green vegetables, and drinking a lot of water.
3. She recommends cutting back on added salt, exercising, relaxing, and getting regular physicals.

 3-06 Read the instructions aloud. Explain that students are going to hear the audio one more time. They should write the words they hear to complete the sentences. Play the audio. Call on volunteers to elicit the answers.

Answers
1. So I need to
2. So I'm supposed to
3. So I should

2 Practice your pronunciation

Pronunciation Extension
10–15 minutes

A **3-07** 1. Write *I'm sure she's had that chest cold and a slight stomachache for a week,* on the board. Say the sentence and ask students to repeat it. Underline the *s* in *sure* and *since* and the *ch* in *chest* and *stomachache*. Say and have students repeat those words. Say: *Now we're going to focus on different pronunciations of s and ch.*

2. Play the audio. Direct students to listen for the pronunciation of *s* and *ch*.

3. Call on volunteers to tell you how the sounds are different.

B **3-08** 1. Have students work individually to choose the correct sound for each word.

2. Play the audio and have students check their answers.

Answers	
1. sh	4. ch
2. s	5. ch
3. k	6. k

C **3-09** Have students take turns saying the sentences with a partner. Play the audio and have students check their pronunciation. Call on volunteers to say the sentences for the class.

3 Use verbs with gerunds and infinitives

Presentation II and Guided Practice II
10–15 minutes

 1. Introduce the new topic. *Now we're going to talk about health using verbs followed by gerunds or infinitives.*

2. Read the instructions aloud. Direct students to study the chart. Read and have students repeat the sentences in the chart. Check comprehension of the chart. Ask: *What is the form of a gerund?* [verb + ing] *What is an infinitive?* [to + verb] *What are verbs that are followed by gerunds?* [quit, consider] *What form of verb follows* plan? [an infinitive] *What form can you use after* like? [either an infinitive or a gerund]

3. Tell students to underline infinitives and circle gerunds and then compare answers with a partner. Go over the answers with the class.

Answers
Underline: to limit, to make, to walk
Circle: smoking, joining, walking

Guided Practice III
15–20 minutes

 Have students work with a partner to complete the sentences. Call on volunteers to read the completed sentences aloud.

Answers
1. exercising
2. to do/doing
3. to change
4. to eat/eating
5. smoking

MULTILEVEL STRATEGIES

Seat higher-level students together for 3B.

• **Higher-level** If these students finish 3B early, provide them with this list of verbs followed by a gerund: *postpone, recommend, can't help* and this list of verbs followed by an infinitive: *deserve, intend, refuse.* Direct them to write a sentence with each of the words. Have volunteers write their sentences on the board to share with the class.

TIP

Provide more practice with infinitives and gerunds after 3B. Write conversation starters on the board. 1. *Tell me about a time you quit doing something.* 2. *What do you always avoid doing?* 3. *Tell me about a time you considered doing something and then changed your mind.* 4. *What have you decided to do recently?* 5. *What do you plan to do this weekend?* 6. *Tell me about something you agreed to do recently.* Direct students to walk around the room and talk to six people. Tell them to use a different conversation starter with each person.

4 Building conversation skills

Guided Practice IV
15–20 minutes

 Direct students to look at the picture and skim the conversation. Build students' schema by asking: *Who is in the picture?* [a patient and a doctor] *Where are they?* [in the doctor's office] *How do you think the patient feels?* [a little nervous] *What do you think is his problem?* [he's overweight] Have them work with partners to identify the purpose of the conversation. Elicit responses and ask: *How do you know?* or *Why do you say that?* to encourage students to state their reasoning.

Possible Answer
The purpose of the conversation is to talk about the patient's health.

B 🔊 **3-10** 1. Ask students to read the instructions and tell you what they are going to do [listen and read and respond to the question]. Play the audio and then elicit the answer to the question.

2. Check comprehension. Ask: *What has Tony been working on?* [losing weight] *What is he worried about?* [diabetes] *How has he lost weight?* [by eating smaller portions] *What does the doctor recommend?* [to try to exercise 30 minutes 5 days a week] *How do you know the patient is listening carefully?* [He repeats some of the doctor's words to check his understanding.]

3. Ask students to read the conversation with a partner. Circulate and monitor pronunciation. Model and have students repeat difficult words or phrases.

4. Ask: *What other suggestions could you make to help someone lose weight?* Point out places where you could make other suggestions. Ask volunteers to point out others.

Possible Answer
He wants to prevent diabetes.

Communicative Practice and Application I
15–20 minutes

C 1. Pair students and have them read the instructions silently. Check their comprehension of the exercise. Ask: *What are the two roles?* [physician's assistant and patient] *Is the conversation at a health center?* [yes]

2. Model and have students repeat the expressions in the *In Other Words* box. Explain that they should use these expressions in their conversations.

3. Draw a T-chart on the board. Label the left column *Physician's assistant* and the right column *Patient*. Elicit examples of what each person might say and make notes on the chart.

4. Set a time limit (three minutes). Have students act out the role-play. Call "time" and have students switch roles.

5. Ask three volunteer pairs to act out their role-play for the class. Tell students who are listening to make a simple table with four rows and three columns. Use the top row to label the columns: *Positive change, Concerns,* and *Advice*. Have students take notes in the chart for each role-play.

MULTILEVEL STRATEGIES

For 4C, adapt the role-play to the level of your students.

• **Pre-level** Provide these students with a simplified role-play.

Physician's assistant: You've _____ since your last visit.

Patient: Well, I'm trying to _____. I'm concerned about _____.

Physician's assistant: That's great.

Patient: Is there anything else you'd recommend?

Physician's assistant: Try _____. You should _____.

Patient: So I should _____, right?

Physician's assistant: Yes, that's it.

5 Focus on listening for details

Presentation and Guided Practice
20–25 minutes

A 1. Direct students to read the poster. Elicit any questions about the vocabulary. Check comprehension. Ask: *What is tetanus?* [a serious disease] *How can people get tetanus?* [from a cut that gets dirty] *How often should adults get a tetanus shot?* [every ten years]

2. Read the instructions and statement aloud. Pair students to discuss their opinions and state reasons.

3. Ask volunteers to tell the class about their discussion.

B Direct students to read the sentences and predict what they will hear. Have students compare ideas with a partner.

C 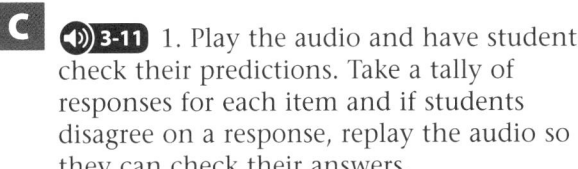 1. Play the audio and have students check their predictions. Take a tally of responses for each item and if students disagree on a response, replay the audio so they can check their answers.

2. Go over the answers with the class.

Answers
1. on a machine
2. ointment
3. more than 20
4. one shot
5. has to

MULTILEVEL STRATEGIES

Replay the audio to challenge on- and higher-level students while allowing pre-level students to catch up.

• **Pre-level** Have these students listen again to go over their answers.

• **On- and Higher-level** Write questions on the board. Tell these students to write the answers. *Does Mr. Gomez need stitches? What other shot is he getting? Why does he need to go back to the doctor's office?* Ask volunteers to write the answers on the board.

6 Discuss

Communicative Practice and Application II
15–20 minutes

A 1. Read the instructions aloud. Draw a sample chart on the board with space for jobs on one side and precautions on the other. Call on volunteers to read the dialogue in 6A. Elicit a precaution nursing home workers should take [e.g., using hand sanitizer] and write it in the chart. Explain that students will make a chart like this one based on their own discussions.

2. Put students into teams of four and assign roles: reporter, manager, administrative assistant, and editor. Verify students' understanding of the roles. Encourage students to use the phrases in the *Speaking Note* during their discussions.

3. Set a time limit for the discussions (ten minutes). Write the sentence frame from 6B on the board. Then circulate and monitor.

B Call "time." Ask the reporter for each team to report the results of their team's discussion, using the sentence frame on the board.

Evaluation
5 minutes

TEST YOURSELF

1. Ask students to complete the checkboxes individually.

2. Tell students that you are going to read each of the items in the checklist aloud. If they are not at all confident with that skill, they should hold up a closed fist. If they are not very confident, they should hold up one finger. If they are somewhat confident, two fingers; confident, three fingers; very confident, four fingers. If they think they could teach the skill, they should hold up five fingers. Read each item in the checklist and identify students that may need further support.

> **TIP**
> For homework, you could ask students to write a sentence or two about what discussion skills they still need to work on or, if they are confident in all of the skills, what skill they are most proud of.

EXTENSION ACTIVITY

Ask Doctor Dora

1. Seat students in mixed-level groups. Tell them that Dr. Dora is a newspaper columnist who gives people health advice. She can't help with emergencies, but she can give general advice about on-going problems. Give each group a large sheet of paper and have them write a letter on the top half of the paper to Dr. Dora about a health concern.

2. Direct groups to pass their papers to another group. Tell students to read the letters and write back on the bottom half of the paper as Dr. Dora. Point out that they can only give general recommendations, including what kind of doctor the person should see. Dr. Dora can't prescribe medicine!

3. Go over the letters with the class and discuss whether Dr. Dora gave good advice.

LESSON 5 READING

Lesson Overview

MULTILEVEL OBJECTIVES

On-, Pre-, and Higher-level: Read about and discuss health insurance

LANGUAGE FOCUS

Grammar: Questions with modals (*What should I look at when I'm trying to choose a health plan?*)

Vocabulary: *Cover, referral, specialist, deductibles, co-payments, network*

For vocabulary support, see these **Oxford Picture Dictionary** topics: Medical Care, page 111; A Hospital, pages 122–123

STRATEGY FOCUS

Use FAQs while reading to scan and locate specific information.

READINESS CONNECTION

In this lesson, students analyze different types of health insurance.

PACING

To compress this lesson: Conduct the word study in 2A as a whole-class activity.

To extend this lesson: Have students practice with verbs to talk about health and illness. (See end of lesson.)

And/or have students complete **Workbook 4 page 63** and **Multilevel Activities 4 Unit 9 pages 104–105**.

Lesson Notes

CORRELATIONS

CCRS: SL.1.B (b.) Follow agreed-upon rules for discussions. (c.) Ask questions to check understanding of information presented, stay on topic, and link their comments to the remarks of others. (d.) Explain their own ideas and understanding in light of the discussion.
SL.2.B Determine the main ideas and supporting details of a text read aloud or information presented in diverse media and formats, including visually, quantitatively, and orally.
SL.6.B Speak in complete sentences when appropriate to task and situation in order to provide requested detail or clarification.
R.1.B Ask and answer such questions as who, what, where, when, why, and how to demonstrate understanding of key details in a text.
R.1.C Refer to details and examples in a text when explaining what the text says explicitly and when drawing inferences from the text.
R.2.B Determine the main idea of a text; recount the key details and explain how they support the main idea.
R.4.B Determine the meaning of general academic and domain-specific words and phrases in a text relevant to a topic or subject area.
R.5.B Know and use various text features to locate key facts or information in a text efficiently.
R.7.C Interpret information presented visually, orally, or quantitatively and explain how the information contributes to an understanding of the text in which it appears.

L.1.B (b.) Explain the function of nouns, pronouns, verbs, adjectives, and adverbs in general and their functions in particular sentences. (g.) Form and use regular and irregular verbs. (l.) Produce simple, compound and complex sentences.
L.1.C (d.) Use modal auxiliaries to convey various conditions.
L.4.B (e.) Use glossaries and beginning dictionaries, both print and digital, to determine or clarify the meaning of words and phrases.
L.6.B Use words and phrases acquired through conversations, reading and being read to, and responding to texts, including using adjectives and adverbs to describe.
RF.4.B (a.) Read grade-level text with purpose and understanding.

ELPS: 1. An ELL can construct meaning from oral presentations and literary and informational text through level-appropriate listening, reading, and viewing. 2. An ELL can participate in level-appropriate oral and written exchanges of information, ideas, and analyses, in various social and academic contexts, responding to peer, audience, or reader comments and questions. 3. An ELL can speak and write about level-appropriate complex literary and informational texts and topics. 4. An ELL can construct level-appropriate oral and written claims and support them with reasoning and evidence. 6. An ELL can analyze and critique the arguments of others orally and in writing. 8. An ELL can determine the meaning of words and phrases in oral presentation and literary and informational text.

Warm-up and Review
10–15 minutes (books closed)

Write *Health Insurance* on the board. Ask students to brainstorm words and phrases that they associate with this topic.

Introduction
5 minutes

1. Ask students to describe the health insurance system in their countries and say whether they think it is the same as the health insurance system in the U.S.

2. State the objective: *Today we're going to read about and discuss health insurance.*

1 Read

Presentation
10–20 minutes

A Read the questions aloud. Call on volunteers to share their ideas.

B 1. Read the words and definitions. Elicit sample sentences for each word or supply them if students can't. Ask students what their insurance covers. Elicit examples of referrals they have gotten. Elicit examples of specialists and write them on the board.

2. Write other words from the reading on the board: *option, provider, network, premium, deductible,* and *co-pay*. Elicit the words students know.

Pre-reading

C Read the instructions aloud and confirm that students understand where the "numbered headings" are. Go over the *Reader's Note*. Check comprehension. Ask: *What does FAQ stand for?* [frequently asked questions] *Why do writers use them?* [to organize information] *How do they help readers?* [Readers can scan to locate specific information.]

2. Have students answer the question individually and then compare answers with a partner. Check the answer with the class. If any students answer incorrectly, ask them to support their answer using information from the article. Establish the correct answer.

Answer
c. Answers to questions about health insurance.

Guided Practice: While Reading
20–30 minutes

 1. Ask students to read the article silently and answer the question.

2. Have volunteers give their answers to the question.

3. After they've finished reading, direct students to underline unfamiliar words they would like to know. Elicit the words and encourage other students to provide definitions or examples.

4. Check comprehension. Ask: *What is the most common type of health insurance?* [HMOS] *What are the different kinds of payments you have to make when you have health insurance?* [monthly premiums, co-pays, deductibles] *What is a co-pay?* [the amount you pay for each doctor's visit]

> **TIP**
>
> After 1D or 1E, look at a coverage summary page from a real health insurance policy description. Have students find the deductibles and co-payments. Go over the coverage categories and discuss the vocabulary.

> **MULTILEVEL STRATEGIES**
>
> Adapt 1D to the level of your students.
> • **Pre-level** Read the text aloud to these students as they follow along.
> • **On- and Higher-level** Pair students and have them read the article aloud to each other, taking turns to read each paragraph.

Guided Practice: Rereading
10–15 minutes

 1. Provide an opportunity for students to extract evidence from the text. Have students reread the article and underline any words or phrases that indicate why the writer chose to ask and answer these questions.

2. Pair students and tell them to compare the words they underlined and report anything they disagree on. Discuss and clarify as needed. Ask if the FAQs answered all of their questions or if they think something important has been left out.

F 1. Have students work individually to write the FAQ that answers each question and then ask and answer the questions with a partner. Go over the answers with the class.

2. Elicit and discuss any additional questions about the reading. You could introduce new questions for class discussion: *What are the advantages of each kind of plan? Which feature is most important to you?*

Answers
1. 1: In an HMO, you see a doctor from the plan's network of health-care providers. In a PPO, you can see a provider outside of your network but you pay an extra cost.
2. 2: A deductible is the amount you have to spend on health services before your insurance company will pay for any costs.
3. 3: Services, choices, and costs
4. 2: $10–$30
5. 1: doctors, hospitals, and pharmacies
6. 1: An HMO will usually not cover the cost if you see a doctor outside of the network (except in an emergency).

MULTILEVEL STRATEGIES

For 2B, seat same-level students together.

• **Pre-level** Direct these students to copy the words from the chart into their notebooks with a definition. Allow them to look in their dictionaries if necessary.

• **Higher-level** If these students finish before the others, ask them to write sentences using the verbs for talking about health and illness in the chart. Ask volunteers to write their sentences on the board.

2 Word study

Guided Practice: Post-reading
10 minutes

A 1. Direct students to look at the chart and identify the topic [verbs for talking about health and illness]. Have students read the chart.

2. Read the first two questions. Elicit questions or sentences for the other expressions in the chart.

3. Have students repeat after you as you say each expression with natural intonation, rhythm, and stress.

4. Direct students to complete the sentences and then compare answers with a partner. Read the correct answers and have students check their work.

Answers
1. see
2. get
3. have, feel/get
4. saw, take

B Direct students to work individually to write a sentence for each topic that includes the underlined word or phrase. Ask volunteers to write their sentences on the board. Have the rest of the class suggest grammar and spelling edits as needed.

3 Talk it over

Guided Practice
15–20 minutes

A Have students look at the table and read the *Reader's Note*. Point out that they need to use the information from the table and the note to complete the sentences and answer the questions. Confirm understanding of key vocabulary: *vary, annual, out-of-pocket, estimated*. Set a time limit (ten minutes). Have students work in pairs to complete the task. Ask volunteers to share their answers with the class.

Answers
1. $4,620
2. $160
3. A, C
4. $9,000
5. $13,800

Communicative Practice
20 minutes

B Read the questions aloud. Set a time limit (ten minutes). Pair students to discuss the questions.

C Ask volunteers to share their ideas with the class.

Application

5–10 minutes

BRING IT TO LIFE

Ask students to brainstorm ways that their community encourages healthy living. Ask volunteers to share their ideas.

EXTENSION ACTIVITY

Practice

Provide additional practice with the verbs for talking about health and illness.

1. Have students write questions using the verbs for talking about health and illness. *When did you last see a doctor?*

2. Pair students and have them ask and answer the questions they wrote. Monitor and provide feedback.

AT WORK

Warm-up and Review
10–15 minutes (books closed)

Begin the lesson by talking about a physical problem you have had because of your work (e.g., carpal tunnel from working on a computer, a sore back from standing a long time, stiffness from sitting in a chair for a long time). Elicit physical problems that students have suffered or know about that are related to work.

Introduction
5 minutes

State the objective: *Today we're going to talk about staying safe and healthy at work.*

Presentation
5 minutes

 Read the instructions aloud. Play the audio. Give students a minute to think about the question. Elicit responses from the class.

Possible Answer
They are discussing a memo about preventing injuries on the job, who is responsible for protecting workers, and how to prevent injuries.

Guided Practice
10–15 minutes

 Read the instructions and actions aloud. Play the audio again. Direct students to listen for each action and put a check next to any that they hear mentioned. Have them compare answers with a partner.

Answers
Checked:
tell a manager if they see a problem
not sit for too long a time
take computer breaks
read the memo about safety

 Read the instructions aloud. Play the audio again, encouraging students to take notes in their notebooks. Set a time limit (five minutes) for students to discuss their answers with a partner. Circulate and monitor.

Presentation and Communicative Practice
10 minutes

 1. Direct students' attention to the *Do/Say* chart and ask them to identify the lesson's soft skill [helping people get quiet]. Ask the class which column has examples of language [right] and which has examples of behaviors [left].

2. Say a phrase from the left and act it out. Say it again and have the class act it out with you. Say it a third time and have the class act it out for you.

3. Model the sentence frames from the right using authentic intonation. Have students practice imitating your inflection.

4. Put students in teams of four and assign each team a question. Assign roles: reporter, manager, administrative assistant, and researcher. (Researchers will ask you questions on behalf of the team.) Verify understanding of the roles. Set a time limit (five minutes) and monitor.

5. Write sentence frames on the board that teams can use to summarize their response. *Our team discussed the following question: _____. We decided _____ because _____.*

6. Call "time" and let reporters rehearse their report for one minute. Direct each reporter to present to three other teams.

Communicative Practice and Application
20–25 minutes

 1. Direct students to work in pairs to take turns describing an issue and offering advice.

2. Elicit other advice for each issue and write it on the board.

 1. Have pairs merge to form teams of four. Tell students that they are going to be having an informal conversation about safety at work.

2. Direct groups to come up with three more possible issues and three suggestions. Each group should select a manager to run the meeting. The other three members should each choose an issue to bring up.

3. As students have their conversations, circulate and monitor. Provide global feedback once the activity ends.

4. Call on volunteers to present issues and suggestions to the class.

TEAMWORK & LANGUAGE REVIEW

Lesson Overview

MULTILEVEL OBJECTIVES

On-, Pre-, and Higher-level: Expand upon and review unit grammar and life skills

LANGUAGE FOCUS

Grammar: Modals of advice (*You ought to exercise more.*)

Vocabulary: Health advice and concerns

For vocabulary support, see these **Oxford Picture Dictionary** topics: Symptoms and Injuries, page 110; Illnesses and Medical Conditions, pages 112–113; Taking Care of Your Health, pages 116–117; Medical Care, page 111; A Hospital, pages 122–123

READINESS CONNECTION

In this review, students cooperate with others and decide how to give advice on health to a loved one.

PACING

To extend this review: Have students complete **Workbook 4 page 64**, **Multilevel Activities 4 Unit 9 page 106**, and **Multilevel Grammar Exercises 4 Unit 9**.

Lesson Notes

CORRELATIONS

CCRS: SL.1.B (a.) Come to discussions prepared, having read or studied required material; explicitly draw on that preparation and other information known about the topic to explore ideas under discussion. (b.) Follow agreed-upon rules for discussions. (c.) Ask questions to check understanding of information presented, stay on topic, and link their comments to the remarks of others. (d.) Explain their own ideas and understanding in light of the discussion.

SL.1.C (b.) Follow agreed-upon rules for discussions and carry out assigned roles.

SL.2.B Determine the main ideas and supporting details of a text read aloud or information presented in diverse media and formats, including visually, quantitatively, and orally.

SL.4.B Report on a topic or text, tell a story, or recount an experience with appropriate facts and relevant, descriptive details, speaking clearly at an understandable pace.

R.1.B Ask and answer such questions as who, what, where, when, why, and how to demonstrate understanding of key details in a text.

R.2.A Identify the main topic and retell key details of a text.

R.7.B Use information gained from illustrations and the words in a text to demonstrate understanding of the text.

L.1.B (l.) Produce simple, compound and complex sentences.

L.1.C (d.) Use modal auxiliaries to convey various conditions.

L.1.D (f.) Explain the function of verbals (gerunds, participles, infinitives) in general and their function in particular sentences. (h.) Form and use verbs in the indicative, imperative, interrogative, conditional and subjunctive mood.

L.6.B Use words and phrases acquired through conversations, reading and being read to, and responding to texts, including using adjectives and adverbs to describe.

RF.4.B (a.) Read grade-level text with purpose and understanding.

ELPS: 2. An ELL can participate in level-appropriate oral and written exchanges of information, ideas, and analyses, in various social and academic contexts, responding to peer, audience, or reader comments and questions. 4. An ELL can construct level-appropriate oral and written claims and support them with reasoning and evidence. 5. An ELL can conduct research and evaluate and communicate findings to answer questions or solve problems. 7. An ELL can adapt language choices to purpose, task, and audience when speaking and writing. 9. An ELL can create clear and coherent level-appropriate speech and text. 10. An ELL can demonstrate command of the conventions of standard English to communicate in level-appropriate speech and writing.

Warm-up and Review
10–15 minutes (books closed)

1. Review *At Work* activity F.

2. Ask students to share the good, not-so-good, and interesting things that happened during the group activity. As students speak, write their responses in a chart on the board.

Introduction and Presentation
5 minutes

1. Pair students and direct them to look at the picture in their book. Ask them to describe what they see to their partner.

2. Ask volunteer pairs to share their ideas with the class.

Guided Practice
15–20 minutes

  1. Model the process for completing the first sentence.

2. Set a time limit (five minutes). Have students work with partners to complete the activity. Direct them to explain their choices. Go over answers with the class.

Answers	
1. must	4. Jill and Kyle must
2. should	5. They ought to
3. Jill ought to	6. should not

  1. Read the instructions aloud. Direct students' attention to the pictures. Elicit what they see.

2. Have students work in pairs to complete the sentences and take turns reading the sentences to each other.

3. Go over the answers with the class.

Answers	
1. to make	5. to have
2. joining	6. to eat
3. riding/to ride	7. smoking
4. taking/to take	8. drinking/to drink

Communicative Practice
30–40 minutes

  1. Group students and assign roles: manager, director, editor, and presenters. Confirm understanding of roles (manager keeps track of time, director facilitates the conversation, editor writes and corrects script, and presenters present the conversation to the class). Explain that students are going to work with their teams to write a conversation between a person with a problem and a friend who offers advice.

2. Read steps 2–5 of the activity aloud. Check comprehension of the task. *What is the first thing you should do?* [choose a problem from the list] *What should the friend in the conversation do?* [give suggestions or advice]

3. Set a time limit (ten minutes) to complete the exercise. Circulate and answer any questions.

4. Have presenters from each team perform their conversations for the class.

  1. Have students walk around the room to conduct the interviews. To get students moving, tell them to interview three people who were not in their team for C.

2. Set a time limit (five minutes) to complete the exercise.

3. Tell students to make a note of their classmates' answers but not to worry about writing complete sentences.

> **MULTILEVEL STRATEGIES**
>
> Adapt the mixer in D to the level of your students.
> - **Pre-and On-level** Pair these students and have them interview other pairs together.
> - **Higher-level** Have these students ask an additional question and write all answers.

  1. Call on individuals to report what they learned about their classmates. Keep a running tally on the board for question 2 on the board.

2. Use your tally for question 2 to create a pie chart on the board. Circulate and answer any questions.

PROBLEM SOLVING
10–15 minutes

A 🔊 3-13 1. Ask: *Do you have any friends or relatives with bad health habits?* Tell students they will read a story about a man whose sister has bad health habits. Direct students to read Ivan's story silently.

2. Ask: *What are Katya's bad habits?*

3. Play the audio and have students read along silently.

B 1. Elicit answers to question 1.

2. Write *He could try...* on the board and ask volunteers to write their ideas under it. Write *He shouldn't try...* and ask volunteers to write their ideas.

3. Pair students. Have them write two lists of what Ivan could and shouldn't try.

4. Go over the lists. Have the class vote on Ivan's best course of action.

Possible Answer
1. Ivan is worried about his sister, Katya, because he thinks she doesn't pay enough attention to her health. His sister is very independent and doesn't like advice, so Ivan doesn't know what to do. 2. Answers will vary.

Evaluation
20–25 minutes

To test students' understanding of the unit language and content, have them take the Unit 9 Test, available on the Teacher Resource Center.

UNIT 10 Get Involved!

Unit Overview

This unit explores community issues and ways to get involved with a range of employability skills and contextualizes indirect information questions.

KEY OBJECTIVES

Lesson 1	Identify and discuss community involvement and community services
Lesson 2	Identify community problems and write an email asking for assistance
Lesson 3	Use indirect information questions to ask about community issues
Lesson 4	Demonstrate understanding of others' feelings about an issue
Lesson 5	Identify ways to get involved in a community
At Work	Disagree at work
Teamwork & Language Review	Review unit language

UNIT FEATURES

Academic Vocabulary	accessible, administration, alternative, dispose, editorial, enforcement, environmental, implement, input, legal, partnership, primary, resident
Employability Skills	• Listen actively • Understand teamwork • Speak so others can understand • Communicate information • Work independently • Communicate verbally • Work with others • Comprehend written material • Analyze information • Think critically • Decide the best way to reach goals • Decide how to solve a problem • Decide how to help resolve community problems

Resources	**Class Audio** CD3, Tracks 14–24
	Workbook Unit 10, pages 65–71
	Teacher Resource Center
	    Multilevel Activities 4 Unit 10
	    Multilevel Grammar Exercises 4 Unit 10
	    Unit 10 Test
	Oxford Picture Dictionary Civic Engagement, Community Cleanup, Career Planning

LESSON 1 VOCABULARY

Lesson Overview

MULTILEVEL OBJECTIVES

On-level: Talk about community involvement and describe community services

Pre-level: Identify community-involvement vocabulary and describe community services

Higher-level: Talk and write about community involvement and community services

LANGUAGE FOCUS

Grammar: Want/need + to-infinitive *(I want to talk to the city manager.)*

Vocabulary: Community involvement and community services

For vocabulary support, see this **Oxford Picture Dictionary** topic: Community Cleanup, pages 152–153.

READINESS CONNECTION

In this lesson, students work with others to conduct research about community services.

PACING

To compress this lesson: Conduct 1B as a whole-class activity.

To extend this lesson: Have students discuss who they would call in certain situations. (See end of lesson.)

And/or have students complete **Workbook 4 page 65** and **Multilevel Activities 4 Unit 10 pages 108–109**.

Lesson Notes

CORRELATIONS

CCRS: SL.1.B (b.) Follow agreed-upon rules for discussions. (c.) Ask questions to check understanding of information presented, stay on topic, and link their comments to the remarks of others. (d.) Explain their own ideas and understanding in light of the discussion.

SL.2.B Determine the main ideas and supporting details of a text read aloud or information presented in diverse media and formats, including visually, quantitatively, and orally.

SL.4.B Report on a topic or text, tell a story, or recount an experience with appropriate facts and relevant, descriptive details, speaking clearly at an understandable pace.

SL.6.B Speak in complete sentences when appropriate to task and situation in order to provide requested detail or clarification.

R.1.B Ask and answer such questions as who, what, where, when, why, and how to demonstrate understanding of key details in a text.

R.4.B Determine the meaning of general academic and domain-specific words and phrases in a text relevant to a topic or subject area.

R.7.B Use information gained from illustrations and the words in a text to demonstrate understanding of the text.

W.7.A Participate in shared research and writing projects.

L.1.B (l.) Produce simple, compound and complex sentences.

L.4.B (a.) Use sentence-level context as a clue to the meaning of a word or phrase.

RF.4.B (a.) Read grade-level text with purpose and understanding.

ELPS: 1. An ELL can construct meaning from oral presentations and literary and informational text through level-appropriate listening, reading, and viewing. 2. An ELL can participate in level-appropriate oral and written exchanges of information, ideas, and analyses, in various social and academic contexts, responding to peer, audience, or reader comments and questions. 3. An ELL can speak and write about level-appropriate complex literary and informational texts and topics. 5. An ELL can conduct research and evaluate and communicate findings to answer questions or solve problems. 8. An ELL can determine the meaning of words and phrases in oral presentation and literary and informational text.

Warm-up and Review
10–15 minutes (books closed)

Get students to start thinking about their communities. Ask: *Do you know your neighbors? What's your relationship like? What do you have in common with your neighbors?*

Introduction
5 minutes

1. Say: *Even if we don't socialize with our neighbors, we still have a lot in common. We are part of a community. We use the same parks and schools, drive down the same streets, and receive the same services.*

2. State the objective: *Today we're going to learn words for community involvement and community services.*

1 Identify community-involvement strategies

Presentation I
20–25 minutes

 1. Write *Ways to Get Involved in the Community* on the board and elicit one example from the whole class. Have students work together and brainstorm in a group. Make a list on the board.

2. Have students identify the best ways to get involved. Elicit ideas and put a checkmark next to the ways students feel are the most important, encouraging them to explain their reasons.

B 1. Direct students to look at the pictures. Ask: *What is the problem in the first picture?* [the area is a mess] Pair students to talk about what is happening in the pictures. Ask: *What happened between the first picture and the last picture?* [The community built a playground in the formerly empty lot with garbage.]

2. Ask volunteers to describe the pictures to the class. To preview vocabulary in the listening, ask: *Why is garbage in an empty lot a problem?* Elicit that it could attract rats. *Is there a problem in your community that bothers you?*

C 1. Read the instructions aloud. Say each phrase and have students repeat. Have students work individually to number the actions in order and then compare answers with a partner.

2. Go over the answers with the class.

Answers
6 implemented the plan
2 discussed alternatives
1 identified a problem
5 got approval
3 proposed a solution
4 developed a plan

Guided Practice I
10–20 minutes

 🔊 3-14 1. Prepare students to listen by saying, *Now you're going to listen to a man tell his friend about how to get involved in his community. While you listen, take notes and check your work in 1C.* Ask students to circle the items in 1C that don't match the listening passage.

2. Have students work in pairs to compare their notes and correct any incorrect answers.

3. Replay the audio and challenge students to listen for the answers to these questions: *What city does the first man live in?* [Riverview] *What was the problem that his friend describes?* [garbage in an empty lot] *What was the solution?* [a new playground] *Who did they need to get permission from?* [city council]

2 Learn about community services

Presentation II
10–20 minutes

 1. Direct students to look at the city directory. Introduce the new topic: *We've talked about ways to get involved. Now we're going to talk about services in the community.*

2. Elicit the names of the departments students see on the directory.

3. Read the instructions and the department names aloud. Ask for examples of when a person might call each department.

4. Elicit answers to the question. Ask students to justify their choices for the department that gets the most calls.

5. Check comprehension. Ask: *Who can I call to get information on a music program?* [Parks & Recreation] *Where can an older person get help with meals?* [Senior Services]

> **TIP**
> If you have access to the Internet in class, have students visit the website for their city. Ask them to make a list of services and departments. Elicit the information and write any ideas not included in the directory in 2A on the board.

Guided Practice II
10–15 minutes

B Have students work individually to complete the sentences and then compare answers with a partner. Go over the answers as a class.

Answers	
1. Administration	5. Public Safety
2. Public Works	6. Health Services
3. Parks & Recreation	7. Legal Services
4. Child Care Services	8. Senior Services

Communicative Practice and Application
20–25 minutes

C 1. If students will use the Internet for this task, establish what device(s) they'll use: a class computer, tablets, or smartphones. Alternatively, print information from the Internet before class and distribute to groups.

2. Write the questions from 2C on the board. Explain that students will work in teams to research and report on these questions. Ask: *Which search terms or questions can you use to find the information you need?* ["qualities of a good leader", "community services" + your city] *What information will you scan for?* [adjectives, names of departments] *How will you record the information you find?* [table, checklist, index cards] Remind students to bookmark or record sites so they can find or cite them in the future.

3. Group students and assign roles: reporter, manager, administrative assistant, and IT support. Verify student understanding of their roles.

4. Give managers the time limit for researching question 1 (ten minutes). Direct the IT support to begin the online research or pick up the printed materials for each team. Direct the administrative assistant to record information for the team using a table, checklist, or index cards.

5. Give a two-minute warning. Call "time." Ask reporters to first answer and then ask each member of the team question 2.

> **TIP**
> When setting up task-based activities, verify that students understand their roles using physical commands. For example: *If you report on your team's work, stand up* [reporter]. *If you keep the team on task, point to the clock* [manager]. *If you write the team's responses, raise your hand* [administrative assistant]. *If you help the team research, hold up your smartphone/tablet* [IT support].

D 1. Copy the sentence frames on the board.

2. Direct teams to help their administrative assistant use the sentence frames to record the team's findings. Direct the reporter to use the recorded information to report the team's findings to the class or another team.

Evaluation
10–15 minutes

TEST YOURSELF

1. Direct Partner A to read prompts 1–3 from 1C on page 148 to Partner B. Partner B should close their book and say and write the prompts. When finished, students switch roles. Partner B reads prompts 4–6 from 1C.

2. Direct both partners to open their books and check their spelling when they finish.

> **EXTENSION ACTIVITY**
> **Discussion**
> Write *Whom should you call?* on the board.
>
> 1. Write a list of situations on the board. *The sidewalks are cracked. There's a suspicious person hanging around the neighborhood. The corner needs a crosswalk. You want your daughter to join the soccer team. A neighbor has a large amount of trash piled up in the yard.*
>
> 2. Pair students and ask them to discuss the community service department they would call for each situation.

LESSON 2 WRITING

Lesson Overview

MULTILEVEL OBJECTIVES

On- and Higher-level: Analyze, write, and edit an email about a community problem

Pre-level: Read and write an email about a community problem

LANGUAGE FOCUS

Grammar: Conditional (*If the light stayed red for five more seconds, everyone would be able to cross safely.*)

Vocabulary: *Primary concern, sincerely*

For vocabulary support, see these **Oxford Picture Dictionary** topics: Civic Engagement, pages 142–143; Community Cleanup, pages 152–153

STRATEGY FOCUS

When you are writing, focus each paragraph on a clear purpose or main idea.

READINESS CONNECTION

In this lesson, students think critically and communicate information by writing an email about a community problem.

PACING

To compress this lesson: Assign the *Test Yourself* for homework.

To extend this lesson: Students have a city council meeting. (See end of lesson.)

And/or have students complete **Workbook 4 page 66** and **Multilevel Activities 4 Unit 10 page 110**.

Lesson Notes

CORRELATIONS

CCRS: SL.1.B (d.) Explain their own ideas and understanding in light of the discussion.

SL.2.B Determine the main ideas and supporting details of a text read aloud or information presented in diverse media and formats, including visually, quantitatively, and orally.

R.1.B Ask and answer such questions as who, what, where, when, why, and how to demonstrate understanding of key details in a text.

W.2.B (a.) Introduce a topic and group related information together; include illustrations when useful to aiding comprehension. (b.) Develop the topic with facts, definitions, and details. (c.) Use linking words and phrases to connect ideas within categories of information. (d.) Provide a concluding statement or section.

W.4.B Produce writing in which the development and organization are appropriate to task and purpose.

W.5.B With guidance and support from peers and others, develop and strengthen writing as needed by planning, revising and editing.

W.6.B With guidance and support, use technology to produce and publish writing (using keyboarding skills) as well as to interact and collaborate with others.

L.1.B (l.) Produce simple, compound and complex sentences.

L.1.C (f.) Use verb tense to convey various times, sequences, states, and conditions.

L.2.B (c.) Use commas in greetings and closings of letters.

L.2.C (a.) Use correct capitalization.

L.6.B Use words and phrases acquired through conversations, reading and being read to, and responding to texts, including using adjectives and adverbs to describe. Acquire and use accurately level-appropriate conversational, general academic, and domain-specific words and phrases, including those that signal spatial and temporal relationships.

RF.4.B (a.) Read grade-level text with purpose and understanding.

ELPS: 1. An ELL can construct meaning from oral presentations and literary and informational text through level-appropriate listening, reading, and viewing. 2. An ELL can participate in level-appropriate oral and written exchanges of information, ideas, and analyses, in various social and academic contexts, responding to peer, audience, or reader comments and questions. 3. An ELL can speak and write about level-appropriate complex literary and informational texts and topics. 4. An ELL can construct level-appropriate oral and written claims and support them with reasoning and evidence. 6. An ELL can analyze and critique the arguments of others orally and in writing.

Warm-up and Review
10–15 minutes (books closed)

Write *Community Problems* on the board and elicit examples from students—possibilities include cracked pavement, potholes, bad lighting, trash, graffiti, old playground equipment, and undesirable businesses. Write the problems on the board.

Introduction
5 minutes

1. Ask students if they think they can do anything about these kinds of problems.

2. State the objective: *Today we're going to read and write a letter about a community issue.*

1 Prepare to write

Presentation
20–25 minutes

A 1. Build students' schema by asking questions about the email. Ask: *Who's writing?* [Alan Hart] *Who is he writing to?* [Ms. Butler] *Is the email formal or informal?* [formal] *How do you know?* [*Dear Ms. Butler* and *Sincerely*]

2. Give students one minute to tell a partner their responses to questions 1 and 2. Elicit responses from the class.

B 🔊 3-15 1. Introduce the model email and its purpose: *You're going to read an email from a community member. As you read, look for the purpose of the email: Why is he writing?* Have students read the email silently.

2. Check comprehension. Ask: *Who is Alan Hart?* [a resident of the Melrose neighborhood] *Is the email offering help or asking for help?* [asking for help] *What is the problem?* [a traffic light changes too quickly at an intersection] *How will keeping the light green for five more seconds help?* [People will be able to cross safely.]

3. Play the audio. Ask students to number the paragraphs as they read along.

Guided Practice I
10 minutes

C 1. Have students work independently to answer the questions about the email and then compare answers with a partner.

2. Point out the *Writer's Note* and ask students to circle the phrases that introduce the reason for the email and the problem. Have students underline the phrases or sentences that explain the situation in detail and the request.

3. Ask a volunteer to write the answers on the board.

Possible Answers
1. He wants to let Ms. Butler know right away why he is writing./He wants to get Ms. Butler's attention.
2. Older people cannot make it across the street in time; parents with children have a difficult time too.
3. He wants the city to increase the time that the light stays red for cars and he wants Ms. Butler to visit his neighborhood.

MULTILEVEL STRATEGIES
For 1C, challenge on- and higher-level students while allowing pre-level students to catch up.
• **On- and Higher-level** While pre-level students are finishing 1C, ask these students to come up with specific examples to explain why the problems on the board from the *Warm-up* are serious. After you go over 1C, ask volunteers to share their ideas with the class.

2 Plan and write

Guided Practice II
15–20 minutes

A 1. Read the questions. Elicit students' answers.

2. Put the students' ideas about whom to write to on the board.

B 1. Direct students to look at the email template and then find the phrases in Alan Hart's email in 1B.

2. Read the instructions aloud.

3. Check comprehension of the exercise. Ask: *What are you writing about?* [community problems] *How many paragraphs does your letter need to be?* [three]

4. Have students write their emails individually.

MULTILEVEL STRATEGIES

Adapt 2B to the level of your students.

- **Pre-level** Provide these students with this letter template:

Dear _____,

I'm writing to ask for your help with a problem in our community. I live in _____. The problem is _____.

I am very concerned because _____. I think we can solve this by _____.

I would like to invite you to visit to see the problem for yourself.

Sincerely,

_____

- **Higher-level** Encourage these students to include an example of something specific that happened or might happen because of the safety problem. Provide sentence frames to help with the register: *As a result of this situation, _____. I am concerned that _____ could _____ as a result of the situation.*

3 Get feedback and revise

Guided Practice III
5 minutes

 Direct students to check their writing using the editing checklist. Tell them to read each item in the list and check their papers before moving onto the next item. Explain that students should not edit their writing at this stage. They should just use the checklist to check their work and mark any areas they want to revise.

Communicative Practice
15 minutes

 1. Read the instructions aloud. Emphasize to students that they are responding to their partners' work, not correcting it.

2. Use the email in 1B to model the exercise. *I think the sentence that says, "Older people who walk with canes or walkers cannot make it across the street in time." describes the problem clearly. I'm not sure I understand this part of the problem…*

3. Direct students to exchange papers with a partner and follow the instructions.

C Allow students time to edit and revise their writing as necessary, using the editing checklist from 3A and their partner's feedback from 3B. If necessary, students could complete this task as homework.

EXTENSION ACTIVITY
City Council Meeting

After completing 3C, hold a "city council meeting" in class. Ask for volunteers to come to the front of the room and explain their problems and proposed solutions. All non-volunteers are "city council members." Ask the council members to listen and take notes. Tell them they need to prioritize the problems. Have the council members come to a consensus about which problem they should deal with first.

Application and Evaluation
10 minutes

TEST YOURSELF

1. Review the instructions aloud. Assign a time limit (five minutes) and have students work independently.

2. Before collecting student work, invite two or three volunteers to share their sentences. Ask students to raise their hands if they wrote similar answers.

LESSON 3 GRAMMAR

Lesson Overview

MULTILEVEL OBJECTIVES

On- and Higher-level: Ask and respond to indirect questions about community issues and listen for information about community services

Pre-level: Recognize and respond to indirect questions about community issues and listen for information about community services

LANGUAGE FOCUS

Grammar: Indirect questions (*Do you know what the mayor wants? Could you tell me if City Hall is open?*)

Vocabulary: Community issues

For vocabulary support, see these **Oxford Picture Dictionary** topics: Civic Engagement, pages 142–143; Community Cleanup, pages 152–153

READINESS CONNECTION

In this lesson, students communicate verbally and use indirect questions to ask about community services.

PACING

To compress this lesson: Conduct 2A and 2B as whole-class activities.

To extend this lesson: Have students practice asking indirect questions depending on different situations. (See end of lesson.)

And/or have students complete **Workbook 4 pages 67–68**, **Multilevel Activities 4 Unit 10 pages 111–112**, and **Multilevel Grammar Exercises 4 Unit 10**.

Lesson Notes

CORRELATIONS

CCRS: SL.1.B (d.) Explain their own ideas and understanding in light of the discussion.

SL.2.B Determine the main ideas and supporting details of a text read aloud or information presented in diverse media and formats, including visually, quantitatively, and orally.

R.1.B Ask and answer such questions as who, what, where, when, why, and how to demonstrate understanding of key details in a text.

R.7.A Use the illustrations and details in a text to describe its key ideas.

L.1.B (l.) Produce simple, compound and complex sentences.

L.1.D (h.) Form and use verbs in the indicative, imperative, interrogative, conditional and subjunctive mood.

RF.4.B (a.) Read grade-level text with purpose and understanding.

ELPS: 2. An ELL can participate in level-appropriate oral and written exchanges of information, ideas, and analyses, in various social and academic contexts, responding to peer, audience, or reader comments and questions. 3. An ELL can speak and write about level-appropriate complex literary and informational texts and topics. 7. An ELL can adapt language choices to purpose, task, and audience when speaking and writing. 9. An ELL can create clear and coherent level-appropriate speech and text. 10. An ELL can demonstrate command of the conventions of standard English to communicate in level-appropriate speech and writing.

Warm-up and Review
10–15 minutes (books closed)

Write *When, Where, What,* and *How* on the board. Ask students to come up with questions they might ask if they were calling their area's city hall or using a community service like the library. Write their ideas on the board.

Introduction
5–10 minutes

1. Ask: *Do you talk to someone you don't know like you do to a friend? Are you more polite to strangers?* Point out that sometimes it's more formal and polite to use an indirect question. Give an example by saying one of the questions on the board as an indirect question.

2. State the objective: *Today we're going to use indirect questions to talk about community issues.*

1 Use indirect information questions

Presentation I
20–25 minutes

1. Direct students to look at the cartoon. Ask: *Where can you see cartoons like this?* [online, in newspapers] *What do editorial cartoons do?* [express an opinion on an issue, usually through humor]

2. Read the instructions and questions aloud. Ask students to read the cartoon and discuss their answers in pairs. Elicit answers from the class.

Answers
1. A woman who is waiting for a bus and a man who is from/represents the government. 2. She wants to know what time the bus is coming. 3. No, he doesn't. His answer is about money for buses; he is not talking about a real bus.

1. Demonstrate how to read the grammar chart. Read each question aloud and have students repeat. Ask: *What is added to the indirect questions?* [do you know, could you please tell me, can you tell me] *In what other way is the indirect question different from the direct question?* [The direct question begins with a *wh-* question word.]

2. Elicit the forms of both questions and write them on the board. Direct questions: *wh-* word + auxiliary/*be* + subject + main verb. Indirect questions: auxiliary + *you* + verb + *wh-* word + subject + main verb.

3. Direct students to underline the indirect question in the cartoon in 1A. Write the question on the board.

4. Pair students and direct them to read the chart aloud to each other. (One partner reads the direct questions and the other reads the indirect questions.) Then read the chart aloud as students follow along.

5. Assess students' understanding of the chart. Ask: *Which is more polite?* [indirect questions] Elicit indirect forms of the questions on the board from the *Warm-up*. Ask volunteers to write the indirect questions on the board.

Answer
Can you tell me when the bus is coming?

Guided Practice I
15–20 minutes

1. Tell students they will collaborate to complete the description of the grammar point. Model collaboration by working with the class to complete the first sentence. Encourage students to look at 1A and 1B before choosing the correct answers.

2. Pair students and have them work together to complete the description.

3. Project or write the completed definition on the board and have pairs verify the accuracy of their responses. Ask volunteers which sentences confused them and discuss.

Answers
indirect, polite, how, before

MULTILEVEL STRATEGIES

For 1C, seat mixed-level students together.

• **Pre-, On-, and Higher-level** Assign pre-level students the role of administrative assistant, on-level students the role of manager, and higher-level students the role of researcher. The administrative assistant fills in the blanks according to the team's decisions, the manager reads the description and manages the team's discussion, and the researcher looks up the definition of the grammar point online or checks against an answer key to verify the team's answers.

Guided Practice II
5–10 minutes

 Read the instructions aloud. Have students work individually to match the situation with an indirect question and then compare answers with a partner. Go over the answers with the class.

Answers	
1. b	3. d
2. a	4. c

TIP
For more practice with indirect information questions before 1E, write scrambled questions on the board. *1. know do you the library finished when will be new 2. school board you tell me where the can meets 3. you is have any the when do next idea election 4. you tell me is my please representative could who*

Ask students to unscramble the words to make questions. Have volunteers write the unscrambled questions on the board. *1. Do you know when the new library will be finished? 2. Can you tell me where the school board meets? 3. Do you have any idea when the next election is? 4. Could you please tell me who my representative is?* Ask any students who finish early to write their own scrambled question and put it on the board.

E 1. Have students form teams of three: manager, administrative assistant, editor. The manager keeps track of time, the administrative assistant writes the corrected sentences, and the editor checks the grammar charts to confirm accuracy. Set a time limit of three minutes.

2. Ask administrative assistants to write the corrected sentences on the board. Provide correction and clarification as needed.

Answers
1. Do you know where the park is?
2. Do you know what the teacher wants?
3. Could you tell me where the post office is?
4. Can you tell me how you get to city hall?

 1. Ask students to work individually to complete the indirect questions and then compare answers with a partner. Call on volunteers for the answers.

2. Direct students to take turns asking and answering the questions with a partner.

Answers
1. Do you know when the meeting is?
2. Do you know where it is?
3. Do you have any idea what the mayor wants to talk about?
4. Could you please tell me what the mayor's proposal cuts?
5. Can you tell me which budgets the city cut?

MULTILEVEL STRATEGIES
For 1F, seat pre-level students together.

- **Pre-level** Work with these students. Underline the section of each answer that needs to be used in the question. Elicit each completion before students write it in their books.

2 Use indirect *yes/no* questions

Presentation II
20–25 minutes

 1. Introduce the new topic. Say: *Now we're going to learn how to ask indirect* yes/no *questions*. Elicit an example of a *yes/no* question and write it on the board. Show students how to rewrite it as an indirect question.

2. Read the direct and indirect questions in the chart. Elicit the form for indirect *yes/no* questions: Auxiliary + *you* + verb + *if/whether* + subject + verb?

3. Ask students to work individually to answer the question. Then have students compare answers with a partner.

Answer
whether

MULTILEVEL STRATEGIES
After 2A, seat students in same-level groups. Provide each group with magazines or with pictures that show people engaged in conversation. Ask the groups to come up with questions that one person might be asking the other.

- **Pre-level** Have these students write direct questions. Before they begin writing, review present- and past-tense questions with them.
- **On- and Higher-level** Have these students write indirect questions. Tell them to be sure to include some information and some *yes/no* questions.

Have a reporter from each group share the group's pictures and questions with the class.

Guided Practice III
10–15 minutes

 Ask students to work individually to complete the indirect questions and then compare their answers with a partner. Ask volunteers to write the completed questions on the board.

Answers
1. if the meeting is at 5:00
2. if/whether they discussed the issue
3. if/whether they are going to approve the budget cut
4. if/whether the mayor was at the meeting
5. if/whether the meeting ended on time
6. if/whether they are going to meet next month

3 Listen for indirect questions to determine the meaning

Guided Practice IV
10–15 minutes

 1. Say: *Now we're going to listen to some questions about community services. Read the instructions aloud.*

2. Play the audio. Direct students to read along silently without writing.

3. Replay the audio. Ask students to circle the letter of the question with the same meaning.

4. Go over the answers as a class.

Answers	
1. a	4. b
2. a	5. b
3. b	6. a

MULTILEVEL STRATEGIES

Replay the audio for 3 to allow pre-level students to catch up while you challenge on- and higher-level students.

- **Pre-level** Have these students listen again to circle the letter of the correct question.
- **On- and Higher-level** Have these students listen and write the questions they hear for numbers 2 and 4.

B Read the instructions aloud. Model the activity with a student. Say 1a from exercise 3A and elicit the indirect question. Pair students to practice asking indirect questions using the questions in 3A.

Possible Answers
1. Do you know when the next public works committee meeting is?
Do you know where the next public works committee meeting is?
2. Do you know why the law clinic is closed?
Do you know when the law clinic is closed?
3. Do you know if/whether they talked about childcare services?
Do you know who I talk to about childcare services?
4. Do you know where the nearest senior center in your city is?
Do you know if your city has any senior centers?
5. Do you know what the city manager wants?
Do you know where the city manager went?
6. Do you know if/whether the public safety committee discussed my idea?
Do you know when the public safety committee discussed my idea?

4 Use indirect questions to ask about community services

Communicative Practice and Application
20–25 minutes

A Brainstorm a list of community services and write them on the board. Read the instructions and example question aloud. Give students time to write five indirect questions about the services on the board.

B 1. Put students in teams and direct them to take turns asking their indirect questions about community services from 4A. Assign roles: manager, reporter, administrative assistant, and researcher. Have the manager keep the team on task and manage time. Have the researcher look online for information to find answers to questions. Tell the administrative assistant to make notes of the team's answers. Model the exercise by asking a volunteer the first question. Have the class tell you how to write the answer in note form.

2. Check comprehension of the exercise. Ask: *Should you ask direct or indirect questions?* Set a time limit for the exercise (four minutes) and observe, taking note of issues that arise.

3. Call on reporters to share their questions and the answers given by their classmates.

> **MULTILEVEL STRATEGIES**
>
> Adapt 4B to the level of your students.
>
> • **Pre-level** Allow these students to ask direct questions.

Evaluation
10–15 minutes

TEST YOURSELF

Ask students to write the questions independently. Collect and correct their writing before they exchange questions with a partner.

> **EXTENSION ACTIVITY**
>
> **Writing**
>
> Provide more practice with indirect questions.
>
> 1. Put up poster paper with a situation at the top of each sheet. *At the Supermarket, At Your Child's School, At a Restaurant, At a Park Entrance, At an Amusement Park, At a Mall Information Booth, At a Police Station, In a College Office, In an Airport, On an Airplane*
>
> 2. Put students in mixed-level groups and assign each group to a poster. Tell them to write one indirect question they might ask in that situation. Have the groups move to a new poster. Continue until there are five questions on each poster.

LESSON 4 EVERYDAY CONVERSATION

Lesson Overview

MULTILEVEL OBJECTIVES

On-, Pre-, and Higher-level: Talk about community issues and listen for directions

LANGUAGE FOCUS

Grammar: Statements with *wh-* and *if/whether* phrases (*I don't know where the meeting is.*)

Vocabulary: *Public hearing, encouraged, proposals, Council Chamber*

For vocabulary support, see these **Oxford Picture Dictionary** topics: Civic Engagement, pages 142–143; Career Planning, pages 152–153

STRATEGY FOCUS

Practice showing understanding and confirming a question before answering.

READINESS CONNECTION

In this lesson, students listen to a recorded message and complete directions.

PACING

To compress this lesson: Conduct *Discuss* as a whole-class activity.

To extend this lesson: Have students practice giving directions. (See end of lesson.)

And/or have students complete **Workbook 4 page 69** and **Multilevel Activities 4 Unit 10 page 113**.

Lesson Notes

CORRELATIONS

CCRS: SL.1.B (a.) Come to discussions prepared, having read or studied required material; explicitly draw on that preparation and other information known about the topic to explore ideas under discussion. (b.) Follow agreed-upon rules for discussions. (c.) Ask questions to check understanding of information presented, stay on topic, and link their comments to the remarks of others. (d.) Explain their own ideas and understanding in light of the discussion.

SL.2.B Determine the main ideas and supporting details of a text read aloud or information presented in diverse media and formats, including visually, quantitatively, and orally.

SL.4.B Report on a topic or text, tell a story, or recount an experience with appropriate facts and relevant, descriptive details, speaking clearly at an understandable pace.

SL.6.B Speak in complete sentences when appropriate to task and situation in order to provide requested detail or clarification.

R.1.B Ask and answer such questions as who, what, where, when, why, and how to demonstrate understanding of key details in a text.

R.2.A Identify the main topic and retell key details of a text.

R.7.B Use information gained from illustrations and the words in a text to demonstrate understanding of the text.

L.1.B (l.) Produce simple, compound and complex sentences.

L.1.C (f.) Use verb tense to convey various times, sequences, states, and conditions.

L.1.D (j.) Explain the function of phrases and clauses in general and their function in specific sentences.

L.3.B (b.) Recognize and observe differences between the conventions of spoken and written standard English.

L.4.B (a.) Use sentence-level context as a clue to the meaning of a word or phrase.

L.6.B Use words and phrases acquired through conversations, reading and being read to, and responding to texts, including using adjectives and adverbs to describe.

RF.4.B (a.) Read grade-level text with purpose and understanding.

ELPS: 2. An ELL can participate in level-appropriate oral and written exchanges of information, ideas, and analyses, in various social and academic contexts, responding to peer, audience, or reader comments and questions. 6. An ELL can analyze and critique the arguments of others orally and in writing. 7. An ELL can adapt language choices to purpose, task, and audience when speaking and writing. 9. An ELL can create clear and coherent level-appropriate speech and text. 10. An ELL can demonstrate command of the conventions of standard English to communicate in level-appropriate speech and writing.

Warm-up and Review
10–15 minutes (books closed)

Using an indirect question, ask a volunteer to give you directions to your area's city hall from school (or to the city center from school). Write the student's directions on the board. Elicit corrections and help from other students as you go.

Introduction
5 minutes

1. Say: *If you want to go to a city council meeting or you want to inquire in person about city services, that's where you need to go.*

2. State the objective: *Today we're going to talk about a community problem and listen for directions.*

1 Learn ways to comment on an issue in the community

Presentation I
10–20 minutes

 1. Direct students to look at the notice. Elicit or provide the meanings for *public hearing* [a public meeting where people have an opportunity to state their case], *proposal* [a plan or suggestion, especially a formal or written one, put forward for others to consider], *Council Chamber* [the room where the City Council meets]. Ask: *What are the three issues they will discuss?* [a plan to build an apartment building, a proposal to reduce a jobs program, and a proposal to close a police station]

2. Read the instructions aloud. Play the audio. Give students a minute to answer the question and then compare answers with a partner. Go over the answer as a class.

Answer
They don't like the plans to build new apartments and cut summer jobs.

Guided Practice I
20–25 minutes

 1. Read the instructions aloud. Play the audio. Ask students to listen for the answers to each question.

2. Ask students to compare their answers with a partner. Circulate and monitor to ensure students understand the audio.

Possible Answers
1. A builder wants to put new apartments near the park.
2. The mayor wants to cut the Summer Jobs for Teens program.
3. The city clerk tells them about public hearings they can go to about the plans.

 Read the instructions aloud. Explain that students are going to hear the audio one more time. They should write the words they hear to complete the sentences. Play the audio. Call on volunteers to elicit the answers.

Answers
1. hear what you're saying
2. I know what you mean

2 Practice your pronunciation

Pronunciation Extension
10–15 minutes

 1. Write the following sentence on the board: *I don't know what you think, but I think we ought to go.* Say the sentence and ask students to repeat it. Ask them to identify the pause. Say: *Now we're going to focus on when to pause in long sentences.*

2. Play the audio. Direct students to listen for the pause.

3. Say and have students repeat the sentences.

 Play the audio. Direct students to listen and mark the pauses. Go over the answers as a class.

Answers
1. Older people who walk with canes or walkers ^ cannot make it across the street in time.
2. The council members discuss the issue ^ to try to find a solution ^ that works for everyone.

Have students take turns saying the sentences with a partner. Monitor and provide feedback on pronunciation.

3 Use statements with *wh-* and *if/whether* phrases

Presentation II and Guided Practice II
10–15 minutes

1. Introduce the new topic. Write the following sentence on the board: *Maria didn't know where the hearing was.* Underline *where the hearing was*. Ask: *Is this a question?* [no] Say: *Now we're going to learn statements with* wh- *and* if/whether *phrases.*

2. Read the instructions aloud. Direct students to look at the picture and the chart. Ask: *What are the man's questions?*

3. Read the statements in the chart and have students repeat. Write the following sentence frame on the board: *He doesn't _____.* Call on a volunteer to give an answer. Elicit completions for the sentence on the board. Read the *Grammar Note*.

4. Elicit the form that follows the expressions in the left column: *wh-* word */if/whether* + subject + verb. Point out that we use statement, not question order, in these sentences.

Possible Answer
He doesn't have any information about the meeting.

Guided Practice III
15–20 minutes

1. Have students work with a partner to circle the best answers to complete the conversation. Tell partners to read the conversation aloud when they finish.

2. Ask a volunteer pair to read the conversation aloud for the class.

Answers
1. it starts
2. it's
3. the issues are
4. they sent

MULTILEVEL STRATEGIES

For 3B, seat same-level students together.

- **Pre-level** Work with this group. Read each sentence in 3B aloud with the correct completion and have students circle the words they hear. Then ask pairs to read the conversation aloud, switch roles, and read it again.

- **On- and Higher-level** When these students finish 3B, ask them to write the *wh-* and *if/whether* phrases in the conversation as direct questions. Have volunteers write the questions on the board. Compare the questions to the statements in the conversation.

4 Building conversation skills

Guided Practice IV
15–20 minutes

A Direct students to look at the picture and skim the phone conversation. Have them work with partners to identify the purpose of the phone call. Elicit responses and ask: *How do you know?* or *Why do you say that?* to encourage students to state their reasoning.

Possible Answer
The woman is calling to ask about a community issue.

 🔊 3-21 1. Ask students to read the instructions and tell you what they are going to do [listen and read and respond to the question]. Play the audio and then elicit the answer to the question.

2. Ask students to read the conversation with a partner. Circulate and monitor pronunciation. Model and have students repeat difficult words or phrases.

3. Say and have students repeat the expressions in the *In Other Words* box. Elicit the placement of the expressions in the conversation. Ask volunteers to read the conversation using expressions from the box.

4. Ask: *In what other situation could you use this conversation?* Point out a few phrases that are not specific to the closing of a police station. Ask volunteers to point out others.

Answer
He says, "I can certainly understand."

Communicative Practice and Application I
15–20 minutes

C 1. Pair students and have them read the instructions silently. Check their comprehension of the exercise. Ask: *What are the two roles?* [resident and city clerk] *Is the conversation at city hall?* [no]

2. Draw a T-chart on the board. Label the left column *resident* and the right column *city clerk*. Elicit examples of what each person might say and make notes on the chart. Remind students to use phrases in the *In Other Words* box.

3. Set a time limit (three minutes). Have students act out the role-play. Call time and have students switch roles.

4. Ask three volunteer pairs to act out their role-play for the class. Tell students who are listening to take notes on the phrases used to show understanding.

> **MULTILEVEL STRATEGIES**
>
> For 4C, adapt the role-play to the level of your students.
>
> • **Pre-level** Provide the beginning of the role-play for these students.
> *A: City Clerk's Office. How can I help you?*
> *B: Hi. I'm calling because I heard that the city is going to close the library.*
>
> • **Higher-level** Have students create role-plays for another community issue involving city council.

5 Focus on listening for details

Presentation and Guided Practice
20–25 minutes

A Read the questions aloud and elicit answers from volunteers. Encourage students to respond to each other's ideas. After one student speaks, ask other students for their opinions: *Do you know of another reason/way?*

B 🔊 3-22 Tell students that they will be listening to information about a meeting. Play the audio. Ask them to circle the correct answers.

Answers	
1. a	3. b
2. a	4. b

C 🔊 3-22 1. Direct students to read the sentences before listening.

2. Replay the audio and have students work individually to complete the sentences. Take a tally of responses for each item and if students disagree on a response, replay the audio so they can check their answers.

Answers
1. F4
2. straight
3. second
4. Hearing Room
5. right, 210

> **MULTILEVEL STRATEGIES**
>
> Replay the directions in 5C to challenge on- and higher-level students while allowing pre-level students to catch up.
>
> • **Pre-level** Have these students listen again to go over their answers.
>
> • **On- and Higher-level** Write questions on the board and have these students listen for the answers. *Where does the bus stop? Where is the parking lot?*

6 Discuss

Communicative Practice and Application II
15–20 minutes

A 1. Read the instructions aloud. Draw a sample chart on the board with space for the relationship on one side and reasons it's important to show concern on the other. Call on volunteer pairs to read the example conversation in 6A. Fill in the chart, writing "clerk and customer" on the left and "good customer service" on the right. Explain that students will make a chart like this one based on their own discussions.

2. Put students into teams of four and assign roles: reporter, manager, administrative assistant, and researcher. Verify students' understanding of the roles. Encourage students to use the phrases in the *Speaking Note* during their discussions.

3. Set a time limit for the discussions (ten minutes). Write the sentence frame from 6B on the board. Then circulate and monitor.

B Call "time." Ask the reporter for each team to report the results of their team's discussion, using the sentence frame on the board.

> **EXTENSION ACTIVITY**
>
> To extend 6B, draw a large blank chart on the board. As each reporter shares with the class, the administrative assistant from that group fills in the chart. If other teams came up with the same answers, they should not enter the information again.

Evaluation
5 minutes

TEST YOURSELF

1. Ask students to complete the checkboxes individually.

2. Tell students that you are going to read each of the items in the checklist aloud. If they are not at all confident with that skill, they should hold up a closed fist. If they are not very confident, they should hold up one finger. If they are somewhat confident, two fingers; confident, three fingers; very confident, four fingers. If they think they could teach the skill, they should hold up five fingers. Read each item in the checklist and identify students that may need further support.

> **TIP**
>
> For homework, you could ask students to write a sentence or two about what discussion skills they still need to work on or, if they are confident in all of the skills, what skill they are most proud of.

LESSON 5 READING

Lesson Overview

MULTILEVEL OBJECTIVES

On-, Pre-, and Higher-level: Read about and discuss community involvement

LANGUAGE FOCUS

Grammar: Verbs and nouns with *-ment* (*I agree. We have an agreement.*)

Vocabulary: *Accessible, announce, dispose, dumping, get rid of, implement, legal, play an active part, sponsor*

For vocabulary support, see these **Oxford Picture Dictionary** topics: Civic Engagement, pages 142–143; Community Cleanup, pages 152–153

STRATEGY FOCUS

Students practice comparing information from different sources.

READINESS CONNECTION

In this lesson, students decide how to help resolve community problems and analyze information.

PACING

To compress this lesson: Conduct the word study in 2A as a whole-class activity.

To extend this lesson: Have students talk about cleanliness problems at school. (See end of lesson.)

And/or have students complete **Workbook 4 page 70** and **Multilevel Activities 4 Unit 10 pages 114–115**.

Lesson Notes

CORRELATIONS

CCRS: SL.1.B (b.) Follow agreed-upon rules for discussions. (c.) Ask questions to check understanding of information presented, stay on topic, and link their comments to the remarks of others. (d.) Explain their own ideas and understanding in light of the discussion.

SL.6.B Speak in complete sentences when appropriate to task and situation in order to provide requested detail or clarification.

R.1.C Refer to details and examples in a text when explaining what the text says explicitly and when drawing inferences from the text.

R.2.B Determine the main idea of a text; recount the key details and explain how they support the main idea.

R.4.B Determine the meaning of general academic and domain-specific words and phrases in a text relevant to a topic or subject area.

R.5.B Know and use various text features to locate key facts or information in a text efficiently.

R.7.B Use information gained from illustrations and the words in a text to demonstrate understanding of the text.

R.8.A Identify the reasons an author gives to support points in a text.

R.9.B Compare and contrast the most important points and key details presented in two texts on the same topic.

W.8.B Recall information from experiences or gather information from print and digital sources; take brief notes on sources and sort evidence into provided categories.

L.1.B (b.) Explain the function of nouns, pronouns, verbs, adjectives, and adverbs in general and their functions in particular sentences.

L.2.B (h.) Use conventional spelling for high-frequency and other studied words and for adding suffixes to base words. (k.) consult reference materials, including beginning dictionaries, as needed to check and correct spellings.

L.4.B (e.) Use glossaries and beginning dictionaries, both print and digital, to determine or clarify the meaning of words and phrases.

L.6.B Use words and phrases acquired through conversations, reading and being read to, and responding to texts, including using adjectives and adverbs to describe.

ELPS: 2. An ELL can participate in level-appropriate oral and written exchanges of information, ideas, and analyses, in various social and academic contexts, responding to peer, audience, or reader comments and questions. 3. An ELL can speak and write about level-appropriate complex literary and informational texts and topics. 4. An ELL can construct level-appropriate oral and written claims and support them with reasoning and evidence. 8. An ELL can determine the meaning of words and phrases in oral presentation and literary and informational text.

Warm-up and Review
10–15 minutes (books closed)

Ask if there are any areas of your city that are dirty. Find out what students see there and elicit their opinions about why that area is dirtier than others.

Introduction
5 minutes

1. Say: *Sometimes an area is dirty because there's nobody around who wants to take responsibility for it.*

2. State the objective: *Today we're going to read about and discuss community involvement.*

1 Read

Presentation
10–20 minutes

A Read the questions aloud. Write students' ideas on the board.

B Read the words and definitions. Elicit sample sentences for each word or supply them if the students can't.

Pre-reading

C Read the instructions aloud and confirm that students understand they are reading two articles and that they know where the "bold headings" are. Have students work in pairs to answer the questions. If any students answer incorrectly, ask them to support their answer using the numbered headings. Establish the correct answers.

Guided Practice: While Reading
20–30 minutes

D 1. Read the *Reader's Note* aloud. Check comprehension by asking: *What are two things you can do to compare information from different sources?* [identify the writer's purpose, distinguish fact from opinion]

2. Check that students understand vocabulary in the reading: *announce, in return, dump, multi-agency, implement,* and *critical.* Have them look up any words they don't know. Point out that there may be other words they don't know, but they should use context to guess their meaning. Ask students to read the articles silently and answer the question.

3. Check answers with the class.

4. Check comprehension. Ask: *How many strategies to clean up Riverview are mentioned in the first article?* [three] *And in the second?* [one] *What is the one clean-up strategy both articles mention?* [stop illegal dumping] *Which one talks about the mayor?* [the second] *Which one mentions the city's website?* [the first]

Answer
illegal dumping

MULTILEVEL STRATEGIES

Adapt 1D to the level of your students.

• **Pre-level** Provide these students with a summary of the first article and have them read the second article independently. *There are three ways to get involved in cleaning up the community. 1. Adopt-a-Road. In this program, your group cleans a section of the road four times a year, and the city puts your group's name on a sign along the road. 2. People often dump large trash items by the road. The Environmental Committee wants to raise the fine for dumping to $500. Support the new law! 3. Four times a year, residents work together on Community Clean-up Days. You can volunteer to help.*

Direct these students to read the summary for the first article while other students are reading the first article.

• **On- and Higher-level** Pair students and have them read the articles aloud to each other, taking turns to read each paragraph.

Guided Practice: Rereading
10–15 minutes

E 1. Provide an opportunity for students to extract evidence from the text. Read the instructions aloud. Have students reread the article and underline any words or phrases that support their answers to the questions.

2. Pair students and tell them to compare the words they underlined and report anything they disagree on. Discuss and clarify as needed.

TIP

Have students go online to find out about community cleanup activities in your city ("community clean-up" + your city).

2 Word study

Guided Practice: Post-reading
10 minutes

> **MULTILEVEL STRATEGIES**
>
> For 1E, work with pre-level students.
>
> • **Pre-level** Ask these students *yes/no* and short-answer information questions about the reading while other students are completing 1E. *What is the name of the city?* [Riverview] *What do they call the program where people clean up a section of a road?* [Adopt a Road] *What kinds of things do people dump?* [furniture, building materials, tires, and trash] *How much is the fine now?* [$50] *How many times a year do they have community clean-up days?* [four] *What is the name of Holly Adams's organization?* [Sunnyside Community Organization] *Who is Alfonso Nunez?* [a community organizer from the Little Hill neighborhood] *What is the mayor's name?* [Ellis]

A 1. Direct students to look at the chart and identify the topic (changing verbs to nouns with *-ment*). Read the verbs in the chart aloud. Have students fill in the noun forms and then compare answers with a partner. Elicit and discuss any questions the students have about the *-ment* suffix. Have students repeat after you as you say each word with natural intonation, rhythm, and stress.

2. Read the first pair of words from the chart and provide example sentences: *I agree with the mayor. The mayor and I have an agreement.* Elicit sentences for the other words in the chart.

4. Direct students to complete the sentences then compare answers with a partner. Read the correct answers and have students check their work.

F Have students work individually to complete the sentences and then compare answers with a partner. Ask volunteers to read the completed sentences and tell you where they found clues to the meanings of the words.

Answers
1. illegal
2. Accessible
3. input
4. Proper
5. enforcement

Answers
announcement, assignment, government, involvement, statement
1. government
2. agreement
3. announcement
4. involvement

B Direct students to work individually to write a sentence for each topic that includes the underlined word. Ask volunteers to write their sentences on the board. Have the rest of the class suggest grammar and spelling edits as needed.

> **MULTILEVEL STRATEGIES**
>
> For 2B, seat higher-level students together.
>
> • **Higher-level** When these students finish 2B, assign or have them choose a word from the chart and have them write sentences with the verb and the noun form. Ask them to put their sentences on the board. Have other students identify the verbs and the nouns.

G 1. Write *Fact* and *Opinion* on the board. Brainstorm ways to tell a fact from an opinion and write the ideas under the appropriate heading (e.g., names and numbers vs. adjectives like *great* and *beautiful*).

2. Have students work individually to mark the statements and then compare answers with a partner. Go over the answers with the class.

3. Elicit and discuss any additional questions about the reading. You could introduce new questions for class discussion: *Which activities would you be more likely to participate in? Why? What other ways can people clean up their communities?*

Answers	
1. O	4. F
2. F	5. F
3. O	

3 Talk it over

Guided Practice
15–20 minutes

Communicative Practice
20 minutes

A Read the questions aloud. Set a time limit (ten minutes). Allow students to think about the questions and then write notes in their notebooks.

B Ask volunteers to share their ideas with the class.

Application
5–10 minutes

BRING IT TO LIFE

Read the instructions aloud. Tell students to visit the city website. If it has a search engine, they can try the search terms *dump, litter, clean-up,* and *Adopt-a-Highway program.* Challenge them to call the city or ask a librarian to help them find the information.

EXTENSION ACTIVITY

Discussion

1. As a class, brainstorm a list of cleanliness problems that often occur at schools. The list might include gum on the floor and under the tables, lunch trash thrown on the school grounds, and graffiti. Write the ideas on the board.

2. Put students in small groups. Tell them to imagine that the school(s) in their community has these problems. They need to draw up a list of at least three proposals for the school principal.

3. Have a reporter from each group share the proposals with the class. Have a class discussion about which are the most practical proposals and which would be most effective.

AT WORK

Warm-up and Review
10–15 minutes (books closed)

Begin the lesson by talking about a disagreement you have had at work. Elicit examples of disagreements that students have had at school or at work.

Introduction
5 minutes

State the objective: *Today we're going to talk about ways to disagree with someone at work.*

Presentation
5 minutes

 Read the instructions aloud. Play the audio. Give students a minute to think about the question. Elicit responses from the class.

Answer
They are discussing a new company volunteer program.

Guided Practice
10–15 minutes

 Play the audio again. Direct students to listen for each idea and put a check next to any that they hear mentioned.

Answers
employees helping in the community
helping children with reading

 Read the instructions aloud. Play the audio again, encouraging students to take notes in their notebooks. Set a time limit (five minutes) for students to discuss their answers with a partner. Circulate to monitor. Ask volunteers to write the corrections on the board.

Answers
cleaning up trash on a road
volunteering on work time

Presentation and Communicative Practice
10 minutes

 1. Direct students' attention to the *Do/Say* chart and ask them to identify the lesson's soft skill [disagreeing with someone]. Ask the class which column has examples of language [right] and which has examples of behaviors [left].

2. Say a phrase from the left and act it out. Say it again and have the class act it out with you. Say it a third time and have the class act it out for you. To confirm understanding, combine phrases: *Take a breath and sigh and roll your eyes.*

3. Model the statements from the right using authentic intonation. Have students practice imitating your inflection.

4. Put students in teams of four and assign each team a question. Assign roles: reporter, manager, administrative assistant, and researcher. (Researchers will ask you questions on behalf of the team.) Verify understanding of the roles. Set a time limit (five minutes).

5. Write sentence frames on the board that teams can use to summarize their response. *Our team discussed the following question: _____. We decided _____ because _____.*

6. Call "time" and let reporters rehearse for one minute. Direct each reporter to present to three other teams.

Communicative Practice and Application
20–25 minutes

 1. Direct students to work in pairs to take turns reading the statements and disagreeing. Remind them to use the expressions in the chart.

2. Read the statements aloud. Elicit disagreement from volunteers.

F 1. Have pairs merge to form teams of four. Tell students that they are going to have a conversation about workplace volunteering.

2. Direct groups to come up with five possible volunteer ideas. Each group should select a manager to run the meeting. The other three members should each choose one or two ideas to bring up.

3. As students carry out their discussions, circulate and monitor.

TEAMWORK & LANGUAGE REVIEW

Lesson Overview

MULTILEVEL OBJECTIVES

On-, Pre-, and Higher-level: Expand upon and review unit grammar and life skills

LANGUAGE FOCUS

Grammar: Indirect questions, *wh-* and *if/whether* statements (*Do you know when the meeting starts? I don't know when it starts.*)

Vocabulary: Community involvement

For vocabulary support, see these **Oxford Picture Dictionary** topics: Civic Engagement, pages 142–143; Community Cleanup, pages 152–153; Career Planning, pages 174–175

READINESS CONNECTION

In this review, students think critically and work with others to solve a neighborhood problem.

PACING

To extend this review: Have students complete **Workbook 4 page 71**, **Multilevel Activities 4 Unit 10 page 116**, and **Multilevel Grammar Exercises 4 Unit 10**.

Lesson Notes

CORRELATIONS

CCRS: SL.1.B (a.) Come to discussions prepared, having read or studied required material; explicitly draw on that preparation and other information known about the topic to explore ideas under discussion. (b.) Follow agreed-upon rules for discussions. (c.) Ask questions to check understanding of information presented, stay on topic, and link their comments to the remarks of others. (d.) Explain their own ideas and understanding in light of the discussion.

SL.1.C (b.) Follow agreed-upon rules for discussions and carry out assigned roles.

SL.2.B Determine the main ideas and supporting details of a text read aloud or information presented in diverse media and formats, including visually, quantitatively, and orally.

SL.4.B Report on a topic or text, tell a story, or recount an experience with appropriate facts and relevant, descriptive details, speaking clearly at an understandable pace.

R.1.B Ask and answer such questions as who, what, where, when, why, and how to demonstrate understanding of key details in a text.

R.2.A Identify the main topic and retell key details of a text.

R.7.B Use information gained from illustrations and the words in a text to demonstrate understanding of the text.

L.1.B (l.) Produce simple, compound and complex sentences.

L.1.C (d.) Use modal auxiliaries to convey various conditions.

L.1.D (h.) Form and use verbs in the indicative, imperative, interrogative, conditional and subjunctive mood.

RF.4.B (a.) Read grade-level text with purpose and understanding.

ELPS: 2. An ELL can participate in level-appropriate oral and written exchanges of information, ideas, and analyses, in various social and academic contexts, responding to peer, audience, or reader comments and questions. 4. An ELL can construct level-appropriate oral and written claims and support them with reasoning and evidence. 5. An ELL can conduct research and evaluate and communicate findings to answer questions or solve problems. 7. An ELL can adapt language choices to purpose, task, and audience when speaking and writing. 9. An ELL can create clear and coherent level-appropriate speech and text. 10. An ELL can demonstrate command of the conventions of standard English to communicate in level-appropriate speech and writing.

Warm-up and Review
10–15 minutes (books closed)

1. Review *At Work* activity F.

2. Ask students to share the good, not-so-good, and interesting things that happened during the role-play. As students speak, write their responses in a chart on the board.

Introduction and Presentation
5 minutes

1. Pair students and direct them to look at the picture in their book. Ask them to describe what they see to their partner.

2. Ask volunteer pairs to share their ideas with the class.

Guided Practice
15–20 minutes

A 1. Model the process for making indirect questions. Write the question in the speech bubble by the information desk on the board: *What are the mall hours?* Ask a volunteer to read the first example of an indirect question.

2. Set a time limit (five minutes). Have students work with partners to complete the activity. Ask volunteers to write the questions on the board.

B 1. Have students work individually to write three new questions.

2. Group students to take turns asking and answering their questions.

C 1. Read the instructions aloud. Direct students to read the story silently and complete the sentences.

2. Have students compare sentences with their teammates. Ask volunteers to write the sentences on the board.

Answers
1. who proposed the clean-up.
2. how much time the repairs took.
3. how much the repairs cost.
4. if the donut shop stayed open during the clean-up.
5. if the shop owners are planning another project.
6. if the mall will be renovated this year.

MULTILEVEL STRATEGIES

Adapt C to the level of your students.

• **Pre-level** Read the story aloud. Ask questions about the content: *What was wrong with City Mall ten years ago?* [It was in terrible condition.] *Who proposed they clean it up?* [one shop owner] *What did they give money to do?* [pay for paint, plants, and benches] *Did all the businesses close during the clean-up?* [no] *How does it look today?* [beautiful]

Communicative Practice
30–40 minutes

 1. Group students and assign roles: manager, director, editor, actors. Explain that students are going to work with their teams to write and perform a conversation.

2. Read steps 2–4 of the activity aloud. Check comprehension of the task. *What is the first thing you should do?* [choose a situation from the list] *Who is going to have a conversation?* [two neighbors]

3. Set a time limit (ten minutes) to complete the exercise. Circulate and answer any questions.

4. Have actors from each team perform the conversation for another team.

 1. Have students walk around the room to conduct the interviews. To get students moving, tell them to interview three people who were not in their team for D.

2. Set a time limit (five minutes) to complete the exercise.

3. Tell students to make a note of their classmates' answers but not to worry about writing complete sentences.

MULTILEVEL STRATEGIES

Adapt the mixer in E to the level of your students.

• **Pre- and On-level** Pair these students and have them interview other pairs together.

• **Higher-level** Have these students ask an additional question and write all answers.

F 1. Call on individuals to report what they learned about their classmates. Keep a running tally on the board for question 2, writing down each service mentioned.

2. Have students work individually to draw bar graphs of the results and then compare graphs with their teammates. Ask volunteers to draw bars of the graph on the board.

PROBLEM SOLVING
10–15 minutes

A 🔊 3-24 1. Ask: *Are your neighbors involved with the community?* Tell students they will read a story about a woman whose neighborhood has many problems. Direct students to read Teresa's story silently.

2. Ask: *What are the problems in her neighborhood?* [trash, cracked sidewalks, broken glass, dead trees] *Does she think they can be fixed?* [yes]

3. Play the audio and have students read along silently.

B 1. Elicit answers to question 1.

2. Put students into groups of three or four. Ask each group to think of three or four possible solutions to Teresa's problems and report them to the class. Ask a volunteer to write all possible solutions on the board.

3. Ask students to write possible indirect questions Teresa could ask based on the solutions on the board. Have a volunteer from each group write one or two indirect questions on the board.

Possible Answers
1. Teresa is worried because her neighborhood has problems. No one is taking care of it and people don't want to go outside. She would like to start a neighborhood organization, but she doesn't know how to start.
2. Answers will vary.
3. Answers will vary.

Evaluation
20–25 minutes

To test students' understanding of the unit language and content, have them take the Unit 10 Test, available on the Teacher Resource Center.

UNIT 11 Find Us Online!

Unit Overview

This unit explores web resources, renting and renter's rights and contextualizes tag questions.

KEY OBJECTIVES	
Lesson 1	Identify web resources and tools
Lesson 2	Identify changes over time and write an essay comparing times
Lesson 3	Use tag questions to ask about personal, work, and academic experiences
Lesson 4	Ask for clarification and offer to help
Lesson 5	Identify and discuss renters' rights
At Work	Help someone understand at work
Teamwork & Language Review	Review unit language

UNIT FEATURES	
Academic Vocabulary	*clarification, discriminate, maintenance, media, negative, range, require, research, secure, security, submit, vary*
Employability Skills	• Speak so others can understand • Understand teamwork • Work with others • Communicate information • Communicate verbally • Listen actively • Cooperate with others • Ask for and give directions • Decide how to give someone feedback on their teaching style

Resources	**Class Audio** CD3, Tracks 25–35
	Workbook Unit 11, pages 72–78
	Teacher Resource Center
	    Multilevel Activities 4 Unit 11
	    Multilevel Grammar Exercises 4 Unit 11
	    Unit 11 Test
	Oxford Picture Dictionary Finding a Home, Apartments, Household Problems and Repairs, Internet Research

LESSON 1 VOCABULARY

Lesson Overview

MULTILEVEL OBJECTIVES

On-level: Talk about the Internet and describe web resources
Pre-level: Identify Internet vocabulary and web resources
Higher-level: Talk and write about the Internet and web resources

LANGUAGE FOCUS

Grammar: Unreal conditional (*If I had a website, I would put my favorite links on it.*)

Vocabulary: Internet and web resources

For vocabulary support, see these **Oxford Picture Dictionary** topics: Finding a Home, pages 48–49; Apartments, pages 50–51; Internet Research, pages 212–213.

READINESS CONNECTION

In this lesson, students work with others to conduct research about websites.

PACING

To compress this lesson: Conduct 1C as a whole-class activity.

To extend this lesson: Have students make and annotate a website list. (See end of lesson.)

And/or have students complete **Workbook 4 page 72** and **Multilevel Activities 4 Unit 11 pages 118–119**.

Lesson Notes

CORRELATIONS

CCRS: SL.1.B (b.) Follow agreed-upon rules for discussions. (c.) Ask questions to check understanding of information presented, stay on topic, and link their comments to the remarks of others. (d.) Explain their own ideas and understanding in light of the discussion.

SL.2.B Determine the main ideas and supporting details of a text read aloud or information presented in diverse media and formats, including visually, quantitatively, and orally.

SL.4.B Report on a topic or text, tell a story, or recount an experience with appropriate facts and relevant, descriptive details, speaking clearly at an understandable pace.

SL.6.B Speak in complete sentences when appropriate to task and situation in order to provide requested detail or clarification.

R.1.B Ask and answer such questions as who, what, where, when, why, and how to demonstrate understanding of key details in a text

R.4.B Determine the meaning of general academic and domain-specific words and phrases in a text relevant to a topic or subject area.

R.5.B Know and use various text features to locate key facts or information in a text efficiently.

R.7.B Use information gained from illustrations and the words in a text to demonstrate understanding of the text.

W.7.A Participate in shared research and writing projects.

L.1.B Demonstrate command of the conventions of standard English grammar and usage when writing or speaking. (l.) Produce simple, compound and complex sentences.

L.4.B (a.) Use sentence-level context as a clue to the meaning of a word or phrase.

RF.4.B (a.) Read grade-level text with purpose and understanding.

ELPS: 1. An ELL can construct meaning from oral presentations and literary and informational text through level-appropriate listening, reading, and viewing. 4. An ELL can construct level-appropriate oral and written claims and support them with reasoning and evidence. 5. An ELL can conduct research and evaluate and communicate findings to answer questions or solve problems. 7. An ELL can adapt language choices to purpose, task, and audience when speaking and writing. 8. An ELL can determine the meaning of words and phrases in oral presentation and literary and informational text. 9. An ELL can create clear and coherent level-appropriate speech and text. 10. An ELL can demonstrate command of the conventions of standard English to communicate in level-appropriate speech and writing.

Warm-up and Review
10–15 minutes (books closed)

Put a picture of a computer on the board or indicate the parts of a real computer. Ask students to name the parts they can and write them on the board. Elicit the parts of a laptop.

Introduction
5 minutes

1. Tell students that the parts they have named are the computer's hardware but that today you're going to focus on aspects of the computer controlled by its software.

2. State the objective: *Today we're going to learn vocabulary for the Internet and web resources.*

1 Identify Internet vocabulary

Presentation I
20–25 minutes

A 1. Direct students to look at the web page and the text. Build students' schema by asking questions. Ask: *What is the web page for?* [renting homes] *What type of information can you find?* [apartments, roommates, houses, movers, rental trucks, community information] *When is the class?* [Monday and Wednesday, 6–9 p.m.] *Can you learn about Internet searches?* [yes] *Can you learn about cyber (or Internet) security?* [yes]

2. Have students work in groups to answer the three questions. Call on volunteers to share their answers with the class. Say each vocabulary word and have students repeat.

Possible Answers
1. Links, ad, pull-down menu, scroll bar, (also possible to click in: search box, URL)
2. Search box, URL
3. Cursor: move to where you want to type. Pointer: click on parts of the page

B Read the instructions aloud. Have students work individually to define *discriminate*, *research*, and *secure* by identifying words that provide context and then compare answers with a partner. Elicit answers from the class.

Possible Answers
discriminate: between types of sites
research: topics
secure: safe and … from threats

Guided Practice I
10–20 minutes

C 1. Prepare students for the listening. Say: *You are going to hear an instructor explain how to use a computer to access the Internet and websites.*

2. Read the instructions aloud. Have students work individually to complete the sentences and then compare answers with a partner. Say: *While you listen, check your work in 1C.* Play the audio.

3. Go over the answers with the class.

Answers
1. pointer
2. pop-up ad
3. scroll bar, pull-down menu
4. URL
5. search box, cursor
6. links

MULTILEVEL STRATEGIES

Adapt 1C to the level of your students.

• **Pre-level** Work with these students as a group. If possible, demonstrate each of the items using a laptop or project on a screen.

• **On- and Higher-level** Play the audio again and have students take notes and then create questions based on their notes. Have students work in pairs to ask and answer their questions.

D Read the instructions aloud. Play the audio and have students discuss the question in pairs. Call on volunteers to share their answers with the class.

E Read the instructions and question aloud. Pair students to ask and answer the question. Call on students to share their answers with the class.

2 Learn website vocabulary

Presentation II
10–20 minutes

A 1. Direct students to look at the website links. Introduce the new topic: *Now we're going to look at parts of a typical website.*

2. Say and have students repeat the words in the website.

3. Ask students to work individually to match the links with the definitions.

4. Call on volunteers to read the matching links and information aloud.

5. Check comprehension. Ask: *Where can you find other websites on the same topic?* [Related Links] *Where can you find the organization's address?* [Contact Us]

Answers	
1. b	4. f
2. a	5. e
3. c	6. d

TIP
Show the class your school's or your district's home page and discuss the website links and what they link to. If you have no way of projecting a computer screen, print the home page out and make a transparency of it.

Guided Practice II
10–15 minutes

B 1. Model the conversation with a volunteer. Model it again using other information from 2A.

2. Set a time limit (three minutes). Direct students to practice with a partner.

3. Call on volunteers to present their version of the conversation for the class.

MULTILEVEL STRATEGIES
Adapt 2B to the level of your students.
- **Pre- and On-level** Pair pre- and on-level students for 2B. Assign pre-level students part A for the first round and then have them switch roles.

Communicative Practice and Application
20–25 minutes

C 1. If students will use the Internet for this task, establish what device(s) they'll use: a class computer, tablets, or smartphones. Alternatively, print information from the Internet before class and distribute to groups.

2. Write the questions from 2C on the board. Explain that students will work in teams to research and report on these questions. Ask: *How can we use the Internet for this task?* [they can look up the websites people mention] *How will you record the information you find?* [table, checklist, index cards] Remind students to bookmark or record sites so they can find or cite them in the future.

3. Group students and assign roles: reporter, manager, administrative assistant, and IT support. Verify students' understanding of their roles.

4. Give managers the time limit for discussing the questions and looking up websites as appropriate (ten minutes). Direct the IT support to begin the online research or pick up the printed materials for each team. Direct the administrative assistant to record information for the team using a table, checklist, or index cards.

5. Give a two-minute warning. Call "time." Tell reporters to first answer and then ask each member of the team question 2.

TIP
When setting up task-based activities, verify that students understand their roles using physical commands. For example: *If you report on your team's work, stand up* [reporter]. *If you keep the team on task, point to the clock* [manager]. *If you write the team's responses, raise your hand* [administrative assistant]. *If you help the team research, hold up your smartphone/tablet* [IT support].

D 1. Copy the sentence frames on the board.

2. Direct teams to help their administrative assistant use the sentence frames to record the team's findings. Direct the supervisor to use the recorded information to report the team's findings to the class or another team.

Evaluation
10–15 minutes

TEST YOURSELF

1. Direct Partner A to read prompts 1–3 from 1C on page 164 to Partner B. Partner B should close their book and write the answers in their notebook. When finished, students switch roles. Partner B reads prompts 4–6 from 1C.

2. Direct both partners to open their books and check their spelling when they finish.

MULTILEVEL STRATEGIES
Target the *Test Yourself* to the level of your students.
- **Higher-level** Direct these students to write instructions for new computer users, directing them to their favorite website. They should use as many target vocabulary words and phrases as they can.

EXTENSION ACTIVITY

Annotated Website List

1. Seat students in mixed-level groups. Tell the students to compile a list of their favorite websites and write a brief description of each one. If you have students who don't use the Internet, assign them to different groups and tell them to take the role of recorder or reporter.

2. Have a reporter from each group share the group's work with the class. Post the lists on the wall so that students can refer to them.

3. Have students vote and choose the most interesting website from the list.

LESSON 2 WRITING

Lesson Overview

MULTILEVEL OBJECTIVES

On- and Higher-level: Analyze, write, and edit an essay about technology use

Pre-level: Read an essay and write responses to questions about technology use

LANGUAGE FOCUS

Grammar: Contrast past and present (*Ten years ago, I didn't use the Internet. Now I use it every day.*)

Vocabulary: Information technology

For vocabulary support, see this **Oxford Picture Dictionary** topic: Internet Research, pages 212–213

STRATEGY FOCUS

When comparing times, use time expressions to make the times clear for the reader.

READINESS CONNECTION

In this lesson, students communicate information by writing about changes in their use of technology.

PACING

To compress this lesson: Assign the *Test Yourself* for homework.

To extend this lesson: Discuss entertainment technology. (See end of lesson.)

And/or have students complete **Workbook 4 page 73** and **Multilevel Activities 4 Unit 11 page 120**.

Lesson Notes

CORRELATIONS

CCRS: SL.1.B (d.) Explain their own ideas and understanding in light of the discussion.

SL.2.B Determine the main ideas and supporting details of a text read aloud or information presented in diverse media and formats, including visually, quantitatively, and orally.

R.1.B Ask and answer such questions as who, what, where, when, why, and how to demonstrate understanding of key details in a text.

W.2.B (a.) Introduce a topic and group related information together; include illustrations when useful to aiding comprehension. (b.) Develop the topic with facts, definitions, and details. (c.) Use linking words and phrases to connect ideas within categories of information. (d.) Provide a concluding statement or section.

W.4.B Produce writing in which the development and organization are appropriate to task and purpose.

W.5.B With guidance and support from peers and others, develop and strengthen writing as needed by planning, revising and editing.

L.1.B (l.) Produce simple, compound and complex sentences.

L.1.C (f.) Use verb tense to convey various times, sequences, states, and conditions.

L.2.C (a.) Use correct capitalization.

L.6.B Acquire and use accurately level-appropriate conversational, general academic, and domain-specific words and phrases, including those that signal spatial and temporal relationships.

RF.4.B (a.) Read grade-level text with purpose and understanding.

ELPS: 1. An ELL can construct meaning from oral presentations and literary and informational text through level-appropriate listening, reading, and viewing. 2. An ELL can participate in level-appropriate oral and written exchanges of information, ideas, and analyses, in various social and academic contexts, responding to peer, audience, or reader comments and questions. 3. An ELL can speak and write about level-appropriate complex literary and informational texts and topics. 6. An ELL can analyze and critique the arguments of others orally and in writing. 9. An ELL can create clear and coherent level-appropriate speech and text. 10. An ELL can demonstrate command of the conventions of standard English to communicate in level-appropriate speech and writing.

Warm-up and Review
10–15 minutes (books closed)

Write these questions on the board and call on volunteers to answer: *When is the last time you went online? What did you do or what site did you look at? Is there something you would like to do online but haven't tried yet?*

Introduction
5 minutes

1. Ask how many students were using the Internet ten years ago.

2. State the objective: *Today we're going to read and write about changes in the use of technology.*

1 Prepare to write

Presentation
20–25 minutes

A 1. Build students' schema by asking questions about the essay. Ask: *What is the title of the essay?* [Technology Then and Now] *Who is the writer?* [Pedro Sanchez] *Have you ever written about technology?*

2. Read the instructions aloud. Give students one minute to tell a partner their responses to questions 1 and 2. Elicit responses from the class.

B 1. Introduce the essay and its purpose: *You're going to read an essay about how someone's use of technology has changed in the last ten years.* Direct students to read the essay silently.

2. Check comprehension. Ask: *What are the two times the writer talks about?* [ten years ago and today] *Is he writing about differences or similarities or both?* [both] *What kind of computer did he use ten years ago?* [a desktop] *What things did he keep track of on the computer in the past?* [family budget and address book] *What devices does he use now?* [a smartphone and a tablet] *What does he keep track of on his devices?* [his activity] *What does his family do at dinnertime?* [turn off all devices]

3. Play the audio. Ask students to number the paragraphs as they read along. Go over the *Writer's Note*. Have students underline the time expressions.

Guided Practice I
10 minutes

C Have students work independently to mark the statements and then compare answers with a partner.

Answers
1. F
2. NI
3. T
4. NI
5. T

MULTILEVEL STRATEGIES

Seat pre-level students together for 1C.

- **Pre-level** While other students are working on 1C, ask these students questions about the reading. *How did the writer keep track of different things ten years ago? What does he use now? Does Pedro talk about paper maps? Did he have the Internet ten years ago? Does Pedro mention an English class? What does Pedro do when he is in line?* Give students time to copy the answers to 1C from the board.

- **On- and Higher-level** Write two column heads on the board: *Ten Years Ago* and *Now*. Direct these students to first complete 1C and write the answers on the board. When they finish, ask them to write ideas for ways that their use of technology has changed in the last ten years.

2 Plan and write

Guided Practice II
15–20 minutes

A 1. Read the questions. Elicit students' answers.

2. Put the students' ideas under the two column heads on the board (*Ten Years Ago* and *Now*). Include ways of using technology as well as kinds of technology.

B 1. Direct students to look back at the essay in 1B. Read through the questions for each paragraph and elicit how the writer in 1B answered them.

2. Draw students' attention to the template and ask them to follow the format as they write in their notebooks.

3. Check comprehension of the exercise. Ask: *How many paragraphs are you going to write?* [three] *Which paragraph will talk about your use of technology today?* [paragraph 2]

4. Have students work individually to write their essays.

> **MULTILEVEL STRATEGIES**
>
> Adapt 2B to the level of your students.
>
> • **Pre-level** Tell these students to compose their essays by writing two sentences in answer to each question.
>
> • **Higher-level** Tell these students to include more than one kind of technology and to provide specific examples of how they used (or use) them.

3 Get feedback and revise

Guided Practice III
5 minutes

 Direct students to check their writing using the editing checklist. Tell them to read each item in the list and check their papers before moving onto the next item. Explain that students should not edit their writing at this stage. They should just use the checklist to check their work and mark any areas they want to revise.

Communicative Practice
15 minutes

B 1. Read the instructions aloud. Emphasize to students that they are responding to their partners' work, not correcting it.

2. Use the letter in 1B to model the exercise. *Your comparison of the things you kept track of on your computer or device ten years ago and now is interesting.*

3. Direct students to exchange papers with a partner and follow the instructions.

C Allow students time to edit and revise their writing as necessary, using the editing checklist from 3A and their partner's feedback from 3B. If necessary, students could complete this task as homework.

> **TIP**
>
> After completing 3C, hold a "technology tutorial" in class. Ask for volunteers to come to the front of the room and describe how they use technology now. All non-volunteers are people who want to use technology in a new way. Ask them to listen and take notes. Tell them they need to choose three new uses of technology to get more training on.

Application and Evaluation
10 minutes

TEST YOURSELF

1. Review the instructions aloud. Assign a time limit (five minutes) and have students work independently.

2. Before collecting student work, invite two or three volunteers to share their sentences. Ask students to raise their hands if they wrote similar answers.

> **MULTILEVEL STRATEGIES**
>
> Adapt the *Test Yourself* to the level of your students.
>
> • **Pre-level** Tell these students to write a one-sentence answer to each prompt.

> **EXTENSION ACTIVITY**
>
> **Discussion**
>
> Talk about entertainment technology. Have a class discussion about how technology has changed entertainment. Ask: *How do you listen to music now? How did people listen to music ten or twenty years ago? How has watching television and movies changed? What are the advantages of the new technology? Are there any disadvantages?*

LESSON 3 GRAMMAR

Lesson Overview

MULTILEVEL OBJECTIVES

On- and Higher-level: Use tag questions to ask for and clarify instructions

Pre-level: Identify and respond to tag questions; use tag questions

LANGUAGE FOCUS

Grammar: Tag questions (*You live here, don't you?*)
Vocabulary: Housing

For vocabulary support, see these **Oxford Picture Dictionary** topics: Household Problems and Repairs, pages 62–63; Internet Research, pages 212–213

READINESS CONNECTION

In this lesson, students use tag questions and speak so others can understand.

PACING

To compress this lesson: Conduct 2A and 2B as whole-class activities.

To extend this lesson: Have students learn more about each other by using tag questions. (See end of lesson.)

And/or have students complete **Workbook 4 pages 74–75**, **Multilevel Activities 4 Unit 11 pages 121–122**, and **Multilevel Grammar Exercises 4 Unit 11**.

Lesson Notes

CORRELATIONS

CCRS: SL.2.B Determine the main ideas and supporting details of a text read aloud or information presented in diverse media and formats, including visually, quantitatively, and orally.

R.1.A Ask and answer questions about key details in a text.

R.7.B Use information gained from illustrations and the words in a text to demonstrate understanding of the text.

L.1.B (l.) Produce simple, compound and complex sentences.

L.2.C (e.) Use a comma to set off the words yes and no, to set off a tag question from the rest of the sentence, and to indicate direct address.

L.1.D (h.) Form and use verbs in the indicative, imperative, interrogative, conditional and subjunctive mood.

RF.4.B (a.) Read grade-level text with purpose and understanding.

ELPS: 2. An ELL can participate in level-appropriate oral and written exchanges of information, ideas, and analyses, in various social and academic contexts, responding to peer, audience, or reader comments and questions. 3. An ELL can speak and write about level-appropriate complex literary and informational texts and topics. 7. An ELL can adapt language choices to purpose, task, and audience when speaking and writing. 9. An ELL can create clear and coherent level-appropriate speech and text. 10. An ELL can demonstrate command of the conventions of standard English to communicate in level-appropriate speech and writing.

Warm-up and Review
10–15 minutes (books closed)

Write sentence frames and ask volunteers to complete them. *Email is _____. Computers are _____. Ten years ago, life was _____. Ten years ago, telephones were _____. Today, life isn't _____. Ten years ago, computers weren't _____. Ten years ago, email wasn't _____.*

Introduction
5–10 minutes

1. Ask students how many of them use email every day, how many use it every week, and how many never use it. Direct tag questions to the students who use email. *It's very convenient, isn't it? They're quick, aren't they?*

2. State the objective: *Today we're going to use tag questions to talk about housing problems and life experiences.*

1 Use tag questions with *be*

Presentation I
20–25 minutes

1. Direct students to look at the picture and conversation. Ask: *Who are these people? What are they doing?* Establish that the relationship is friendly, perhaps classmates or colleagues, and that they are working on computers.

2. Read the instructions aloud. Ask students to read the conversation silently and answer the questions.

3. Read the first question aloud. Call on a volunteer for the answer. Ask the volunteer where in the conversation they found the answer. Read the rest of the questions aloud, calling on a different volunteer for each answer.

Answers
1. Yes, she does.
2. Yes, he does. No, he isn't.

1. Demonstrate how to read the grammar chart. Read each question aloud and have students repeat.

2. Direct students to underline the tag questions in the conversation in 1A. Write the questions on the board.

3. Elicit the form for both affirmative and negative statements and write them on the board: Subject + (auxiliary) + main verb…, aux + subject pronoun? And Subject + auxiliary + *not* + main verb…, + aux + *not* + subject pronoun? Check for understanding. Ask: *When the statement is affirmative, is the tag affirmative or negative?* [negative] *What are the two parts of a tag?* [auxiliary/*be (not)* + subject pronoun] *How do you disagree with a negative statement?* [an affirmative short answer]

4. Pair students and direct them to read the chart aloud to each other. (One partner reads the questions and the other responds by agreeing or disagreeing.) Then read the chart aloud as students follow along.

5. Assess students' understanding of the chart. Ask them to convert the statements on the board from the *Warm-up* into tag questions. Call on volunteers to say the tag questions and tell other volunteers to agree or disagree.

Answers
Underline: aren't you?; isn't he?

Guided Practice I
15–20 minutes

1. Tell students they will collaborate to complete the description of the grammar point. Model collaboration by working with the class to complete the first sentence. Encourage students to look at 1A and 1B to see if the negative tag is used after an affirmative or negative statement.

2. Pair students and have them work together to complete the description.

3. Project or write the completed definition on the board and have pairs verify the accuracy of their responses. Ask volunteers which sentences confused them and discuss.

Answers
an affirmative, Negative, yes, an affirmative, comma

MULTILEVEL STRATEGIES

For 1C, seat mixed-level students together.

- **Pre-, On-, and Higher-level** Assign pre-level students the role of administrative assistant, on-level students the role of manager, and higher-level students the role of researcher. The administrative assistant fills in the blanks according to the team's decisions, the manager reads the description and manages the team's discussion, and the researcher looks up the definition of the grammar point online or checks against an answer key to verify the team's answers.

Guided Practice II
10–15 minutes

1. Model the first item. Ask: *How do you know which tag to use?* [look at the pronoun and whether the statement is negative or affirmative]

2. Have students work individually to match the parts of the question and then compare answers with a partner. Go over the answers with the class.

3. Have students practice asking and answering the questions in pairs.

Answers	
1. b	4. d
2. e	5. a
3. c	

MULTILEVEL STRATEGIES

Target 1D to the level of your students.

- **Pre-level** Direct these students to underline the verb *be* in the first part of each question. As their classmates read the completed questions aloud, point out that the tag has the same verb form as the first part of the question, but if the first part is negative, the verb in the tag is positive and vice versa.

 1. Read the instructions and the model aloud.

2. Have students work individually to complete the statements with tag questions and then compare answers with a partner. Go over the answers with the class.

3. Have students practice asking and answering the questions in pairs.

4. Provide clarification or feedback to the whole class as needed.

Answers
1. isn't it
2. was he/was she
3. aren't you
4. weren't they
5. is it

2 Use tag questions with *do* and *did*

Presentation II
20–25 minutes

 1. Introduce the new topic. *Now we're going to learn tag questions with do, does, and did.*

2. Read and have students repeat the questions and answers in the chart. Point out that the form for these tag questions is the same as the tag questions in 1B, but the auxiliaries are *do/does* and *did*, rather than *be*.

3. Direct students to work individually to complete the tag questions and then compare answers with a partner. Ask volunteers to write the answers on the board.

Answers	
1. didn't he	4. does he
2. do you	5. doesn't he
3. didn't she	6. don't they

TIP

Provide practice with tag questions after going over the chart. Make cards with each of the tags from the charts in 1B and 2A. Put students in groups and provide each group with a complete set of tags. Make statements and have the students in each group take turns holding up the group's tag to go with the sentence. Give groups time to discuss and make their choices before they hold up a tag. Possible statements: *You don't work Mondays. He doesn't attend this class. The computer crashed. The homework was difficult.* If students have difficulty choosing the correct tag, elicit the verb you used and write it on the board. Refer students to the charts in 1B and 2A to find the correct tag.

MULTILEVEL STRATEGIES

For 2A, give pre-level students time to catch up while challenging on- and higher-level students.

- **Pre-level** Read each completed tag question aloud twice to allow these students time to fill in any missing tags.
- **On- and Higher-level** Call on these students to answer your tag questions. The first time, tell the student to agree; the second time, tell the student to disagree.

Guided Practice III
10–15 minutes

 1. Elicit the importance of accuracy. Tell students they will be building their accuracy in this task.

2. Organize students into groups. Assign roles: manager, administrative assistant, and reporter. Demonstrate how to correct the sentence using the first example.

3. Have team members work together to correct the sentences. Have the manager keep track of the time (ten minutes). Have the administrative assistant write down the group's edited sentence. Circulate and monitor teamwork.

4. Have reporters share the corrected sentences.

Answers
1. You called me, didn't you?
2. Your doorbell doesn't work, does it?
3. The people in 3A just moved in, didn't they?
4. That looks better, doesn't it?
5. You don't need anything else, do you?

MULTILEVEL STRATEGIES

After 2B, provide more practice with tag questions. Put up sheets of poster paper around the room. Write a topic at the head of each paper. Possible topics: *Landlords, Renters, Apartments, Email, Computers*, etc. Have students line up in front of a poster. Tell the first person in line to write a simple-present or simple-past statement related to the topic. Tell the next student to add a tag to the statement to make it a question. To make this activity more challenging, "outlaw" the verb *be*. Have a reporter from each line read the completed questions aloud. Call on other students to agree or disagree.

• **Pre-level** Put these students in the first and/or third position in line so they will be writing statements, not tags.

3 Listen for the verb to determine the tag question

Guided Practice IV
10–15 minutes

🔊 **3-27** 1. Say: *Now we're going to listen to some statements about a class. You'll need to choose the correct tag to turn the statement into a question.*

2. Play the audio. Direct students to read along silently without writing.

3. Replay the audio. Ask students to choose the correct tag.

4. Have students work in pairs to compare their answers. Call on volunteers for the answers.

Answers	
1. a	6. b
2. a	7. a
3. b	8. b
4. a	9. a
5. b	

MULTILEVEL STRATEGIES

Replay the audio for 3 to allow pre-level students to catch up while you challenge on- and higher-level students.

• **Pre-level** Have these students listen again to choose the correct tag.

• **On- and Higher-level** Have these students take notes on the questions. When you go over the answers, call on these students to reconstruct the first part of the question.

4 Use tag questions to talk about life experience

Communicative Practice and Application
20–25 minutes

A Pair students. Direct students to work independently to predict their partners' answers. Tell students to write their answers without speaking to their partners. Encourage them to make guesses even if they have no idea.

B 1. Elicit the tag questions that students will ask their partners.

2. Read the *Speaker's Note*. Read the model conversation with a volunteer and point out how the speakers are asking for and giving extra information. Tell students that we often use tag questions to get a conversation going.

3. Direct students to ask their partners the questions. Tell them to make notes of each other's answers. Model the exercise by asking a volunteer the first question.

4. Check comprehension of the exercise. Ask: *What kind of questions are you asking?* [tag] *Are you going to give a yes/no answer or are you going to add information?* [add information] Set a time limit for the exercise (four minutes) and observe and take note of issues that arise.

C 1. Have the partners from 4B join with another pair. Model the exercise with two volunteers. First play the role of A and then play the role of B to demonstrate that A asks a regular question and B responds with a tag question.

2. Set a time limit (five minutes). Monitor and provide feedback.

Evaluation

10–15 minutes

TEST YOURSELF

1. Brainstorm names of famous people and write them on the board.

2. Ask students to write the five tag questions independently. Then pair students and have them ask their partners the questions they wrote.

3. Collect and correct their writing.

MULTILEVEL STRATEGIES

Target the *Test Yourself* to the level of your students.

- **Pre-level** Encourage these students to write tag questions with the verb *be*.

Ask students to write the sentences independently. Collect and correct their writing.

EXTENSION ACTIVITY

Discussion

After the *Test Yourself*, group students and have them write tag questions for each of the members of their group to confirm what they know about them. For example: They can confirm their likes or dislikes, where they are from, or other observations about their classmates.

LESSON 4 EVERYDAY CONVERSATION

Lesson Overview

MULTILEVEL OBJECTIVES

On-, Pre-, and Higher-level: Ask for and clarify instructions about Internet use and listen for information in a talk show interview

LANGUAGE FOCUS

Grammar: Use question words for clarification (*From where?*) Tag questions (*That's a good website, isn't it?*)

Vocabulary: Internet and housing words, *premises*

For vocabulary support, see these **Oxford Picture Dictionary** topics: Apartments, pages 50–51; Internet Research, pages 212–213

STRATEGY FOCUS

Practice language to offer help and keep a conversation going.

READINESS CONNECTION

In this lesson, students listen actively and focus on listening for details.

PACING

To compress this lesson: Conduct *Discuss* as a whole-class activity.

To extend this lesson: After completing 6B, have students complete a chart as a class. (See end of lesson.)

And/or have students complete **Workbook 4 page 76** and **Multilevel Activities 4 Unit 11 page 123**.

Lesson Notes

CORRELATIONS

CCRS: SL.1.B (a.) Come to discussions prepared, having read or studied required material; explicitly draw on that preparation and other information known about the topic to explore ideas under discussion. (b.) Follow agreed-upon rules for discussions. (c.) Ask questions to check understanding of information presented, stay on topic, and link their comments to the remarks of others. (d.) Explain their own ideas and understanding in light of the discussion.

SL.2.B Determine the main ideas and supporting details of a text read aloud or information presented in diverse media and formats, including visually, quantitatively, and orally.

SL.4.B Report on a topic or text, tell a story, or recount an experience with appropriate facts and relevant, descriptive details, speaking clearly at an understandable pace.

SL.6.B Speak in complete sentences when appropriate to task and situation in order to provide requested detail or clarification.

R.1.B Ask and answer such questions as who, what, where, when, why, and how to demonstrate understanding of key details in a text.

R.2.A Identify the main topic and retell key details of a text.

R.4.B Determine the meaning of general academic and domain-specific words and phrases in a text relevant to a topic or subject area.

R.7.B Use information gained from illustrations and the words in a text to demonstrate understanding of the text.

L.1.A (k.) Understand and use question words (interrogatives).

L.1.B (l.) Produce simple, compound and complex sentences.

L.3.B (b.) Recognize and observe differences between the conventions of spoken and written standard English.

L.4.B (a.) Use sentence-level context as a clue to the meaning of a word or phrase.

L.5.B (b.) Identify real-life connections between words and their use.

L.6.B Use words and phrases acquired through conversations, reading and being read to, and responding to texts, including using adjectives and adverbs to describe.

RF.4.B (a.) Read grade-level text with purpose and understanding.

ELPS: 2. An ELL can participate in level-appropriate oral and written exchanges of information, ideas, and analyses, in various social and academic contexts, responding to peer, audience, or reader comments and questions. 4. An ELL can construct level-appropriate oral and written claims and support them with reasoning and evidence. 7. An ELL can adapt language choices to purpose, task, and audience when speaking and writing. 9. An ELL can create clear and coherent level-appropriate speech and text. 10. An ELL can demonstrate command of the conventions of standard English to communicate in level-appropriate speech and writing.

Warm-up and Review
10–15 minutes (books closed)

Display and elicit the purpose of different websites. If you don't have a means of projecting a computer screen, print and make transparencies of the home pages of different sites—for example, a search engine, a map finder, a weather page, a news site, a blog, an online game, and a fan site.

Introduction
5 minutes

1. Ask: *Who knows the most about computers and technology in your house?*

2. State the objective: *Today we're going to learn ways to offer and respond to help and clarify information.*

1 Learn ways to offer and respond to help

Presentation I
10–20 minutes

 3-28 1. Direct students to look at the picture. Build students' schema. Ask: *Who are these people?* [friends or colleagues] *What are they doing?* [working on computers]

2. Play the audio. Tell students to ask and answer the questions with a partner. Go over the answers with the class.

Answers
Abby wants to send an email to her landlord. Leo's suggestions are: "Make the message short." And "If you don't hear back from the landlord today, call again and send another email tomorrow."

Guided Practice I
20–25 minutes

 3-28 1. Read the instructions aloud. Have students read the list of tasks before listening. Play the audio. Ask students to listen for and check the tasks.

2. Ask students to compare their answers with a partner. Circulate and monitor to ensure students understand the audio.

Answers
Check: typing in the landlord's address the length of the message sending an email

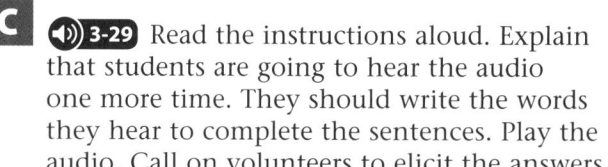 3-29 Read the instructions aloud. Explain that students are going to hear the audio one more time. They should write the words they hear to complete the sentences. Play the audio. Call on volunteers to elicit the answers.

Answers
1. can I suggest something 2. Can I make another suggestion

2 Practice your pronunciation

Pronunciation Extension
10–15 minutes

 3-30 1. Write *You have the landlord's email address, don't you?* on the board. Say the question twice—once with rising and once with falling intonation. Ask students to identify which time you were not sure of the answer. Say: *Now we're going to focus on two ways to say tag questions.*

2. Play the audio. Direct students to listen for the rising and falling intonation.

B 3-31 1. Play the audio and ask students to check the correct column.

2. Replay the audio. Stop after each question so that students can check their answers. Ask for a show of hands to see how many chose *fairly sure* or *not sure*. Replay any questions that caused difficulty.

Answers	
1. not sure	4. not sure
2. fairly sure	5. not sure
3. fairly sure	6. fairly sure

C Have students practice the questions in 3A with a partner. Call on volunteers to say the questions for the class and have the class guess whether the student is fairly sure or not sure.

3 Use questions words for clarification

Presentation II and Guided Practice II
10–15 minutes

 1. Introduce the new topic. Say: *Now we're going to use* what *and* where *in questions for clarification.* Read the conversations in the chart aloud. Point out that repeating the words when giving clarification helps the listener understand.

2. Have students work individually to complete the questions with *what* or *where* and then compare answers with a partner. Go over the answers as a class.

Answers
1. what
2. where

Guided Practice III
15–20 minutes

B Have students work with a partner to match the sentences with the clarification questions. Go over the answers as a class.

Answers	
1. e	4. d
2. a	5. b
3. c	

> **TIP**
>
> After 3B, practice clarification questions as a class. Make statements and mumble the endings. Call on students to ask clarification questions. *I went to the (mumble). I talked to (mumble) yesterday. I bought new (mumble). I want to go to (mumble).*

4 Building conversation skills

Guided Practice IV
15–20 minutes

 Direct students to look at the picture and skim the conversation. Ask: *What are they doing?* [One person is helping the other with something on the computer.] Have them work with partners to identify the purpose of the conversation. Elicit responses and ask: *How do you know?* or *Why do you say that?* to encourage students to state their reasoning.

Possible Answers
The purpose is to help a co-worker with a computer problem. He is pointing at her computer and showing her something.

B 🔊 **3-32** 1. Ask students to read the instructions and tell you what they are going to do [listen and read and respond to the question]. Play the audio and then elicit the answer to the question.

2. Ask students to read the conversation with a partner. Circulate and monitor pronunciation. Model and have students repeat difficult words or phrases.

3. Ask: *In what other situations could you use this conversation?* Point out a few phrases that are not specific to a problem with a document on the computer. Ask volunteers to point out others.

Possible Answer
Arnie says, "Can I make a suggestion?"

Communicative Practice and Application I
15–20 minutes

C 1. Pair students and have them read the instructions silently. Check their comprehension of the exercise. Ask: *What are the two roles?* [an employee and a co-worker] *What is the problem?* [finding a company's hours on the website]

2. Model and have students repeat the expressions in the *In Other Words* box. Explain that they should use these expressions in their conversations.

3. Draw a T-chart on the board. Label the left column *Employee* and the right column *Co-worker*. Elicit examples of what each person might say and make notes on the chart.

4. Set a time limit (three minutes). Have students act out the role-play. Call time and have students switch roles.

5. Ask three volunteer pairs to act out their role-play for the class. Have students who are listening take notes in the chart for each role-play.

5 Focus on listening for details

Presentation and Guided Practice
20–25 minutes

 1. Read the statement aloud and model a discussion with a volunteer. Ask: *Do you agree that the best way to find a new home is to use the Internet?... Why? / Why not? ... I agree because... / I disagree because...*

2. Pair students and tell them to discuss their ideas about the statement. Circulate and monitor. Then call on students to share their ideas with the class.

B 🔊 3-33 1. Direct students' attention to the picture. Build students' schema by asking: *Where are they?* [a radio station] *How do you know?* [they have microphones and headsets]

2. Read the instructions and questions aloud. Play the audio. Have students answer the questions and then compare answers with a partner. Call on volunteers to answer the questions.

Answers
1. They are talking about a website that Malia designed for finding an apartment.
2. Malia

C 🔊 3-33 1. Direct students to read the sentences before listening.

2. Replay the audio and have students work individually to complete the sentences and then compare answers with a partner. Take a tally of responses for each item and if students disagree on a response, replay the audio so that they can check their answers.

Answers	
1. college	4. six
2. landlord	5. a lot of
3. hard	6. hundreds

> **MULTILEVEL STRATEGIES**
>
> Adapt 5C to the level of your students.
>
> • **Pre-level** Before these students listen, provide them with the answers to 5C written out of order. Have them write the words in the correct sentence as they listen.

6 Discuss

Communicative Practice and Application II
15–20 minutes

A 1. Read the instructions aloud. Draw a sample chart on the board with space for jobs on one side and technology skills on the other. Call on volunteers to read the sample sentences in 6A. Fill in the chart, writing "cashiers" on the left and "use a cash register" on the right. Explain that students will make a chart like this one based on their own discussions.

2. Put students into teams of four and assign roles: reporter, manager, administrative assistant, and researcher. Verify students' understanding of the roles. Encourage students to use the phrases in the *Speaking Note* during their discussions.

3. Set a time limit for the discussions (ten minutes). Write the sentence frame from 6B on the board. Then circulate and monitor.

B Call "time." Ask the reporter for each team to report the results of their team's discussion, using the sentence frame on the board.

> **EXTENSION ACTIVITY**
>
> To extend 6B, draw a large blank chart on the board. As each reporter shares with the class, the administrative assistant from that group fills in the chart. If other teams came up with the same answers, they should not enter the information again.

Evaluation
5 minutes

TEST YOURSELF

1. Ask students to complete the checkboxes individually.

2. Tell students that you are going to read each of the items in the checklist aloud. If they are not at all confident with that skill, they should hold up a closed fist. If they are not very confident, they should hold up one finger. If they are somewhat confident, two fingers; confident, three fingers; very confident, four fingers. If they think they could teach the skill, they should hold up five fingers. Read each item in the checklist and identify students that may need further support.

> **TIP**
>
> For homework, you could ask students to write a sentence or two about what discussion skills they still need to work on or, if they are confident in all of the skills, what skill they are most proud of.

LESSON 5 READING

Lesson Overview

MULTILEVEL OBJECTIVES

On-, Pre-, and Higher-level: Read about and discuss renters' rights and responsibilities

LANGUAGE FOCUS

Vocabulary: *Check up on, claim, routine, tenant*

For vocabulary support, see these **Oxford Picture Dictionary** topics: Apartments, pages 50–51; Household Problems and Repairs, pages 62–63; Internet Research, pages 212–213

STRATEGY FOCUS

Practice previewing an article to predict its content and read with a purpose.

READINESS CONNECTION

In this lesson, students ask for and give help with rental problems.

PACING

To compress this lesson: Conduct the word study in 2A as a whole-class activity.

To extend this lesson: Have students discuss renters' rights and responsibilities. (See end of lesson.)

And/or have students complete **Workbook 4 page 77** and **Multilevel Activities 4 Unit 11 pages 124–125**.

Lesson Notes

CORRELATIONS

CCRS: SL.1.B (b.) Follow agreed-upon rules for discussions. (c.) Ask questions to check understanding of information presented, stay on topic, and link their comments to the remarks of others. (d.) Explain their own ideas and understanding in light of the discussion.

SL.2.B Determine the main ideas and supporting details of a text read aloud or information presented in diverse media and formats, including visually, quantitatively, and orally.

SL.6.B Speak in complete sentences when appropriate to task and situation in order to provide requested detail or clarification.

R.1.B Ask and answer such questions as who, what, where, when, why, and how to demonstrate understanding of key details in a text.

R.1.C Refer to details and examples in a text when explaining what the text says explicitly and when drawing inferences from the text.

R.2.B Determine the main idea of a text; recount the key details and explain how they support the main idea.

R.4.B Determine the meaning of general academic and domain-specific words and phrases in a text relevant to a topic or subject area.

R.5.B Know and use various text features to locate key facts or information in a text efficiently.

R.7.B Use information gained from illustrations and the words in a text to demonstrate understanding of the text.

W.8.B Recall information from experiences or gather information from print and digital sources; take brief notes on sources and sort evidence into provided categories.

L.1.B (l.) Produce simple, compound and complex sentences.

L.4.B (a.) Use sentence-level context as a clue to the meaning of a word or phrase. (b.) Determine the meaning of the new word formed when a known prefix is added to a known word. (e.) Use glossaries and beginning dictionaries, both print and digital, to determine or clarify the meaning of words and phrases.

RF.3.B (c.) Identify and know the meaning of the most common prefixes and derivational suffixes.

RF.4.B (a.) Read grade-level text with purpose and understanding.

ELPS: 1. An ELL can construct meaning from oral presentations and literary and informational text through level-appropriate listening, reading, and viewing. 2. An ELL can participate in level-appropriate oral and written exchanges of information, ideas, and analyses, in various social and academic contexts, responding to peer, audience, or reader comments and questions. 3. An ELL can speak and write about level-appropriate complex literary and informational texts and topics. 4. An ELL can construct level-appropriate oral and written claims and support them with reasoning and evidence. 8. An ELL can determine the meaning of words and phrases in oral presentation and literary and informational text.

Warm-up and Review
10–15 minutes (books closed)

Ask your students how many of them are renters and how many are homeowners. Call on volunteers to share if they have a good relationship with their landlords. Find out if any of your students are landlords. Ask about their relationship with their tenants.

Introduction
5 minutes

1. Explain that landlords and tenants often disagree about certain issues and that most of those issues are covered by laws. Point out to students that they may find themselves in situations where it would be useful to know about renters' rights and responsibilities.

2. State the objective: *Today we're going to read about and discuss renters' rights and responsibilities.*

1 Read

Presentation
10–20 minutes

A Read the questions aloud. Write students' ideas on the board.

B Read the words and definitions. Elicit sample sentences for each word or supply them if the students can't.

Pre-reading

C Read the instructions aloud and confirm that students understand what the URL is and where the headings are. Go over the *Reader's Note*. Have students write questions individually and then compare questions with a partner. Elicit questions from the class and write them on the board.

Possible Answers
What rights do renters have? What are landlords allowed and not allowed to do?

Guided Practice: While Reading
20–30 minutes

D 1. Ask students to read the article silently and answer the question.

2. Check answers with the class.

3. After they've finished reading, direct students to underline unfamiliar words they would like to know (e.g., *vary, advance, property, common areas, maintain*). Elicit the words and encourage other students to provide definitions or examples.

4. Check students' comprehension. Ask: *When can a landlord enter your home without advance notice?* [during an emergency] *Who has to keep the inside of the home clean?* [the tenant] *Why should you make a checklist of the condition of things in your home?* [in case the landlord wants to keep your deposit]

Answers
Laws protect renters by protecting their rights to privacy, to a home in good condition, and to a refund of their security deposit when they move out if there is no damage to the home.

MULTILEVEL STRATEGIES

Adapt 1D to the level of your students.

- **Pre-level** Provide these students with a summary of the ideas in the reading. *Renters' rights are different in different states, but here are some laws that are true in most states: 1. Unless there is an emergency, a landlord must tell you ahead of time if he or she is going to enter your home. 2. Landlords are responsible for keeping the property in good condition. Renters are responsible for keeping their areas clean. 3. The landlord must refund your security deposit when you move out unless you have damaged property.*

Direct students to read the summary while other students are reading 1D.

Guided Practice: Rereading
10–15 minutes

E 1. Provide an opportunity for students to extract evidence from the text. Have students reread the article and underline the answers.

2. Pair students and tell them to compare the words they underlined and report anything they disagree on. Discuss and clarify as needed.

Answers
The landlord has a right to enter a home without advance notice in an emergency. The landlord has the right to keep part of a security deposit if a renter has damaged a home.

1. Have students work individually to choose the best answer and then compare answers with a partner. Go over the answers with the class.

2. Elicit and discuss any additional questions about the reading. You could introduce new questions for class discussion: *Why is it important to know your rights as a renter? Have you ever had difficulties with your landlord?*

Answers
1. a
2. b
3. b

MULTILEVEL STRATEGIES

Target 1F to the level of your students.

- **Pre-level** Tell these students to use their summaries to complete the exercise.

- **Higher-level** Give these students questions to discuss with a partner when they finish 1F. *What should be on your checklist for things to look for before you move in? How does the tenant/landlord relationship compare?*

TIP

Have students go online to find out about tenants' rights in your area. Decide which device(s) students will use and elicit search terms ("tenants' rights" + your city).

2 Word study

Guided Practice: Post-reading
10 minutes

1. Direct students to look at the chart and identify the topic (the prefix *re-*). Have students read the chart.

2. Read the sentences in the chart. Elicit the root for each underlined word [*-boot, -imburse, -new, -certify*]. Ask which ones are words on their own.

3. Have students repeat after you as you say each word with natural intonation, rhythm, and stress.

4. Direct students to complete the sentences and then compare answers with a partner. Read the correct answers and have students check their work.

Answers
1. reorganize
2. renew
3. rewrite/redo
4. reapply
5. Reimburse, refund

Direct students to work individually to write a sentence for each topic that includes the underlined word. Ask volunteers to write their sentences on the board. Have the rest of the class suggest grammar and spelling edits as needed.

3 Talk it over

Guided Practice
15–20 minutes

1. Read the instructions aloud. Have students read the emails.

2. Go over the *Reader's Note*. Have students underline examples of informal language in the emails [*OK, Hi*]. Ask: *What is the tone?* [informal] *What is the writer's purpose?* [to get a quick answer to a question]

3. Set a time limit (ten minutes). Have students work in pairs to complete the task. Ask volunteers to share their answers with the class.

Answers
Renthelp101 will probably tell New York renter that the landlord had the right to enter the apartment because the smoke alarm went off and that could mean/have meant an emergency.
Renthelp101 will probably tell Miami1016 that the landlord can keep some of the deposit because the renter caused damage to the house.

Communicative Practice
20 minutes

Read the questions aloud. Set a time limit (ten minutes). Allow students to think about the questions and then write their answers in their notebooks.

C Ask volunteers to share their ideas with the class.

> **TIP**
> Before students do the *Bring It to Life* assignment, have them work in groups to brainstorm a list of important questions they would want to ask before renting an apartment or buying a new home. Have each group write the questions on a large sheet of paper. Keep the questions for the follow-up to *Bring It to Life*.

Application
5–10 minutes

BRING IT TO LIFE

Read the instructions aloud. Tell students who are going to look on the Internet to try typing *home buying checklist, rental checklist,* and *apartment checklist* into a search engine.

> **EXTENSION ACTIVITY**
> **Discussion**
> Write a list of situations that deal with renters' rights and responsibilities on the board.
> 1. The ceiling leaks every time it rains or snows. 2. There are grease stains all over the kitchen from cooking. 3. A table lamp is broken. 4. The trash is piling up by the side of the house. 5. A step in the staircase leading into the apartment building is broken.
>
> Put students in pairs. Ask them to discuss who is probably responsible for the situation. Tell them to come up with things that the landlord or renter might do in each case. Call on volunteers to share their ideas with the class.

AT WORK

Warm-up and Review
10–15 minutes (books closed)

Ask: *Have you ever taken any classes or training online?* Elicit students' experiences with online training and then brainstorm the kinds of training people might be able to take online. Make sure students understand the concept—that online training typically consists of lessons and assessment.

Introduction
5 minutes

State the objective: *Today we're going to talk about online training for the workplace.*

Presentation
5 minutes

A **3-34** Read the instructions aloud. Play the audio. Give students a minute to think about the question. Elicit responses from the class.

Possible Answer
They are co-workers.

Guided Practice
10–15 minutes

B **3-34** Play the audio again. Direct students to listen for each word or phrase and match it to its definition. Have them compare answers with a partner. Check answers with the class.

Answers	
1. c	4. a
2. d	5. b
3. e	

C **3-34** Read the instructions aloud. Play the audio again, encouraging students to take notes in their notebooks. Set a time limit (five minutes) for students to discuss their answers with a partner. Circulate to monitor.

Possible Answers
Neela understands the new requirement best. Hank understands online training best. Hank needs help with the training requirements. Roy needs help with online training.

Presentation and Communicative Practice
10 minutes

D 1. Direct students' attention to the *Do/Say* chart and ask them to identify the lesson's soft skill [helping someone understand]. Ask the class which column has examples of language [right] and which has examples of behaviors [left].

2. Say a phrase from the left and act it out. Say it again and have the class act it out with you. Say it a third time and have the class act it out for you. To confirm understanding, combine phrases: *Point to the item and spell the item.*

3. Model the questions and sentence frame from the right using authentic intonation. Have students practice imitating your inflection.

4. Put students in teams of four and assign each team a question. Assign roles: reporter, manager, administrative assistant, and researcher. (Researchers will ask you questions on behalf of the team.) Verify understanding of the roles. Set a time limit (five minutes) and monitor.

5. Write sentence frames on the board that teams can use to summarize their response. *Our team discussed the following question:_____. We decided _____ because_____.*

6. Call "time" and let reporters rehearse their report for one minute. Direct each reporter to present to three other teams or the class.

Communicative Practice and Application
20–25 minutes

E 1. Read the instructions aloud. Check comprehension of the task: *What do you need to make a list of?* [three more kinds of training] *How many people will be knowledgeable about each kind of training?* [one] *What will the others do?* [ask questions and bring up concerns]

2. Point to one of the training topics you wrote on the board in the *Warm-up*. Have three students model the example conversation.

3. Put students in groups to list three training topics and then have a conversation about each, taking turns being knowledgeable and asking questions/bringing up concerns. Remind students to use the expressions in the chart.

Lesson Plans 4

4. Circulate and monitor. When students are finished, provide global feedback.

> **MULTILEVEL STRATEGIES**
>
> Form mixed groups.
>
> **Pre-level** Have these students only ask questions and bring up concerns. On-level and higher-level students can perform the role of the knowledgeable employee.

TEAMWORK & LANGUAGE REVIEW

Lesson Overview

MULTILEVEL OBJECTIVES

On-, Pre-, and Higher-level: Expand upon and review unit grammar and life skills

LANGUAGE FOCUS

Grammar: Tag questions and clarification questions (*She lives in Lakewood, doesn't she? She lives where?*)

Vocabulary: Housing and the Internet

For vocabulary support, see these **Oxford Picture Dictionary** topics: Apartments, pages 50–51; Household Problems and Repairs, pages 62–63; Internet Research, pages 212–213

READINESS CONNECTION

In this review, students work together to give someone feedback on their teaching style.

PACING

To extend this review: Have students complete **Workbook 4 page 78**, **Multilevel Activities 4 Unit 11 page 126**, and **Multilevel Grammar Exercises 4 Unit 11**.

Lesson Notes

CORRELATIONS

CCRS: SL.1.B (a.) Come to discussions prepared, having read or studied required material; explicitly draw on that preparation and other information known about the topic to explore ideas under discussion. (b.) Follow agreed-upon rules for discussions. (c.) Ask questions to check understanding of information presented, stay on topic, and link their comments to the remarks of others. (d.) Explain their own ideas and understanding in light of the discussion.

SL.1.C (b.) Follow agreed-upon rules for discussions and carry out assigned roles.

SL.2.B Determine the main ideas and supporting details of a text read aloud or information presented in diverse media and formats, including visually, quantitatively, and orally.

SL.4.B Report on a topic or text, tell a story, or recount an experience with appropriate facts and relevant, descriptive details, speaking clearly at an understandable pace.

R.1.B Ask and answer such questions as who, what, where, when, why, and how to demonstrate understanding of key details in a text.

R.2.A Identify the main topic and retell key details of a text.

R.7.B Use information gained from illustrations and the words in a text to demonstrate understanding of the text.

L.1.A (k.) Understand and use question words (interrogatives) (e.g., who, what, where, when, why, how).

L.1.B (l.) Produce simple, compound and complex sentences.

L.1.C (d.) Use modal auxiliaries to convey various conditions.

L.1.D (h.) Form and use verbs in the indicative, imperative, interrogative, conditional and subjunctive mood.

L.2.C (e.) Use a comma to set off the words yes and no, to set off a tag question from the rest of the sentence, and to indicate direct address.

RF.4.B (a.) Read grade-level text with purpose and understanding.

ELPS: 2. An ELL can participate in level-appropriate oral and written exchanges of information, ideas, and analyses, in various social and academic contexts, responding to peer, audience, or reader comments and questions. 4. An ELL can construct level-appropriate oral and written claims and support them with reasoning and evidence. 5. An ELL can conduct research and evaluate and communicate findings to answer questions or solve problems. 7. An ELL can adapt language choices to purpose, task, and audience when speaking and writing. 9. An ELL can create clear and coherent level-appropriate speech and text. 10. An ELL can demonstrate command of the conventions of standard English to communicate in level-appropriate speech and writing.

Warm-up and Review
10–15 minutes (books closed)

1. Review *At Work* activity E.

2. Ask students to share the good, not-so-good, and interesting things that happened during the conversations. As students speak, write their responses in a chart on the board.

Introduction and Presentation
5 minutes

1. Pair students and direct them to look at the pictures in their book. Ask them to describe what they see to their partner.

2. Ask volunteer pairs to share their ideas with the class.

Guided Practice
15–20 minutes

1. Model the process for creating tag questions (e.g., *They're having a party, aren't they?*).

2. Set a time limit (five minutes). Have students work with partners or in teams to complete the activity. Elicit tag questions from volunteers.

Possible Answers
1. There's a party, isn't there?
2. They are noisy, aren't they?
3. There's a meeting tonight, isn't there?
4. The renters got in trouble, didn't they?
5. The renters cleaned up, didn't they?

1. Have students work individually to match the sentences with tag clarification questions and then compare answers with their teams. Students should explain their choices.

2. Ask volunteer pairs to read the questions and answers for the class. Ask students to explain why they answered the way they did. Provide feedback on pronunciation.

Answers	
1. c	4. a
2. f	5. b
3. e	6. d

1. Have students work individually to write the tag questions. Ask them to check the tag questions with their teams.

2. Go over the answers. Then have students work in pairs to take turns asking and answering the tag questions.

Answers
1. I have to let my current landlord know, don't I?
2. My current landlords are going to give back my security deposit, aren't they?
3. The new building doesn't have cable TV, does it?
4. The rent for the new apartment includes utilities, doesn't it?
5. The rent is due on the 15th of the month, isn't it?
6. The new landlord speaks both Spanish and Farsi, doesn't she/he?
7. The lease said no parties on weeknights, didn't it?
8. The upstairs neighbors are planning to move out, aren't they?

MULTILEVEL STRATEGIES

For 1B and 1C, seat same-level students together.

- **Pre-level** Give these students extra time to complete 1B. Work with them as a group to write the tag questions for 1C.

- **On- and Higher-level** When these students finish 1B and 1C, have them write original tag questions. Tell them to imagine that they are being shown around a new home. Have them write tag questions they might ask a rental or real-estate agent. *Utilities are paid for, aren't they?*

Communicative Practice
30–40 minutes

1. Group students and assign roles: manager, editor, and actors. Explain that students are going to work with their teams to write and perform a conversation about a problem.

2. Read steps 2–4 of the activity aloud. Check comprehension of the task. *What is the first thing you should do?* [choose a computer problem from the list] *Who is going to have a conversation?* [someone who needs help and a person who knows how to help]

3. Set a time limit (ten minutes) to complete the exercise. Circulate and answer any questions.

4. Have actors from each team perform the conversation for another team.

E 1. Have students walk around the room to conduct the interviews. To get students moving, tell them to interview three people who were not in their team for D.

2. Set a time limit (five minutes) to complete the exercise.

3. Tell students to make a note of their classmates' answers but not to worry about writing complete sentences.

> **MULTILEVEL STRATEGIES**
>
> Adapt the mixer in E to the level of your students.
>
> • **Pre-and On-level** Pair these students and have them interview other pairs together.
>
> • **Higher-level** Have these students ask an additional question and write all answers.

F 1. Call on individuals to report what they learned about their classmates. Keep a running tally on the board for each question, noting the number of affirmative and negative answers to each.

2. Use your tally for question 2 to create a pie chart on the board. Instruct students to draw pie charts for questions 1 and 3 in their notebooks. Circulate and answer any questions.

PROBLEM SOLVING
10–15 minutes

 3-35 1. Ask: *Have you ever had a family member teach you a new skill? Was he or she a good teacher?* Tell students they will read a story about a man who wants to learn computer skills from his brother. Direct students to read Eric's story silently.

2. Ask: *Why is Louis not a good teacher for Eric?* [He talks quickly and he doesn't let Eric try things for himself.]

3. Play the audio and have students read along silently.

B 1. Elicit answers to question 1.

2. Put students into groups of three or four. Ask each group to think of some possible solutions to Eric's problem and report them to the class. Ask a volunteer to write all possible solutions on the board.

3. Pair students and have them write a conversation between Eric and his brother. Call on volunteer pairs to read their conversations to the class.

Possible Answers
Eric isn't good with computers and he would like to be able to use social media and the Internet. His brother is good with computers, but it's hard for Eric to learn from him. So far, he hasn't learned anything.

Evaluation
20–25 minutes

To test students' understanding of the unit language and content, have them take the Unit 11 Test, available on the Teacher Resource Center.

UNIT 12 How Am I Doing?

Unit Overview

This unit explores achievement and leadership with a range of employability skills and contextualizes gerunds after prepositions.

KEY OBJECTIVES	
Lesson 1	Identify and describe achievements and leadership qualities
Lesson 2	Identify goals and achievements and write a formal essay describing them
Lesson 3	Use gerunds to talk about achievements in the workplace
Lesson 4	Give and respond to feedback
Lesson 5	Identify ways people can succeed in non-traditional roles
At Work	Agree at work
Teamwork & Language Review	Review unit language

UNIT FEATURES	
Academic Vocabulary	challenge, communication, conclusion, convincing, distribution, dominate, ethnicity, facilitate, focus, maintain, professional, summarize, topic, tradition, transportation
Employability Skills	• Decide when to talk about your achievements • Understand teamwork • Work with others • Determine whether feedback is positive or negative • Communicate information • Communicate verbally • Listen actively • Decide on your priorities in life • Determine how to give back to your community

Resources	**Class Audio** CD3, Tracks 36–46
	Workbook Unit 12, pages 79–85
	Teacher Resource Center
	    Multilevel Activities 4 Unit 12
	    Multilevel Grammar Exercises 4 Unit 12
	    Unit 12 Test
	Oxford Picture Dictionary Life Events and Documents, Schools and Subjects

LESSON 1 VOCABULARY

Lesson Overview

MULTILEVEL OBJECTIVES

On-level: Describe and talk about achievements and leadership qualities

Pre-level: Identify and describe achievements and leadership qualities

Higher-level: Talk and write about achievements and leadership qualities

LANGUAGE FOCUS

Grammar: Adjectives (*I am confident.*)

Vocabulary: Achievements and leadership qualities

For vocabulary support, see this **Oxford Picture Dictionary** topic: Life Events and Documents, pages 40–41

READINESS CONNECTION

In this lesson, students work with others to conduct research on achievements and leadership qualities.

PACING

To compress this lesson: Conduct 1B as a whole-class activity.

To extend this lesson: Have students write about someone they admire. (See end of lesson.)

And/or have students complete **Workbook 4 page 79** and **Multilevel Activities 4 Unit 12 pages 128–129**

Lesson Notes

CORRELATIONS

CCRS: SL.1.B (b.) Follow agreed-upon rules for discussions. (c.) Ask questions to check understanding of information presented, stay on topic, and link their comments to the remarks of others. (d.) Explain their own ideas and understanding in light of the discussion.

SL.2.B Determine the main ideas and supporting details of a text read aloud or information presented in diverse media and formats, including visually, quantitatively, and orally.

SL.4.B Report on a topic or text, tell a story, or recount an experience with appropriate facts and relevant, descriptive details, speaking clearly at an understandable pace.

SL.6.B Speak in complete sentences when appropriate to task and situation in order to provide requested detail or clarification.

R.1.B Ask and answer such questions as who, what, where, when, why, and how to demonstrate understanding of key details in a text.

R.4.B Determine the meaning of general academic and domain-specific words and phrases in a text relevant to a topic or subject area.

R.5.B Know and use various text features to locate key facts or information in a text efficiently.

R.7.B Use information gained from illustrations and the words in a text to demonstrate understanding of the text.

W.7.A Participate in shared research and writing projects.

L.1.B (l.) Produce simple, compound and complex sentences.

L.4.B (a.) Use sentence-level context as a clue to the meaning of a word or phrase. (e.) Use glossaries and beginning dictionaries, both print and digital, to determine or clarify the meaning of words and phrases.

L.6.A Use words and phrases acquired through conversations, reading and being read to, and responding to texts, including using frequently occurring conjunctions to signal simple relationships.

RF.4.B (a.) Read grade-level text with purpose and understanding.

ELPS: 4. An ELL can construct level-appropriate oral and written claims and support them with reasoning and evidence. 5. An ELL can conduct research and evaluate and communicate findings to answer questions or solve problems. 7. An ELL can adapt language choices to purpose, task, and audience when speaking and writing. 9. An ELL can create clear and coherent level-appropriate speech and text. 10. An ELL can demonstrate command of the conventions of standard English to communicate in level-appropriate speech and writing.

Warm-up and Review
10–15 minutes (books closed)

Write *Famous Person* and *Person I Know* on the board. Ask students to name people they admire and write the names in the correct column. (For *Person I Know*, include the relationship—my mother, my friend Joe, etc.)

Introduction
5 minutes

1. Ask volunteers to talk about why they admire the people on the board. Say: *We usually admire people for their achievements and their qualities.*

2. State the objective: *Today we're going to talk about achievements and leadership qualities.*

1 Identify achievements

Presentation I
20–25 minutes

A Elicit students' answers to questions 1 and 2. Write the things they are proud of on the board.

B 1. Direct students to look at the pictures. Ask: *Do you think the person is successful? Why or why not?*

2. Pair students to talk about the pictures. Check comprehension. Ask: *What is he thinking about in the first picture?* [becoming a mayor] *What does he get in the second picture?* [a check] *What kind of business is in the third picture?* [an electronics store] *What happens to the store?* [It burns and he rebuilds it.] *Does he become mayor?* [yes] *Why is he with the baseball team in the last picture?* [He's giving them some money.]

Possible Answers
Answers should be in simple past.   When he was young, he wanted to win an election/be elected some day.   He won/got a scholarship/money for college.   He opened a store.   His store had a fire/burned down, but he rebuilt it.   He became the mayor.   He gave money to a children's baseball team.

C Have students work with their partners to number the events in the order they happened. Elicit definitions for *adversity, goal, overcome,* and *scholarship*.

Answers
1. have a dream   2. win a scholarship   3. start a business   4. overcome adversity   5. achieve a goal   6. give back to the community

Guided Practice I
10–20 minutes

D 🔊 3-36 1. To prepare students for listening, tell them: *We're going to listen to Mr. Moya talk to a reporter about his life. While you listen, check your work in 1C.* Elicit or provide definitions for unfamiliar vocabulary: *elected, ecstatic, run for.*

2. Play the audio. Confirm answers with the class.

E 🔊 3-36 Read the instructions aloud. Direct students to read the sentences about Mr. Moya. Play the audio again as students listen and complete the sentences. Have students compare answers with a partner. Go over the answers with the class.

Answers
1. to be elected   2. go to college   3. started, business   4. store burned   5. achieved his goal   6. give back to the community

F 1. Group students. Assign roles (manager, administrative assistant, researcher, reporter). Confirm responsibilities: the manager will keep track of time and manage the group, the administrative assistant will take notes and write the achievements on the board, and the reporter will report to the class. Read the instructions aloud. Elicit or provide examples of achievements and write them on the board (e.g., won a competition, started a club, attended a summer program, etc.).

2. Set a time limit of five minutes. Researchers should look up any unfamiliar words.

3. Call on reporters to read the team's list to the class. Ask administrative assistants to write the achievements on the board.

2 Learn about leadership qualities

Presentation II
10–20 minutes

1. Direct students to look at the checklist. Introduce the new topic. Say: *Now we're going to look at a checklist of leadership qualities. Read through it and check the words that describe you.*

2. Say and have students repeat the words. Check comprehension. Ask: *What word means you'll try something even if it's difficult or scary?* [courageous] *What word means that you know what things can and can't be done?* [practical]

Guided Practice II
10–15 minutes

1. Model the conversation with a volunteer. Model it again using other information from 2A.

2. Set a time limit (three minutes). Direct students to practice with a partner.

3. Call on volunteers to present their version of the conversation for the class.

> **TIP**
> After 2B, ask students to apply the vocabulary from 2A to the famous people they mentioned during the *Warm-up*. Ask: *Which words describe _____? Why?* Encourage students to supply specific examples of how the person demonstrates the leadership quality.

Communicative Practice and Application
20–25 minutes

1. If students will use the Internet for this task, establish what device(s) they'll use: a class computer, tablets, or smartphones. Alternatively, print information from the Internet before class and distribute to groups.

2. Write the questions from 2C on the board. Explain that students will work in teams to research and report on these questions. Ask: *Which questions can you research?* [both] *Which search terms or questions can you use to find the information you need?* ["achievement" + name of person; "leadership qualities" + name of person] *How will you record the information you find?* [table, checklist, index cards] Remind students to bookmark or record sites so they can find or cite them in the future.

3. Group students and assign roles: reporter, manager, administrative assistant, and IT support. Verify student understanding of their roles.

4. Give managers the time limit for researching question 1 (ten minutes). Direct the IT support to begin the online research or pick up the printed materials for each team. Direct the administrative assistant to record information for the team using a table, checklist, or index cards.

5. Give a two-minute warning. Call "time." Tell reporters to first answer and then ask each member of the team question 2.

> **TIP**
> When setting up task-based activities, verify that students understand their roles using physical commands. For example: *If you report on your team's work, stand up* [reporter]. *If you keep the team on task, point to the clock* [manager]. *If you write the team's responses, raise your hand* [administrative assistant]. *If you help the team research, hold up your smartphone/tablet* [IT support].

D 1. Copy the sentence frames on the board.

2. Direct teams to help their administrative assistant use the sentence frames to record the team's findings. Direct the reporter to use the recorded information to report the team's findings to the class or another team.

Evaluation
10–15 minutes

TEST YOURSELF

1. Direct Partner A to read prompts 1–3 from 1E on page 180 to Partner B. Partner B should close their book and write the answers as they listen in their notebook. When finished, students switch roles. Partner B reads prompts 4–6 from 1E.

2. Direct both partners to open their books and check their spelling when they finish.

> **EXTENSION ACTIVITY**
> **Group Writing**
> Put students in mixed-level groups and have them write about someone they admire. Tell the group to choose a famous person they all admire. Direct them to work together to write a list of the person's achievements and leadership qualities. Have a reporter from each group share the group's work with the class.

LESSON 2 WRITING

Lesson Overview

MULTILEVEL OBJECTIVES

On- and Higher-level: Analyze, write, and edit an application essay in response to a prompt

Pre-level: Read an application essay and write a short essay in response to a prompt

LANGUAGE FOCUS

Grammar: Past and present tense (*I studied hard and now I speak very well.*)

Vocabulary: Achievements

For vocabulary support, see this **Oxford Picture Dictionary** topic: Life Events and Documents, pages 40–41

STRATEGY FOCUS

When writing a formal essay, the first paragraph introduces the topic and the middle paragraph(s) include supporting information and details.

READINESS CONNECTION

In this lesson, students communicate information about their achievements and goals.

PACING

To compress this lesson: Assign the *Test Yourself* for homework.

To extend this lesson: Have students talk about their partners' achievements. (See end of lesson.)

And/or have students complete **Workbook 4 page 80** and **Multilevel Activities 4 Unit 12 page 130**.

Lesson Notes

CORRELATIONS

CCRS: SL.1.B (d.) Explain their own ideas and understanding in light of the discussion.

SL.2.B Determine the main ideas and supporting details of a text read aloud or information presented in diverse media and formats, including visually, quantitatively, and orally.

R.1.B Ask and answer such questions as who, what, where, when, why, and how to demonstrate understanding of key details in a text.

W.2.B (a.) Introduce a topic and group related information together; include illustrations when useful to aiding comprehension. (b.) Develop the topic with facts, definitions, and details. (c.) Use linking words and phrases to connect ideas within categories of information. (d.) Provide a concluding statement or section.

W.4.B Produce writing in which the development and organization are appropriate to task and purpose.

W.5.B With guidance and support from peers and others, develop and strengthen writing as needed by planning, revising and editing.

W.8.B Recall information from experiences or gather information from print and digital sources; take brief notes on sources and sort evidence into provided categories.

L.1.B (h.) Form and use the simple verb tenses. (l.) Produce simple, compound and complex sentences.

L.1.C (f.) Use verb tense to convey various times, sequences, states, and conditions.

L.2.C (a.) Use correct capitalization.

L.6.B Acquire and use accurately level-appropriate conversational, general academic, and domain-specific words and phrases, including those that signal spatial and temporal relationships.

RF.4.B (a.) Read grade-level text with purpose and understanding.

ELPS: 1. An ELL can construct meaning from oral presentations and literary and informational text through level-appropriate listening, reading, and viewing. 3. An ELL can speak and write about level-appropriate complex literary and informational texts and topics. 6. An ELL can analyze and critique the arguments of others orally and in writing. 9. An ELL can create clear and coherent level-appropriate speech and text. 10. An ELL can demonstrate command of the conventions of standard English to communicate in level-appropriate speech and writing.

Warm-up and Review
10–15 minutes (books closed)

Ask students what they think is required to get into a four-year college. Ask them what tuition is like in their countries and if scholarships are available. Have students discuss the things they need to do to get a scholarship. Write their ideas on the board.

Introduction
5 minutes

1. If students mentioned *writing an essay*, circle it on the board. If they didn't mention it, write it. Say: *Many people don't realize that a very important part of a four-year college application is the essay you write to get in. In addition, many scholarships are won because of a student's ability to write a convincing essay.*

2. State the objective: *Today we're going to read and write a scholarship application essay.*

1 Prepare to write

Presentation
20–25 minutes

A 1. Build students' schema by asking questions about the prompt and the essay in 1B. Ask: *How many questions does the writer have to answer in the essay?* [three] *Who gives scholarships?* [individuals, organizations, colleges] *Who is writing the essay?* [Victoria Sanchez] *Who should apply for scholarships?* [anyone who would like financial help]

2. Give students one minute to tell a partner their responses to questions 1 and 2. Elicit responses from the class.

3. Point out that although many people are uncomfortable talking about their achievements, in an application essay (as well as in a resume and cover letter), it's important to be able to describe them.

B 1. Introduce the model essay and its purpose: *You're going to read an essay in response to a prompt in a scholarship application.* Have students read the essay silently.

2. Check comprehension. Ask: *Why is she applying for the Joseph Martin Scholarship?* [education is the first step in reaching her goals] *What award did she receive?* [Outstanding Volunteer] *What is her dream?* [to be a lawyer] *Why does she want to contribute to her community?* [because it has helped and supported her]

3. Play the audio. Ask students to number the paragraphs as they read along with the audio.

Guided Practice I
10 minutes

C 1. Have students work independently to underline the answers to the questions in the essay.

2. Point out the *Writer's Note* and ask students to annotate the information they underlined with the phrases *topic, main point,* and *supporting detail.*

Possible Answers
1. She is introducing her reason for applying for the scholarship. 2. Paragraph 2: She makes the point that she works hard to achieve her goals. She gives examples from her school, from her work, and from her volunteer work. Paragraph 3: She makes the point that she has goals and dreams. She supports her point by explaining why she has the dream to be a lawyer. 3. Her conclusion is that she believes that this scholarship would help her reach her goal.

2 Plan and write

Guided Practice II
15–20 minutes

A 1. Read the instructions and questions aloud. Give students a few minutes to take notes on their answers. Then have students discuss their answers with a partner.

2. Call on volunteers to share their answers with the class. Write examples on the board under the headings: *Recent Achievements, How Achieved, Goals,* and *Ways Scholarship Will Help.*

B 1. Point out that each sentence and sentence frame introduces a new paragraph. Direct students to look back at the essay in 1B and identify the sentences and sentence frames.

2. Tell students to follow the essay template as they write their essay in their notebooks.

3. Check comprehension of the exercise. Ask: *How many paragraphs are you going to write?* [four]

4. Have students work individually to write their essays.

> **MULTILEVEL STRATEGIES**
>
> Adapt 2B to the level of your students.
>
> • **Pre-level** Tell these students to compose their essays by writing completions to the sentences in the template.

3 Get feedback and revise

Guided Practice III
5 minutes

 Direct students to check their writing using the editing checklist. Tell them to read each item in the list and check their papers before moving onto the next item. Explain that students should not edit their writing at this stage. They should just use the checklist to check their work and mark any areas they want to revise.

Communicative Practice
15 minutes

 1. Read the instructions aloud. Emphasize to students that they are responding to their partners' work, not correcting it.

2. Use the essay in 1B to model the exercise. *I think the sentence that says, "I studied hard and now I speak English well." is convincing because it shows what she did to reach that goal.*

3. Direct students to exchange papers with a partner and follow the instructions.

 Allow students time to edit and revise their writing as necessary, using the editing checklist from 3A and their partner's feedback from 3B. If necessary, students could complete this task as homework.

> **TIP**
>
> Look online for a scholarship search website. These sites provide services that allow students, ages 13 and up, to complete a profile and then get a list of scholarships for which they might be eligible. The list includes all of the necessary application information. Such sites can be an excellent source of higher-education funding, but students should not use them unless they are from a reputable source.

Application and Evaluation
10 minutes

TEST YOURSELF

1. Review the instructions aloud. Assign a time limit (five minutes) and have students work independently.

2. Before collecting student work, invite two or three volunteers to share their sentences. Ask students to raise their hands if they wrote similar answers.

> **EXTENSION ACTIVITY**
>
> **Discussion**
>
> Have students work in groups to create a scholarship for college. Have them decide who can apply, the things that applicants must do, and how the group will choose the final candidate.
>
> Have one student (the reporter) from each group present the scholarship to the class. Have another student (the administrative assistant) write key points from the presentation on the board. Have the class discuss which scholarship they would like to apply to.

LESSON 3 GRAMMAR

Lesson Overview

MULTILEVEL OBJECTIVES

Pre-, On-, and Higher-level: Use gerunds after prepositions to interpret evaluations and give feedback

LANGUAGE FOCUS

Grammar: Gerunds after prepositions (*She knows a lot about working the front desk.*)

Vocabulary: Employment words, *performance review*

For vocabulary support, see this **Oxford Picture Dictionary** topic: Life Events and Documents, pages 40–41

READINESS CONNECTION

In this lesson, students verbally communicate using gerunds after prepositions.

PACING

To compress this lesson: Conduct 2A and 2B as whole-class activities.

To extend this lesson: Have students use gerunds after prepositions to discuss occupations. (See end of lesson.)

And/or have students complete **Workbook 4 pages 81–82, Multilevel Activities 4 Unit 12 pages 131–132,** and **Multilevel Grammar Exercises 4 Unit 12**.

Lesson Notes

CORRELATIONS

CCRS: SL.2.B Determine the main ideas and supporting details of a text read aloud or information presented in diverse media and formats, including visually, quantitatively, and orally.

R.1.B Ask and answer such questions as who, what, where, when, why, and how to demonstrate understanding of key details in a text.

R.5.A Know and use various text features to locate key facts or information in a text.

R.7.A Use the illustrations and details in a text to describe its key ideas.

W.8.B Recall information from experiences or gather information from print and digital sources; take brief notes on sources and sort evidence into provided categories.

L.1.B (b.) Explain the function of nouns, pronouns, verbs, adjectives, and adverbs in general and their functions in particular sentences. (l.) Produce simple, compound and complex sentences.

L.1.C (a.) Explain the function of conjunctions, prepositions, and interjections in general and their function in particular sentences.

L.1.D (f.) Explain the function of verbals (gerunds, participles, infinitives) in general and their function in particular sentences.

L.6.B Use words and phrases acquired through conversations, reading and being read to, and responding to texts, including using adjectives and adverbs to describe.

RF.4.B (a.) Read grade-level text with purpose and understanding.

ELPS: 2. An ELL can participate in level-appropriate oral and written exchanges of information, ideas, and analyses, in various social and academic contexts, responding to peer, audience, or reader comments and questions. 3. An ELL can speak and write about level-appropriate complex literary and informational texts and topics. 7. An ELL can adapt language choices to purpose, task, and audience when speaking and writing. 9. An ELL can create clear and coherent level-appropriate speech and text. 10. An ELL can demonstrate command of the conventions of standard English to communicate in level appropriate speech and writing.

Warm-up and Review
10–15 minutes (books closed)

Ask: *What are you good at?* Write students' answers on the board. Ask: *What do you know a lot about?* Write the answers on the board. If a student supplies a simple verb, change it to a gerund. For example: *good at writing, know a lot about using computers.*

Introduction
5–10 minutes

1. Circle any gerunds that are on the board. Say: *We use this form here because* good at *and* know about *have prepositions at the end.*

2. State the objective: *Today we're going to use gerunds after prepositions to discuss performance reviews.*

1 Use gerunds after prepositions

Presentation I
20–25 minutes

 Read the instructions and the questions aloud. Discuss the meaning of *performance review*. Ask students to read the performance review silently to find the answer to the questions and then compare answers with a partner. Elicit the answers. Check comprehension. Ask: *What is her job?* [desk clerk] *Who is her manager?* [M. Perez] *What month is her review?* [July]

Answers
1. She welcomes guests and answers questions very well. 2. She needs to be more careful when she takes messages. 3. She should work on managing multiple tasks at the same time if she wants to get an "excellent" rating on her next review.

 1. Read the sentences in the chart aloud. Ask: *What is a gerund?* [an *-ing* form of a verb which functions as a noun]

2. Direct students to circle the examples of gerunds after prepositions in 1A and then compare answers with a partner. Go over the answers as a class.

3. Pair students and direct them to read the chart aloud to each other. Then read the chart aloud as students follow along.

4. Assess students' understanding of the chart. Write these sentence frames on the board: *We talked about _____. She's an expert at _____. I thanked him for _____. They succeeded in _____. I'm used to _____.* Tell pre-level students to complete the sentences with *make* (in gerund form). Have on- and higher-level students complete the sentences with other verbs. Elicit their ideas and write them on the board.

Answers
Circle: welcoming, helping, recording, taking

Guided Practice I
15–20 minutes

 1. Tell students they will collaborate to complete the description of the grammar point. Model collaboration by working with the class to complete the first sentence. Encourage students to look at 1A and 1B to see which ending gerunds have.

2. Pair students and have them work together to complete the description.

3. Project or write the completed description on the board and have pairs verify the accuracy of their responses. Ask volunteers which sentences confused them and discuss.

Answers
-ing, after, verb, helping

MULTILEVEL STRATEGIES

For 1C, seat mixed-level students together.

- **Pre-, On-, and Higher-level** Assign pre-level students the role of administrative assistant, on-level students the role of manager, and higher-level students the role of researcher. The administrative assistant fills in the blanks according to the team's decisions, the manager reads the description and manages the team's discussion, and the researcher looks up the definition of the grammar point online or checks against an answer key to verify the team's answers.

Guided Practice II
5–10 minutes

D Ask students to work individually to complete the paragraph and then compare answers with a partner. Ask volunteers to write the answers on the board.

Answers	
1. greeting	5. sitting
2. asking	6. looking
3. calling	7. making
4. asking	

MULTILEVEL STRATEGIES

After 1D, seat students in same-level pairs.

- **Pre-level** Tell these students to complete these sentences about their partner: *She/He is good at _____. She/He knows a lot about _____. She/He cares about _____. She/He is looking forward to _____.*
- **On- and Higher-level** Have these students write five sentences about their partners using any preposition + gerund combination.

E Ask students to work individually to match the sentence parts and then compare answers with a partner. Have volunteers read the complete sentences aloud.

Answers	
1. b	3. a
2. c	4. d

MULTILEVEL STRATEGIES

Adapt 1E to the level of your students.

Pre-level Work with this group. Read each sentence beginning aloud and have students match the correct ending before moving on to the next item.

2 Use gerunds after *be* + adjective + preposition

Presentation II
20–25 minutes

 1. Introduce the new topic. Say: *Now we're going to look at more gerunds after prepositions, this time with adjectives.*

2. Read the instructions. Read the sentences in the chart aloud and elicit the answer to the question. Pair students and direct them to read the chart aloud to each other.

3. Read the *Grammar Note*. Check understanding: *Which preposition comes after the adjective in the example?* [in]

Answer
be

Guided Practice III
10–15 minutes

 1. Read and have students repeat the list of adjectives + prepositions.

2. Have students work individually to complete the sentences and then compare answers with a partner. Ask partners to take turns reading conversations. Have volunteer pairs read the conversations aloud.

Answers
1. good at
2. nervous about, interested in
3. tired of, proud of

MULTILEVEL STRATEGIES

For 2B and 2C, use mixed-level pairs.

- **Pre-level** For 2B, have these students complete as many of the sentences as they can. Tell them to check with their partners for the answers they don't know.

  For 2C, encourage these students to write short answers to the questions. Have them ask their partners the questions and listen to the answers before they answer the questions themselves.

- **On- and Higher-level** For 2B, ask these students to assist their partners before they read the conversations aloud.

  For 2C, tell these students to answer the questions first to provide a model for their partners.

C Ask students to work individually to write their answers to the questions. Have them ask and answer the questions with a partner.

> **MULTILEVEL STRATEGIES**
>
> After 2C, provide more practice with gerunds after prepositions. Target the practice to the level of your students.
>
> - **Pre-level** Give these students scrambled sentences. When they finish unscrambling them, ask them to write the sentences on the board. *1. new learning not afraid he's of things.* [He's not afraid of learning new things.] *2. class interested taking they're another in* [They're interested in taking another class.] *3. a lot furniture about building knows he* [He knows a lot about building furniture.] *4. trying best believes she in her* [She believes in trying her best] *5. nervous I front about in am of class the speaking* [I am nervous about speaking in front of the class.]
>
> - **On-level** Ask these students to write a new conversation using the expressions in the word box in 2B. Ask volunteer pairs to read their conversations aloud for the class.
>
> - **Higher-level** Ask these students to write a new conversation using these adjective or verb + preposition phrases followed by a gerund: *thank you for, sorry about, worried about, believe in, plan on*. Ask volunteer pairs to read their conversations aloud for the class.

3 Listen for the gerunds to determine the meaning

Guided Practice IV
10–15 minutes

◁)) 3-38 1. Say: *Now we're going to listen to some sentences about a man named Michael. Michael is thinking about his goals.*

2. Play the audio. Direct students to read along silently without writing.

3. Replay the audio. Ask students to circle the letter of the sentence with the same meaning as the sentence they hear and then compare answers with a partner.

4. Go over the answers as a class.

Answers	
1. a	4. b
2. b	5. b
3. a	6. a

> **MULTILEVEL STRATEGIES**
>
> Replay the audio for 3 to allow pre-level students to catch up while you challenge on- and higher-level students.
>
> - **Pre-level** Have these students listen again to choose the sentence with the same meaning.
>
> - **On- and Higher-level** Have these students listen again and write the preposition + gerund combination that they hear.

4 Use gerunds after prepositions to talk about your life experience

Communicative Practice and Application
20–25 minutes

A 1. Direct students to look at the photos. Ask what each person is doing. Ask which activity looks more interesting.

2. Read the questions aloud. Ask students to think about and note their answers.

B Put students in pairs and have them work together to write two more questions.

C 1. Have each pair join another pair. Tell them to make notes of each other's answers. Model the exercise by asking a volunteer the first question. Encourage students to give complete sentences as answers.

2. Check comprehension of the exercise. Ask: *Are you giving short answers or having a conversation?* [having a conversation] Set a time limit for the exercise (four minutes) and observe and take note of issues that arise.

3. Call on individuals to share some interesting things they learned about their partners.

Evaluation

10–15 minutes

TEST YOURSELF

Ask students to write the sentences independently. Collect and correct their writing.

MULTILEVEL STRATEGIES

Target the *Test Yourself* to the level of your students.

- **Pre-level** Provide sentence frames for these students to complete. *(partner's name) is good at _____. (partner's name) is thinking about _____. (partner's name) is tired of _____. (partner's name) is planning on _____.*

- **Higher-level** Have these students write a paragraph in response to the prompt and the accompanying instructions: *What are some similarities and differences between you and your partner? Use at least three preposition + gerund combinations in your paragraph.*

EXTENSION ACTIVITY
Conversation

Use preposition + gerund combinations to describe occupations. Ask students what occupations they think are interesting and write them on the board. Put students in pairs. Have them talk with their partners about what people in each profession are good at, what they know a lot about, what they are probably interested in, and what they probably get tired of doing. Call on volunteers to share their ideas with the class.

LESSON 4 EVERYDAY CONVERSATION

Lesson Overview

MULTILEVEL OBJECTIVES

On-, Pre-, and Higher-level: Respond to positive feedback and criticism in a performance review

LANGUAGE FOCUS

Grammar: Requests and suggestions with gerunds (*I suggest taking the training.*)

Vocabulary: Work and feelings

For vocabulary support, see this **Oxford Picture Dictionary** topic: Life Events and Documents, pages 40–41

STRATEGY FOCUS

Practice language to respond to feedback and ask for detail and elaboration.

READINESS CONNECTION

In this lesson, students determine whether feedback is positive or negative.

PACING

To compress this lesson: Conduct *Discuss* as a whole-class activity.

To extend this lesson: After completing 6B, have students practice giving suggestions to a problem. (See end of lesson.)

And/or have students complete **Workbook 4 page 83** and **Multilevel Activities 4 Unit 12 page 133**.

Lesson Notes

CORRELATIONS

CCRS: SL.1.B (b.) Follow agreed-upon rules for discussions. (c.) Ask questions to check understanding of information presented, stay on topic, and link their comments to the remarks of others. (d.) Explain their own ideas and understanding in light of the discussion.

SL.2.B Determine the main ideas and supporting details of a text read aloud or information presented in diverse media and formats, including visually, quantitatively, and orally.

SL.4.B Report on a topic or text, tell a story, or recount an experience with appropriate facts and relevant, descriptive details, speaking clearly at an understandable pace.

SL.6.B Speak in complete sentences when appropriate to task and situation in order to provide requested detail or clarification.

R.1.B Ask and answer such questions as who, what, where, when, why, and how to demonstrate understanding of key details in a text.

R.2.A Identify the main topic and retell key details of a text.

R.4.B Determine the meaning of general academic and domain-specific words and phrases in a text relevant to a topic or subject area.

R.7.B Use information gained from illustrations and the words in a text to demonstrate understanding of the text.

L.1.B (l.) Produce simple, compound and complex sentences.

L.1.D (f.) Explain the function of verbals (gerunds, participles, infinitives) in general and their function in particular sentences.

L.3.B (b.) Recognize and observe differences between the conventions of spoken and written standard English.

L.4.B (a.) Use sentence-level context as a clue to the meaning of a word or phrase.

L.6.B Use words and phrases acquired through conversations, reading and being read to, and responding to texts, including using adjectives and adverbs to describe.

RF.4.B (a.) Read grade-level text with purpose and understanding.

ELPS: 2. An ELL can participate in level-appropriate oral and written exchanges of information, ideas, and analyses, in various social and academic contexts, responding to peer, audience, or reader comments and questions. 4. An ELL can construct level-appropriate oral and written claims and support them with reasoning and evidence. 5. An ELL can analyze and critique the arguments of others orally and in writing. 6. An ELL can adapt language choices to purpose, task, and audience when speaking and writing. 7. An ELL can create clear and coherent level-appropriate speech and text. 8. An ELL can demonstrate command of the conventions of standard English to communicate in level-appropriate speech and writing.

Warm-up and Review
10–15 minutes (books closed)

Put adjectives from the previous lesson on the board: *nervous, tired, good, proud, interested, afraid, responsible, happy.* Elicit the prepositions that go with the adjectives; then elicit a sentence using the combination with a gerund.

Introduction
5 minutes

1. Ask students if they've ever had a performance review. Ask: *Would you be nervous about going through one?*

2. State the objective: *Today we'll learn to ask and answer questions in a performance review and listen for feedback from the boss.*

1 Learn ways to participate in a performance review

Presentation I
10–20 minutes

 3-39 Have students look at the picture. Build students' schema by asking: *Who is in the picture?* [Kim and the manager] *How does Kim feel?* [concerned, worried] Read the questions aloud. Play the audio. Give students a minute to ask and answer the questions with a partner. Go over the answers as a class.

Possible Answers
Kim hears positive feedback about her work, about contributing to the team, and about how much she has learned about working in a hotel. She hears negative feedback about being late sometimes.

Guided Practice I
20–25 minutes

 3-39 1. Read the instructions and questions aloud. Play the audio. Ask students to listen for the answers to each question.

2. Ask students to compare their answers with a partner. Circulate and monitor to ensure students understand the audio. Go over the answers with the class. Check comprehension. Ask: *What is the period of time of the review?* [six months] *What does Kim do that affects the rest of the team?* [She is late to work.]

Possible Answers
1. The manager offers an opportunity to take a leadership training class.
2. The class could help her move into a management position.
3. He wants her to be on time.
4. She says that she will try taking an earlier bus.

 3-40 Read the instructions aloud. Explain that students are going to hear the audio one more time. They should write the words they hear to complete the sentences. Play the audio. Call on volunteers to elicit the answers.

Answers
1. for saying so
2. didn't realize anything was wrong
3. I'll try to do better

2 Practice your pronunciation

Pronunciation Extension
10–15 minutes

A **3-41** 1. Write *I'd recommend talking to your supervisor about the position you're interested in.* on the board. Say the sentence and ask students to repeat it. Draw a carat (^) between *supervisor* and *about*. Point out that the last part of the sentence is a separate word group and that there's a slight pause after *supervisor*. Say: *Now we're going to focus on word groups.*

2. Play the audio. Direct students to listen for the pauses. Have students repeat the sentences.

B **3-42** Play the audio. Ask students to mark the pauses. Go over the answers as a class.

Answers
1. I'd like to see some changes ^ in the way you deal with customers.
2. Is a training class for cooks ^ something you'd be interested in?
3. She helps out her co-workers ^ by looking for extra work to do.
4. I've learned a lot ^ about working in a restaurant ^ since I got this job.

C Have students work with a partner to practice saying the sentences in 2A and 2B.

3 Use polite requests and suggestions with gerunds

Presentation II and Guided Practice II
10–15 minutes

1. Introduce the new topic: *Now we're going to make polite requests and suggestions with gerunds.*

2. Read the instructions aloud. Then read the sentences in the chart aloud and elicit the answer to the question. Ask: *What form follows the verbs* suggest *and* recommend? [gerunds]

3. Read the sentences again and have students repeat them.

4. Check comprehension. Write a series of common commands on the board. *Bring a pencil to school. Listen to the teacher. Come to class on time. Take notes.* Call on students to turn the commands into polite requests and suggestions using gerunds.

Answers
May I suggest, Would you mind

Guided Practice III
15–20 minutes

B Have students work in pairs to write polite requests and suggestions. Have volunteers write their sentences on the board.

Answers
1. May I suggest applying for a management position?
2. Would you mind giving me some more information?
3. I would suggest/I'd recommend thinking about your long-term goals.
4. I would suggest/I'd recommend making a plan to reach your goals.

MULTILEVEL STRATEGIES
Adapt 3B to the level of your students.
• **Pre-level** Provide these students with sentence frames for the items.
2. Would you mind _____?
3. I would suggest _____.
4. I'd recommend _____.

TIP
For further practice with requests and suggestions, read this story to your class: *You own a restaurant. One of your workers is a waitress named Nancy. She's very nice and you'd like her to keep her job, but you'd like for her change some of her habits. Listen to this information about Nancy; then write some suggestions for her. Here is the story: Nancy usually arrives at work just at the moment her shift is supposed to start, but she's out of uniform. She goes into the bathroom to change into her uniform and ends up starting her shift ten minutes late. She's very friendly and sometimes she gets so interested in talking to one customer that she forgets about her other customers. She doesn't work very efficiently. She does one thing at a time. For example: She takes one order, gives it to the kitchen, and then comes back to take another order.*
Have students work with a partner to write polite requests and suggestions with gerunds, directing them at Nancy. Call on volunteers to share their sentences.

4 Building conversation skills

Guided Practice III
15–20 minutes

A Direct students to look at the picture and skim the conversation. Ask: *Who do you see?* [a man and a woman] *Where are they?* [at work, a design firm] *What is their relationship?* [employee and manager] Have them work with partners to identify the purpose of the conversation. Elicit responses and ask: *How do you know?* or *Why do you say that?* to encourage students to state their reasoning.

Answers
The purpose is for the manager to give the employee feedback on his work. She tells him what he is doing well and what he should improve.

1. Ask students to read the instructions and tell you what they are going to do [listen and read and respond to the question]. Play the audio and then elicit the answer to the question.

2. Check comprehension. Ask: *What is he good at?* [developing new sites and making suggestions for new projects] *What does he need to do better?* [asking for help]

3. Ask students to read the conversation with a partner. Circulate and monitor pronunciation. Model and have students repeat difficult words or phrases.

4. Ask: *In what other situation could you use this conversation?* Point out a few phrases that are not specific to this job. Ask volunteers to point out others.

Possible Answers
Luke says, "I appreciate your saying so.", "I'm sorry. I didn't know there was a problem." and "I'll try to do better at asking."

Communicative Practice and Application I
15–20 minutes

C 1. Pair students and have them read the instructions silently. Check their comprehension of the exercise. Ask: *What are the two roles?* [manager and employee] *Where is the conversation?* [at a store]

2. Model and have students repeat the expressions in the *In Other Words* box. Explain that they should use these expressions in their conversations.

3. Draw a T-chart on the board. Label the left column *Manager* and the right column *Employee*. Elicit examples of what each person might say and make notes on the chart.

4. Set a time limit (three minutes). Have students act out the role-play. Call time and have students switch roles.

5. Ask three volunteer pairs to act out their role-play for the class. Tell students who are listening to make a simple table with four rows and three columns. Use the top row to label the columns: *Positive feedback*, *Negative feedback*, and *Responses*. Have students take notes in the chart for each role-play.

MULTILEVEL STRATEGIES
For 4C, adapt the role-play to the level of your students. • **Pre-level** Give these students the beginning of the role-play. A: You've done a great job of keeping the store neat and handling money. B: Thanks for saying so. A: However, I'd like you to try _____.

5 Focus on listening for details

Presentation and Guided Practice
20–25 minutes

A Read the questions aloud and elicit answers from volunteers. Write their ideas on the board.

B 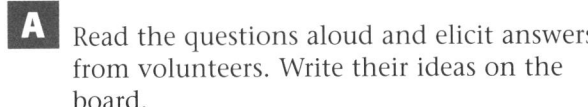 Say: *Now we're going to listen to a manager giving positive feedback and criticism to an employee.* Direct students to listen to the audio and mark the correct column in the chart and then compare answers with a partner. Go over the answers as a class.

Answers
1. negative feedback
2. positive feedback
3. negative feedback
4. positive feedback
5. negative feedback
6. positive feedback

C 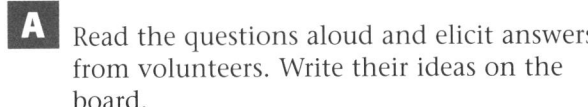 Direct students to read the sentences before listening. Replay the audio and have students work individually to choose the best response. Go over the answers as a class. Take a tally of responses for each item and if students disagree on a response, replay the audio so they can check their answers.

Answers	
1. b	4. a
2. a	5. b
3. b	6. b

MULTILEVEL STRATEGIES
Replay the audio to challenge on- and higher-level students while allowing pre-level students to catch up. • **Pre-level** Have these students listen again to go over their answers. • **On- and Higher-level** Ask these students to make quick notes about what the manager says. Elicit what the manager said before you go over each response.

6 Discuss

Communicative Practice and Application II
15–20 minutes

 1. Read the instructions aloud. Give students two minutes to think about their rankings.

2. Put students into teams of four and assign roles: reporter, manager, administrative assistant, and editor. Verify students' understanding of the roles. Encourage students to use the phrases in the *Speaking Note* during their discussions.

3. Set a time limit for the discussions (ten minutes). Write the sentence frame from 6B on the board. Then circulate and monitor.

 Call "time". Ask the reporter for each team to report the results of their team's discussion, using the sentence frame on the board.

Evaluation
5 minutes

TEST YOURSELF

1. Ask students to complete the checkboxes individually.

2. Tell students that you are going to read each of the items in the checklist aloud. If they are not at all confident with that skill, they should hold up a closed fist. If they are not very confident, they should hold up one finger. If they are somewhat confident, two fingers; confident, three fingers; very confident, four fingers. If they think they could teach the skill, they should hold up five fingers. Read each item in the checklist and identify students that may need further support.

> **TIP**
> For homework, you could ask students to write a sentence or two about what discussion skills they still need to work on or, if they are confident in all of the skills, what skill they are most proud of.

> **EXTENSION ACTIVITY**
> To extend this lesson, have students write on slips of paper about a problem they are having at school or at work (e.g., *I have difficulty remembering new vocabulary.* or *I am afraid to ask questions when I don't understand.*). Collect the slips of paper and redistribute. Tell students to write polite requests and suggestions with gerunds in response (e.g., *May I suggest keeping a vocabulary notebook?* or *I would suggest making a note of your question and asking the teacher after class.*). Call on students to read the problem and the suggestion to the class.

LESSON 5 READING

Lesson Overview

MULTILEVEL OBJECTIVES

On-, Pre-, and Higher-level: Read about and discuss non-traditional occupations

LANGUAGE FOCUS

Grammar: Past tense (*She grew up in California.*)

Vocabulary: *Challenge, distribution, dominate, eventually, pioneer, non-traditional*

For vocabulary support, see this **Oxford Picture Dictionary** topic: Life Events and Documents, pages 40–41

STRATEGY FOCUS

Bold headings usually summarize the main idea for each section of a text.

READINESS CONNECTION

In this lesson, students communicate information about distribution in occupations.

PACING

To compress this lesson: Conduct the word study in 2A as a whole-class activity.

To extend this lesson: Have students brainstorm and discuss people for the *Bring It To Life* activity. (See end of lesson.)

And/or have students complete **Workbook 4 page 84** and **Multilevel Activities 4 Unit 12 pages 134–135**.

Lesson Notes

CORRELATIONS

CCRS: SL.1.B (b.) Follow agreed-upon rules for discussions. (c.) Ask questions to check understanding of information presented, stay on topic, and link their comments to the remarks of others. (d.) Explain their own ideas and understanding in light of the discussion.

SL.2.B Determine the main ideas and supporting details of a text read aloud or information presented in diverse media and formats, including visually, quantitatively, and orally.

SL.6.B Speak in complete sentences when appropriate to task and situation in order to provide requested detail or clarification.

R.1.B Ask and answer such questions as who, what, where, when, why, and how to demonstrate understanding of key details in a text.

R.1.C Refer to details and examples in a text when explaining what the text says explicitly and when drawing inferences from the text.

R.2.B Determine the main idea of a text; recount the key details and explain how they support the main idea.

R.4.B Determine the meaning of general academic and domain-specific words and phrases in a text relevant to a topic or subject area.

R.5.B Know and use various text features to locate key facts or information in a text efficiently.

R.7.C Interpret information presented visually, orally, or quantitatively and explain how the information contributes to an understanding of the text in which it appears.

L.1.B (b.) Explain the function of nouns, pronouns, verbs, adjectives, and adverbs in general and their functions in particular sentences. (l.) Produce simple, compound and complex sentences.

L.4.B (e.) Use glossaries and beginning dictionaries, both print and digital, to determine or clarify the meaning of words and phrases.

L.6.B Use words and phrases acquired through conversations, reading and being read to, and responding to texts, including using adjectives and adverbs to describe.

RF.4.B (a.) Read grade-level text with purpose and understanding.

ELPS: 1. An ELL can construct meaning from oral presentations and literary and informational text through level-appropriate listening, reading, and viewing. 2. An ELL can participate in level-appropriate oral and written exchanges of information, ideas, and analyses, in various social and academic contexts, responding to peer, audience, or reader comments and questions. 6. An ELL can analyze and critique the arguments of others orally and in writing. 8. An ELL can determine the meaning of words and phrases in oral presentation and literary and informational text.

Warm-up and Review
10–15 minutes (books closed)

Write *Women's Jobs* and *Men's Jobs* on the board. Ask volunteers to write in each column the jobs that are dominated by men and dominated by women.

Introduction
5 minutes

1. Ask students which of the jobs on the board they think are most interesting. Point out there can be many barriers in the way for a woman doing a male-dominated job or a man doing a female-dominated job. This can create more work for the person breaking the barriers.

2. State the objective: *Today we're going to read about and discuss this kind of personal achievement.*

1 Read

Presentation
10–20 minutes

A Read the question aloud. Use ideas from the *Introduction* to help guide discussion.

B Read the words and definitions. Elicit sample sentences for each word or supply them if the students can't. Refer to the list on the board and ask: *Which jobs do men often dominate? Do you know of any women who have been pioneers in one of these jobs?*

Pre-reading

 1. Have students look at the photos. Ask: *What do you see?* [sushi, race cars]

2. Read the *Reader's Note* and instructions aloud. Confirm that students understand where the "bold headings" are. Have students answer the question individually and then compare answers with a partner. Check answers with the class. If any students answer incorrectly, ask them to support their answer using the bold headings. Establish the correct answer.

Answer
c. Women can succeed in jobs that are more often held by men.

Guided Practice: While Reading
20–30 minutes

 1. Check students' understanding of vocabulary in the article: *advance, distribution, challenge, current, vehicle.*

2. Ask students to read the article silently and answer the question and then compare answers with a partner.

3. Check answers with the class.

4. Check comprehension. Ask: *How many people does the article discuss?* [two] *What are their professions?* [chef and race-car mechanic] *Are female sushi chefs unusual?* [yes] *What did one customer do when he saw Nakayama behind the sushi bar?* [walked out] *What did she change in her current restaurant?* [the kitchen isn't open]

Answers
chef, racing mechanic, other answers will vary

MULTILEVEL STRATEGIES

Adapt 1D to the level of your students.
- **Pre-level** Read the text aloud to these students as they follow along.
- **On- and Higher-level** Pair students and have them read the article aloud to each other, taking turns to read each paragraph.

Guided Practice: Rereading
10–15 minutes

 1. Elicit the meaning of the idiom "to break a glass ceiling." Provide an opportunity for students to extract evidence from the text. Have students reread the article and underline any words or phrases that indicate the women are breaking a glass ceiling.

2. Pair students and tell them to compare the words they underlined and report anything they disagree on. Discuss and clarify as needed.

TIP

Have students go online to find out about any women or men doing nontraditional jobs in your area. Decide which device(s) students will use and elicit search terms ("nontraditional job" + "pioneer" + your city).

1. Have students work individually to put the events in order. They should then write the line number(s) where they found the answer. Write the answers on the board.

2. Elicit and discuss any additional questions about the reading. You could introduce new questions for class discussion: *What qualities do you think it takes to be a pioneer in a field? Would you want to be a pioneer? Why or why not?*

Answers	
1. 5, lines 25–26	4. 3, lines 23–24
2. 2, lines 19–20	5. 1, lines 18–19
3. 4, lines 24–25	

MULTILEVEL STRATEGIES

For 1F, work with pre-level students.

• **Pre-level** Ask these students *yes/no* and short-answer information questions about the reading while other students are completing 1F. *What is Niki Nakayama's job?* [sushi chef] *Where is her restaurant?* [Los Angeles] *What is Chatten's job?* [race-car mechanic] *Does she like it?* [yes] Have these students copy the answers to 1F from the board.

2 Word study

Guided Practice: Post-reading
10 minutes

1. Direct students to look at the chart and identify the topic (using hyphens to make compound adjectives). Elicit the meaning of a compound adjective. Have students read the chart.

2. Have students repeat after you as you say each word with natural intonation, rhythm, and stress. Elicit example sentences for each compound adjective.

3. Direct students to complete the sentences and then compare answers with a partner. Read the correct answers and have students check their work.

Answers
1. long-term
2. one-year
3. male-dominated
4. real-life

Direct students to work individually to write a sentence for each topic that includes the underlined word. Ask volunteers to write their sentences on the board. Have the rest of the class suggest grammar and spelling edits as needed.

3 Talk it over

Guided Practice
15–20 minutes

1. Have students look at the graph and read the note. Check comprehension. Ask: *What year does the graph show?* [2010] *What occupations did they study?* [management, professional; sales and office; natural resources, construction, maintenance; production, transportation; material moving; service] *If you work in a hotel, what occupation is that?* [service] *What field are lawyers in?* [professional] *What color is "sales and office"?* [purple] *Do more Hispanics or more Asians work in service jobs?* [Hispanics]

2. Point out that they need to use the information from the graph and the note to complete the sentences and answer the questions. Set a time limit (ten minutes). Have students work in pairs to complete the task. Ask volunteers to share their answers with the class.

Answers
1. sales and office, service
2. natural resources, construction and maintenance
3. 77
4. Gap
5. Information about the difference in earnings between men and women

Communicative Practice
20 minutes

1. Read the questions aloud. Set a time limit (ten minutes). Pair students to discuss the questions.

2. Ask volunteers to share their ideas with the class.

Application

5–10 minutes

BRING IT TO LIFE

Read the instructions aloud. Ask the class to brainstorm names of people they might want to look up. Write the names on the board. Tell students that if they are going to search the Internet, they should type the person's name plus *short biography* into a search engine. (Otherwise they are apt to get biographies that are many pages long.)

EXTENSION ACTIVITY

Discussion

After the class brainstorms the names of people to look up for their *Bring It to Life* assignment, have students talk about what they already know about the people.

1. Have students tell a partner, *I'm going to look up* _____. Direct the partner to ask questions about the person. Have students talk to several partners.

2. Tell students to make a note of the questions they couldn't answer. They can search for those answers in the biography.

AT WORK

Warm-up and Review
10–15 minutes (books closed)

Elicit the meaning of *improvement*. Ask: *What kind of improvements do you think are needed in most workplaces?* Brainstorm with the class. Elicit ideas and write them on the board.

Introduction
5 minutes

State the objective: *Today we're going to talk about agreeing with someone at work.*

Presentation
5 minutes

 3-45 Read the instructions aloud. Play the audio. Give students a minute to think about the question. Elicit responses from the class.

Possible Answer
They are discussing ideas about communication and collaboration at work.

TIP
Write vocabulary on the board: *engagement, focus group, facilitator, officially, collaboration, effectively*. Play the audio again and have students use the context to guess the meaning of words and phrases they don't know.

Guided Practice
10–15 minutes

B 3-45 Play the audio again. Direct students to listen for each idea or suggestion and put a check next to any that they hear mentioned.

Answers
Check:
tell employees about things that are happening
put important information in writing
consider everyone's ideas equal

 3-45 Read the instructions aloud. Play the audio again, encouraging students to take notes in their notebooks. Set a time limit (five minutes) for students to discuss their answers with a partner. Circulate to monitor.

Presentation and Communicative Practice
10 minutes

 1. Direct students' attention to the *Do/Say* chart and ask them to identify the lesson's soft skill [agreeing with someone]. Ask the class which column has examples of language [right] and which has examples of behaviors [left].

2. Say a phrase from the left and act it out. Say it again and have the class act it out with you. Say it a third time and have the class act it out for you.

3. Model the phrases from the right using authentic intonation. Have students practice imitating your inflection.

4. Put students in teams of four and assign each team a question. Assign roles: reporter, manager, administrative assistant, and researcher. (Researchers will ask you questions on behalf of the team.) Verify understanding of the roles. Set a time limit (five minutes) and monitor.

5. Write sentence frames on the board that teams can use to summarize their response. *Our team discussed the following question: _____. We decided _____ because_____.*

6. Call "time" and let reporters rehearse their report for one minute. Direct each reporter to present to three other teams.

Communicative Practice and Application
20–25 minutes

E 1. Direct students to work in pairs to take turns reading the issues, discussing the consequences, and come up with suggestions for improvement.

2. Invite volunteers to share their suggestions.

 1. Have pairs merge to form teams of four. Tell students that they are going to be role-playing a staff meeting where they will suggest solutions for issues at work.

2. Direct groups to come up with three issues and three solutions. Each group should select a facilitator to run the meeting. The other three members should each choose an issue to bring up.

3. As students carry out the role-play, circulate and monitor. Provide global feedback once the activity ends.

TEAMWORK & LANGUAGE REVIEW

Lesson Overview

MULTILEVEL OBJECTIVES

On-, Pre-, and Higher-level: Expand upon and review unit grammar and life skills

LANGUAGE FOCUS

Grammar: Gerunds after prepositions. (*He's worried about losing his job.*)

Vocabulary: Accomplishments and work

For vocabulary support, see these **Oxford Picture Dictionary** topics: Life Events and Documents, pages 40–41; Schools and Subjects, pages 200–201

READINESS CONNECTION

In this review, students solve a problem and think of ways to give back to the community.

PACING

To extend this review: Have students complete **Workbook 4 page 85**, **Multilevel Activities 4 Unit 12 page 136**, and **Multilevel Grammar Exercises 4 Unit 12**.

Lesson Notes

CORRELATIONS

CCRS: SL.1.B (a.) Come to discussions prepared, having read or studied required material; explicitly draw on that preparation and other information known about the topic to explore ideas under discussion. (b.) Follow agreed-upon rules for discussions. (c.) Ask questions to check understanding of information presented, stay on topic, and link their comments to the remarks of others. (d.) Explain their own ideas and understanding in light of the discussion.

SL.1.C (b.) Follow agreed-upon rules for discussions and carry out assigned roles.

SL.2.B Determine the main ideas and supporting details of a text read aloud or information presented in diverse media and formats, including visually, quantitatively, and orally.

SL.4.B Report on a topic or text, tell a story, or recount an experience with appropriate facts and relevant, descriptive details, speaking clearly at an understandable pace.

R.2.A Identify the main topic and retell key details of a text.

R.7.B Use information gained from illustrations and the words in a text to demonstrate understanding of the text.

W.2.A Write informative/explanatory texts in which they name a topic, supply some facts about the topic, and provide some sense of closure.

L.1.B (l.) Produce simple, compound and complex sentences.

L.1.C (a.) Explain the function of conjunctions, prepositions, and interjections in general and their function in particular sentences. (d.) Use modal auxiliaries to convey various conditions.

L.1.D (f.) Explain the function of verbals (gerunds, participles, infinitives) in general and their function in particular sentences.

RF.4.B (a.) Read grade-level text with purpose and understanding.

ELPS: 2. An ELL can participate in level-appropriate oral and written exchanges of information, ideas, and analyses, in various social and academic contexts, responding to peer, audience, or reader comments and questions. 4. An ELL can construct level-appropriate oral and written claims and support them with reasoning and evidence. 5. An ELL can conduct research and evaluate and communicate findings to answer questions or solve problems. 7. An ELL can adapt language choices to purpose, task, and audience when speaking and writing. 9. An ELL can create clear and coherent level-appropriate speech and text. 10. An ELL can demonstrate command of the conventions of standard English to communicate in level-appropriate speech and writing.

Warm-up and Review
10–15 minutes (books closed)

1. Review *At Work* activity F.

2. Ask students to share the good, not-so-good, and interesting things that happened during the staff meeting. As students speak, write their responses in a chart on the board.

Introduction and Presentation
5 minutes

1. Pair students and direct them to look at the pictures in their book. Ask them to describe what they see to their partner.

2. Ask volunteer pairs to share their ideas with the class.

Guided Practice
15–20 minutes

A 1. Read the instructions. Go over the vocabulary in the pictures.

2. Group students to write a review of the restaurant. Assign roles: manager, reporter, editor, researcher. The editor will check spelling and grammar, and the researcher will ask you questions and/or do research.

3. Set a time limit (five minutes). Call on reporters to read the review to the class. Have the class vote on the best one.

B 1. Have students work individually to complete the email and then compare emails with a partner.

2. Go over the answers with the class.

Answers
offering, pursuing, mind telling, suggest contacting, recommend getting, baking, taking

Communicative Practice
30–40 minutes

C Read the instructions aloud. Pair students to write questions for the interview. Elicit questions and write them on the board.

D Have each pair take turns role-playing an informational interview. Ask volunteers to perform their role plays for the class.

E 1. Group students and assign roles: manager, writer, editor, actors. Explain that students are going to work with their teams to write a conversation.

2. Read steps 2–4 of the activity aloud. Check comprehension of the task. *What is the first thing you should do?* [choose one of the pictures] Elicit what is going on in each situation. Ask: *What qualities should the speakers have?* [leadership qualities from Lesson 1]

3. Set a time limit (ten minutes) to complete the exercise. Circulate and answer any questions.

4. Have actors from each team perform their team's conversation for another team. As the other teams perform, tell students to listen and write down the qualities they observe in the speakers.

F 1. Have students walk around the room to conduct the interviews. To get students moving, tell them to interview three people who were not in their team for E.

2. Set a time limit (five minutes) to complete the exercise.

3. Tell students to make a note of their classmates' answers, but not to worry about writing complete sentences.

> **MULTILEVEL STRATEGIES**
>
> Adapt the mixer in F to the level of your students.
> - **Pre-and On-level** Pair these students and have them interview other pairs together.
> - **Higher-level** Have these students ask an additional question and write all answers.

G Call on individuals to report what they learned about their classmates. Record each student's achievements and dates. Then have students work together to make a timeline of the class's achievements.

PROBLEM SOLVING
10–15 minutes

A 🔊 3-46 1. Ask: *Are you working on your goals right now?* Tell students they will read a story about a man who has achieved many of his goals and now has a new one. Direct students to read Jafari's story silently.

2. Ask: *Why wasn't life easy when Jafari first came to the U.S.? What has he achieved?*

3. Play the audio and have students read along silently.

B 1. Elicit answers to question 1.

2. Put students into groups of three or four. Ask each group to make a list of things Jafari could do, and the pros and cons of each, and report them to the class. Ask a volunteer to write all ideas on the board.

Possible Answer
1. Jafari has worked hard and reached his goals, and now he wants to get involved and give back to his community, but he doesn't know where to start.
2. Answers will vary.

TIP

Have students write letters giving advice to Jafari. Pair students and ask them to read their partners' letters. Call on volunteers to share any differences between the letter they wrote and the one they read.

Evaluation
20–25 minutes

To test students' understanding of the unit language and content, have them take the Unit 12 Test, available on the Teacher Resource Center.